THE EUROPEAN UNION SERIES

General Editors: Neill Nugent, William E.

The European Union series provides an authorita[tive] ranging from general introductory texts to definiti[ve] [...]tutions and actors, issues, policies and policy processes, and th[e] [...]member states.

Books in the series are written by leading scholars in their fields and reflect the most up-to-date research and debate. Particular attention is paid to accessibility and clear presentation for a wide audience of students, practitioners and interested general readers.

The series editors are **Neill Nugent**, Professor of Politics and Jean Monnet Professor of European Integration, Manchester Metropolitan University, and **William E. Paterson**, Founding Director of the Institute of German Studies, University of Birmingham, and Chairman of the German–British Forum. Their co-editor until his death in July 1999, **Vincent Wright**, was a Fellow of Nuffield College, Oxford University.

Feedback on the series and book proposals are always welcome and should be sent to Steven Kennedy, Palgrave Macmillan, Houndmills, Basingstoke, Hampshire RG21 6XS, UK, or by e-mail to s.kennedy@palgrave.com

---

General textbooks

Published

Desmond Dinan **Encyclopedia of the European Union**
[Rights: Europe only]

Desmond Dinan **Europe Recast: A History of European Union**
[Rights: Europe only]

Desmond Dinan **Ever Closer Union: An Introduction to European Integration (3rd edn)**
[Rights: Europe only]

Mette Eilstrup Sangiovanni (ed.) **Debates on European Integration: A Reader**

Simon Hix **The Political System of the European Union (2nd edn)**

Paul Magnette **What is the European Union? Nature and Prospects**

John McCormick **Understanding the European Union: A Concise Introduction (3rd edn)**

Brent F. Nelsen and Alexander Stubb **The European Union: Readings on the Theory and Practice of European Integration (3rd edn)**
[Rights: Europe only]

Neill Nugent (ed.) **European Union Enlargement**

Neill Nugent **The Government and Politics of the European Union (6th edn)**
[Rights: World excluding USA and dependencies and Canada]

John Peterson and Elizabeth Bomberg **Decision-Making in the European Union**

Ben Rosamond **Theories of European Integration**

Forthcoming

Laurie Buonanno and Neill Nugent **Policies and Policy Processes of the European Union**

David Howarth **The Political Economy of the European Union**

Philippa Sherrington **Understanding European Union Governance**

Series Standing Order (outside North America only)
ISBN 0-333-71695-7 hardback
ISBN 0-333-69352-3 paperback
Full details from www.palgrave.com

Visit Palgrave Macmillan's EU Resource area at
www.palgrave.com/politics/eu

The major institutions and actors

Published

Renaud Dehousse **The European Court of Justice**

Justin Greenwood **Interest Representation in the European Union (2nd edn)**

Fiona Hayes-Renshaw and Helen Wallace **The Council of Ministers (2nd edn)**

Simon Hix and Christopher Lord **Political Parties in the European Union**

David Judge and David Earnshaw **The European Parliament**

Neill Nugent **The European Commission**

Anne Stevens with Handley Stevens **Brussels Bureaucrats? The Administration of the European Union**

Forthcoming

Simon Bulmer and Wolfgang Wessels **The European Council**

The main areas of policy

Published

Michelle Cini and Lee McGowan **Competition Policy in the European Union**

Wyn Grant **The Common Agricultural Policy**

Martin Holland **The European Union and the Third World**

Jolyon Howorth **Security and Defence Policy in the European Union**

Brigid Laffan **The Finances of the European Union**

Malcolm Levitt and Christopher Lord **The Political Economy of Monetary Union**

Bart Kerremans, David Allen and Geoffrey Edwards **The External Economic Relations of the European Union**

Stephen Keukeleire and Jennifer MacNaughtan **The Foreign Policy of the European Union**

Janne Haaland Matláry **Energy Policy in the European Union**

Jörg Monar **Justice and Home Affairs in the European Union**

John Vogler, Richard Whitman and Charlotte Bretherton **The External Policies of the European Union**

Also planned

Political Union

Social Policy in the European Union

The member states and the Union

Published

Carlos Closa and Paul Heywood **Spain and the European Union**

Alain Guyomarch, Howard Machin and Ella Ritchie **France in the European Union**

Forthcoming

Simon Bulmer and William E. Paterson **Germany and the European Union**

Phil Daniels and Ella Ritchie **Britain and the European Union**

Brigid Laffan **The European Union and its Member States**

Brigid Laffan and Jane O'Mahoney **Ireland and the European Union**

Luisa Perrotti **Italy and the European Union**

Baldur Thorhalsson **Small States in the European Union**

Issues

Published

Derek Beach **The Dynamics of European Integration: Why and When EU Institutions Matter**

Forthcoming

Thomas Christiansen and Christine Reh **Constitutionalizing the European Union**

Steven McGuire and Michael Smith **The USA and the European Union**

Also planned

Europeanization and National Politics

Security and Defence Policy in the European Union

Jolyon Howorth

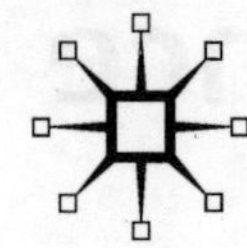

First published 2007 by
PALGRAVE MACMILLAN
Houndmills, Basingstoke, Hampshire RG21 6XS and
175 Fifth Avenue, New York, N.Y. 10010
Companies and representatives throughout the world

PALGRAVE MACMILLAN is the global academic imprint of the Palgrave Macmillan division of St. Martin's Press, LLC and of Palgrave Macmillan Ltd. Macmillan® is a registered trademark in the United States, United Kingdom and other countries. Palgrave is a registered trademark in the European Union and other countries.

ISBN-13: 978-0–333–63911–5 hardback
ISBN-10: 0–333–63911–1 hardback
ISBN-13: 978–0–333–63912–2 paperback
ISBN-10: 0–333–63912–X paperback

This book is printed on paper suitable for recycling and made from fully managed and sustained forest sources. Logging, pulping and manufacturing processes are expected to conform to the environmental regulations of the country of origin.

A catalogue record for this book is available from the British Library.

A catalog record for this book is available from the Library of Congress.

10 9 8 7 6 5 4 3 2 1
16 15 14 13 12 11 10 09 08 07

Printed and bound in China

For Vivien

Contents

List of Tables, Figures and Boxes

Tables

Figures

Boxes

List of Abbreviations

AFSouth	Allied Forces South (NATO Southern Command, Naples)
AMIS	African Mission in Sudan
AMM	Aceh Monitoring Mission
ASEAN	Association of South East Asian Nations
AU	African Union
AVF	All-Volunteer Force
BAM	Border Assistance Mission
BG	Battle Group
BiH	Bosnia-Herzegovina
C^4I	Command, Control, Communications, Computers and Intelligence
CCM	Civilian Crisis Management
CDM	Council of Defence Ministers
CDS	Centre for Defence Studies (King's College, University of London)
CER	Centre for European Reform (London-based think-tank)
CFSP	Common Foreign and Security Policy
CHG-*2008*	Civilian Headline Goal *2008*
CHODs	Chiefs of the Defence Staff
CIVCOM	Committee for Civilian Aspects of Crisis Management
CJTF	Combined Joint Task Forces
CMI	Crisis Management Initiative
CMPC	Civil–Military Planning Cell
COPS	Comité de Politique et de Sécurité (French acronym for the Political and Security Committee)
COPPS	Coordinating Office for Palestinian Police Support
COREPER	Committee of Permanent Representatives
CPCO	Centre de Planification et de Conduite des Opérations (French PJHQ)
CRT	Civilian Response Team

CS	Combat Support
CSCE	Conference on Security and Cooperation in Europe
CSIS	Center for Strategic and International Studies (Washington DC)
CSS	Combat Service Support
DDR	Disarmament, Demobilization and Re-Integration
DRC	Democratic Republic of Congo
DSACEUR	Deputy Supreme Allied Commander (NATO)
EAS	External Action Service (EU Diplomatic Corps)
EC	European Commission
ECAP	European Capability Action Plan
EDA	European Defence Agency
EDC	European Defence Community
EEC	European Economic Community
EGF	European Gendarmerie Force
ENEC	European Network Enabling Capability
EP	European Parliament
EPC	European Political Cooperation
ERRF	European Rapid Reaction Force
ESDC	European Security and Defence College
ESDI	European Security and Defence Identity
ESDP	European Security and Defence Policy
ESS	European Security Strategy
EU	European Union
EUFOR-RDC	European Force in Congo
EU-ISS	European Union Institute for Security Studies (Paris)
EUMC	European Union Military Committee
EUMS	European Union Military Staff
EUPAT	European Union Police Advisory Team
EUPM	European Union Police Mission (in FYROM)
EUSR	European Union Special Representative
FAC	Foreign Affairs Council
FCO	Foreign and Commonwealth Office (London)
FYROM	Former Yugoslav Republic of Macedonia

GAC	General Affairs Committee
GAERC	General Affairs and External Relations Committee
GAM	Free Aceh Movement (Indonesia)
GDP	Gross Domestic Product
GOI	Government of Indonesia
GOS	Government of Sudan
HG *2010*	Headline Goal *2010*
HGTF	Headline Goal Task Force
HHG	Helsinki Headline Goal
HQ	Headquarters
HR-CFSP	High Representative for the Common Foreign & Security Policy
HRW	Human Rights Watch
ICG	International Crisis Group
IDP	Internally Displaced Person
IGC	Inter-Governmental Conference
IISS	International Institute for Strategic Studies (London)
IRRI–KIIB	Belgian Royal Institute for International Relations
IPTF	International Police Task Force
IR	International Relations
ISTAR	Intelligence, Surveillance and Target-Acquisition
JEM	Justice and Equality Movement (Sudan)
KFOR	Kosovo Force (NATO force in Kosovo)
LOT	Liaison and Observation Team
MEDA	Euro-Mediterranean Partnership
MENA	Middle East and North Africa (as a region)
MFA	Ministry of Foreign Affairs
MILREPs	Military Representatives (delegating for CHODs on EUMC)
MOD	Ministry of Defence
MONUC	UN Mission in Congo
MSF	Médecins Sans Frontières ('Doctors Without Borders')
NAC	North Atlantic Council (NATO political command)
NACC	North Atlantic Coordination Committee
NATO	North Atlantic Treaty Organization

NEC	Network Enabling Capability
NGO	Non-Governmental Organization
NORTHAG	Northern Army Group (Central European NATO Command)
NPT	(Nuclear) Non-Proliferation Treaty
NRF	NATO Response Force
OEF	Operation Enduring Freedom (US mission in Afghanistan)
OSCE	Organization for Security and Cooperation in Europe
P-5	Permanent Members of the United Nations Security Council
PfP	Partnership for Peace
PGM	Precision-Guided Munition
PJHQ	Permanent Joint Headquarters
PNA	Palestinian National Authority
PSC	Political and Security Committee (see COPS)
Quai	Quai d'Orsay (French MFA)
QDR	Quadrennial Defense Review (US)
QMV	Qualified Majority Voting
RCP	Rafah Crossing Point
Relex	Directorate General for External Relations (European Commission)
RS	Republika Srpska (Serbian part of BiH)
SAA	Stabilisation and Association Agreement
SACEUR	Supreme Allied Commander Europe (NATO European Command)
SDS	Serbian Democratic Party
SFOR	Stabilization Force (NATO force in BiH)
SHAPE	Supreme Headquarters Allied Powers Europe (NATO Central Planning HQ)
SIPRI	Stockholm International Peace Research Institute
SLM/A	Sudan Liberation Movement/Army
SSR	Security Sector Reform
TBMD	Theatre Ballistic Missile Defence
UESD	Union Européenne de Sécurité et de Défense
UK	United Kingdom
UMFA	Union Minister for Foreign Affairs
UN	United Nations
UNSC	United Nations Security Council

UNPROFOR	United Nations Protection Force (in Bosnia-Herzegovina)
USA	United States of America
USCOMEUR	United States Commander Europe (Commander of all US forces in Europe)
WEU	Western European Union
WMD	Weapons of Mass Destruction

Preface and Acknowledgements

This book has had a long gestation. For two decades I specialized in *French* defence policy, a topic which fascinated me because it was so very different both from the European mainstream and from US defence policy. After the fall of the Berlin Wall, I began to track the gradual realization, within the French political establishment, that the very features of the Cold War which had allowed French defence policy to blaze an autonomous trail no longer afforded such a luxury in the very different environment of the post-Cold War world. French defence policy gradually adopted a twin-track strategy: ever closer cooperation with NATO in the context of the renewal of military conflict on the European continent, and ever closer cooperation with France's European partners, as the EU strove to emerge as a significant actor on the world stage. My focus switched to the gradual emergence of a *European* security and defence project, discernible from the mid-1990s and then gathering pace at the turn of the century. In 2000 I wrote one of the first overall studies of the emerging European security project (Howorth, 2000) and in 2003 John Keeler and I edited one of the first major collective volumes on ESDP (Howorth and Keeler, 2003). But the writing of a substantial single-author volume requires both time and focus – which the peculiar circumstances of those years did not seem to allow.

In the immediate aftermath of the fall of the Berlin Wall, friends and colleagues occasionally chided me for my continuing interest in security and defence. At a time when the talk was of the 'end of history' and of 'peace dividends', was this not a subject with little future? The reverse rapidly proved to be the case as violent military conflict shattered the pacifistic illusions of the post-Cold War world. By the mid-1990s an entire cottage industry was developing around the new field of 'security studies'. Invitations came in to write articles and chapters on this and that aspect of rapidly evolving events, to mount courses and draft briefings, to attend conferences and colloquia. Over the past ten years I have attended and given papers on aspects of European security and defence at over 150 international conferences in 20 different countries. This proved to be a major obstacle to producing a general overview in the guise of a monograph. However, the urging of friends and colleagues eventually prevailed and in particular Steven Kennedy at Palgrave Macmillan gradually persuaded me to sit down and write this book.

Many people have assisted me in all sorts of ways over many years. Bath University, where I served as a Professor for 20 years, provided an institutional base and generous travel and research facilities without which my work would not have been possible. Thanks in particular are due to Michael Scriven, Roger Eatwell, Stefan Wolff and Ian Jamieson, all of whom encouraged and assisted me in important ways. My students at Bath, and particularly generations of Euromasters students, with whom I engaged in seminars on European security, also deserve special thanks. Without the support of Jill O'Brien and Ann Burge, life at Bath would have been much more difficult and far less pleasant. The Department of European Studies granted me one year's sabbatical leave (1999–2000) during which my work on ESDP gathered speed. During that sabbatical year, I was fortunate to be hosted in Paris by the *Institut Français des Relations Internationales* (IFRI), where I have been a Senior Research Associate ever since. Thanks are due to Thierry de Montbrial, IFRI's founding Director, to Dominique David, currently its Executive Director, to Dominique Moïsi, Etienne de Durand, Fréderic Bozo, Florent Baran and Françoise Thomas, all of whom have either clarified my thinking and/or facilitated my endeavours in important ways. In spring 2000, I also spent two stimulating months as Senior Research Associate at the EU's Institute for Security Studies in Paris. I am grateful to the Institute's Director, Nicole Gnesotto, both for appointing me to this key European think-tank and for encouraging me to write a Chaillot Paper. From colleagues at the Institute, who became and have remained friends – Antonio Missiroli, Julian Lindley-French, Burkard Schmitt – I learned, and continue to learn, a great deal.

In the United States, I have benefited enormously from a long-term association with Harvard University's Center for European Studies, where, as a Visiting Scholar in the early 1980s I first became seriously interested in security and defence issues and where, since 2002, I have been a Faculty Affiliate. Thanks are due to Stanley Hoffmann, an inspirational beacon, and to Peter

Hall for his unfailing support and good humour over the years. In spring 2001, I was appointed as the Marshall-Monnet Visiting Professor of Political Science at the University of Washington where John Keeler and I consolidated a strong and close working relationship (and friendship) which has led to several security and defence-related projects. In the autumn of 2002, I was appointed to the Consortium Visiting Professorship of European Studies at New York University and Columbia University. Thanks are due to Martin Schain and Volker Berghahn for offering me this invaluable opportunity to work in post-9/11 America. The students who took my seminars on ESDP at all these institutions have had more influence than they could imagine on my own intellectual development. Since January 2003 I have worked uninterruptedly as Visiting Professor of Political Science at Yale University, where my colleagues and graduate students in the Political Science Department and in the International Relations seminar have offered an intellectual context of unparalleled vibrancy. I would like to thank Ian Shapiro for appointing me in the first place, David Cameron for his unflagging support and much appreciated friendship, Bruce Russett for stimulating discussions on IR issues, and Bill Foltz and Peter Swenson for their manifold assistance in my endeavours. My students at Yale are simply a joy to teach and I suspect that I have learned as much from them as they have from me in my seminars on European and Transatlantic security issues.

Other support has been forthcoming from the UK's Economic and Social Research Council, which, in 1998, awarded a group of us (Stuart Croft, Terry Terriff, Mark Webber and me) a major research grant for a project on 'Security Governance in the EU'. Thanks are due to Helen Wallace, the overall Director of the ESRC's 'One Europe or Several?' programme and to Stuart, Terry and Mark for being an endless source of stimulation and friendship. At the *Institut d'Etudes Politiques* (Sciences-Po) in Paris, I have also been a regular visiting professor, teaching ESDP to annual cohorts of international students. Thanks to Renaud Dehousse for his support over the years.

The Universities, think-tanks and research institutes in many countries which have invited me to participate in workshops and seminars have also been an important influence on my thinking. They are too numerous to name but I would especially like to thank the Geneva Centre for Security Policy, ARENA (Oslo), the

Bertelsmann Foundation (Gütersloh), *Institut für Europäische Politik* (Berlin), MGIMO (Moscow), the Netherlands Institute for International Relations (Clingendael), the Royal Institute of International Affairs (London), the Royal Institute for International Relations (Belgium), and Cirpes (Paris).

Over the past ten years, I have conducted over 200 interviews with major individuals in European security and defence policy: senior military officers, leading officials from Ministries of Defence and Foreign Affairs in various European capitals, officials of the European Union's many agencies – the Commission, Council Secretariat, Parliament, Political and Security Committee, Military Committee and from the offices of the High Representative for the Common Foreign and Security Policy, especially the Policy Unit – researchers from leading think-tanks and specialists in security affairs from the worlds of academia and the media. I have listed these, along with their functions, on the Palgrave website. A heartfelt thanks to all of them.

Finally, I would like to thank a number of individuals with whom, over the years, I have engaged in exchanges about European security issues: Franco Alghieri, Robert Art, Sven Biscop, Yves Boyer, Michael Brenner, André Brigot, Klaus Brummer, Michael Clarke, Dominique David, Anne Deighton, Simon Duke, André Dumoulin, Philip Gordon, Charles Grout, Giovanni Grévi, Jean-Yves Haine, François Heisbourg, Daniel Keohane, Gustav Lindstrom, Alex McCleod, Jenny Medcalf, Anand Menon, Frédéric Mérand, Hanna Ojanen, John Peterson, Barry Posen, John Roper, Kori Schake, Jane Sharp, Thierry Tardy, Sunniva Tofte, William Wallace, Stephen Walt, Rob de Wyk, David Yost. Those many colleagues whose work I have plundered in the pages that follow will recognize the immense debt I owe to them. I alone, of course, am responsible for the mistaken assessments made in the pages that follow.

The bedrock of love and emotional stability which has been the indispensable context within which the book was written has been provided by my wife, Vivien Schmidt, to whom the book is dedicated.

JOLYON HOWORTH

The author and publishers would like to thank the following who have kindly given permission for the use of copyright material: Phil Alexander for Box 2.2; The International Institute for Strategic Studies for the use of data in Tables 4.1, 4.2 and 4.5. Box 2.1 is reproduced with the permission of the controller of Her Majesty's Stationery Office under the click licence CO1W0000276. Figure 4.1 is copyright of the European Defence Agency; Appendix 1, Box 3.1, Box 3.2, Box 5.1 and Box 6.1 are European Union copyright.

Chapter 1

Introduction: A New Security Actor on the World Stage

Coming to terms with ESDP

In 1999, Europe and the rest of the world witnessed the emergence of a new and unprecedented political project: the European Security and Defence Policy (ESDP). This book analyses the multifaceted reality of this new policy area, its many different policy instruments, and, where appropriate, its relationship with the *national* security and defence policies of the European Union's (EU's*) member states. For the first time in modern history, a number of sovereign states have elected, of their own volition and with no external threats compelling them to form a traditional alliance, to coordinate their activities in the field of security and – perhaps one day – defence. It must be made clear from the outset that ESDP has not *superseded* the national security and defence policies of the EU's member states. ESDP is a political and strategic project, with a common body of instruments which all member states – except Denmark – agree to implement collectively and which has acquired its own distinct profile and footprint. This book is therefore primarily concerned with the *coordinated* and increasingly *integrated* security and defence policy initiatives of the EU member states under the aegis of ESDP. It would be somewhat tedious to attempt, in one volume, to cover the distinct security and defence policies of all

---

* The European Union was the title bestowed upon the European integration process by the Treaty of Maastricht in 1992. Prior to that, the process had been called the European Communities (1950s to 1960s), the European Economic Community (1960s to 1970s) and the European Community (1970s to 1990s). For the sake of simplicity, I shall refer to it throughout this book, with reference to the entire period, as the European Union.

27 EU member states. While these continue to enjoy *de jure* sovereignty, in practice the differences between them are fairly minimal. As the EU has grown in international stature, the interests of its member states have converged. The most interesting phenomenon of the past decade has been the gradual emergence of this collective endeavour to construct and implement an EU security and defence policy. This has already assumed a considerable measure of distinctiveness. Since 2003, the EU has progressively mounted overseas missions under the collective guise of ESDP, some military, some civilian, and some involving a mix of civilian and military elements. We shall assess the significance of these missions, which represent the concrete implementation of ESDP, in Chapter 6.

However, these developments have not been without controversy. Many, both in Europe and in the United States, have deplored the advent of ESDP as a step in the wrong direction for an EU which had hitherto steered resolutely clear of any involvement in military affairs. Many have seen in this emerging force a threat to the North Atlantic Treaty Organization (NATO). Traditional theorists of international relations, for whom only states or alliances of states can engage in security and defence activities, have scratched their heads in disbelief as this new actor, which is clearly less than a state but more than an alliance, has taken the stage. Others have applauded the EU's initiative. Having already emerged as a major international actor in the fields of trade, economics, competition and other policy areas, the EU, in this view, was only taking the logical next step by assuming responsibility for regional (and to a certain extent global) stability and security. Some have hoped that these new responsibilities will hasten the moment when the EU will be forced to transform itself into a supranational federal structure. Others have looked on in bewilderment, unsure of the precise intentions of this new development or of its implications. More significantly, a majority of European citizens, and an even larger majority of people elsewhere in the world, have probably never even heard of ESDP.

For fifty years, the European Union remained a purely 'civilian' actor. By this expression, analysts have indicated the Union's focus on the core policy areas of trade and economics, its existence as an institutions-driven project rooted in international law, and its total absence from the arena of military ambition or coercive diplomacy (Whitman, 1998; Manners, 2005). To the extent to which the EU member states attempted, from the 1970s onwards, to coordinate their foreign policy preferences and maximize their coherence, this was essentially done through the relatively informal channels of European Political Cooperation (EPC – Nuttall 1992) in which consensus-seeking and lowest common denominator decision-making were the order of the day. EPC, it should be stressed, took place entirely outside the formal institutions of the EU. Even after the Union itself decided, at the Maastricht European Council meeting in December 1991, to develop a Common Foreign and Security Policy (CFSP), the civilian dimension continued to dominate – both as a result of the institutional structures devised for the new policy area (intergovernmental bargaining) and as a result of the member states' initial difficulties in reaching agreement on an appropriate format for the introduction of a tentative military arm. CFSP as a policy area was proposed in February 1990, but it was almost a decade before a framework was developed for the institutional and practical requirements behind the 'S' (Security) component. We shall examine the details of these institutional developments in Chapter 2.

One key question posed by this passage from entrenched civilian status to aspirant military status was that of knowing whether the shift would fundamentally alter the essence of the EU as a project (Cornish and Edwards, 2001, 2005; JEPP, 2006/1). The answers to that question will become clearer in Chapter 5. Suffice it to say, for the moment, that no definitive answer is yet possible. While there seems little reason to imagine that the EU, as it develops its military muscle, will either emulate or (still less) rival the USA in global military force projection, and while all the empirical evidence points to the emergence of a security and defence profile which is both *sui generis* and very different from anything previously witnessed in the realm of international relations, it must be stressed – as it will be periodically throughout this volume – that the EU as a security actor is still in its early infancy. The precise form it eventually assumes will be governed by a host of imponderables (the evolution of transatlantic relations, the impact of future enlargement, the emergence of other regional actors and, perhaps above all, the resolution – or lack thereof – of the various crises in the Middle East) as much as by any design scheme in Brussels or in leading national capitals. There is little point in bending over the cradle of this infant actor and speculating as to its detailed professional orientation 25 or 50 years hence.

Nevertheless, ESDP continues to generate controversy. Academics, policy analysts and practitioners pore over every detail of its existence and activities in an attempt to understand precisely what it is and where it is heading. Academics in particular – and, through them, an entire generation of students – have been fascinated by what is widely seen as a relatively dramatic development. The literature on ESDP (witness the Bibliography at the end of this book) is already voluminous considering the short lifespan of the project. Robert Cooper, the Director General for External and Politico-Military Affairs in the European Council, remarked to the author in a conversation in Oxford in May 2006 that his Brussels staff of 200 'effectively "do" ESDP', whereas there appear to be many thousands of academics and students all over the world who engage in study of the subject. The questions asked by academics generally differ from those posed by analysts and yet again from those of interest to practitioners. Where academics labour over theory, analysts tend to delve into political and strategic implications and practitioners deal with planning and organizational realities. This book will attempt to bring in insights from all three of these communities, but it will lean more towards the empirical, political and strategic side of the debate than towards the pure theory.

It is a truism to date the birth of the EU as a security actor from the Franco-British summit in Saint Malo in December 1998. This seminal event gave rise, throughout 1999, to intense discussions on the development of an *autonomous* institutional and military capacity for EU force generation and deployment. The word autonomous implied relative freedom from American leadership. The institutional bases of ESDP were fixed by the Cologne European Council meeting in June 1999 and the military capacity objectives by the Helsinki European Council meeting in December 1999. Thus, within a mere 12 months, at the very dawn of the new century, the EU succeeded in reaching agreement on arrangements over which it had simply avoided discussion for over 50 years.

It is worth recalling that the European integration project actually began with defence. The first 'European Treaty' after the end of the Second World War was the Franco-British Defence

Treaty of Dunkirk in 1947 (Greenwood 1989), followed by the (essentially defence-oriented) Treaty of Brussels in 1948 between France, the UK and the Benelux countries. The first impassioned intra-European debate, between 1950 and 1954, was over the European Defence Community (Fursdon 1980). Despite these origins, the EU as an entity remained untouched, throughout the Cold War, by security and defence policy. The reason for this was simple. NATO, as a collective defence alliance, underwrote the existential security of its member states and, by extension, of the European continent as a whole. That security guarantee was largely provided by the United States, which rapidly assumed the leadership of the Atlantic Alliance. But as the Cold War began to fade, the transatlantic relationship also shifted, both in its underpinnings and in its objectives. As Europe ceased to be the epicentre of US security policy, the ties began to weaken (Walt, 1998–9). From around 1987 to 1997, the EU debated endlessly – and unsuccessfully – the appropriate framework for the potential assumption of security responsibilities (mainly involving some formula for the mobilization of the Western European Union – WEU: see Box 1.1). But it was only after the Saint Malo summit in December 1998 that the Union bestowed upon itself the wherewithal to become a credible and autonomous security actor. The European Security and Defence Policy, as it became known from mid-1999, has moved and is still moving rapidly

Box 1.1 The Western European Union

The Western European Union arose from the Treaty of Brussels in 1948 as a body designed to coordinate the defence policies of the five signatory countries (UK, France, Belgium, Netherlands, Luxembourg). It was effectively superseded by NATO in 1949 as a significant defence organization, but was re-launched when Germany and Italy joined NATO in 1955 as an oversight organization to monitor compliance (especially German) with the terms of the Treaty. It became an organization grouping members of the EU which were also NATO members, but remained relatively dormant until it was 're-activated' in the 1980s. Most of its activities were effectively phased out in 1999 and transferred to the EU. See Deighton (1997).

from infancy to adolescence and on to budding maturity. We shall examine in Chapter 2 the reasons why this new policy area has developed so fast when in many other policy areas and institutional/constitutional aspects, the EU has recently appeared to be slowing down or even grinding to a halt. Some even believe that ESDP could infuse new life into the integrationist elements of a project which, for so long, set its teeth firmly against any military ambition at all (Alliot Marie 2005).

The genesis of ESDP

Why did the EU become a security actor? For a brief moment, at the end of the Cold War, some believed in the advent of a 'new world order' (Bush and Scowcroft, 1998) or even in the 'end of history' (Fukuyama, 1992). The talk was of 'peace dividends' and the worldwide triumph of liberal democracy. It was not to last. Within nine months of the fall of the Berlin Wall, Saddam Hussein had invaded Kuwait, provoking the first major military confrontation since the end of the Vietnam War. In late 1990, a coalition force of some 550,000 troops from 30 countries mustered in Saudi Arabia to force the Iraqi President to withdraw. European militaries realized, during the Gulf War of February–March 1991, just how dependent they were on US military technology and how ineffective and even inappropriate their own armed forces were for the type of post-Cold War 'crisis management' epitomized by the coalition to oust Saddam Hussein from Kuwait. Scarcely had that objective been achieved, however, when war broke out anew, this time in Europe itself. The violence which engulfed former Yugoslavia from the summer of 1991 to the autumn of 1995 was a wake-up call for the whole of Europe. War, it seemed, far from disappearing with the fall of the Berlin Wall, was as present as ever in a world where ethnic tensions, border disputes and strategic rivalries had, from 1949 to 1989, merely been suspended in the permafrost of superpower confrontation. And Europe, far from being able to assume the challenge of containing this new threat, as many assumed it could and would, proved, on the contrary, to be incapable of action. Meanwhile, storm clouds mustered around the EU's periphery, from the Maghreb to Kosovo, from the Caucasus to the Baltic. The US was preoccupied elsewhere.

Europe, ultimately, had little choice but to assume responsibility for the stabilization of its hinterland.

The period after Saint Malo was marked by a constant succession of major international developments, constituting a highly turbulent context within which the infant ESDP project was obliged to emerge. Significantly, most of these developments tended to enhance divisions either between the EU and the USA or among the EU member states – or both. These events included: the 1999 Kosovo crisis and NATO military operations in former Yugoslavia; growing tensions between the EU and the USA over missile defence schemes; the 2000 election of President George W. Bush and the advent of a new, less 'Euro-friendly' administration in Washington; the 11 September 2001 terrorist attacks on New York and Washington; the war in Afghanistan and the ensuing global 'war on terrorism'; the massive increase in US military capacity outlined in the October 2001 Quadrennial Defense Review (QDR); the launch of the €uro in 2002; the September 2002 US National Security Strategy with its emphasis on the new doctrine of *preemptive* warfare; the escalating crisis between Israel and the Palestinian Authority; a radical renewal of NATO's membership, structures and remit; the 2002 international crisis over Iraq, leading to the 2003 war and US occupation, and the concomitant crises of United Nations legitimacy and European unity; the 2003 Convention on the Future of Europe and the Intergovernmental Conference on a European Constitution followed in 2005 by the negative referendum results in France and the Netherlands; nuclear alerts in North Korea and Iran; the 2003 launch of the first ever European Union military missions; and the drafting of the EU's first security strategy document. Rarely can a single five-year period have been marked by so many portentous events. To say that the circumstances surrounding the ESDP's birth were unpropitious would be an understatement. And yet this policy area forged steadily ahead. To understand why, we need to situate it within the broader context of transatlantic relations.

While, throughout the 1990s, the EU sought to discover the necessary and possible framework for its security policy ambitions, most member states continued in practice to look for their security and defence requirements to NATO. In 1990, there were 12 EU member states, of which only one, Ireland, was not also a member of NATO. In 1995, with the accession of Sweden,

Finland and Austria, the increasingly inappropriately labelled 'neutrals' grew to four out of a total membership of 15 (27%). In 2004, however, with the advent of the predominantly Central and Eastern European accession states, the proportion of NATO members rose once again, to 19 out of a total of 25 (76%). That ratio changed again in 2007 when the EU embraced 21 NATO member states out of 27 (84%) (Table 1.1). If around 80 per cent of EU member states were reliant for their defence on NATO, why was there any necessity for the EU to embark on its own security project? This is a question we shall examine more fully in Chapter 4. It goes to the heart of the controversy surrounding the new EU policy area. Many adversaries of ESDP have pointed to the fact that, during the mid-1990s, the EU had attempted to organize its security arrangements entirely *within* the NATO framework by developing a European Security and Defence Identity (ESDI) based on European-only forces, a European-only command chain, and complex arrangements for borrowing essential assets from the Alliance. The buzz word for this arrangement was 'separable but not separate', a formula which consciously eschewed any suggestion of *autonomy* – the cardinal feature of ESDP. The object of the ESDI exercise was to provide for circumstances – of which the Bosnian war in the early 1990s was a prime example – where the EU needed to (and wished to) deploy military force, but in which the US did not wish to be directly involved. Why, many subsequent critics of ESDP later asked, did the Union feel the need to go beyond the NATO-friendly framework of ESDI and to develop the autonomous capabilities required by ESDP?

The detailed explanation for this shift will be examined in Chapter 3, but three key pointers can be highlighted immediately. The first is that the formal arrangements under which the EU might be able to 'borrow' crucial military assets from NATO (which remain classified to this day) were felt to be unsatisfactory for both parties. The second is that the identification of the WEU as the pivotal structure within such arrangements was an understandable but ultimately misguided choice. It was understandable in that the WEU was the only existing security structure which acted as an interface between the EU and NATO. But it was misguided in that the WEU was too weak politically, too insignificant militarily and too unwieldy institutionally to be able to carry out the major responsibilities which were being

Table 1.1 *EU and NATO Memberships, 1994–2007*

Date	*EU & NATO*	*Non-NATO EU*	%*	*Non-EU NATO*
1994	UK, France, Germany, Italy, Spain, Portugal, Belgium, Netherlands, Luxembourg, Denmark, Greece	Ireland	92%	Turkey, Norway, Iceland
1995	UK, France, Germany, Italy, Spain, Portugal, Belgium, Netherlands, Luxembourg, Denmark, Greece	Ireland, Austria, Finland, Sweden	73%	Turkey, Norway, Iceland (joined in 1999 by Czech, Hungary, Poland)
2004	Above, plus: Poland, Hungary, Czech, Latvia, Lithuania, Estonia, Slovenia, Slovakia	Ireland, Austria, Finland, Sweden, Malta, Cyprus	76%	Turkey, Norway, Iceland, Bulgaria, Romania
2007	Above, plus Bulgaria, Romania	Ireland, Austria, Finland, Sweden, Malta, Cyprus	84%	Turkey, Norway, Iceland

* Percentage of EU member states which are also members of NATO.

thrust upon it. The third reason is that NATO itself, while undergoing a constant process of self re-invention from 1989 onwards (Yost, 1998; Rynning, 2005; Rupp, 2006), failed ultimately to convince its major partners – on either side of the Atlantic – that it remained the key Atlantic security instrument for the rapidly unfolding new world in which powers were finding themselves required to act. The emergence of ESDP was, to this extent, in large part the result of the absence of suitable existing alternatives in a world which was changing rapidly from year to year. However, it is important to understand that, unlike NATO, ESDP is not a response to a sense of existential threat hanging over Europe. It does not involve the creation of a potentially offensive or aggressive armed force poised to fight major wars with other powers. ESDP represents the generation of a range of instruments appropriate to the task of 'crisis management'. By this term is meant the development or outbreak of a political or even military crisis between two forces within the boundaries of what is considered to be Europe's strategic space. The management of that crisis might involve the deployment of diplomatic or economic instruments, the despatch of police or administrative agents, or even the deployment of combat troops. Most often, it involves the mobilization of all of these instruments. ESDP is therefore a policy area akin to risk management on a regional basis. To that extent, it is a new development in international relations, comparable only in scope and range to the United Nations as a peace-keeping body, but potentially more effective than the UN in that it represents the collective will of its own member states who have agreed to bestow upon themselves the necessary instruments to enforce that will.

The basic structure of the book

This book is structured by the major interrogations which ESDP engenders, some of which have been referred to in the preceding paragraphs.

Drivers behind ESDP

Chapter 2 addresses immediately some of the major misperceptions and misunderstandings which have arisen. There are several reasons for the confusion which has accompanied the emergence of ESDP. First, national politicians, through lack of an appropriate discourse aimed at *explaining* ESDP, have, in most countries, failed to enlighten their national publics as to the real motivations behind the project. At the same time, newspaper proprietors, chasing circulation figures, have created the mythology of a dramatically problem-ridden ESDP. In short, there has been enormous public misinformation about the principal drivers behind the project. I have devoted an early section of Chapter 2 to the issue of *what ESDP is not*. Because ESDP is so controversial, various constituencies have detected in it motivations which they find alarming. Some 'blame' unscrupulous and/or misguided politicians who, it is alleged, embarked on the project out of personal political ambition without realizing what perils they were unleashing. Others (mainly in the USA) worry that ESDP is a strategy to 'balance' against US power or that it is, in some way, designed to undermine, subvert, or replace the NATO alliance. ESDP also worries those (predominantly but not exclusively in Europe) who fear that the entire European integration project is leading inexorably to some type of European melting-pot in which national distinctiveness and above all national *sovereignty* is being seriously eroded. Among these critics are those who dread the emergence of some mythical 'Euro-army' which will both (effectively) put an end to centuries of regimental and national glory and (ineffectually) set about the task of defending the territory of the EU member states from some ill-defined external existential threat.

This same chapter will seek to allay many of these fears by setting the project squarely in the twin contexts of its natural gestation. On the one hand, it is the logical offspring of exogenous forces deriving from the end of the Cold War – most notably the lessening strategic importance of Europe for the USA and, as a consequence, the diminishing relative military significance attached by Washington to European security. Since long before the end of the Cold War, and intensively after 1989, the USA admonished the Europeans to take greater responsibility for their own regional security (Gompert and Larrabee, 1997). This is what eventually happened after 1998. At the same time, that development meshed neatly with the endogenous dynamics of the European Union itself as it ceased to be simply a market and aspired to emerge as a political actor on the world stage. The development of a modicum of military capacity was probably an inevitable concomitant of that ambition. The rest – the details – have been stimulated by 'events': the lessons of the Balkans; the inherent evolution of both the EU and NATO; the rise of new threats and unforeseen risks; the emergence of dangerous non-state actors; 9/11 and the new world disorder; US-led preemptive wars and their repercussions for European security.

ESDP, after initial teething troubles, emerged in the early years of the twenty-first century as a credible project. It has institutions which work reasonably well; it is acquiring usable and relevant military capacity; it has taken on (successfully) a growing number of overseas operations: military, policing, training and assistance, border control and peace monitoring. It is beginning to specialize in *Civilian Crisis Management*. It has given itself both an embryonic strategy and a number of procurement objectives; and it has successfully devised a procedure (structured cooperation) to allow for the maximization of available inputs from all member states. Of course there are different agendas for ESDP in different national capitals. It is impossible to generalize in any meaningful way, but certain realities are widely accepted. The ESDP project does not aspire to become a military superpower comparable in any way to the USA. It does not aim to become a 'European army' responsible for collective territorial defence. It is conceived as a *capacity* – political, civilian and military – which extends the range of instruments at the EU's disposal for essential crisis management operations in the Union's immediate neighbourhood and to some extent beyond. Any military operations envisaged will be conducted, where relevant, in consistency with NATO, a body with which the EU now has a comprehensive understanding about shared and distinct security responsibilities. Civilian operations will be tightly coordinated with the United Nations.

It is now over 20 years since the 'Gorbachev effect' first began to turn the world on its head. Few (if any) analysts foresaw in 1985/6 the dramatic developments which have punctuated the last 20 years. We can be fairly certain that the next twenty will be equally difficult to call. Meanwhile, the ESDP project will develop along the pathway implicit in its infancy: natural in gestation, limited in scale, unique in genre, *sui generis* in purpose.

The politico-institutional framework

Chapter 3 will offer a fresh analysis of the reasons why the ESDP project has taken the politico-institutional course it has – *rather than other available courses*. It will seek to demonstrate the inherent logic behind current politico-institutional developments. There were three main options available towards the end of the Cold War, when it became clear that the Europeans could not continue (and no longer wished) indefinitely to cling to US apron-strings (Wyatt-Walter, 1997). The first was simply to ignore the strategic challenges of the post-Cold War, to continue to concentrate on what the EEC/EC/EU had always been – a civilian, 'soft' power – and to bask in the sunshine of the 'end of history'. That illusion was shattered in the deserts of Arabia and the mountains of the Balkans. The second, given the relative inappropriateness and inadequacies of European military capacity (for forty years geared to fighting a line-based conventional defensive war on the great European plain – now the one scenario which could be ruled out as highly improbable) was to find some means of identifying, from inside NATO, the command structures, the forces and the instruments which would allow *Europeans* to cope in their own regional backyard, and *Americans* to deploy elsewhere – where more urgent challenges awaited them. This led to widespread assumptions that the one institution in existence with specific responsibility for European security coordination – the Western European Union – in cooperation with NATO, would be an obvious part of the solution. It informed the five year attempt (1994–9) to find a politico-institutional arrangement via the emergence of a European Security and Defence Identity (ESDI) inside NATO. Alas, the attempts to find an institutional framework through the WEU were doomed.

The demise of ESDI led inevitably to the third option: the European Security and Defence Policy (ESDP) which posited autonomous political and military capacity *for the EU itself*. Chapter 3 will examine the existing institutional framework for foreign and security policy-making which pre-dated the Saint Malo summit, as well as assessing the new institutions which emerged from the processes unleashed by that summit. It will not seek to conceal the disagreements and divergences between European leaders over institutional processes, nor will it gloss over the complexity of security decision-making under the present multi-level institutional framework. But it will argue that, as a result of readily understandable developments, the eventual structures which emerged proved to be workable if not ideal. The chapter will follow institutional developments through from 2000 (Treaty of Nice) to 2007 (Constitutional Treaty impasse). It will conclude with a critical analysis of the new politico-institutional instruments called for in the Constitution and their likely impact on the efficiency and course of the ESDP project. It will also argue that the very complexity of the ESDP institutional labyrinth rules out the possibility of any actor or nation-state dominating policy. Everything that is agreed is agreed 'at twenty-six' – Denmark being the only EU member state which does not take part in ESDP.The significant feature is that, despite the institutional maze, many significant and robust agreements are reached and implemented.

Military and civilian capacity

Chapter 4 will begin with an inventory of EU military capacity at the end of the Cold War, demonstrating how, even though the member states collectively were spending huge sums on 'defence', their ability to deal with the new types of security threat which characterized the post-Cold War period, all of which required force projection, mobility, rapidity and coordination, potentially over long distances, was extremely limited. This therefore required major transformation. While most European nations greeted the end of the Cold War with calls for a 'peace dividend' and defence budgets began to fall, others saw immediately that new challenges were emerging. The new direction was initially indicated by a small number of countries (UK, France, Belgium and the Netherlands) which, through a succession of programme reviews, nudged their armed forces towards the new world order. All of this took place before the ESDP project emerged. The chapter will therefore chart the evolution and progress of thinking in Europe about military capacity: from the CJTF concepts of ESDI (essentially stemming from reflections on Bosnia), to the Helsinki Headline Goal 'force catalogue' of 1999 (strongly influenced by reflections on Kosovo), to the current ambitions of *Headline Goal 2010* with its emphasis on usable battle-groups (designed to meet the real challenges of limited crisis management in areas such as the Balkans and the Democratic Republic of Congo). It will analyse the outcomes of the various 'commitment conferences' of the early twenty-first century, which sought to identify and eliminate the major shortfalls in EU military capacity, and it will chart the gradual emergence of usable military assets at the disposal of the Union. It will evaluate the relevance and appropriateness of the principal EU missions – the so-called 'Petersberg tasks' (humanitarian responses, peace-keeping and peace-making tasks) – to the potential challenges facing the EU. It will outline the still inchoate 'debate' within the EU over the *type and style* of military capacity that the EU needs to acquire: classical conventional or fully digitized US-style 'network-centred'. It will address the problems facing EU military planners at the level of procurement and will offer an initial evaluation of the activities and challenges of the new European Defence Agency.

In a second section, this chapter will also look at the non-military instruments of ESDP – the instruments of *civilian crisis management*. Since most scholarly attention has been focused on the EU's emergence as a military actor, there has been a tendency to neglect its growing capacity to re-inject necessary judicial, administrative and civilian protection mechanisms into crisis situations – either pre-conflict or post-conflict. This side of the ESDP equation is in some ways more important than the military side. In the post-modern world we are entering, the instruments available to the 'international community' to intervene in crisis situations and assist in 'nation-building' or 'state-building' are overwhelmingly instruments such as police forces, judges, lawyers, civil administrators, penitentiary officers and disaster relief agents. Quietly but surely, and somewhat away from the spotlight, the EU has been developing these capabilities since the birth of ESDP in 1999. Ten of the 16 overseas missions already embarked on as this book went to press had come within this framework. Finally, this chapter will assess the necessary – and uniquely *European* – capacity to coordinate both the military dimension and the civilian dimension of crisis management. For the two should not artificially be separated. They remain tightly interdependent.

ESDP and transatlantic relations

Chapter 5 will analyse the confused and quasi-schizophrenic manner in which both the EU and the USA have faced up to the new challenges of their evolving security relationship. It will assess the various contrasting US schools of thought on ESDP (ranging from the overtly enthusiastic to the vigorously opposed) primarily in order to make the twin points that the USA has not reacted in unitary fashion and that this is hardly surprising in view of the unprecedented nature of the implied new relationship. Hegemonic powers have difficulty accepting a shift to balanced partnerships, realists understand 'balancing' as 'threatening'. All too few Americans take the project seriously in its own terms and all too many (still) consider it as either utopian or insignificant (or both). This range of opinion reflects the fact that nobody really knows what ESDP portends – other than that it constitutes a significant step in a new and unfamiliar direction. But the US confusion is reflected back across the Atlantic not only in the dichotomous line-up of 'Atlanticist' and 'Europeanist' countries within the EU, but also in the fact that important nuances to that line-up exist around the margins: a Denmark which combines rejection of the ESDP project politically with espousal of its ethos culturally and which prefers NATO while asking serious questions about the USA; a Netherlands which combines Euro-federalist and Euro-Atlanticist impulses; a Norway and Turkey which, from a starting position of enthusiastic Atlanticism, have begun to look upon ESDP as a future potential; a series of Central and Eastern European countries which were hailed by Donald Rumsfeld as 'new Europe' but are already shifting the balance of their security preferences in the direction of their new *alma mater*, the EU.

The plain fact is that, for Americans as for Europeans, the emergence from the Cold War has presided over an end to the aberrant relationship which obtained from 1949 to 1989 (and which persisted to 1999), based on *hegemony* and *dependency*. That relationship was aberrant in that the USA demanded unquestioned leadership but complained about lack of burden-sharing; and in that the Europeans enjoyed a period of free-riding (which effectively reduced their sense of responsibility for security and defence) while complaining constantly about US hegemony. It was a relationship imposed by the realities of the

Cold War with which neither side was satisfied. But no one country any more than any one individual has any clear idea of how that relationship will eventually be restructured. Meanwhile, 'events' will dictate its actual course and configuration. The chapter will assess various different approaches to the new and constantly evolving transatlantic security relationship.

Chapter 5 will also evaluate the evolution of relations between ESDP and NATO, arguing, essentially, that while in the early days of ESDP, the new-born infant seemed destined to grow up in the shadow of its 50-year-old cousin, the balance of that relationship has shifted constantly. NATO has moved into radical new territory since the Prague summit in November 2002. It has given itself a global remit; it has declared war on terrorism; and it has equipped itself with a new rapid reaction force. But to an increasing number of observers, this seems to amount to being 'all dressed up and nowhere to go'. The Alliance, which had initially been designed to deliver US commitment to European security, has imperceptibly been transformed into an Alliance implicitly configured to deliver European commitment to US global strategy. After 2003, the politics of NATO operationality became hostage to the overall state of the transatlantic relationship. With 26 member states, it has become harder to imagine the circumstances under which a NATO deployment could command political consensus let alone unanimity. There have been calls for NATO forces to be deployed to Iraq, to Gaza, to Kashmir, to Darfur, to the Caucasus and even beyond. But no political consensus proved possible among the member states for such arrangements. The only place where NATO was able to deploy was Afghanistan, the one country on earth where, in the wake of the terrorist attacks of 11 September 2001, virtually no state objected to an American military presence. In 2006, NATO adopted a 'stand or fall' policy in Afghanistan. On the other hand, ESDP, beginning in 2003, became involved in some 15 to 20 missions in over a dozen countries on three continents. ESDP seemed to have become more 'usable' than NATO itself. ESDP has, since December 2002, enjoyed a formal working arrangement with NATO. On paper, the arrangements seem perfectly sensible and they have worked well in areas such as the Balkans where European forces have gradually replaced NATO forces while still being reliant on NATO for back-up in the event of an aggravation of the situation. However, major problems still exist between the two forces. Since there is a finite pool of troops and other forces on which, currently, both NATO and the EU can call, what happens if both entities call on them at the same time? These are just some of the issues which currently lie at the heart of an increasingly complex relationship. However, the chapter will argue that, despite today's lack of clarity in apprehending the precise future of transatlantic relations, the picture that will emerge is one in which ESDP will complement rather than compete with, enhance rather than weaken, and facilitate rather than complicate the strategic efforts of the US and of the evolving Atlantic Alliance.

A European strategic culture?

Chapter 6 assesses the consequences in terms of 'strategic culture' of the ongoing creation of the European Security and Defence Policy. The ways in which national collectivities think about defence and security, the role of armies, the function of war and the likelihood of peace are subtly different from one country to another. The chapter begins by considering the vast differences in what is called 'strategic culture' between the EU's member states. In recent years, a substantial and sophisticated literature has appeared addressing the question of whether the very recent development of ESDP is or is not leading to a new, trans-European, strategic culture. There is no overall consensus on this, some analysts detect divergence, others convergence. We shall assess this literature and the problems it raises. Those approaching ESDP from a realist perspective tend to adopt criteria appropriate to the analysis of nation-states and thus often fail to come to terms with the very different reality epitomized by the EU in general and ESDP in particular. When assessed against the expectations and assumptions peculiar to the behaviour of a unitary nation-state, ESDP is, not surprisingly, often found wanting. Most theoretical work on EU strategic culture nevertheless comes out of the constructivist (see pp. 191–8) camp. Here too, there is a potentially important problem in that constructivists like to work from the basis of an identifiable and coherent cultural unit – which most often presents a sense of collective identity. Clearly, such a coherent identity has not yet emerged in the EU. On the other hand, if the debate is framed less around issues of identity and more around those of capacity, objectives and implementation, there are grounds for concluding that convergence is already taking place. Some important constructivist work, notably by Bastien Giegerich (2005) and by Christoph Meyer (2006), has recently been carried out. Both conclude, tentatively and provisionally, but unequivocally, that clear signs of convergence can be detected.

In a second section of Chapter 6, we will evaluate the seminal December 2003 document known as the European Security Strategy (ESS) which set out in geo-political terms the normative strategic thinking behind ESDP (see Appendix, pp. 260–70). We shall examine the origins and composition of the ESS, setting the document in its historical context (the War in Iraq). We shall see that the ESS offers a different approach to international security from traditional nation-state actors, emphasizing normatively different issues such as comprehensive security, global public goods and human security and offering up a vast and integrated range of policy instruments with which to tackle security challenges by emphasizing multilateralism, prevention, global scope and a new definition of power. The chapter will conclude by asking to what extent we can detect clear signs that all these developments are forging a coherent new EU-wide cultural approach to the task of underwriting regional – and potentially global security.

The EU's overseas missions

Chapter 7 will offer an initial assessment of the overseas missions which had, at time of going to press, been conducted by the EU under the aegis of ESDP. Since January 2003, the EU has mounted no fewer than 16 civil-military missions in as many countries on three continents. With the exception of the purely military operations, which have generally mobilized several thousand troops (Operation *Althea* in Bosnia-Herzegovina involved up to 7,000 troops), the majority of these missions have mobilized between several dozen and several hundred individuals (all in all about 1,500). The most distant, and the only operation in Asia, is the EU Monitoring Mission in Aceh (AMM) which has, since September 2005, overseen the peace agreement between the Indonesian government and the Free Aceh Movement (GAM) which put an end to 30 years of civil war. The EU projected its norms to a distant part of the world that has been at war since decolonization. A different story emerges from Central/East Africa, however. After many hesitations (and several false starts) the EU abandoned any intention of mounting a major military mission in Sudan, judging the strategic challenges in Darfur to be too constraining in a situation where, in any case, a definitive settlement will require a serious political breakthrough in Khartoum. The EU therefore restricted its involvement (as did NATO) to offering military assistance and training to the forces of the African Union. A similar decision was initially taken in Congo, where for months the EU restricted itself to assistance for the AU. However, on 12 June 2006, the Council finally decided to authorize Operation EUFOR RD Congo, involving 2,000 soldiers in support of a UN mission of 17,000 (MONUC) to enhance security during the crucial elections in Congo on 30 June. This mission is limited in scope and has been denounced by those who feel that the EU ought to be capable of a much more robust and muscular involvement (Haine and Giegerich, 2006). However, the mission has to be seen as part of a holistic EU policy, embracing both diplomatic and institutional support for the peace and democratic process. As such, whatever its actual shortcomings, it is certainly in line with the new normative approach sketched in this book.

Elsewhere, the EU has taken on less challenging tasks. Two missions to train judges, jurists and penitentiary officers in Georgia (300 officials) and Iraq (800) were technically concluded, although questions remain as to the overall impact of such initiatives. Symbolically, but also in a practical way, the EU's involvement underscored the importance in these countries emerging from various forms of arbitrary authority of the existence of the rule of law based on competent personnel. Two other missions have focused on border control in critically unstable regions: Moldova/Ukraine and Gaza/Egypt. In both cases, the porous borders have been transmission belts for traffickers of various sorts and this concentration on limiting international criminal or terrorist activities once again demonstrates a practical operationalization of the ESS. The EU's emerging speciality in crisis management has become that of the police mission, the trailblazer of civilian crisis management. This has been the key contribution of the EU in Macedonia, Bosnia, DRC (Kinshasa) and in the Palestinian Authority. To deploy a force sufficiently sizeable to reassure traumatized populations (in Bosnia more than 500 agents were dispatched) and to train local police forces is a genuine novelty for the international community, strong on symbolism but also very necessary and practical. However, these missions have revealed serious problems and a very steep learning curve.

Finally, there have been four strictly military missions – in Macedonia, Bosnia and two missions in Congo. These missions have allowed the EU to hone and demonstrate its ability to project force – even into 'non-permissive' theatres such as the DRC – at considerable distances from Brussels. These are not expeditionary forces destined to shift political balances, still less invasions by conquering armies. These are crisis-management missions which have succeeded in mobilizing EU troops selected from almost all member states and indeed from 14 non-EU states, projecting them externally, taking charge of planning (either with or without NATO assistance), sustaining them in the theatre and deploying them within a clear political framework (Giegerich and Wallace, 2004). This EU apprenticeship in military force projection remains limited for the moment, but it is real, has proven successful and carries with it the seeds of future crisis management missions. Crucially, these operations are almost all coordinated with and complemented by civilian assets designed to provide the elements of post-conflict reconstruction which is the real trademark of the EU and of ESDP. As of 2007, as many as 15 EU battle groups will be ready for deployment, theoretically allowing the EU to engage in two medium-sized operations simultaneously. To repeat: the military instrument is not the primary instrument of ESDP. But it is an instrument which is essential as an underpinning of the overall thrust of the EU's CFSP.

The major challenges ahead

Chapter 8 will assess the major challenges ahead. A number of studies were published in 2006 which attempted to peer into the future and predict the contours of the world in which the EU will have to function in 2025. For security and defence planners, a bewildering number of factors have to be entered into the overall calculation. The bottom line is that, 20 years hence, the environment in which the EU will be competing will be much less hospitable than it is today. To begin with, the EU's assets will all have declined, at least relatively, against her main competitors. Economically and commercially, Europe will have been overtaken by new rising poles like China and possibly also India, with Brazil and perhaps even Russia coming up fast. Demographically, Europe's declining and ageing population will pose massive challenges in terms of immigration as well as domestic spending (with concomitant pressures on external or security spending). At the same time, the EU will become ever more dependent on energy sources from some of the least stable areas on earth, and will have to compete for those sources with rising giants like China which will have an insatiable thirst for scarce fossil fuels. Environmental problems will increase, affecting the agricultural yield of the EU. In science and technology, without a radical increase in funding for education and for research and development, the EU is likely to be left far behind by the USA and Japan and to have been overtaken by China and India. The new multi-polar structure of the world will in itself bring new sources of tension, which the individual member states alone will have no chance of stabilizing. The pressures for the EU to speak to the rest of the world with a single voice will become intense. The refusal to make collective EU choices in the world of 2025 will be tantamount to an abdication of sovereignty. The EU's immediate neighbourhood will be likely to be even more volatile than it is today, with a Russia seeking to re-assert itself in the new multi-polar pecking order, a Middle East in a state of constant ebullition and an African continent, both north and south of the Sahara, brimming with social discontent and, hence, migratory threats. Turkish membership of the EU would take its borders to some of the seriously unstable parts of Asia Minor and force the Union to become a serious player towards its immediate neighbours, the Caucasus, Iran, Iraq, Syria. This will require ever more sophisticated and robust military instruments. Finally, terrorism is predicted to increase as a security threat, while becoming more and more of an internal than an external challenge. How, under these circumstances, will the EU succeed in husbanding its shrinking resources to maximize their effectiveness? Rationalization and pooling of security and defence budgets seems inevitable.

Empirical reality and political theory

As the above summary and the following chapters make clear, ESDP has emerged overwhelmingly as a series of empirical reactions to historical events. While visionaries in London, Paris, Brussels and other cities dreamed up blueprints for ESDP's short and medium-term trajectory, which political leaders worked hard to shape, it was the dual movement of history's tectonic plates on the two symbolic dates of 9/11 (9 November 1989 – fall of the Berlin Wall – and 11 September 2001 – the terrorist attacks on New York and Washington) that acted as principal fertilizer and incubator. Among the many consequences of those twin earthquakes, one which stemmed equally strongly from both of them was the relative disengagement of the USA from its 50-year role as guarantor of European security. Not only did the 1989 fall of the Berlin Wall remove Europe as the central blip on the US radar screen, but the 2001 Al-Qaeda attacks obliged Washington to concentrate its available resources and forces elsewhere. While teleology should be firmly rejected as an explanatory factor (nothing is inevitable *solely* because of historical forces), this volume will argue strongly that 'events' were largely responsible for the specific course ESDP has taken. When, in 1958, the UK Prime Minister was asked by a young journalist what had been the most difficult problem to cope with in his first year in Downing Street, Harold Macmillan replied: 'Events, dear boy! Events!' Since November 1989, and especially since September 2001, 'events' have run way ahead of the capacity of politicians and statesmen – even strong ones – to determine their precise course. In the area of security and defence, events have also ridden roughshod over most of the established theories of European integration.

Attentive readers may have noted that the approach I have outlined so far is essentially empirical. I have not sought to situate my analysis of developments in European security and defence explicitly within the framework of any particular school of International Relations theory or of European Integration theory. This is for two main reasons. First, my work has almost always been grounded first and foremost in empirical research, which then informs my theoretical considerations. I make no apology for this. That is the work I enjoy doing and it is, in my view, the best way properly to get to grips with what is actually happening. My approach is essentially inductive, pursuing relentlessly the concrete realities of coordination and even integration of security and defence policy – on the ground, in government offices, in ministries, in the various EU agencies in Brussels, among soldiers and diplomats in the field. It is based largely on official documents, political speeches and government statements and on interviews with many actors at many different levels. This approach is supplemented by close contact with the many security and defence think-tanks across Europe and in the United States where policy analysts constantly monitor and interpret the evolving reality. That is the raw material of ESDP from which, to the extent to which I believe it is possible to derive an overarching theory, my own theoretical approach stems.

The writings of political scientists and theorists provide an interesting and necessary context within which my own theoretical observations can be situated, but they do not, except on rare occasions, influence my inductive analysis of the concrete reality that is ESDP. That statement should in no way be read as critical of those who choose to prioritize theory. Most scholars thrive on the intellectual challenge of constructing theoretical models which are then offered as explanatory frameworks behind complex historical and political reality. Others strive to situate their research findings within one or other of these theoretical models or frameworks. Such activities are indispensable. Theory is a valuable way of making cognitive sense of complex reality. However – and this is the second reason for my relative downplaying of the theoretical dimension – existing academic theories have had enormous difficulty in explaining the existence of ESDP. Indeed, most theorists, from most schools, have long insisted that, whatever other policy areas might one day come under the aegis of European integration, security and defence will not be among them. In other words, what most theorists over the years have focused on and 'explained' is the *absence* of ESDP (Ojanen, 2006: 58–60). A brief incursion into the domain of theory is therefore necessary at this point in order to understand the generally unsatisfactory – or even plainly erroneous – analysis of ESDP in some of the scholarly literature. Several serious and highly illuminating attempts have already been made to situate ESDP within existing theoretical frameworks (Manners, 2002b; Mérand, 2003; Giegerich, 2005; Meyer, 2005; Ojanen, 2006; JEPP, 2006). To date, however, none has been wholly satisfactory. Those readers who are keen to discover the main outlines of the book itself may prefer to skip this theoretical incursion at this point and go forward to Chapter 2, returning to ponder theory when they have understood more closely the empirical reality.

Box 1.2 The Westphalian system

The Treaty of Westphalia (1648) ended the Thirty Years War, and posits four basic principles:

(1) The principle of the sovereignty of nation-states and the concomitant fundamental right of political self-determination; (2) the principle of (legal) equality between nation-states; (3) the principle of internationally binding treaties between states; and (4) the principle of non-intervention of one state in the internal affairs of other states.

For these reasons, the Treaty of Westphalia is crucial in the history of international political relations. It formed the basis for the modern international system of independent nation-states. It marked the beginning of an international community of law between sovereign states of equal legal standing, guaranteeing each other their independence and the right of their peoples to political self-determination. The two most innovative principles being proclaimed were the principle of sovereignty and the principle of equality among nations.

The Treaty defined these new principles of sovereignty and equality among states in order to establish a durable (eternal) peace and friendship among them, within a mutually acceptable system of international law, based on internationally binding treaties. This was a revolutionary approach to international relations. For the first time, it established a system that respected peoples' rights and that relied on international law, rather than on brute force and the right of the strongest to regulate interactions between states.

Source: Adapted from *Wikipedia*.

In the case of *international relations* theory, none of the existing schools seems to come close to explaining the 'ESDP effect'. *Structural realism*, so long the dominant force in US international relations theory (Waltz, 1979; Mearsheimer, 2001), has no convincing explanation for the phenomenon whereby sovereign state actors pool their sovereignty and, apparently ignoring the rules of the Westphalian system (Box 1.2), elect to intervene in the internal affairs of neighbouring – or even in some cases quite distant – sovereign countries. For structural realists (also known as *neo-realists*), state actors alone can engage in security and defence – that is, military – activities, either individually, or as part of a military alliance. A body such as the European Union, in this conception, is not only inappropriate for but theoretically quite incapable of engaging in security and defence policy. Indeed, the most recent 'grand tome' from the structural realist camp, *The Tragedy of Great Power Politics*, by John Mearsheimer (2001: 392–6), gives little credence to European integration and tends to assume, on the contrary, that the EU, as a result of the end of the Cold War, is likely to go 'back to the future' and revert to the type of nationalist jostling for position we saw in the nineteenth and early twentieth centuries. ESDP is, in any case, hardly studied by neo-realists for the simple reason that it does not fit into their vision of things. The principal explanation offered – that the EU is 'balancing' against US dominance (Posen, 2004; Art, 2004; Walt, 2005) – is not hard to refute (Brooks and Wohlforth, 2005; Lieber and Alexander, 2005; Howorth, 2006a). I shall return to this debate in Chapter 2.

Other scholars from within the realist family tend to see European integration as a standard process of inter-state bargaining with a view to furthering the national interest. This school, among scholars of European integration, is known as *intergovernmentalism*. Stanley Hoffmann argued forty years ago that integration could only take place in policy areas where state gains constantly outweighed losses. This, he predicted, would not and could not be the case in the area of 'high politics', of which defence was the ultimate example (Hoffmann, 1966). This approach was taken to its ultimate theoretical conclusion – in the very year of Saint Malo – by Andrew Moravcsik (1998) in *The Choice for Europe*, his ground-breaking work of *liberal intergovernmentalism*. Moravcsik argues that although actors other than just states – social actors of many types – can bargain at the international level for more rational policy coordination, ultimately, decisions are taken by the state. Once again, foreign, security and defence policy is regarded as the prime policy area where coordination and (still less) integration will *not happen*. That received wisdom was also accepted by the other main school of European integration theory, *neo-functionalism*, which excluded from its key processes of spillover the entire field of foreign and security policy – considered as the last bastions of sovereignty. Spillover is the process whereby the successful functioning of integration in a given policy area is believed to create pressures in connected policy areas for a similar measure of integration. Hanna Ojanen has recently suggested that all these theorists were so focused on finding a reason for the empirical *absence* of integration in security and defence that they failed to realize that their own theories could in fact *explain* a phenomenon such as ESDP if they simply jettisoned the distinction between high and low politics (Ojanen, 2006: 61). There is no reason, she suggested, if they perceived their national interests as being better served by coordination, why sovereign states should not cooperate. One problem with such an approach, however, as Frédéric Mérand (2003: 13–17) has argued, is that it would imply the likelihood of much more explicit inter-state bargaining in the realm of security and defence than has actually taken place. Would states, hard pressed for resources and struggling to justify their sizeable but ultimately ineffectual militaries, not logically have made much more of an effort to coordinate force generation, troop deployment, defence expenditure, equipment procurement if this rational intergovernmental approach were the principal motor behind ESDP developments? Manifestly, this is not happening. One has to look elsewhere than to the realists for an explanation.

Neo-liberalism, with its emphasis on trade and economics as the twin pillars of interdependence and soft power (Keohane and Nye, 1972, 1977), while offering useful interpretations of the purely civilian actor the EU *used to be*, has its work cut out trying to explain why the EU has now chosen to don the accoutrements of *military power*. Neo-liberal approaches are, at one level, geared to explaining the absence of war and the presence of peace in complex multilateral organizations. Their focus on *soft power* is informed by a belief that military instruments have been over-analysed in IR and that the significant aspects of the present are the features of attractiveness and exemplarity of which the EU is a model (Nye, 2004). These approaches appear to lend themselves awkwardly to the analysis of ESDP which at first glance seems to run against the grain of neo-liberal theory. On the other hand, *supranationalists* are also hard put to come to terms with a European reality in which the main actor in their integrationist system – the European Commission – has little more than a bit part to play in ESDP (Stone-Sweet *et al.*, 2001). As with the realists, one discovers that neo-liberals and supranationalists have tended to neglect or eschew analysis of this key policy area whose very existence poses a challenge to the bases of their theoretical approach. Moreover, both liberal intergovernmentalists and supranationalists have striven to stake out a territory fenced by a dominant or mono-causal explanatory factor for European cooperation (the former) or integration (the latter): on the one hand the sovereign state as a unitary actor involved in political bargaining; on the other hand supranational institutions with diverse actors at multiple levels involved in functional integration. The key element here is that each of these two camps believes that *its* dominant explanation trumps that of the other. However, it is not clear why scholars would wish to detect mono-causal or even dominant drivers behind complex political and historical processes. ESDP is certainly such a process.

As for those who eschew any prior theory in favour of methodology, in particular the more social-scientific approach of the *behaviourist* school, there are two main obstacles to the application of its methodology to the European Union in general and to ESDP in particular. The first is that behaviourists also tend to reason in terms of inter-state relations and have difficulty fitting into their framework complex multilateral bodies such as the EU. The second is that their analysis relies crucially on massive data-sets which can be analysed inductively. Such quantitative data simply do not exist for either CFSP or ESDP at this point. Nevertheless, objectively, one of the bedrocks of this recent work – democratic peace theory which argues that democracies do not wage war on one another – ought logically to allow for serious application to the EU (Russett, 1994; Russett and Oneal, 2001). Unfortunately, to date, no major work has been done on ESDP from within this perspective, although some initial research findings have been published and doctoral dissertations are in train (Donno, 2006).

To the extent to which the recent wave of *constructivism* has addressed these issues, it has been to suggest that international relations can be understood in more value-based or normative terms (rather than as a simple clash of interests), and that in this sense EU security integration is theoretically unproblematic. Where neo-realists and neo-liberals insist that states have more or less fixed preferences dictated by unchanging factors such as the international system or national interests, constructivists have insisted that those preferences are in fact *socially constructed* through forces such as identity, ideas, normative beliefs and socialization – which are in a state of constant evolution. As Glarbo (1999: 649) argued, 'social integration is emerging as the natural historical product of the day-to-day practices of political co-operation'. Yet, for years, constructivists seemed, for the most part, somewhat ill-at-ease with the EU as their focal point and tended to fight shy of delving too deeply into this recent, swiftly flowing and somewhat murky current. Two of the major tomes of constructivist theory (Wendt, 1999, and Katzenstein, 1996) fail even to look at the European Union as such. Constructivism has, since the mid-1980s, succeeded in broadening national concepts of security (Buzan *et al.*, 1998) with the result that there has been some measure of convergence between neo-realist and neo-liberal approaches on the one hand, and the newer, sociologically-derived theories of international relations on the other, not least because constructivism has made some significant concessions to rationalism (Smith, S., 2000). Thus, as Mérand, who is himself closely connected to the constructivist school, has pointed out, 'pure' constructivists cannot really explain in theoretical terms *why* state preferences change, nor can they explain factors such as the 2002–03 decision on the part of both Tony Blair and José-Maria Aznar to pursue policies over the Iraq War which were fundamentally at odds with the identity and ideals of their electorates. Constructivism as an overall method or approach remains very much mired in pure theory, with the result that it remains far more idealist and prescriptive than analytical and descriptive. There are a few very recent notable and successful exceptions which deal tellingly with specific issues or case studies (Croft, 2000; Risse, 2002; Mérand, 2003; Keating, 2004; Giegerich, 2005; Berenskoeter, 2005; Tofte, 2005; Meyer, 2006), to which I shall return where appropriate in the chapters that follow. For what it is worth, my own feeling is that constructivism will increasingly reveal deep insights into ESDP.

Two other approaches must be mentioned, even though they relate more to foreign policy than to security and defence policy. The first is the approach which sees a central role for political leaders. There is no question but that, at key moments in history, no matter how seemingly compelling may be the constraints of path dependency or systemic forces, individual leaders can make a significant difference. Thus, to ignore the role of Mikhail

Gorbachev – or, more indirectly, of Ronald Reagan – in bringing an end to the Cold War would be to discount one critical factor among others. To underestimate the role of Tony Blair in breaking, at Saint Malo, with fifty years of traditional British refusal to countenance a security and defence role for the EU would be to miss a fundamental element behind ESDP. But it is crucially important here not to misread the stimuli which motivated the individual. Those, for instance, who argue that Blair crossed the European Rubicon out of some sort of European mission, have failed to recognize the most important motivating factor behind his visit to Saint Malo: pressure from Washington DC as a result of the historical forces unleashed by the end of the Cold War. Leaders are fascinating to study, but it is important not to misunderstand their deeper motivations. The second final theoretical approach, which builds on leader narratives but goes beyond it, is that of Foreign Policy Analysis. This approach concentrates on the wider policy-making and institutional context of decision-making. The domestic and international political contexts within which decision-makers function constitute a central element in this approach, as do the complexities and bureaucratic peculiarities and above all the inter-agency tensions behind ultimate security and defence policy-making. While this approach has been largely confined to foreign policy (Hill, 2003), it offers considerable potential for application to security and defence policy (Rynning, 2002; Mérand, 2003). All of these theories and approaches have their uses and their values and the present volume will refer to them as and where appropriate. But it does not consider itself to be fully identifiable as part of any of these schools.

In one of the earliest studies of ESDP, I coined the concept of 'supranational inter-governmentalism' (Howorth, 2000: 36, 84). By that I meant the phenomenon whereby a profusion of agencies of inter-governmentalism take root in Brussels and, through dialogue and socialization processes, reaction to 'events' and a host of other dynamics, gradually create a tendency for policy to be influenced, formulated and even driven, from within that city. This is close to the idea of 'Brusselsization' used by other commentators (Allen, 2004; Nuttall, 2000). Governments, often against their wishes, are constantly being forced in directions they had not anticipated. Vivien Schmidt (2002: 63–7) has outlined a variety of 'mediating factors' which help explain such changes in government policy on major issues. Although her factors were devised for the European political economy, they are easily adaptable to other policy areas, including security. *Vulnerability* – in strategic terms – is a factor which, in the last 15 years, has risen dramatically to the top of security policy-makers' agendas. It is largely exogenous and a prime example of 'events'. *Political-institutional capacity* – an endogenous ability to impose or negotiate change – has also evolved markedly in the field of ESDP. European statesmen, even the most powerful, have demonstrated time and again that national institutions are inadequate to the task of driving forward a coherent *European* response to the external environment. New European institutions and agencies have recently popped up like mushrooms to fill the gap. *Policy legacies and preferences* – the extent to which long-standing approaches remain valid – are likewise factors to which even the most powerful statesmen have been forced to submit. Consider the irony of it being a *Gaullist* president, Jacques Chirac, who reversed his socialist predecessor's inhibitions about bringing France back into the NATO fold in 1995; or of it being a *British* Prime Minister, Tony Blair, who, at Saint Malo in 1998 acted as midwife to European defence integration. Above all, *discourse* – the ability to change preferences by altering actors' perceptions of the available options – has proven to be an immensely powerful factor in driving forward the ESDP process (Howorth, 2004). Policy preferences which, only a few years previously, would have seemed unimaginable to many a leading actor, have in recent years and in this crucial policy area rapidly been embraced, constructed and integrated into the mainstream.

The moves towards coordination in that last bastion of 'sovereignty' – security and defence policy – with all their limitations and caveats, constitute a sea-change in the way the EU and its member states will henceforth relate to the outside world. The reality is deeply empirical and lends itself awkwardly to theoretical speculation. It belies the prescriptions of most main schools of theory. As this book will show, there is no question that *coordination* is taking place. Coordination is a term much favoured by intergovernmentalists because it meshes with their rational-choice methodology. One question which analysts nevertheless return to frequently is this: will there come a time when the intensity, scope and scale of coordination across a range of issue areas in security and defence becomes so intense that it amounts, *de facto*, to *integration*. Integration, of course, is the notion favoured by neo-functionalists because it does, precisely, lead to a new supranational structure. Hanna Ojanen (2006) has recently presented the outline of a case for concluding that coordination might well lead to integration (providing, according to her analysis, NATO does not first succeed in re-absorbing and fusing with ESDP, thereby snatching it back into an Atlantic context). The overlap between coordination and integration has been, to some extent, theorized by neo-functionalists; but the precise distinctions, and above all the dividing line at which point the process shifts from one to the other have not. It might be helpful for the discussion if a new term were to be coined which highlights the complex and symbiotic forces at play: *coordigration*. My view is that ESDP demonstrates a great deal of coordigration. But, as we shall see below, it also has a very long way to go . . .

Chapter 2

Disputed Origins: True and False Drivers behind ESDP

The Saint Malo revolution

Around three o'clock in the morning on Friday 4 December 1998, officials of the French and British governments slipped under the bedroom doors of President Jacques Chirac and Prime Minister Tony Blair, both fast asleep in the French seaside town of Saint Malo, a document which was to revolutionize both the theory and the practice of European security and defence (Whitman, 1999; Shearer, 2000; Author's interviews London and Paris, 2000). The document had been written from scratch during the late afternoon and evening of 3 December by the Political Directors of the UK Foreign and Commonwealth Office and the French *Quai d'Orsay*, respectively Emyr Jones Parry and Gérard Erreira. The *Saint Malo Declaration* (Box 2.1), as the text was to be known, initiated a new political process and a substantial new policy area for the European Union. This new venture was soon to be called the European Security and Defence Policy (ESDP). The key sentences from the Saint Malo Declaration are the following:

1 The European Union needs to be in a position to play its full role on the international stage . . .
2 To this end, the Union must have the capacity for autonomous action, backed up by credible military forces, the means to decide to use them, and a readiness to do so, in order to respond to international crises.
. . . In strengthening the solidarity between the member states of the European Union, in order that Europe can make its voice heard in world affairs, while acting in conformity with our respective obligations in NATO, we are contributing to the vitality of a modernized Atlantic Alliance which is the foundation of the collective defence of its members.

Box 2.1 The British-French Summit, Saint Malo, 3–4 December 1998

JOINT DECLARATION

The Heads of State and Government of France and the United Kingdom are agreed that:

1 The European Union needs to be in a position to play its full role on the international stage. This means making a reality of the Treaty of Amsterdam, which will provide the essential basis for action by the Union. It will be important to achieve full and rapid implementation of the Amsterdam provisions on CFSP. This includes the responsibility of the European Council to decide on the progressive framing of a common defence policy in the framework of CFSP. The Council must be able to take decisions on an intergovernmental basis, covering the whole range of activity set out in Title V of the Treaty of European Union.

2 To this end, the Union must have the capacity for autonomous action, backed up by credible military forces, the means to decide to use them, and a readiness to do so, in order to respond to international crises.

In pursuing our objective, the collective defence commitments to which member states subscribe (set out in Article 5 of the Washington Treaty, Article V of the Brussels Treaty) must be maintained. In strengthening the solidarity between the member states of the European Union, in order that Europe can make its voice heard in world affairs, while acting in conformity with our respective obligations in NATO, we

→

How can we understand the historical origins of ESDP? In one of the earliest published studies of ESDP, I noted that 'the story of European integration began with defence' (Howorth, 2000: 1). This story punctuates the European Union's constantly frustrated attempts to forge a coordinated defence capacity back from the negotiation of the Treaty of Dunkirk (1947), through the Brussels Treaty (1948), the European Defence Community (EDC 1950–54),

→ are contributing to the vitality of a modernized Atlantic Alliance which is the foundation of the collective defence of its members.

Europeans will operate within the institutional framework of the European Union (European Council, General Affairs Council, and meetings of Defence Ministers).

The reinforcement of European solidarity must take into account the various positions of European states.

The different situations of countries in relation to NATO must be respected.

3 In order for the European Union to take decisions and approve military action where the Alliance as a whole is not engaged, the Union must be given appropriate structures and a capacity for analysis of situations, sources of intelligence, and a capability for relevant strategic planning, without unnecessary duplication, taking account of the existing assets of the WEU and the evolution of its relations with the EU. In this regard, the European Union will also need to have recourse to suitable military means (European capabilities pre-designated within NATO's European pillar or national or multinational European means outside the NATO framework).

4 Europe needs strengthened armed forces that can react rapidly to the new risks, and which are supported by a strong and competitive European defence industry and technology.

5 We are determined to unite in our efforts to enable the European Union to give concrete expression to these objectives.

Source: Reproduced from Rutten (2001: 8–9), and on http://www.iss-eu.org/chaillot/chai47e.pdf.

the Fouchet Plan (1962), the process of European Political Cooperation (EPC 1970s), the re-launch of the Western European Union (WEU 1980s) to the first glimmerings of the Common Foreign and Security Policy (CFSP) in the 1990s (Howorth and Menon, 1997: 10–22; Duke, 2000; Andréani *et al.*, 2001; Cogan, 2001; Quinlan, 2001; Duke, 2002; Hunter, 2002; Salmon and Shepherd, 2003; Bonnen, 2003; Dumoulin *et al.*, 2003).

That Europe should have sought to maximize its own security and defence capacity seems logical enough and, as indicated above, several attempts were made. Why did they all fail? At this point, suffice it to say that the most significant factor which stymied earlier efforts, particularly during the Cold War, was the contradiction between the respective positions of France and the UK. For 50 years (1947–97), Britain and France effectively stalemated any prospect of serious European cooperation on security issues by their contradictory interpretations of the likely impact in Washington of the advent of serious European military muscle. I have called this the *Euro-Atlantic Security Dilemma* (Howorth, 2005b). London tended to fear that if Europe demonstrated genuine ability to take care of itself militarily, the USA would revert to isolationism. The British fears were exacerbated by a feeling in London that the Europeans on their own would never be able to forge a credible autonomous defence. Paris, on the other hand, expressed confidence that the USA would take even more seriously allies who took themselves seriously. Both approaches were based on speculation and on normative aspirations rather than on hard strategic analysis. Prior to the Saint Malo summit of December 1998, a robust *European* Security and Defence Policy simply could not exist. As long as France and Britain, Europe's only two serious military powers, remained at loggerheads over the resolution of the *Euro-Atlantic Security Dilemma*, impasse reigned.

The Saint Malo summit was therefore revolutionary in two ways. First, it removed the blockage which, for decades, had prevented the European Union from embracing security and defence as a policy area and therefore from evolving and maturing as a global political actor. For several leading member states of the EU, like the United Kingdom, the Netherlands and Portugal, European security and defence had long been the *exclusive* prerogative of NATO – end of discussion. This had been the case since the late 1940s and nothing much had changed since then. At most, 'Atlanticist' countries might have been prepared to allow for greater coordination of EU security planning through the Western European Union (WEU; see Box 1.1), but for these countries there could be no thought, well into the 1990s, of the EU itself adopting security and defence as a policy area. For these states, the EU was seen as an entirely separate actor from NATO and one that should not challenge the

Alliance's monopoly of security and defence policy. Saint Malo put an end to all that, and in the pages that follow we shall seek to understand what drove its architects to head off in this new historical direction.

However, the second revolutionary consequence of Saint Malo was the widespread debate it unleashed. The relatively dramatic – and certainly unprecedented – prospect of the Union emerging as a military actor in its own right gave rise immediately to major controversies. What did this imply for the Union's deeply-etched ethos as a civilian actor relying on normative and transformative power (rather than on hard power) to achieve its objectives both internally and externally? What were the implications for European integration of the prospect of pooling resources in this first and last bastion of state sovereignty? How would such a decision impact on NATO, on the Alliance and on the United States? Could the Franco-British couple, so central to the launch of ESDP, remain united despite their very real differences over its deeper significance? Above all, where would it all lead? What was the *finalité* behind ESDP? The debates on all these issues were immediately engaged. They are still ongoing and will remain ongoing for years to come. The simple truth is that there are no definitive, or even obvious, answers to any of the questions just posed. But these questions about 'what?' and 'how?', important though they are, and to which we shall endeavour to respond in the following Chapters, have clouded our understanding of the key question: 'why?' Chou En Lai famously quipped in 1956, in answer to a question about the historical consequences of the French Revolution, 'it's too soon to say'. Less than a decade after Saint Malo, it is far too soon to speculate about its long-term consequences. But it is not impossible to understand where ESDP came from, to evaluate its fundamental drivers.

Misleading allegations

The question remains, therefore: Where *is* ESDP coming from? In order to begin to answer that question it is first necessary to dispel a number of major misunderstandings about motivations and to make it quite clear where ESDP *is not coming from.* Many of ESDP's critics have succeeded in confusing its true sources and motivations by attributing to it false origins or intentions. Four basic charges have been levelled, all of which are fundamentally misguided. ESDP is not a *mistake* and it is far from being *irrelevant*; it is not an attempt to create a *European army*; it is not designed to undermine or *weaken NATO*; and it is not intended to *rival the USA* or to engage in 'balancing' against USA power. The following sections will address these red herrings sequentially.

Neither a mistake nor irrelevant

One puzzle which many have pondered is: why did Tony Blair sign off on the Saint Malo Declaration and apparently jettison 50 years of consistent UK policy rejecting any regional security role for the EU? Many political opponents who have sought reasons to denounce ESDP have suggested that the whole project was a *mistake*, entered into for the wrong reasons by a naïve and inexperienced Prime Minister who did not realize what he was doing. This type of argument is often voiced in British or other European Eurosceptic circles by those who deplore the implicit departure from a long history of Anglo-Atlantic security priorities. A former UK Conservative Defence and Foreign Affairs 'shadow' minister argued that it was 'very clear' to him that ESDP was designed 'to get the government some good European coverage for not joining the single currency a month later. *And that was what it was all about* [my emphasis]' (New Europe, 2001: 65). The idea that ESDP arose from a Blair quest to secure a European role for the UK is widely encountered in the mainstream literature on the topic (Hunter, 2002: 29). This is a misleading notion. To argue that it is misleading is not to rule out the rather different proposition that Britain in general and Tony Blair in particular were, in the early days of the New Labour government, casting around for some sort of European role – which is undoubtedly true. But it is to reject the simplistic notion, usually advanced in Eurosceptic circles, that this was *the fundamental driver* behind the project – and that the prime minister did not understand the consequences of what he was doing. Blair's European aspirations undoubtedly *facilitated* a development which, as we shall see shortly, arose from the movement of history's tectonic plates. But they did not *generate* that development. It cannot, deep down, be attributed to Blair's search for a

European role. This is a very important distinction. Another allegation which is even further from reality comes from those not infrequent US commentators who, in one way or another, have dismissed the project as irrelevant , usually on the grounds that it is simply never going to 'work' – 'working' often being defined in terms of US military criteria (Hamilton, 2004: 150). For years, Washington officials tended to deride ESDP as hardly worthy of their attention: 'an exercise in photocopying machines' as one US official called it (Giegerich, 2005: 75). At a seminar on Europe's CFSP in Washington DC in September 2003, the author was astonished to hear a senior US official introduce the discussion with the injunction: 'And please, let's not waste time talking about ESDP! It used to be interesting. Then it became irritating. Today we see it as irrelevant'. Another example of this attitude is provided by Washington analyst de Jonge Oudraat who, in a concluding remark to a section of her study on ESDP headed (forthrightly) 'An Irrelevant Irritant' states: 'The lack of strong support from the major European powers for ESDP points to its irrelevance. European governments should . . . remove a prominent irritant in US–European security relations' (de Jonge Oudraat, 2004: 23). Quite apart from the inconvenient detail that the 'major European powers' have in fact all been extremely supportive of ESDP, these sorts of critics have unfortunately missed the point altogether. ESDP may well irritate its critics, but to dismiss it as 'irrelevant' is to fail even to begin to understand its origins.

Not a 'European Army'

The second red-herring stems from the widely-hawked suggestion that the real motivation was the desire to create a 'European army' – usually referred to in the popular press as the 'Euro-Army' (Echikson, 1999; Evans-Pritchard and Jones, 2002). This is both the easiest and the hardest criticism to refute. It is the easiest in the sense that there has never been any question that national military assets would be detached from national command and permanently re-assigned to a European command. There has never been any question of creating a 'standing European army', nor is there any question of forging common European ownership of weapons systems or other assets, nor (to date) any serious thought of developing a

European defence budget. Europe does not have a single unified political executive. Therefore a 'European army' in the strict sense of the term is logically inconceivable and it is unwise to use the expression lightly (Salmon and Shepherd, 2003). Each military or civilian mission mounted by ESDP has had (and any future mission will have) its own terms of reference, its own volunteers from a range of EU member states (and indeed from a range of non-EU member states as well), its own logistics and command arrangements and its own lifetime. When the mission is terminated, the resources, both human and material, initially assigned to it, revert to their national owners. Some critics of the 'Euro-army' assume that the project in some way amounts to the transposition, to the European level, of the role and function of traditional national armies with their responsibilities for national, *territorial* defence – in other words that the project is geared to 'defending' the EU space against an existential external threat (Casey, 2001; Cumming, 2004). For this reason, it is often alleged, it will not work because no Italian, or Spaniard, or Slovene or Pole will be prepared to 'die for Europe' (Assinder, 2000). The absence of European *identity*, in this view, is the Achilles heel of ESDP. Only *national armies* work.

There are three major flaws in this line of argument. It fails, on the one hand, to address the reality that, today, virtually no individual nation-state in Europe could 'defend' itself alone against a major external existential threat were one to arise. This has been the case since the dawn of the atomic era. So much for the national 'sovereignty' of 'defence'! Secondly, it also fails to understand that, in the absence of such an existential threat, but in the presence of regional crises, such as the wars in the Balkans, which require management, ESDP amounts not to a traditional army based on citizen conscripts but to a professional fire-fighting force acting in the interests of the Union or even of the 'international community'. No 'citizen' is being asked to 'die for Europe'. Professional soldiers – volunteers one and all – are being asked to do a necessary and sometimes dangerous job. These are very different phenomena. The third flaw in this argument is that there is just not one shred of evidence to support it. Every official EU statement about European defence (including a consistent line from France) stresses that the territorial defence of the European landmass (to the extent to which it faces an existential threat) remains the responsibility of NATO. Nobody in a

Box 2.2 Laughter at the 'Euro-Army's' expense

We are the Euro-army
The fighting force of today
We work together, take orders in English
That is, except les Français

We'll fight alongside the Germans
If we ever go to war
And if the image seems kind of familiar
Well, we've fought 'with' 'em one or two times before

We're working out rules of engagement
Addressing all our members' fears
And soon we'll be ready for battle
In only nine or ten years

So join in the Euro-army
From no conflict will we baulk
So come on you Spanish, Italians and Belgians
Ready!
Aim!
Talk!

Source: Phil Alexander, the author of the parody, who authorizes its reproduction here. From http://www.amiright.com/parody/60s/tomlehrer7.shtml.

position of authority in Europe has ever suggested that the EU should assume responsibility for the territorial defence of the Union. From this perspective, the 'Euro Army' argument is almost always overwhelmingly emotive and designed to evoke strong visceral reactions (Marsden, 2000). A website in the UK – www.euro-army.co.uk – allows readers to sample and judge for themselves some of the whackiest nonsense about the project.

However, there can be no denying that what is being created is a European armed force, for use on behalf of the European Union, under a European commander, flying the European flag, and using exclusively European military assets. At the time of writing, the EU, under ESDP, had mounted some five or six military missions. It is also true that, through the deliberations of a variety of 'top-down' agencies such as the European Defence Agency (EDA), the Council of Defence Ministers (CDM), the office of the High Representative for the Common Foreign and Security Policy (HR-CFSP), and the Political and Security Committee (COPS), which we shall examine in Chapter 3, an ever greater degree of coordination and even integration of policy planning and force planning has been taking shape. In time, this could well lead to a more *integrated* set of arrangements and mechanisms for the more efficient delivery of foreign and security policy objectives. Does this amount to *coordigration* (see above, Introduction, p. 31)? Perhaps, but given that the EU has now embarked on ESDP, surely it is logical that it implement the policy as efficiently and as cost-effectively as possible? The price of failure could be extremely high for the entire EU project. And there is no political risk in success. The ESDP process is destined to remain strictly voluntary, consensual and intergovernmental for as long as the Union remains a body which falls short of fully fledged federalism. All talk of a 'Euro-Army' is little more than politically motivated chatter.

Not designed to undermine NATO

The third major charge which has been levelled at ESDP is that it is in some devious way designed to undermine or weaken NATO (Weston, 2000; Menon, 2003; Cimbalo, 2004). This theme, which consistently points the finger at France, has run continuously since 1998. It has never been satisfactorily refuted and has never really gone away. For hard-line Atlanticists in every country, the emergence of ESDP has always been assumed to be necessarily prejudicial to NATO. The idea was forcefully articulated by Strobe Talbott in his premonitory speech on the new developments at Chatham House in October 1999:

> We would not want to see an ESDI that comes into being first within NATO but then grows out of NATO and finally grows away from NATO, since that would lead to an ESDI that initially duplicates NATO but that could eventually compete with NATO. (Talbott, 1999)

Talbott uses ESDI because at the time he spoke the acronym ESDP had not yet entered the scene. But what he is talking about is clearly ESDP and *not* ESDI. Prime Minister Blair has devoted himself tirelessly to countering this allegation. Virtually his every

utterance on ESDP contains (at some point) the defensive a
reassuring mantra that the project remains entirely consiste
with NATO (Box 2.3). Much of this 'undermining of NATO
criticism revolves around the argument that the original NATO
arrangements involving ESDI ('separable but not separate')

Box 2.3 Tony Blair's speeches on ESDP

'Committed to Europe, reforming Europe' – Ghent City Hall, Belgium, 23 February 2000

'In 1998, Britain and France took the initiative to strengthen Europe's common defences in a way that also strengthens NATO. EU Member States are now looking at ways of enhancing their military capabilities against headline goals. NATO will always remain the cornerstone of European defence. Both of our countries know only too well the importance of the transatlantic alliance for maintaining peace in Europe. But Europe needs to take on more responsibility and share more of the burden within NATO. And Europe needs to be able to act when the Alliance as a whole is not engaged.' (Blair, 2000)

'A clear course for Europe', London, 28 November 2002

'the orientation of Europe toward the United States is absolutely at the core of whether Europe can become effective in foreign and security policy. We need to be clear about where we stand. I know some European colleagues think I am being unnecessarily difficult over European defence and its relations with NATO. But believe me, unless it is clear from the outset it is complementary to NATO, working with it, adding to our defence capabilities, not substituting Europe for NATO, then it will never work or fulfil its potential.' (Blair, 2002)

Prime Minister's speech on Europe in Warsaw, 30 May 2003

'Thirdly, we want a Europe capable of sharing the burden of defending our way of life and freedom but doing so in a way fully consistent with our membership of NATO. NATO will continue to be the bedrock of our defence, in Britain as in Poland. That is why together we have been putting forward plans to reform it so that it can do the different tasks asked of it today. But we need a vastly improved European defence capability so that we can play our part better in NATO and also where NATO chooses not to be engaged, to undertake actions in our own right.' (Blair, 2003) constituted a better formula than ESDP for European security. ESDI, it is argued, accommodated both 'the desire to increase Europe's defence contribution' and the ability for 'Europeans to carry out missions not considered "primary" by the US' (Sangiovanni, 2003: 195). What these critics fail to recognize is that ESDI was transcended and replaced by ESDP *because ESDI did not work*. Not only was it dependent for political direction on a body – the WEU – which lacked political clout, political legitimacy and political credibility, but it also relied for military capacity on borrowing, from the USA, assets which were either jealously guarded by the Joint Chiefs of Staff or (especially after 9/11) simply not available because they were urgently needed by the US military itself. Moreover, ESDI had no real answers to the requirements of EU-only missions. ESDI was, furthermore, predicated on a far-reaching reorganization of NATO's command chain which the USA was simply not prepared to accept. In short, the inadequacies of ESDI were themselves a major driver behind the emergence of ESDP (Howorth and Keeler, 2003).

The suspicion that France, ever the 'reluctant ally', is somehow the *éminence grise* behind this 'anti-NATO' project has fuelled the notion that ESDP is a scheme designed in Paris to weaken the Alliance. The problem with this argument is reality. The reality is that, while France has never sought to *weaken* the Alliance (even at the height of Gaullism – Vaisse, 1996), in the early 1990s in particular Paris was extremely keen to re-integrate NATO's structures (Grant, 1996). Moreover, President Chirac and other French leaders have consistently stated that France considers NATO a vitally important ally (Villepin, 2003a: 345–6). Of course, a sceptic would scoff at France's protestations of NATO 'purity': 'They would say that, wouldn't they?' While pretending to take NATO seriously, the suspicion lurks, France is all the while secretly planning to undermine it. What this reasoning fails to appreciate is the totally changed circumstances of France's relationship with NATO in the interventionist climate of the post-Cold War world. This became self-evident in Bosnia and has remained true ever since. Intervention in Bosnia meant that membership of NATO's alliance oversight committees, especially the Military Committee, far from being a constraint on French action (as had been considered to be the case during the inactivity of the Cold War) had become a strategic and political necessity (Brenner and Parmentier, 2002: 42). Increasingly,

French soldiers were finding themselves, *de facto*, under NATO command. In these circumstances, as Defence Minister Pierre Joxe made clear, France's absence from NATO decision-shaping structures had become a serious liability. Joxe once jokingly remarked, in the context of NATO's increasing embrace of its former Warsaw Pact adversaries, that he would soon be the only defence minister in the whole of Europe not to take part in NATO meetings. He was rebuked by Mitterrand for his un-Gaullist sense of humour (Brenner and Parmentier, 2002: 133 f/n 21). The reality is that France has played a key role in all NATO's military operations since the end of the Cold War. It was Jacques Chirac who persuaded Bill Clinton to use NATO in a serious way to end the Bosnian conflict (Holbrooke 1998: 67, 330). It was France which provided the lion's share of NATO's *European* military assets during the Kosovo conflict in 1999. France has, for the last ten years, provided at any given moment either the largest or the second largest contingent of NATO peace-keeping forces. A French general has assumed the command of both of NATO's key missions: in Kosovo and in Afghanistan. It was France which took the leading role in instrumentalizing the *NATO Response Force*. What further proof could sceptics require that France actually takes NATO seriously?

France may have multiple motives for wishing to cosy up to NATO. The ability to experience combat alongside US troops is not absent from the calculation. Nor is France's long-standing quest for prestige. But the bottom line is that, for the foreseeable future, it is in France's national interests to make her practical contributions to regional (and even global) security as effective as possible. That means accepting NATO as a force which is both 'strong and effective' (Interview with General Patrice de Rousiers, Paris July 2006). This is not seen in Paris as incompatible with the parallel development of ESDP. On the contrary, the two are seen as mutually reinforcing.

Not 'balancing' against the USA

The final allegation which needs to be laid to rest is also the most serious and potentially the most explosive. 'The Euro Army stands on the threshold of becoming the greatest combat force of modern times. The EU has every intention of being the economic and military rival of the United States', argued one polemicist

(Cumming, 2004). Had such motivations been alleged only by the wackier web-sites, the charge could be dismissed as unworthy of comment. However, both US officials and US academics have feared something similar. Concern lay at the heart of the first official US reaction to the Franco-British initiative. In an article in *The Financial Times* three days after Saint Malo, US Secretary of State Madeleine Albright enunciated what became known as the 'three-Ds':

> As Europeans look at the best way to organize their foreign and security policy cooperation, the key is to make sure that any institutional change is consistent with basic principles that have served the Atlantic partnership well for 50 years. This means avoiding what I would call the Three Ds: decoupling, duplication, and discrimination.
>
> First, we want to avoid decoupling: Nato is the expression of the indispensable transatlantic link. It should remain an organization of sovereign allies, where European decision-making is not unhooked from broader alliance decision-making.
>
> Second, we want to avoid duplication: defence resources are too scarce for allies to conduct force planning, operate command structures, and make procurement decisions twice – once at Nato and once more at the EU. And third, we want to avoid any discrimination against Nato members who are not EU members. (Albright, 1998)

This initial reaction reflected concern in Washington (where there had been no prior warning that the Saint Malo initiative was imminent) that ESDP might aim to rival the USA in various ways. Robert Hunter notes that the 'risk' of the EU coming to rival the USA 'should have appeared to be minimal. But as a political matter, it gained greater currency in Washington and, rightly or wrongly, has been a source of concern ever since' (Hunter, 2002: 35). Albright's article amounted to a pre-emptive strike both to avoid ESDP's assuming its own distinct profile and to maintain US hegemony over European security developments (see Chapter 5, pp. 143–5). Ironically, where Washington feared ESDP *moving away* from US norms, the 'normative power Europe' theorists feared it being *sucked into* them. One (largely untested) assumption here seems to be that once the EU sets off down the military road, there is nothing to prevent it from 'degenerating' into a full-blown military power *à la* USA (Smith, 2002; Manners, 2004). In the USA, however, fears of genuine rivalry rapidly oscillated towards the opposite fear: that ESDP could prove to be an 'empty institutional distraction' leading to 'impotence and recrimination' (Gordon, 2000).

Yet the worries about motivations concerning competition and rivalry never completely disappeared. They resurfaced with a vengeance at the time of the Quadripartite summit between France, Germany, Belgium and Luxembourg on 29 April 2003 at the height of the Iraq War (Sands, 2003; Black, 2003; *Le Monde*, 2003). This event marked the nadir of ESDP in that the United Kingdom did not attend, and the EU-4 appeared to make very ambitious noises (Chapter 4, pp. 111–12). Many analysts at the time feared that the four intended to forge ahead with the project for a vastly ambitious European defence capacity – in the absence of any British restraining influence. Some critics indulged in straw-man tactics, ridiculing the alleged European 'pipe-dream' of 'rivalling the United States' (Moravcsik, 2003), but others saw it as a genuine threat to American strategic interests (Bremner, 2003; Geyde and Evans Pritchard, 2003). Such fears are quite unfounded – for two reasons. First, because, once again, nowhere in any official document issuing from the EU or even from a member state in the context of ESDP has there been expressed any intention of developing more than *peace support capacities* for the purpose of regional crisis management via the 'Petersberg tasks' – so designated at a WEU meeting near Bonn in June 1992, and covering 'humanitarian and rescue tasks; peacekeeping tasks; tasks of combat forces in crisis management, including peacemaking'. Some have seen the third of these Petersberg tasks as representing a step too far in the direction of militarization (Manners, 2004: 20). The American political scientist Robert Art equates 'peacemaking' with 'waging war' (Art, 2006: 182). However, when questioned on this very point, the British Chief of the General Staff, General Sir Mike Jackson explained that in order to carry out the first two Petersberg tasks efficiently, troops need to be trained to deal with the third: 'It is very easy to come down from a war-fighting posture to something below that. . . but if you settle for a 'Peace Support Army' and then you want to go into war-fighting, forget it! You will have the wrong equipment, the wrong training. You will have the wrong mindset' (Interview, London, June 2004). This does not mean that, in normative terms, the most robust capacity determines the very ethos of the whole. On the contrary, in order to have a *different* normative footprint, from a purely empirical perspective it is essential to have capacity which goes somewhat beyond that footprint.

Secondly, such an allegation misses the point that the EU long ago turned its back on military conquest or overseas adventures. To the extent to which a discernible EU *strategic culture* will eventually emerge, there is no question but that this culture will be restricted to the 'Petersberg tasks', will be heavily influenced by 'civilian–military' synergies, and will explicitly eschew any prospect of a return to great power military posturing (Chapter 6). Even in the most 'muscular' of the various theoretical scenarios for the future use of ESDP (EU-ISS, 2004; Venusberg, 2004; Everts *et al.*, 2004) there is no suggestion of the EU developing military capacity which could remotely aspire to rival or compete with the US military. The debate in terms of European capabilities is about what the EU will need to do in order to turn itself into an *effective* regional crisis management force (Everts *et al.*, 2004; Biscop, 2005a). The real challenge for the EU is not to close the gap with the USA but to close the gap between, on the one hand, Europe's own security environment, its requirements and its objectives, and on the other hand its current capabilities.

While US officials and journalists worried about empirical military rivalry, US scholars and academics worried about 'balancing'. Balance of power theory is a central pillar of structural realism – the dominant school in the American IR community (Waltz, 1979; Mearsheimer, 2001). Throughout history, it is argued, whenever a great power rises significantly above its rivals, second-tier states will try to 'balance' against it, either by developing their internal resources or by forming balancing coalitions. Stephen Walt has outlined the central puzzle – for structural realists – of the contemporary period: that 'power in the international system is about as unbalanced as it has ever been, yet balancing tendencies have been comparatively mild' (Walt, 2005: 123). Since the end of the Cold War, under the administrations of Presidents George H.W. Bush (1988–92) and then Bill Clinton (1992–2000), the USA – the world's only 'hyperpower' – appeared to have been exempt from balancing efforts on the part of second tier powers. This posed a real theoretical dilemma for structural realism. However, under the Presidency of George W. Bush, theorists from this school began detecting various forms of balancing, one of which was ESDP. Since it was difficult to portray this as classical 'hard' balancing (preparation for a potentially warlike show-down between the EU and the USA), the notion of 'soft balancing' was devised to categorize 'looser' types of resistance to the hegemonic power.

The primary exponent of the balancing thesis, Barry Posen, argues that ESDP is, to a considerable extent, driven by European concern over 'the hegemonic position of the US' and concludes that 'viewed in this light, ESDP is a form of balance of power behaviour, albeit a weak form' (Posen, 2004: 17). He is careful to distinguish between traditional 'hard' balancing against a perceived military threat and (although he does not use the term) a 'softer' type of balancing:

> The EU is balancing against US power, regardless of the relatively low European perception of an actual direct threat emanating from the US . . . US strategists and citizens should thus follow carefully the EU's efforts to get into the defense and security business. The Europeans are useful to the US, but if present trends continue, they will have the wherewithal to decamp, and they could even conceivably cause some mischief. (Posen, 2004a: 2–7)

Robert Art, in similar vein, sees ESDP as a form of soft balancing:

> ESDP represents the institutional mechanism to achieve the following aims: a degree of autonomy in defense matters; a hedge against either an American military departure from Europe or an American unwillingness to solve all of Europe's security problems if it remains in Europe; a mechanism to keep the United States in Europe and to have more influence over what America does there by showing that Europe will bear more of the defense burden; and ultimately a vehicle to help further progress . . . in the European Union project. (Art, 2004: 4)

Stephen Walt agrees with the assessment that ESDP is a case of 'soft' balancing:

> Although the original motivation for this policy was not anti-American, Europe's ability to chart its own course in world politics – and to take positions at odds with US preferences – will be enhanced if it becomes less dependent on US protection and able to defend its own interests on its own. A more unified European defense force would also increase Europe's bargaining power within existing transatlantic institutions, which is why US officials have always been ambivalent about European efforts to build autonomous capabilities. (Walt, 2005: 129)

Let us now assess these propositions by measuring them against the definitions of 'soft-balancing' put forward by its proponents. The first definition – and in some ways the narrowest – is that of Pape ('it aims to have a real, if indirect, effect on the military prospects of a superior state' Pape, 2005: 36). In the case of ESDP, this would imply an effort to constrain or diminish US military power. However, all the official statements about ESDP have explicitly argued the opposite. The Saint Malo Declaration stated that its objective was to contribute to 'the vitality of a modernised Atlantic Alliance, which is the foundation of the collective defence of its members' (Rutten, 2001: 8). The landmark European Union-NATO Declaration on ESDP of December 2002 states that the two organizations 'reaffirm that a stronger European role will help contribute to the vitality of the Alliance' and adds that 'the crisis management activities of the two organizations are mutually reinforcing' (Haine, 2003: 178). The seminal European Security Strategy document of December 2003 goes even further in stating that:

> The transatlantic relationship is irreplaceable. Acting together, the European Union and the United States can be a formidable force for good in the world. Our aim should be an effective and balanced partnership with the USA. This is an additional reason for the EU to build up further its capabilities and increase its coherence.

There is little room for ambiguity in these statements: the objective of ESDP is to relieve the US army from regional crisis management responsibilities in Europe in order to allow Washington to make better use of its military elsewhere in the world. *Partnership* is the keyword. This may be a partnership which the USA is unsure it *welcomes* but that is another matter. If a conceptual term from IR were to be applied to this approach, it would be bandwagoning, which 'takes place when weaker powers decide not to challenge the dominant power through balancing, but, on the contrary, to join forces with it as junior partners' (Walt, 2005: 183–7).

Another flaw in the balancing argument advanced by the structural realists quoted above is connected with *intentionality*. Robert Art argues that '[i]ncreases in a state's power relative to other states have consequences for the balance of power among them *irrespective of the state's intentions* [my emphasis]. In a balance of power system, the consequences of behavior ultimately override the intentions behind the behavior' (Art, 2005/6: 180). The problem with the 'intentionality argument' is that it simply cannot provide any convincing evidence that balancing US power was a major and explicit political driver behind ESDP. The problem with the 'outcome argument' is that it redefines balancing in an all-embracing way. If *any* action by *any* state which increases that state's relative power *vis-à-vis* another one is to be defined as 'balancing', then, as Brooks and Wohlforth (2006) and others have argued, it essentially strips the term of any conceptual or analytical usefulness.

Those US scholars who detect in the recent policies of the EU, and particularly in the ESDP project, evidence of balancing have, as we saw, lined up a series of hypotheses concerning the eventual effect of those policies: that the EU may acquire greater influence in Washington (Art), that Europeans may be in a better situation to influence the agenda in NATO, and eventually take positions at odds with US preferences (Walt), that they might even 'decamp' or 'cause some mischief' (Posen). Some or even all of these predictions may in fact prove – over time – to be correct. However, in terms of understanding what ESDP is and where it comes from, it must be stressed that all such considerations are outcomes – and only *potential outcomes* – of the project, rather than drivers. They are hypothetical consequences rather than motivating forces or intentions. They are not what the project *is about*. The EU, as an actor, has no experience of and no capacity for the sorts of considerations of power politics which are inherent to structural realist logic and which lie at the very heart of 'balancing'. Strategies of bandwagoning, buckpassing or balancing are not prominent (assuming they even exist) in European planners' minds. The EU is not a nation-state and does not behave like one. The guiding principles of ESDP are pragmatic, institutional, multilateral, multi-level, international, diplomatic, rules-based and transformative rather than strategic, coercive, narrowly self-interested, parochial or military. ESDP has been overwhelmingly a process of *reacting to* historical events, events which, since 1989, have tended to race ahead in 'fast forward' mode. It is simply not the case that ESDP has been driven by considerations of how to deal with overwhelming American power. Such considerations have not been absent, but they have not been primary. So where does ESDP come from? What *are* the underlying drivers?

The underlying drivers behind ESDP

There are four fundamental reasons why the European Union became a security actor. First, ESDP is the logical offspring of exogenous forces deriving from the end of the Cold War – most notably the lessening strategic importance of Europe for the USA and, as a consequence, the diminishing political and military significance attached by Washington to European security. The most salient consequence of that shift was eventual US military disengagement from the old continent. As long as the Cold War persisted, Europe was, *de facto*, at the heart of global geo-strategic reality. European security was the stakes in the global confrontation between 'East' and 'West'. All Europeans were concerned to ensure ongoing US commitment to that security. But US commitment inevitably implied US leadership. And although the West Europeans shared much more of the burden than the USA was prepared to recognize (Sharp, 1990), it was US leadership which defined the relationship. Hegemony mirrored by dependence. This was an unnatural – even aberrant – situation. There is nothing *automatic* about European-American harmony. For much of the period between the founding of the US Republic in 1776 and the end of the Second World War in 1945, the picture was one of regular wars between the USA and all the major European powers – Britain, Spain, Germany, Italy, Russia. Niall Ferguson has argued that the founding fathers of the USA clearly perceived the new state as a rising empire which would challenge Europe's empires for world markets, resources and power (Ferguson, 2004: 34–5). From 1945 until 1989, hot wars were replaced by a cold war with another major European power: the USSR. It is true that the main reasons for these conflicts – European imperialism, the US drive for 'open-door' trade policies, and the rise of potential hegemons within Europe – have all now disappeared. Moreover, the level of economic and investment interdependence between the USA and the EU is unprecedented in the history of the world (Quinlan, 2003).

Nevertheless, at the turn of the century, Euro-American harmony – while intuitively 'natural' – cannot simply be taken for granted. Witness the Iraq war of 2003. The quest for European security 'autonomy' is an entirely logical consequence of the end of the Cold War. Moreover, the USA had long been urging some form of it upon the Europeans. Persistently throughout the Cold War, and intensively thereafter, the USA admonished the Europeans to take greater responsibility for their own regional security (Sloan, 2003). Why should the US taxpayer continue to underwrite the security of a political entity with a greater population than that of the USA and a comparable GDP – particularly since there was no longer any apparent 'threat'? While the French had long been urging greater autonomy on their European partners, it required Tony Blair to cross a Rubicon for this to happen. His crossing was assisted by two major factors. The first was that, by late 1997, the new UK government was beginning to receive a very clear message from Washington. Far from a European security capacity being perceived in DC as prejudicial to the Alliance (as London had believed for 50 years), it was now being openly touted as the very salvation of the Alliance: unless Europe got its security act together, NATO was dead in the water. This was an idea that galvanised British security cultural thinking. The author was told by a senior FCO official in 2000 that, had the UK not been convinced that the Alliance was in serious trouble, 'we would not have touched Saint Malo with a bargepole' (Howorth, 2004: 220–2). The second factor urging Blair to embrace ESDP was the rising storm-cloud in Kosovo (see below). The fact that the EU collectively embraced the entirely logical need to look to its own regional security was a quasi-inevitable consequence of the end of the Cold War. A vacuum was forming which had to be filled. This was not strategic calculation; it was historical necessity. In

2004, the US *Global Posture Review* exercise completed the logic of this process by drastically reducing the US military presence in Europe ([IISS] 2004). One of the secondary consequences of these developments has been a series of question marks hanging over both NATO itself and its relationship with ESDP. This we will deal with in detail in Chapter 5.

A second and rather more normative driver behind ESDP also followed from the fall of the Berlin Wall. The 'new world order' called into being by President George H.W. Bush in 1990 was one in which some of the old rules of the Westphalian system (see Box 1.3) came to be questioned. The 'international community', which a reinvigorated United Nations appeared to conjure into existence, began to think in terms of intervention in the internal affairs of sovereign states in order to safeguard human rights and right humanitarian wrongs (Wheeler, 2000). This was to happen regularly throughout the 1990s – in Kurdistan (1991), Bosnia (1992), Somalia (1993), Sierra Leone (1997), Kosovo (1999), East Timor (1999). In Chicago, in April 1999, at the height of the Kosovo crisis of that spring, Tony Blair attempted for the first time to lay down guidelines for what he called 'the doctrine of international community':

> We are witnessing the beginnings of a new doctrine of international community. By this I mean the explicit recognition that today more than ever before we are mutually dependent, that national interest is to a significant extent governed by international collaboration and that we need a clear and coherent debate as to the direction this doctrine takes us in each field of international endeavour. (Blair, 1999)

This amounted, in effect, to re-drafting, for the twenty-first century, some of the oldest precepts of Thomas Aquinas's 'just war' theory (Walzer, 2000). The main thrust was to generate a politico-intellectual rationalization for transcending the state sovereignty which underlay the Westphalian system. The concept of 'crisis management' entered the IR lexicon (Lindborg 2002). This consideration meshed easily with the multilateral internationalism which typified most aspects of the EU's activities. After 40 years of institutional bargaining, the EU had become genetically incapable of not thinking in such terms. The desire to write the new normative rules of the game – especially the international legal, institutional, regulatory, interventionist and ethical – rules came naturally to Europeans who believed that they had finally put their own unruly house in order. Moreover, the European Union, as an integral part of the 'international community', was destined to need well-trained intervention forces in order to stabilize not only its own periphery and near-abroad but also, potentially, regions further afield.

The third fundamental driver behind the birth of ESDP was, of course, the reappearance of military conflict on the continent of Europe. In June 1991, Serbia and Slovenia fought a brief war, followed by a much longer war between Serbia and Croatia. In 1992, a conflict broke out in Bosnia Herzegovina which was to engulf the region for the next three years. When, in response to these events, the Luxembourg Foreign Minister Jacques Poos, temporarily chairing the EU's Council of Ministers, famously declared, 'It is the hour of Europe, not of America', few Europeans suspected the extent to which those words would acquire an aura of historical ridicule. Most assumed that the nations of Western Europe, which collectively were then spending almost $230 billion on 'defence', would rapidly put an end to this little local crisis. The fact that they did not – and *could not* – goes directly to the heart of Europe's security dilemma. In posturing in traditional Cold War military-power terms, the EU found itself both confronting an absent adversary and incapable of dealing with a very present and destabilising security environment. It would require a major shift in security thinking, military procurement and normative approaches for the EU to be able to take on the challenge which actually presented itself. The crises in the Balkans, which dominated the entire decade of the 1990s, were to create a powerful exogenous stimulus behind ESDP. I say exogenous, but it should not be overlooked that the geographical space occupied by former Yugoslavia is situated *inside* today's European Union – with Greece to the south, Italy to the west, Austria and Hungary to the north, and Bulgaria and Romania to the east. Sooner or later, the Western Balkans will become an integral part of the Union. While United States officials could declare with reason that their country did not 'have a dog in this fight' (Holbrooke, 1998: 27), this was, of necessity, very much the European Union's business. Reflections on the wars in former Yugoslavia have had a major impact on the development of ESDP. Appropriately, the Balkans proved, from 2003 onwards, to be the theatre of the EU's first incursions into military operations under an EU flag.

At the same time, these three developments, all responses to exogenous factors, meshed neatly with the endogenous dynamics of the European Union itself as it ceased to be 'just' a market and aspired to emerge as a political actor on the world stage (McCormick, 2006). This is the fourth underlying factor behind ESDP. Some have argued that the EU can never be a fully-fledged international actor unless and until it acquires credible military capacity (Cooper, 2003; Freedman, 2004; Salmon, 2005). This is a significant claim which we shall examine in more detail in Chapter 4. It is not immediately clear how or why the acquisition of military 'teeth' enhances the EU's credibility or viability as an international actor whose influence had previously derived from softer, transformative methods of exerting influence – such as its own attractiveness as a model – particularly for potential members (Vachudova, 2005) – or its use of financial and commercial levers (Youngs, 2004; Leonard, 2005). But the correlation between *political* unity and strength and the development of military instruments seems, on the surface, logical enough – particularly in the context of a revival of turbulence on the European continent. The development of a modicum of military capacity was probably an inevitable concomitant of that political ambition and that historical context. The rest – the details – were stimulated by 'events': the lessons of the Balkans; the inherent evolution of both the EU and NATO; the rise of new 'threats' and non-state actors; 9/11 and the new world disorder; US-led 'preemptive' wars and their repercussions for European security.

One final (indirect) stimulus came from another indigenous source: the European defence industry. Throughout the Cold War, many European nation-states had retained a number of defence-related companies producing everything from rifles to fighter aircraft. In most cases, these companies depended for their very existence on orders from 'their' national government which often sought to bring down unit costs to an affordable level through an aggressive export policy. France had developed this approach into an art form (Kolodziej, 1987). However, as the Cold War ended and defence spending around the world plummeted, this demand-led approach became doomed. The United States proceeded rapidly in the late 1980s and early 1990s to the restructuring and rationalization of its many defence industries. By the mid-1990s, there were only a handful of major players left (Susman and O'Keefe, 1998). The EU, if it was to retain anything approaching a cutting industrial edge, if it was to avoid being relegated to the status of sub-contractor to US companies, and if it was to safeguard hundreds of thousands of jobs, had little alternative but to rationalize as well (Schmitt, 2000). The Saint-Malo Declaration speaks explicitly of the need to forge 'a strong and competitive European defence industry and technology' (Rutten, 2001: 9). From 1996 to 2003, the EU reduced its own defence industrial base to four major players capable of competing on reasonably level terms with their US counterparts. The forging of a trans-national European defence industry has also – albeit painfully slowly – had a major impact on the course of ESDP (Schmitt, 2003, 2003a).

Conclusion

In its brief career, ESDP has had to cope with a large number of false accusations, misunderstandings, straw-men and crossed-wires. The truth is that ESDP as an embryonic actor disturbs and offends as many people as it satisfies or reassures. It disturbs those (mainly but not exclusively in the USA) who believe that American hegemony is both an entitlement and a necessary underpinning of lasting stability, and who feel that the proper place for any EU military capacity is as an adjunct to US capacity and leadership rather than as an autonomous actor. It also offends many (predominantly in Europe) who are basically opposed to the entire project for European integration and who see the military dimension of it as particularly alarming. Those who are uncomfortable with the integrationist dynamics of the European Union also fear that the 'pooling' of that first and last bastion of national sovereignty (security and defence) will, *ipso facto*, lead to ever more intensive federalism within the EU. There are others who worry that the ESDP narrative will close a chapter on their own vested interests – as professional officials of *national* foreign and defence ministries or other security structures with vast corporatist interests. Many of these critics have claimed the 'impossibility' of reaching political and strategic consensus among 15 and later 25 sovereign nation-states. Finally, the ESDP project worries numbers of 'ordinary' citizens across the Union who perceive in it an ill-thought-out scheme, dreamed up by elites with no consultation and no – or inadequate – popular explanation.

It is hardly surprising that national leaders and statesmen, elected by their national constituencies to defend and promote the national interest, should find it hard to construct a discourse which explains to those same citizens why cooperation in the field of *European* security should be in everybody's interest. For this is tantamount to recognizing limitations on their own power and influence. It amounts to a recognition that nation-states are no longer the only actors in the international system and that the rules of the game have changed. Most national leaders, on the contrary, have a vested interest in pretending that the rules of the game remain the same (Schmidt, 2006). This constitutes a problem for ESDP, which has been presented to different national publics in the various member states in very different ways. In France, it has been put across as enhancing and 'multiplying' French power and influence. In the UK, it has been presented as a limited measure only to be implemented in urgent cases where the United States does not wish to be involved. In Germany, it has increasingly been put across as corresponding to the new normative security culture which has epitomized the country since 1945: non-aggressive, legalistic and humanitarian. In some of the Central and Eastern European countries, it is cast in the light of a necessary step towards membership of the Union. Other countries have their own somewhat different takes (Giegerich, 2005; Meyer, 2006). Newspaper proprietors with global reach might be thought to be opposed to the EU project precisely because, being global in their operations, they do not wish to be constrained by regional entities. The reality is that they believe scare-mongering articles about the 'Euro-army' are good for sales. Once the evidence points uncontrovertibly towards the emergence of a European public which accepts ESDP on its merits, one might expect the negative editorializing to cease.

The surprising factor is that European publics, in every country, have little difficulty in accepting that 'security and defence' is a policy area which logically should be handled at European level. Figure 2.1 shows that the *average* level of support for ESDP among the different member states of the EU is extremely high. Although there are significant differences in the level of support among the EU member states, even in 'sceptical' countries like

Figure 2.1 Support for a common defence and security policy among the European Union member states

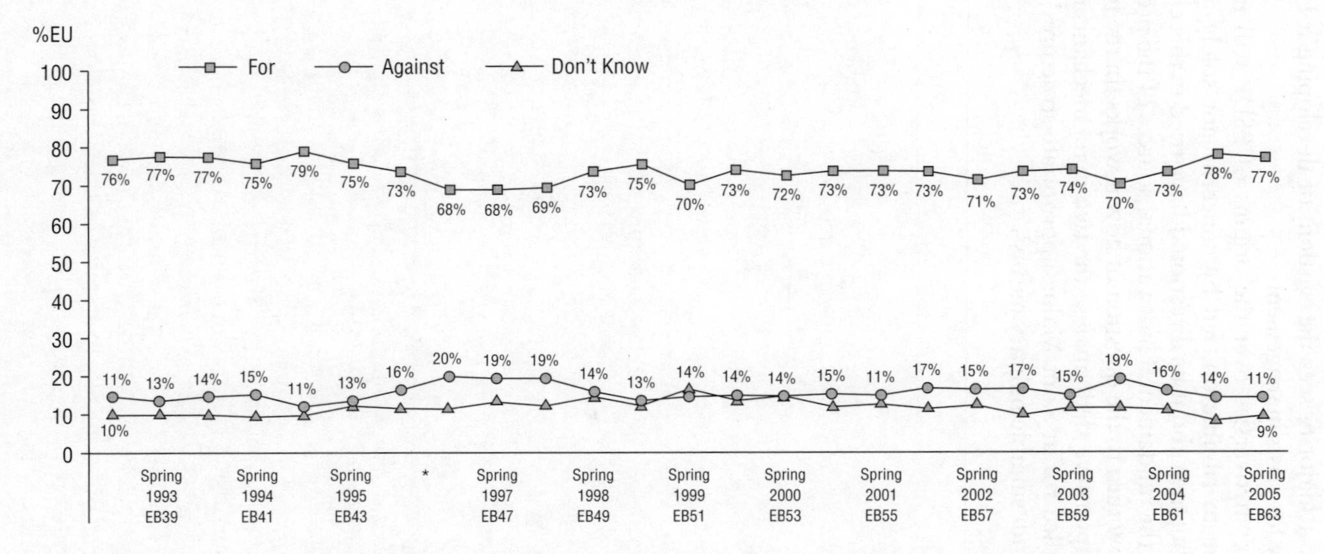

Notes: Spring 2005 support figure breaks down as EU-15 75%; 2005 accession states 85%. * No reading for spring 1996.
Source: Eurobarometer (report number as indicated).

the UK, a majority sees the wisdom of developing a European capacity for crisis management.

The controversies over the origins of ESDP will no doubt continue to rumble on, fed by concerns not solely about its source but also about its direction. I have tried in this chapter to present the fundamental motivational sources of the project. We must now turn to the question of how it works. In the following two chapters we shall analyse the two main mechanisms which were called for at Saint Malo: 'appropriate structures' (institutions) and 'suitable military means'.

Chapter 3

Decision-Making: The Political and Institutional Framework

Institutions and wiring diagrams

Under the 'Westphalian system' following the Treaty of Westphalia in 1648 (Box 1.2), only two types of actors have engaged in security and defence policy: nation-states and military alliances. There is no precedent for a grouping of sovereign nation-states such as the European Union taking upon itself responsibility for a security and defence policy. At the time of Saint Malo, the Union, as we saw in Chapter 2, had been striving to discover a way of engaging in this policy area from within the NATO alliance by engineering an institutional arrangement known as ESDI via the WEU. The decision – implicit in Saint Malo – to phase out the WEU and to give the EU direct responsibility for this highly sensitive policy area posed two immediate institutional challenges. The first was to devise a new framework which would allow for rapid and efficient collective decision-making. The second was to see whether such an arrangement could actually be made to work. The latter problem will be addressed in Chapter 7. It is the former problem which constitutes the central inquiry of this chapter.

The Saint Malo Declaration in December 1998 stated that:

> In order for the European Union to take decisions and approve military action where the Alliance as a whole is not engaged, the Union must be given the appropriate structures and a capacity for analysis of situations, sources of intelligence, and a capability for relevant strategic planning.

Over the following 18 months, beginning at the European Council in Cologne in June 1999, a series of brand new institutions was developed to respond to this prompting. Yet the business of institution-building itself was not without an element of controversy. When, under the German Presidency of the EU in early 1999, officials were busy working out the new institutional framework for what had not yet (quite) been labelled ESDP, the then Secretary General of NATO, Lord George Robertson, took pleasure in teasing his new-found security colleagues from the other side of Brussels. Insisting that what was really important in the field of security and defence was *military capacity*, he gently mocked what he saw as a misguided preoccupation in the European Council with institution-building. He warned against 'the narrow and sterile institutional debate that has so often dominated this subject' and insisted that it was 'political will plus the ability to act that matter first and foremost, rather than the way they are wired together'. 'You cannot', he quipped, 'send a wiring diagram to a crisis' (Robertson, 1999, 1999a). Robertson's comment was intended only half seriously. The British were not opposed to institutions, but from London's perspective the overwhelming reason for implementing Saint Malo was to create usable military capacity. We shall examine that capacity in Chapter 4.

The half serious aspect of Robertson's observation had two sides to it. The first was an implicit reminder that the EU had in the past made several attempts at creating new security institutions – the European Defence Community (EDC) in the 1950s, the Fouchet Plan in the 1960s, an attempt to refloat WEU in the 1970s (Howorth and Keeler, 2003: 6). Those early attempts at institutional engineering had not perceptibly advanced the cause itself. The second was a veiled warning to his continental colleagues not to attempt, via the subterfuge of ESDP, to promote the advance of European integration. This second message was echoed by the US administration. At a private seminar in Paris in May 2000, the US Ambassador to NATO, Alexander Vershbow, was even more explicit:

> If ESDP is mostly about European construction, then it will focus more on institution-building than on building new capabilities, and there will be a tendency to oppose the 'interference' of NATO and to minimize the participation of non-EU Allies. The danger here is that, if autonomy becomes an end in itself, ESDP will be an ineffective tool for managing crises, and transatlantic tensions will increase. (Lindley-French, 2000)

In short, security institution-building, from this perspective, was believed to carry within it potentially self-defeating propensities.

The existing institutional framework

Before examining in some detail the new institutions devised in 1999, it is helpful to remind ourselves of the preexisting institutional framework which had been established over the decades for intra-EU cooperation in the field of foreign and security policy. After all, CFSP had been in operation since the ratification of the Treaty on European Union (Maastricht Treaty) in 1992, and European Political Cooperation (EPC) had existed since the 1970s. Prior to Saint Malo, in addition to the longstanding *national* institutions in each member state such as ministries of defence and foreign affairs, defence chiefs and so on, there were already no fewer than nine *European* bodies with inputs to EU foreign and security policy. At the highest level, of course, stand the trimestrial European Council meetings of heads of state and government with ultimate decision-making and political responsibility for all matters connected with foreign and security policy. It was agreed in the Maastricht Treaty (and subsequently confirmed by the Treaty of Amsterdam (1997), the Treaty of Nice (2000) and the Draft Constitutional Treaty (2004)) that CFSP/ESDP would be conducted by a special *intergovernmental* pillar of the EU in which the Heads of State and Government, voting unanimously, would take all ultimate policy decisions. During the negotiations leading up to Maastricht, several EU member states had wished to 'communitarize' this new policy area along the same lines as those governing trade and the single market: in other words, to subject CFSP decision-making to qualified majority voting in the first pillar. The intergovernmental unanimity procedures agreed under the second pillar reflected the absolute refusal of countries such as the UK and France to accept such arrangements. Young Europeans cannot be sent into combat by qualified majority voting. Not surprisingly, institutionalization of ESDP further reinforced the control of the member states over this new policy area (Wessels, 2001: 77).

Below the European Council comes the General Affairs Council (GAC), which originally derived from the procedures of

EPC (Nuttall 1992). This body meets monthly and comprises the EU's 25 foreign ministers. It is, in practice, the main decision-taking body for CFSP and ESDP. However, by the turn of the century, its agenda had become overloaded (in part as a result of the launch of ESDP), compromising its ability to remain abreast of the minutiae of foreign and security policy. From 2003, it was renamed the General Affairs and External Relations Council (GAERC) and divided into two separate sessions, usually on successive days, dealing first with 'General Affairs', covering the overall 'internal' coordinating work of the Council and secondly with 'External Relations', covering the EU's policy towards various parts of the world and towards specific foreign or security policy issues or crises. Traditionally, the meetings of the GAC/GAERC have been prepared by the Committee of Permanent Representatives (COREPER) formally comprising the ambassadors (referred to in this context as permanent representatives) of the member states to the European Union. This committee, the third of our longstanding foreign and security policy institutions, meets at least once a week in Brussels, and has traditionally enjoyed considerable influence over the policy-shaping process. Any items on which the permanent representatives agree unanimously are normally adopted by the GAERC without discussion. However, as we shall see below, COREPER's influence has waned somewhat since the advent of the new post-Saint Malo institutions of ESDP.

A fourth body of real significance used to be the Political Committee (which also emerged out of the EPC process) comprising the Political Directors of the member state Ministries of Foreign Affairs (MFAs). Prior to 2000, this body had traditionally met monthly, with a view to coordinating foreign and security policy at senior MFA level. However, much of its *security and defence* agenda was subsequently taken over by the new body established after Saint Malo – the Political and Security Committee (COPS, see below). Occasionally the COPS itself can be convened at the level of the Political Directors. The fifth pre-1999 institution is the Council Secretariat, which dates from the Single European Act of 1985 when it was felt necessary to establish a permanent secretariat to coordinate the foreign policy implications of the EU's growing trade and economic relations with the rest of the world. Prior to 1999, the Council Secretariat was primarily responsible for overseeing and servicing CFSP. It has subsequently had to redefine its brief to concentrate on the more juridical aspects of foreign and security policy. The Secretariat which involves some 2,500 officials from across the EU, supports and advises both the European Council and the GAERC.

The sixth institutional input comes from the rotating Presidency of the EU, which has responsibility for galvanizing and even initiating policy during its six-month term of office, and for drafting the 'Presidency Conclusions' which are presented at the final European Council meeting of each semester. The 'ESDP Annexes' to the Presidency Conclusions cumulatively represent the stages of development of the ESDP *acquis*. In addition to these six separate agencies of intergovernmentalism, there is, of course, the supranational European Commission (EC), which is largely responsible for the *delivery* and *implementation* of CFSP via the Directorate General for External Relations (Relex) and the Commissioner for External Relations. In many ways, since the single largest element of European foreign policy involves trade and economic policy, the Commission is also a key player in CFSP. For ESDP purposes, it has established a Conflict Prevention and Crisis Management Unit which monitors data relating to looming crises and aims to foster coherence in response. The eighth institutional input comes from the European Parliament (EP). According to the terms of the Treaty (article 21), the views of the EP on all aspects of CFSP/ESDP 'are duly taken into consideration' but parliamentarians have complained bitterly about the inadequacy and tardiness of information flows. In practice any voice which the EP does raise in foreign and security policy tends to come via its different specialist committees (Human Rights, Foreign Affairs, and Common Security and Defence Policy) (Duke, 2002: 127–30; Cutler and Von Lingen, 2003: 14).

The ninth pre-Saint Malo institution is the post of High Representative for the Common Foreign and Security Policy (HR-CFSP), which from its inception has been occupied by Javier Solana. The need for such a position had been felt ever since the 1970s when Henry Kissinger famously remarked that he did not know the telephone number of the European Union. The post was created by the Amsterdam European Council in June 1997 – although the appointment of its first incumbent in the summer of 1999 had to await the outcome of a political battle among the national capitals over the level of seniority and the political remit of the appointee. France had hoped that a high-profile heavyweight such as a former French President (the name of Valéry Giscard d'Estaing was often mentioned in this connection) would succeed in injecting a clear French voice into Europe's common message to the outside world. The UK, on the other hand, had wanted the post to be filled by a mid-career civil servant who could be kept by the Foreign Office on a relatively tight political leash. In the event, the choice of Javier Solana derived from his diplomatic skills and consensus-forming successes as Secretary General of NATO during the Kosovo War of spring 1999. The HR-CFSP is assisted by a small 26-member Policy Unit (PU), also created by the Amsterdam Council with the formal title of the Policy Planning and Early Warning Unit. The PU's function is to assist the HR-CFSP in assessing situations and in formulating policy responses. One important role of the HR-CFSP himself has been to act as the external face of the EU and to help forge consensus on policy issues within the Council. At this, within the limits of his remit, Solana has been highly successful. 'Quietly and almost unnoticed' commented a leading weekly, 'Javier Solana has done the unthinkable: he has created a European foreign policy' (*Newsweek*, 2002). But Solana has been disadvantaged by the inadequate size of his staff and of his budget and of course by the existence of competing agencies with high stakes in the formulation of CFSP and ESDP (the European Commission, NATO, and above all governments and ministries in national capitals).

One final – but increasingly important – mechanism, which lies entirely outside the Treaties and has no official status, is what has been called 'intensive transgovernmentalism' (Wallace and Wallace, 2000: 33–5). Since the late 1990s, significant strides have been taken, both bilaterally and multilaterally, across European ministries in knitting together the finer points of security policy. Exchange diplomats and officials have spent extended periods in 'sister' ministries in foreign capitals and specialized teams working on European issues have been established in all these ministries. These teams have acquired the habit of communicating regularly, via e-mail, telephone or more formal conferences, with their opposite numbers around the EU. All this has resulted in far greater awareness, in the major capital cities at least, of the respective positions of the different partner countries on security policy issues. This is far from suggesting that differences can easily be ironed out. But there can be no doubt that each member government has a very clear understanding of the positions of its EU partners. It is difficult to quantify the role this process plays in decision-making and in the coherence of ESDP. But it is certainly important. I have analysed elsewhere the role of these 'epistemic communities' in generating the new ideas which actually led to the break-through at Saint Malo (Howorth, 2004). Their work continues.

The post-Saint Malo institutions

One might have imagined, given this multi-level and already extremely cumbersome decision-making apparatus, that the advent of ESDP and the call in Saint Malo for 'appropriate structures' would have presented a golden opportunity for institutional rationalization. However, the intergovernmental conference leading up to the Treaty of Nice was already in train and was essentially concentrating on the institutional consequences of enlargement which was foreseen for 2004. Therefore, Nice simply acknowledged what had been decided throughout 1999 at meetings of the GAC, and added three new institutional organs to the already complex nexus we have just outlined.

Political and security committee

The most important of these was the Political and Security Committee (COPS – the French acronym is normally used) which was enshrined in the Treaty of Nice under Article 25:

> a Political and Security Committee shall monitor the international situation in the areas covered by the common foreign and security policy and contribute to the definition of policies by delivering opinions to the Council at the request of the Council or on its own initiative. It shall also monitor the implementation of agreed policies . . . this Committee shall exercise, under the responsibility of the Council, political control and strategic direction of crisis management operations.

COPS as an institution was first convened on an interim basis in March 2000, becoming permanent in January 2001. The detailed remit for its activities was contained in the *Presidency Report on ESDP* which was annexed to the Presidency Conclusions of the Nice European Council. COPS has already established itself as the key institution in this entire policy area. It has been aptly described in the first detailed scholarly studies of its activities as the 'linchpin' (Duke, 2005) and as 'the work-horse in ESDP decision-shaping and control' (Meyer, 2006: 116). The 15 (now 27) permanent representatives, with the rank of ambassador, meeting twice to three times a week in Brussels, embarked on the work of monitoring the international situation, contributing to the formulation of policies by drafting opinions for the Council and also overseeing the implementation of the agreed policies. However, an important caveat is immediately in order. Despite its centrality to the decision-shaping process, the COPS can easily be short-circuited by national capitals in the event of a real crisis which rules out member-state consensus. During the Iraq crisis of 2002–3, for instance, the COPS, notwithstanding the text of article 25 of the Treaty stating that it should contribute to the definition of policies by 'delivering opinions to the Council', was kept entirely at arm's length from what was certainly the most significant foreign and security policy issue of the entire five-year period following Saint Malo. Many COPS ambassadors received 'very strict instructions' (Interviews in Brussels June 2004) from their respective MFAs that Iraq was to be kept rigorously off the agenda. This stark reality speaks volumes about the relative salience of *national* security policies as opposed to *European* policy on security when push really comes to shove.

Indeed, the overall political sensitivity of this new institutional departure was clear from the outset in the differences of opinion manifest in various European capitals over the potential influence of the COPS. In a repeat of the discussions over seniority after the 1997 decision to create the post of HR-CFSP, the big debate during the Finnish Presidency (June to December 1999) was over the level of representation of the ambassadors to the COPS. France, confident that the very existence of COPS would consecrate 'l'Europe de la défense', leaned towards 'senior ambassadorial' representation. Paris never doubted for a moment the Quai d'Orsay's capacity to keep its own senior

Figure 3.1 CFSP/ESDP institutional structures

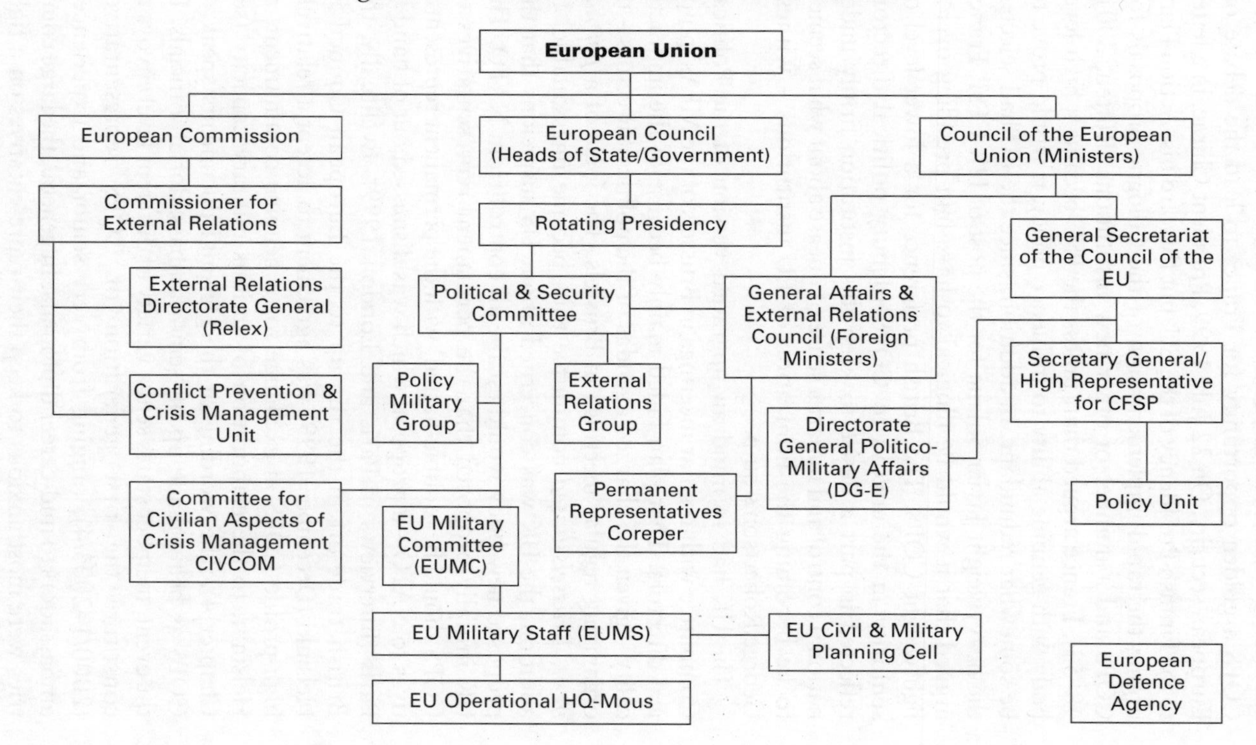

ambassador 'on message', and by the same token it saw in the COPS a golden opportunity for France to lead the debate on European security. On 22 July 1999, President Chirac, in a letter to the Finnish Presidency of the EU, put forward his 'Action Plan' urging the rapid implementation of the Cologne proposals for COPS and a number of other new institutions (Rutten, 2001: 48–53). France argued that, unless the PSC became a high-level body with genuine ability to influence policy, it would prove to be somewhat redundant. In addition, since the EU had selected the heavyweight Javier Solana for the post of HR-CFSP, France argued that it would be illogical to have him presiding over a lightweight COPS. The British preference for a lower level of seniority in the envoys to COPS (deputy political director) reflected in part a desire to keep this institution firmly under national control and in part a sense of unease about what seemed to be becoming the lionization of EU institutions – witness George Robertson's quip.

The UK had in mind an upgraded version of the Political Committee with regular meetings in Brussels of the MFAs' political directors. That plan faded mainly because of the impracticality – given the charged agendas of the political directors – of organizing regular meetings in Brussels. The logic of a *permanent, Brussels-based* committee thus became unassailable. In addition, the UK was concerned about US suspicions that the proposed new body would escape all control from NATO. The UK initially proposed that the permanent representatives to COPS should be 'double-hatted' with the permanent representatives to NATO – a proposal which was dismissed out of hand in Paris (Interviews in Paris and London 1999). Eventually, the British trade-off in the run-up to the European Council in Helsinki (December 1999) was agreement to accept a relatively high-profile COPS in exchange for a genuine commitment, at Helsinki, to the elaboration of serious military capacity (see Chapter 4). The wording of the Helsinki documents speak of COPS as being made up of 'senior/ambassadorial' officials. In the event, member states sent a variety of different level envoys to constitute the first generation of COPS representatives (2000/1–2003/4), ranging from very senior and experienced ambassadors to mid-career diplomats. In general, the large countries were most anxious to keep their representatives on a tight leash and tended to send more junior officials than some of the smaller countries eager to help develop CFSP/ESDP and willing to engage a senior ambassador. The issue nevertheless highlights a problem frequently encountered both in European integration in general and in CFSP/ESDP in particular. The member states, having decided for a variety of external constraining reasons that it was necessary to set up a 'centralizing' institution, immediately became nervous of their own temerity and began trying to keep the new body under their own firm control.

The sensitive issue of the division of labour between COREPER and COPS, both of whom found themselves juridically responsible for preparing Council meetings (Duke, 2005: 10–12), was partially resolved at the Seville European Council in June 2002 by the introduction of the distinction mentioned above between the 'internal' and 'external' agendas of the retitled General Affairs and External Relations Council (GAERC). The former meeting is now essentially prepared by COREPER and the latter by COPS (in collaboration with COREPER). Although this is an improvement on the previous overloaded agenda of the GAC, the situation remains unsatisfactory given the growing volume of business in the strictly security and defence field. Further modifications to the workings of COPS were suggested under the aegis of the Constitutional Treaty of 2004. These we shall examine below.

COPS thus theoretically deals with all aspects of the common foreign and security policy, although interviews with current and former ambassadors suggest that it works best in what is considered its 'core business' – the planning, preparation and oversight of operations, whether civilian or military. Some ambassadors feel that the body works less well when it ventures over-ambitiously into broad-ranging generalities about the future scope and direction of CFSP. A representative of the Commission is also present to ensure cross-pillar consistency and coherence and meetings are attended by four representatives of the Council Secretariat. The work of the committee is assisted by 'European Correspondents' based in the MFAs who form a liaison between the political directors and the representatives to COPS (Duke, 2005: 20). The agenda is agreed by the rotating Presidency and by the Council Secretariat and the committee meets at least twice a week on Tuesdays and Fridays, with additional meetings being convened as necessary. Meetings are regularly attended by Robert Cooper, the Director-General of DG-E within the

Council, who is considered to be Javier Solana's closest adviser. The wide-ranging remit of the committee generates a vast amount of paperwork, creating an intensive workload for its members. This pressure is 'somewhat alleviated' by the assistance of the Politico-Military Working Party, comprising officials from both MFAs and MODs and which convenes up to four times per week, dealing with both the diplomatic aspects and the technical details of planned operations, including relations with NATO. In addition, the meetings of COPS are prepared by a preparatory group (sometimes referred to as the 'Nicolaidis group' after its first chairperson during the Greek Presidency in early 2003). This group fixes the most logical order for discussion of agenda items and indicates in advance where member states have concerns that they wish to raise.

How influential is this 'linchpin', this 'work-horse' in forging a consensual European strategic culture? Christoph Meyer has produced the first detailed scholarly analysis of the workings of the Committee (Meyer, 2006: chapter 5). His findings are important. His research set out to establish to what extent the working of the COPS 'has set in motion dynamics of social influence that can mould a group of national officials into a socially cohesive policy community with shared objectives and increasingly shared attitudes concerning the use of force' (p. 112). Employing recent research methods in the field of social psychology, he has examined the extent to which two dynamics are at work: 'compliance or normative pressures, which make group members conform in public to dominant attitudes or views; and personal acceptance of these group norms through informational influence based on better arguments or superior expertise of in-group persuaders' (Meyer, 2006: 117). This approach was supported by 28 semi-structured interviews with COPS ambassadors. My own research, based on a dozen interviews with ambassadors from the first and second generation of envoys, concurs with Meyer's more 'scientific' conclusions, based on considerations of group characteristics, discursive dynamics and capacity to persuade.

First, the COPS ambassadors have felt themselves to be pioneers in a very important policy area and, given that their remit was to seek consensus, their propensity to compete with one another has been kept in check. The frequency of their meetings in various official formats rose from an average of ten per month in 2001 to an average of over 15 in 2005. There were also ample opportunities for less formal as well as for purely social interaction. Meyer concluded that COPS constitutes 'an unusually cohesive committee with a club atmosphere, high levels of personal trust and a shared "esprit de corps" driven by a common commitment to pioneer cooperation in a new, labour-intensive and particularly sensitive policy-field' (Meyer, 2006: 124). In terms of discursive dynamics, the tendency of newly-appointed ambassadors in their early meetings simply to read out instructions from the national capital rapidly fades and is soon replaced by a consensus-seeking discursive approach which results in even envoys from major countries shifting their initial stance in the greater cause of forging an EU policy. Although both Paris and London are keen to 'tele-guide' their envoys, they are also keen to ensure that ESDP be made to work. Thus, the language and codes through which the meetings are conducted (80% in English and 20% in French) were rapidly established in a form which actively promotes group cohesion. Finally, individual ambassadors, for a wide variety of reasons – seniority, longevity on the committee, personal charm, in-depth knowledge, relevance of their country to the issue under discussions (the Baltic states and Poland have been instrumental in taking forward policy towards Russia) – have found that they have considerable potential to influence the group by the strength of their argument, so long as it is couched within a collectively recognized normative framework. Meyer's conclusion is tentative but unequivocal: The COPS

> has developed into a multiplier of social influence, both through informational influence as well as peer pressure. It has managed to manufacture consent and broker compromises even in areas where national strategic norms would initially indicate incompatibility. [It] remains one of the most important ideational transmission belts of a gradual Europeanisation of national foreign, security and defence policies. (Meyer, 2006: 136–7)

In Chapter 6 we shall see how the committee succeeded in overriding national reticence in a number of key decision-making discussions.

Military committee and military staff

Two other institutions were created in 1999 alongside COPS. The European Union Military Committee (EUMC) is the highest EU military body. It is established within the Council and is formally composed of the Chiefs of the Defence Staff (CHODs) of the member states meeting at least biannually, but normally attended by their military representatives (MILREPs) who, in most cases, are double-hatted with each nation's NATO representative. France is the significant exception to this practice. This Committee rapidly imposed itself as a vital mechanism in the policy-making process. Its ultimate function is to deliver to the European Council, via the COPS, the unanimous advice of the 25 CHODs on all matters with a military dimension as well as recommendations for action. Such unanimity is essential to the commitment of EU forces to any military operation. The EUMC is the designated 'forum for consultation and cooperation between the member states in the field of conflict prevention and crisis management'. Its advice and recommendations pertain to

> the development of the overall concept of crisis management in its military aspects; the . . . political control and strategic direction of crisis management operations and situations; the risk assessment of potential crises; the military dimension of a crisis situation and its implications, in particular during its subsequent management . . . the elaboration, the assessment and the review of capability objectives according to agreed procedures; the EU's military relationship with non-EU European NATO Members, the other candidates for accession to the EU, other states and other organizations, including NATO; and the financial estimation for operations and exercises. (Rutten, 2001: 193–4)

These terms of reference are essentially drawn from those of NATO's Military Committee. The EUMC thus emerges as the key decision-shaping body in crisis management situations, drawing up and evaluating strategic military options, overseeing the elaboration of an operational plan and monitoring operations throughout the mission. It is also responsible for giving advice on the termination of an operation.

The Chairman of the EUMC is a four-star flag officer,

normally a former Chief of Defence of a member state. The first appointee (2001) was the Finnish General Gustav Hagglund, succeeded in April 2004 by General Rolando Mosca Moschini of Italy and in June 2006 by General Henri Bentegeat of France. The Chairman participates, as appropriate, in meetings of the COPS, the Council and the NATO Military Committee as well as liaising with the Presidency.

The European Union Military Staff (EUMS) comprises some 150 senior officers from the 25 member states. It provides military expertise and capacity, including during the conduct of EU-led military operations. The EUMS works under the political direction of the European Council (through the COPS) and under the military direction of the EUMC. Although the EUMS does not act as an operational HQ, it performs the operational functions of early warning, situation assessment and strategic planning and provides in-house military expertise for the HR-CFSP. The EUMS is in fact a General Directorate within the Council General Secretariat and is the only permanent integrated military structure of the European Union. Established on 11 June 2001, the EU Military Staff has had three Directors-General – the German General Rainer Schuwirth (2001), succeeded in March 2004 by the French General Jean-Paul Perruche and in February 2007 by UK General David Leakey, the former commander of the EU's military operation in Bosnia-Herzegovia, EUFOR-*Althea*. Initially, all these new institutions used to be housed in the Council building, Justus Lipsius, near Rond-Point Schuman in Brussels. However, for many civilian officials, the shock to the system created by the sight of military officers in that inner sanctum of civilian power, added to the rapid discovery on the part of the military officers themselves that, in terms of security, Justus Lipsius was, to quote Javier Solana, 'as full of holes as Swiss cheese', led to the wholesale relocation, in 2002, of all ESDP bodies and activities to highly secured purpose-built accommodation in the nearby Rue Cortenberg.

One final post-1999 innovation which has become a regular institutional feature although still with informal status is the Council of Defence Ministers. In February 2002, it had been agreed that defence ministers would be authorized to meet under the aegis of the General Affairs Council (the monthly meeting of the EU foreign ministers) to discuss 'certain agenda items, limited to . . . military capabilities'. The very fact that member states recognized the necessity of such top-down meetings constituted a major step forward. In democratic systems, defence ministers are generally kept strictly subordinate to foreign ministers and, of course, prior to Saint Malo there had never been any prospect of the Council of Ministers meeting in defence minister format. Since February 2002, they have tended to meet several times a year to oversee the development of military capabilities and they have gradually become significant security policy-shapers. They were instrumental in helping move the debate on capacity away from the raw numbers of the HHG and towards a clear set of qualitative criteria. The defence ministers also meet regularly in another format – as the Steering Board of the European Defence Agency, which we shall discuss in Chapter 4.

Institutional engineering in the Constitutional Treaty of 2004

One of the reasons why, at the dawn of the twenty-first century, the EU agreed simply to add on new layers of institutional complexity in the security field – rather than attempt a wholesale institutional rationalization – was that it had already become clear, whatever the outcome of the Nice Treaty, that yet another intergovernmental conference would have to be convened in advance of the accession of the ten candidate countries from Central and Eastern Europe in 2004. Enlargement dictated another wholesale revision of the institutional framework. This recognition eventually gave birth to the Convention on the Future of Europe (2002–3), which itself engendered the Constitutional Treaty of 2004. Given the institutional complexity we have just examined, one of the greatest potential challenges to the drafters of the EU Constitution came in the area of security and defence. The debates of the Convention allowed for very wide-ranging discussion on all aspects of the institutional dimensions of security and defence and it is via these debates that one can see most clearly how different countries perceived the stakes and the available options. It is paradoxical that, in the event, security and defence proved to be the policy area in which clear and substantial progress on the Constitutional Treaty was arguably the most consensual. Such progress was by no means predictable. Two huge coordination challenges arose: military capabilities and security policy itself. The ongoing tensions between the different dyads of EU member states – allies and neutrals, Atlanticists and Europeanists, 'extroverts' and 'introverts', 'bigs' and 'smalls', countries with professional armed forces and countries still reliant on conscripts – hardly augured well for a smooth constitutional ride. Moreover, in the context of enlargement, the necessary stages towards a concomitant deepening were far from obvious. The military capabilities of most accession states were in a different league from those of many EU member states. Furthermore, the Iraq War of 2003 was widely believed to have driven a wedge between 'new' and 'old' Europeans. It was widely assumed, therefore, that there would be fierce constitutional squabbles not only over *decision-making* but also over the very *scope* of ESDP. Meanwhile, on the ground, in 2003–4 for the first time ever, EU military forces, under an EU flag, were engaging in peacekeeping and combat missions – and preparing to engage in further missions. If ESDP was to make progress towards the stark new world of operational capacity, new forms of flexible cooperation would be required – forms which would preserve the EU's political unity and control while allowing variegated 'coalitions of the willing' to engage in real military operations, forms which would help the disparate – and growing – range of agencies and actors involved in this policy sector to coordinate decision-making, not only in the field of armaments and military capabilities, but also in the overall area of security policy. A central challenge was to ensure that cooperative ventures and coalitions, as well as policy-making itself, were subsumed *within the EU framework* rather than electing, as had so often been the case in the past, to function *outside of it*.

Facilities for 'flexibility' had been introduced in the mid-1990s within the IGC discussions preceding the Amsterdam Treaty (Missiroli, 2000). The 1990s indeed saw many variants on 'flexible' combinations of member states: based on *time* ('multi-speed'), *space* ('variable geometry') and *matter* (Europe *à la carte*). The differences between the latter – in many ways choices between opting in and opting out – were explained by Stubb (1996: 289):

> Variable geometry exemplifies the middle ground between multi-speed and *à la carte* . . . By definition, variable geometry

is more integrationist than *à la carte*. The former can create a hard core, which drives for deeper integration in a specific policy area, the latter is usually characterized by miscellaneous co-operation in areas that are not considered to intrude on national sovereignty.

Through the introduction of new instruments such as 'enhanced cooperation', 'constructive abstention' and explicit 'opt-outs' (Denmark was granted an opt-out at Maastricht from any involvement with a common security and defence policy and from any CFSP measures having defence implications), the Amsterdam Treaty of 1997 had attempted to facilitate methods of short-circuiting the increasingly constraining need for unanimity in this critical policy area. Yet, the *danger* in all these procedures was that the EU would break up into an inner core and an outer fringe. At the time, though, these measures had little bearing on ESDP. Since even in the mid-1990s serious security and defence policy cooperation was still little more than a gleam in the eye of a handful of defence planners, little could be done in practice to kick-start a policy area that many still wished to keep out of the EU altogether.

All that changed in December 1998 with Saint Malo and with the UK government's decision to embrace EU defence and security cooperation. For two or three years, despite ongoing differences between EU member states, both over military substance and over eventual political objectives, cooperation and indeed integration appeared to be increasingly the name of the game. However, it was by no means plain sailing. By the time the Constitutional Convention convened in early 2002, several major strains were threatening to complicate the infant ESDP's progression towards adolescence and maturity. First, France's continuing pursuit of maximalist ambitions – with ESDP progressively perceived as a potential alternative to NATO – was still causing ructions with the UK (the necessary partner in driving the ESDP process forward). Second, the UK's apparent shift of focus after 9/11 to a more global approach to security issues exacerbated these tensions with Paris (Howorth, 2003). Third, the continuing reluctance of Germany to move towards a more interventionist security policy and to increase defence spending, was putting a brake on the ESDP process and encouraging other, smaller member states, themselves more wedded to 'softer' forms of power projection, to question some of the EU's military ambitions (Longhurst, 2005). Fourth, the prospect of embracing ten new member states, nine of which, at that time, possessed armed forces of questionable military value raised the prospect of deep divisions within ESDP between the included and the excluded.

The Convention's draft Constitutional Treaty of July 2003 was nevertheless a minor triumph in terms of squaring some of these circles. Diedrichs and Jopp (2003: 29) considered it

> a major breakthrough . . . that would have seemed unachievable only two years ago . . . New opportunities for flexibility probably represent one of the most impressing [sic] innovations for CFSP and ESDP in the draft Constitutional Treaty. The member states now possess a range of options that enable them to go ahead without waiting for all partners to follow.

Significantly, things got even better over the following year. At least six instruments of flexibility were eventually incorporated into the consolidated constitutional draft (August 2004). (For the text of the 6 August 2004 Treaty Establishing a Constitution for Europe, see http://ue.eu.int/igcpdf/en/04/cg00/cg00087.en04.pdf.) Some of these new elements of flexibility had explicitly been ruled out in the penultimate draft of the Constitutional Treaty as drawn up by the Convention. In the pages that follow, I shall examine two main areas of innovation each of which demonstrated the increasing willingness of the major European states to draw the practical conclusions from their decision to promote ESDP and to force through significant progress. The first, *structured cooperation*, is less an 'institution' as such than a mechanism, but it has acquired quasi-institutional status. The second, the post of *Union Minister for Foreign Affairs*, is currently on hold.

Structured cooperation

Structured cooperation is a mechanism which allows a small number of member states, which are able and willing to mount overseas operations, to do so in the name of the entire EU. A major driver behind the notion was the determination of a handful of countries to forge ahead with a 'core group' in the area of security and defence. In particular, France and Germany, for different reasons, were keen to promote a security 'Euro-zone' and during the Convention deliberations had put forward a paper in the Working Group on Defence proposing a similar process to that which had been introduced for the Euro: membership would depend on meeting certain 'capacity criteria' and others could join as and when they met those criteria. For some of the new accession countries, however, the very notion of a 'core group' was unacceptable (Hübner, 2002; Piks, 2003). Unlike 'constructive abstention', which was mainly a mechanism to assist decision-making, structured cooperation appeared to have clear integrative implications. Furthermore, many participants in the Working Group were suspicious of the proponents' motivations, the fear being that *exclusion* of the weaker member states was part of the strategic plan. However, the Working Group's Chairman, Michel Barnier, included in his Final Report the proposal that:

> the new treaty should consequently provide for a *form of closer cooperation between Member States* [emphasis in original], open to all Member States wishing to carry out the most demanding tasks and fulfilling the requirements for such a commitment to be credible. One of the conditions for taking part in this 'defence Euro-zone' would have to be a form of presumption that pre-identified forces and command and control capabilities would be available. (European Convention, 2002)

The implications of this wording seemed ominous to the dissenters. Not only did it look like a 'self-electing club', but it looked like one which intended to try to embark on autonomous military operations in the name of the EU, yet with little or no control by non-participating states. These features, real or imaginary, nevertheless also made their way into the Convention's June 2003 Draft Constitutional Treaty (Article III-213), despite attempts by up to 30 Convention members (from the UK, Ireland, Sweden, Finland, Estonia and Latvia) to delete the entire article. Structured cooperation was conceived amid considerable controversy.

The controversy was heightened by the general impact on EU cohesion of the Iraq War and above all by the four-party 'summit' in Brussels on 29 April 2003 between France, Germany, Belgium and Luxembourg. Widely denounced at the time as divisive (both of the EU and of NATO) and provocative (in that it seemed to imply an EU defence core which *excluded* the UK), the summit Declaration was in fact relatively anodyne. Far from constituting an attack on NATO, the Declaration stressed, in its opening paragraph, the 'shared values and ideas' which constituted the 'transatlantic partnership', characterized as a 'strategic priority' for Europe (Déclaration Commune, 2003). However, the centrepiece of the summit was the proposal to create a 'European Union of Security and Defence' (UESD) involving a number of objectives on the part of its members, most of which were uncontentious, but including an EU operational planning unit to be located at Tervuren near Brussels. It was around this last proposal that controversy was to rage (see pp. 111–12). A number of other initiatives were proposed, most of which were subsequently to find themselves written into the Constitutional Treaty. Aside from the planning cell, the most controversial part of the text – at least potentially – was the proposal that the states joining UESD would make a mutual defence pact, would systematically harmonize their positions on security and defence, and would coordinate their efforts both on military capacity and on investment and procurement. Although the detail remained vague (and contained many devils), the thinking behind UESD clearly seemed modeled on economic and monetary union: a core group of countries would forge ahead (including in the preparation of military operations) and would leave others with the choice of joining or being left out. In the climate of the time, it was hard not to see it as 'exclusionary', and difficult to believe that it would enhance the role of NATO. The combined effect of the 29 April summit and the 18 July Conventional Draft was to imply a major struggle between Europeanists and Atlanticists over the heart and soul of ESDP.

Yet this did not happen. Over the course of the summer 2003, both sides moved towards one another. British enthusiasm for developing military capacity, for early warning systems, for appropriate planning facilities, including the strengthening of HQ capacity, for a defence agency and other military objectives were all entirely compatible with the main UESD proposals. In a

'Food for Thought' paper circulated to an informal meeting of defence ministers in Rome in August 2003, it was clear that London remained concerned about the implication, in 'structured cooperation', that a small number of self-selected states could short-circuit decision-making 'at 25' and that the initiative was really designed as an alternative to NATO (Missiroli, 2003: 204–7). At the same time, France in particular knew that a UESD without the UK would be but a pale shadow of what it could be with the British on board. The desire to have the UK involved was equally strong in Berlin for slightly different reasons. Pragmatism prevailed. At the Rome meeting a number of misperceptions were dispelled. Blair, Chirac and Schroeder then set their 'sherpas' working on a trilateral compromise which was duly agreed at a summit in Berlin on 20 September 2003. Although press comment focused on the continuing differences of opinion between the three men over Iraq policy, the real significance of the trilateral summit came on ESDP. In a nutshell, there was a trade-off. In exchange for solid reassurances from Chirac and Schroeder that 'structured cooperation' would be neither exclusionary nor inimical to NATO, Blair dropped his opposition both to the proposal itself (in which, with misperceptions dispelled, he could actually detect great potential) and to the EU operational planning cell (which most felt was primarily symbolic).

Consequently, the Italian Presidency was able to bring forth new drafts of a text on what was now to be called 'permanent structured cooperation' (Missiroli, 2003: 432–44). The main issue was the decision-making procedure for establishing initial and subsequent membership of the format as well as facilities for suspending membership if any country failed to honour its commitments. The changes brought in (rejection of the proposal to *list* the participating countries in the Protocol, removal of the requirement for participants to have to fulfil 'higher military capability criteria', ability for countries to join and to leave) all succeeded in making *explicitly inclusive* a procedure which had previously seemed implicitly exclusive. The UK was sufficiently confident that structured cooperation would help operationalise ESDP that it even agreed to decision-making under this project taking place through QMV. More significant, however, were the terms of the Protocol annexed to the Treaty which governed the criteria for membership. The criteria for membership were restricted explicitly to the development of military capacity. The conduct of military operations was to depend on a unanimous vote in the Council.

At the end of the day, the successful inclusion of the procedures on structured cooperation reflected parallel and ultimately compatible desires on the part of the UK (not to be sidelined and to ensure that ESDP be 'entirely consistent with NATO'), Germany (to bring the UK back into the loop and to pursue anything which smacked of integrative potential) and France (to re-establish its defence partnership with Europe's leading military power and to push ahead with the creation of a defence vanguard). The smaller EU and NATO countries, especially the new accession states, were reassured by the lead taken by the UK and objections to structured cooperation effectively vanished. The capabilities required for membership were identified as either a niche contribution or delivery of (or participation in) one of the 'Battle Groups' planned under the new *Headline Goal 2010* (p. 108). Most EU member states subsequently found a way of associating themselves with structured cooperation. Clearly, the large military powers will bear the main brunt, especially in the early years. But, as a UK FCO official put it, 'if a crisis arose in South-Eastern Europe which could be appropriately handled by a coalition comprising Romania, Hungary, Poland, Italy and a niche contribution from one or two Baltic states, fantastic! Why shouldn't they?' (Interview FCO 28 June 2004). Structured cooperation aims to bring as many member states as possible militarily 'up to speed' as rapidly as possible. No member state will be forced to do anything. But the potential to do lots – in the name and under the flag of the EU – is considerable. This represented a minor revolution in EU affairs. Moreover, despite the failure of the Constitutional Treaty, the procedures of structured cooperation can be implemented by multilateral agreement.

Union Minister for Foreign Affairs

The most important change proposed by the Constitutional Treaty was the attempt to define an overarching position able to coordinate the work of the many different CFSP/ESDP agencies. The Union Minister for Foreign Affairs (UMFA) emerged from the Convention and IGC processes as – at least potentially – an

Box 3.1 The Union Minister for Foreign Affairs

Article I-28 (Constitutional Treaty)

1 The European Council, acting by qualified majority, with the agreement of the President of the Commission, shall appoint the Union Minister for Foreign Affairs. The European Council may end his or her term of office by the same procedure.

2 The Union Minister for Foreign Affairs shall conduct the Union's common foreign and security policy. He or she shall contribute by his or her proposals to the development of that policy, which he or she shall carry out as mandated by the Council. The same shall apply to the common security and defence policy.

3 The Union Minister for Foreign Affairs shall preside over the Foreign Affairs Council.

4 The Union Minister for Foreign Affairs shall be one of the Vice-Presidents of the Commission. He or she shall ensure the consistency of the Union's external action. He or she shall be responsible within the Commission for responsibilities falling to it in external relations and for coordinating other aspects of the Union's external action. In exercising these responsibilities within the Commission, and only for these responsibilities, the Union Minister for Foreign Affairs shall be bound by Commission procedures to the extent that this is consistent with paragraphs 2 and 3.

immensely powerful figure. There are no fewer than 65 references to the functions of this post in the text of the Treaty. Moreover, it is not insignificant that whereas, in the Convention draft, his functions were often referred to as 'responsibilities', in the Constitutional text, these became 'powers'. Opposition to the creation of the post was forthcoming essentially from the smaller member states which feared yet another 'super-post' with the potential to deliver *ukases*. The post-holder's basic functions are laid out in article I-28 (Box 3.1).

With the defeat of the referenda in France and the Netherlands in June 2005, the precise status of this position went into limbo.

Most commentators and analysts argued that, if anything should be retrieved from the debris of the referendum fiasco, it should be this important ministerial post. The likelihood is strong that, whatever happens to the Constitutional Treaty, some version of UMFA will be introduced in some other form – maybe through a European Council meeting – within the next few years. For this reason, in the paragraphs that follow I have used the future rather than the conditional tense. The post-holder, elected for a five-year term, will replace the previous six-monthly rotating Presidency, thus accumulating considerable authority. At the European Council in June 2004 it was agreed that the first post-holder will be Javier Solana. He will combine the current responsibilities of both the HR-CFSP and the Commissioner for External Relations, thus having one foot in the Council and one (as Vice-President) in the Commission. This will allow him to coordinate the two main thrusts of the EU's external policy: security and overseas aid. The UMFA will also contribute both to the preparation of and to the implementation of CFSP/ESDP and will chair the newly created Foreign Affairs Council (FAC), scheduled to replace the GAERC. He will represent the Union in international organizations and at international conferences, will 'conduct political dialogue' on the Union's behalf, and can convene an emergency meeting of the FAC within 48 hours (or, in a real crisis, even sooner). Moreover, the UMFA will preside over a 'European External Action Service', which was intended to be introduced within one year after entry into force of the Treaty. There are many significant obstacles to the creation of such an EU Diplomatic Service which are too complex to enter into here (Duke, 2002a). They involve extremely delicate negotiations between the Commission (Relex) and the Council, not to mention the Parliament and the national capitals. The remit of the Service is referred to in Constitutional Treaty article III-296(3):

> In fulfilling his or her mandate, the Union Minister for Foreign Affairs shall be assisted by a European External Action Service. This service shall work in cooperation with the diplomatic services of the Member States and shall comprise officials from relevant departments of the General Secretariat of the Council and of the Commission as well as staff seconded from national diplomatic services of the Member States. The

organization and functioning of the European External Action Service shall be established by a European decision of the Council. The Council shall act on a proposal from the Union Minister for Foreign Affairs after consulting the European Parliament and after obtaining the consent of the Commission.

Establishing this service was always going to be a major task of the UMFA's first year in office. It, too, has been on hold since the negative referendums of 2005. But such an EU diplomatic service is also inevitable, sooner or later.

Some have questioned whether the vast range of responsibilities accruing to the Foreign Minister's post would be within the physical and mental powers of a single individual. There is a danger that the post-holder would be so torn between the different agencies to which he is attached that the result would be dysfunctional blockage (Duke, 2003: 16). Delegation will be indispensable. If delegation can be properly organized, however, the advantages of having this central pillar of cohesion will outweigh the disadvantages of inter-agency complexity. The bottom line is clear. The requirements of coordination in the broad field of CFSP and in the more critical field of ESDP are now so urgent that the creation of this post literally imposed itself. Yet its very existence – even if still only hypothetical – raises some big problems.

How will the UMFA handle relations with powerful national foreign ministries such as the Quai d'Orsay or the FCO? As we saw, Javier Solana as HR-CFSP was totally sidelined during the 2003 Iraq crisis. However, the fact that subsequent to that crisis all EU member states concurred in the creation of this central post implies at the very least that they see the urgent need for greater coordination in this increasingly vital policy area. During the Lebanon crisis of July 2006, Javier Solana emerged as a key player in the international efforts to find a diplomatic solution. Two further issues arise. First, how will this new office-holder cooperate with the Constitutional Treaty's other major institutional innovation: the President of the European Council (Box 3.2). In determining how these two new posts might cooperate, an analogy often deployed is that of the US President and the Secretary of State. This is doubly misleading. Both those office-holders exercise clear lines of authority, whereas their new EU

Box 3.2 President of the European Council

1 The European Council shall elect its President, by a qualified majority, for a term of two and a half years, renewable once. In the event of an impediment or serious misconduct, the European Council can end his or her term of office in accordance with the same procedure.

2 The President of the European Council:
(a) shall chair it and drive forward its work;
(b) shall ensure the preparation and continuity of the work of the European Council in cooperation with the President of the Commission, and on the basis of the work of the General Affairs Council;
(c) shall endeavour to facilitate cohesion and consensus within the European Council;
(d) shall present a report to the European Parliament after each of the meetings of the European Council.

The President of the European Council shall, at his or her level and in that capacity, ensure the external representation of the Union on issues concerning its common foreign and security policy, without prejudice to the powers of the Union Minister for Foreign Affairs.

3 The President of the European Council shall not hold a national office.

(Constitutional Treaty Article I-22)

'counterparts' would still have to coexist with powerful heads of state and government and with influential foreign ministers. Moreover, between the US President and the Secretary of State there is a hierarchical relationship entirely missing from the new EU postitions. The best way round any potential clash of responsibilities would be a *de facto* division of labour whereby the President of the European Council concentrates on the preparation and implementation of essentially non-CFSP/ESDP aspects of Council business, leaving most foreign and security policy coordination to the UMFA. In this way, the two executives could come together to coordinate CFSP/ESDP issues whenever such coordination became essential. External representation would follow the norms of protocol. The US President would not expect to interact with the UMFA; whereas the latter would expect to be received by the Chinese foreign minister.

Second, how would the UMFA interact with the President of the Commission who has also traditionally sought to represent the EU in foreign parts and who equally has the right to attend sessions of the European Council? There are fears that the dual-hatting of the UMFA could compromise the collegiality of the Commission. Although he will be a Commissioner like all the others, he will also *not* be like them in that he will at the same time carry all of the gravitas of the Council. In instances of conflict between these two agencies, the UMFA will decide for himself (or herself) on which side of the fence to come down. Moreover, the explicit fusing of the civil and military aspects of the EU's external action at the heart of the UMFA's portfolio could have one of two results. Either it will help consolidate the coherence of the EU's foreign and security policy; or it will spark a renewed struggle for preponderance between the Council and the Commission, particularly with respect to the more civilian tasks hitherto exclusively managed by the latter. One way round this potential minefield is for the Commission President to concentrate on *implementation* and *delivery* of EU policy (both by the member states and by the Union) while the UMFA focuses on *elaboration and policy-initiative.*

Although turf-battles between these many powerful institutions seem written into the fabric of the Constitutional Treaty, at the same time their very existence bears witness to their genuine need. To paraphrase Voltaire, since the post of UMFA did not exist, it was necessary to invent it. Assuming this post materializes, it will be the first time in the history of the European project that the supranational and the intergovernmental functions have been merged in a single individual. The post-holder will have to demonstrate extraordinary diplomatic skills. Much, in all of these instances of potential clash, would depend on the personalities of the individuals involved. When a complex dish is being prepared, it is good to have numerous cooks in the kitchen. But, for the dish to be a culinary masterpiece, there has to be a head chef. Increasingly, that will not just involve following somebody else's recipe. It will involve having a major hand in the writing of the recipe.

There were two other major discussions in the Convention

and Constitutional proceedings, which have a clear *institutional* dimension. These were the proposals to introduce a Solidarity Clause and a European Defence Agency (EDA). The former, which is really more procedural than institutional, has implications for any potential move that the EU might make towards assuming a common approach to *defence* (as opposed to security). The latter, which has already become a key institution, is overwhelmingly occupied with rationalizing the EU's instruments of intervention. For this reason, discussion of these significant constitutional innovations will be included in Chapter 4 which addresses the mechanisms of intervention.

Conclusion

George Robertson's quip about 'wiring diagrams', with which we began this chapter, carried two messages. The first was that, despite the importance of institutions as such, what mattered in European security and defence was political will and military might. This might be perceived as a very British approach to the problem: if the EU is going to get into the defence business at all, it needs to have clear objectives, strong leadership and first-rate military capacity. This message was in fact somewhat contradicted by the second one, which was that the EU should avoid using the institutional discussions as a smokescreen behind which to accelerate integration: do not attempt to turn the EU into a powerful form of centralized political leadership. As we have seen, these tensions have lain at the heart of the institutional debates of the period 1999–2006. The member states – even the biggest and most powerful of them – have clearly recognized the need to intensify cooperation and thereby accelerate the advent of an EU which is more capable of intervening on the international stage. At the same time, they have been reluctant to sacrifice or even downgrade agencies and mechanisms of *national control* and have consciously sought to perpetuate the tense balance between the supranational functions of the Commission and the intergovernmental functions of the Council – while constantly tipping the balance of real power further and further in the direction of the latter. The climax of this process was the proposal to create that Centaur-like figure, the UMFA, a post which is half supranational and half intergovernmental.

What all this tells us is that member states have attempted to sail a perilous course between the Scylla of centralized EU coherence and the Charybdis of uncoordinated national unilateralism. Collective decision-making is complex and time-consuming, particularly where the stakes involve high-value assets and issues of life and death. How is it possible, given the complex institutional nexus we have just outlined, for policy decisions to be shaped – and actually taken – at all? The answer is that what emerges is a largely unplanned synthesis of multiple inputs at manifold levels, involving constant negotiation and compromise. Yet it works! Institutional analyses of the more general functioning of the EU are legion (Moravcsik, 1998; Stone Sweet *et al.*, 2001; Pollack, 2003, Pierson, 2004; Schmidt, 2006). Yet virtually none of this theoretical literature has examined the problems of decision-making in ESDP. The challenge is almost overwhelming! As this chapter has demonstrated, the picture is one whose complexity is such not only as to render rational design problematic at best, but also as to cast wholesale doubt on 'heroic' claims regarding the nature and ambitions of ESDP. The notion, often advanced by adversaries of ESDP, that somehow the Union might be creating a military monster over which it will have no control, is another empty scarecrow. The shaping and taking of decisions in ESDP is seriously constrained by three institutional processes.

The first is inter-agency competition. Although, as we have seen, the member states formally set policy, many different agencies are involved both upstream and downstream in shaping and moulding it (Menon, 2006). Thereafter, implementation is often skewed by turf wars – particularly between the Commission and the Council Secretariat. This has become a major problem in the area of Civilian Crisis Management where there is a desperate need for coherence and an end to turf-wars (Nowak, 2006). The second problem derives from the complex politico-institutional relations between the member states and the EU itself. Much of the theoretical literature treats the EU – wrongly – as a nation-state or at least as an actor with the attributes of a nation-state. Yet even in those areas where it enjoys competence, it is more like a system of 'governance without government' characterized by a striking dispersion of power between and among its various institutions (Sbragia, 2007). In the area of foreign and security policy, competence rests – politically – with the member states.

Unlike in federal systems such as the United States, the ultimate bases of political authority and legitimacy in this multi-tiered system of governance are the parts, not the centre. This places real limits on the scope for an EU security and defence policy. It generates a tension between, on the one hand, the need increasingly recognized by all member states for the EU to be more effective, and, on the other, the fundamental problems involved in achieving greater coherence when the centre remains – at their insistence – so weak. We saw this repeatedly with member states deciding that a central institutional organism was unavoidable (the post of HR-CFSP or the COPS) and then worrying that the new body would escape their control.

The process is therefore one in which a policy initiative may be proposed by a variety of different agencies (governments, the COPS, the Council Secretariat, the Commission), examined by all member states, filtered through recommendations and nuances generated by specialist working groups, COREPER, COPS or a variety of other bodies, sent up to COPS for general discussion, forwarded to the GAERC and eventually approved by the European Council. Along the way, the policy initiative is likely to be modified substantially. In any case, it will only be accepted if it is couched in a form that makes it acceptable to all member states, even if sometimes they may need to be persuaded in roundabout ways. This is not a policy area in which an individual, a single country or a specific type of approach can impose its view. European security policy – unlike traditional 'heroic' notions of defence and security policy – is in a very real way *leaderless* (Menon, 2006). And even if there were such actors, with such a clear blueprint for their strategy, for it to emerge intact out of the EU's institutional labyrinth would be nothing short of miraculous. In short, what emerges as European Security and Defence Policy is a series of decisions which genuinely reflect the political ambitions and the political will of all 27 member states. As we shall see in the next chapter, that amounts to a very great deal. The system actually works.

Chapter 4

The Instruments of Intervention: Military and Civilian Capabilities

Had anybody predicted, as 1998 drew to a close, that within five years the European Union (EU) would be engaging in autonomous military and policing missions in 'non-permissive' theatres, under a European command chain and the European flag, they would have been regarded by most serious analysts as wild-eyed dreamers. The years 1997 and 1998 probably represented a low-point in European hopes of establishing a military capacity which would allow the Union to engage in peace-keeping and crisis management missions independently of the US (Gnesotto, 1998; Gordon, 1997–98). In 1999, the brief campaign in Kosovo demonstrated unequivocally that, compared with the US military, European forces could hope to do little more than play a facilitating or back-up role (Brawley and Martin, 2000; Bozo, 2003). The Franco-British summit in Saint Malo in December 1998, which effectively kick-started the drive towards a serious European security and defence project, was immediately followed by the chaotic and ineffectual international conference on Kosovo, convened at Rambouillet and co-chaired by France and the UK. The event signally failed to avert the Kosovo war, for which the Europeans were so manifestly unprepared. Yet in late 2001, the European Council declared its objective of being able to field operational combat-ready troops by 2003. The reaction from strategic experts around the world was one of serious scepticism (CDS, 2001; IISS, 2001). Nevertheless, the 2003 deadline was met and by 2006 the EU had engaged in 16 missions in as many countries on three continents. We shall analyse these missions in detail in Chapter 7. The current chapter charts the transformation of the EU's instruments of intervention from the end of the Cold War to the present day. There were two major strands to this transformation, the first military and the second civilian. We shall deal with these sequentially, even though it must be stressed that the fundamental distinctiveness of ESDP is its combination of military and civilian instruments.

While much attention has been focused on the EU's development of military muscle, it is a serious mistake to see this as the most important component of ESDP. As the European project has taken shape, the US armed forces have intervened massively in Iraq and in Afghanistan. Those interventions, by a military power that spends more than the next 15 military powers combined (Table 4.1), whose navy is larger than the rest of the world's navies combined, and whose mastery of real-time digitized warfare is relatively absolute, have nevertheless demonstrated that the usefulness of military force alone has serious limits. In particular, military power on its own – however massive – cannot solve complex political and human problems. Some have mocked the EU's soft power and argued that, without hard power to back it up, little can be achieved. The reverse is probably true. As we have seen in the Western Balkans, in the Middle East and in Afghanistan, without the complementary deployment of *civilian* instruments of crisis management, the application of naked military power can often lead to failure. Civilian crisis management is a concept which has only recently entered the political lexicon. It refers to the entire range of non-military instruments which are called for in crisis situations – whether pre-conflict or post-conflict. Police forces, state-building capacity, trained judges, lawyers, civil administrators, customs officials, civil protection and disaster relief agents, demobilization and reintegration specialists, security sector reform instruments: all these and other capacities are subsumed under the generic title of civil crisis management (CCM). It covers a much broader range of instruments than the military component of ESDP and involves a much greater degree of institutional flexibility, since it calls on agencies from all three of the 'pillars' of the TEU. This is at least as important a component of ESDP as the strictly military element – and many would argue that it is ultimately more important. Yet its emergence has gone largely unheralded. The EU's achievement in assembling all these instruments is remarkable, especially since it was carried out in a context in which, on both sides of the Atlantic, critics tended to view the Union as woefully unprepared to face the test of

Table 4.1 *World military expenditure, 2004*

Military spending	*Expenditure in US$ millions*	*US$ per capita*	*% of GDP (and trend ↓ since 2003)*
1 United States	455,908	1,555	3.8 ↑
2 China	62,539	48	3.7 ↓
3 Russia	61,900	429	4.3 ↓
4 France	51,698	855	2.5 ↓
5 UK	49,618	823	2.3 ↓
6 Japan	45,151	354	1.0 –
7 Germany	37,790	458	1.4 ↓
8 Italy	30,537	525	1.8 ↓
9 Saudi Arabia	20,910	810	8.8 ↓
10 India	19,647	18	3.0 ↑
11 South Korea	16,398	339	2.4 ↓
12 Australia	14,310	718	2.3 –
13 Spain	12,588	312	1.2 –
14 Canada	11,418	351	1.1 –
15 Turkey	10,115	146	3.3 ↓
16 Israel	9,682	1,561	8.2 ↓
17 Netherlands	9,607	588	1.6 –
18 Brazil	9,232	50	1.5 ↓
19 Indonesia	7,553	31	2.9 ↓
20 Taiwan	7,519	330	2.74 ↓
NATO	702,684	819	2.8 –
NATO Europe	235,358	442	1.9 –
EU 25	229,907	364	1.5 ↓
Middle East and North Africa	59,645	189	5.7 ↓
Central and South Asia	29,299	19	2.8 ↓
East Asia + Australia	180,496	85	2.0 ↓
Caribbean, Central and South America	25,659	47	1.3 ↓
Sub-Saharan Africa	8,694	13	1.7 ↓

Note: US expenditure is equal to that of the next 15 countries combined (China to Israel); it is equal to the rest of the entire world (minus NATO Europe), totalling $456 billion. EU 25 expenditure of $229.907 billion is equal to the total of China plus Russia plus Japan plus Saudi Arabia plus India plus South Korea (which together total $226.545 billion).
Source: IISS, *The Military Balance 2005–2006*, pp. 353–8.

overseas engagement, let alone the harsh strategic reality of the post-9/11 world.

Transforming EU military capabilities

Emerging from the cold war

After the Cold War, all European nations were compelled to transform their militaries. The type of military forces and other instruments required for the territorial defence objectives of the Cold War were quite inappropriate for the new crisis management and peace-keeping missions of the post-Cold War world. In 1988, as the Cold War was ending, the NATO alliance had almost 5.4 million active-duty service personnel, backed up by over 7 million reservists. Of these, the European members of NATO contributed the vast bulk, with 3.1 million active-duty service members and 5.5 million reservists. Against these forces were ranged over 5 million active-duty troops from the Warsaw Pact, backed by 6.2 million reservists.* However, within three years, both the Warsaw Pact and the Soviet Union had disappeared and a dozen years later, the numbers of armed forces in the NATO alliance had been radically reduced. By 2003, total European forces numbered only 4.9 million, a 43 per cent decrease. The paradoxical reality about these forces, however, was that substantial numbers of the 12 million men and women under arms at the height of Cold War tensions virtually never saw action, whereas by 2006 their counterparts – from both the United States and the European Union (EU) – were seriously overstretched, large numbers of them being at one stage or another of the three-stage cycle of deploying, resting, or preparing to deploy. Moreover, whereas in 1989 the 'peace' was kept essentially by mass divisions of conscripts dug-in across the Iron Curtain and backed by a nuclear deterrent, in

* Source for military statistics: International Institute for Strategic Studies, *The Military Balance 1989–1990*, London: Brassey's, 1989, pp. 208–9. Other military statistics cited in this chapter are taken from the appropriate annual volume of *The Military Balance*, Oxford, Oxford University Press.

2006, crisis management operations were being carried out by professional soldiers using sophisticated conventional equipment demanding high levels of technical skills and ongoing training.

The fundamental shift was from quantity to quality. As the United Kingdom's 1998 'Strategic Defence Review' stated: 'defence is a highly professional, increasingly high technology, vocation.' The challenge was to recruit highly motivated people, to train them appropriately and to a very high standard, to equip them properly, and to retain both their motivation and their services (UK MOD, 1998). This chapter will examine the process whereby the EU member-states, both individually and collectively, shifted their military thinking away from the fixed 'legacy' weapons and systems of the Cold War years and towards the power-projection and crisis-management 'enablers' of the present. The professional soldier of 2007 and beyond will require a range of skills – not just military skills, but also political, social and even cultural and linguistic skills – undreamed of only two decades earlier. We have witnessed a wholesale transformation of the EU's plans, structures, weapons systems and equipment: in short, its entire military mindset.

The challenge of transformation was especially acute for Europe. During the Cold War, European forces were rarely deployed far from home (indeed almost never, if 'home' is taken to mean Europe); they spent most of their time on exercises and virtually none of it on active combat duty. General de Gaulle, justifying France's decision to spend around 40 per cent of its defence budget on nuclear weapons, had coined the formula 'nuclear weapons mean the absence of battle'. As a result, when the Gulf War overtook them in 1991, French forces, although among the most robustly trained and experienced in Europe, were shocked to discover that very few were actually deployable: just 15,000 out of a total armed force of 289,000. Their vaunted AMX-300 combat tanks were badly in need of servicing; only 40 were combat-ready out of a notional 1,300 in service. When the lightly armed *Daguet* division finally arrived in Saudi Arabia, it found that its AMX-10RC light armoured vehicles were quite literally blind to the topography of the desert theatre until equipped with American global positioning (GPS) guidance systems. When, less than six months later the

Europeans were again caught off guard with the outbreak of the Balkan wars, it came as an even harsher revelation to many – even within the security community – that the Europeans were far from able, as Luxembourg's Foreign Minister Jacques Poos had imprudently implied they were, to take over from the Americans responsibility for European security. Lacking strategic transport systems, they were unable even to project any forces to a region which lay, technically, within the geographical bounds of the EU itself.

The basic explanation for this state of affairs is simple. Whereas US forces throughout the twentieth century had devoted massive effort – financial, technological, and logistical – to a capacity for 'force projection' across both the world's great oceans, European forces since 1945 had been configured for line-defence across the great European plain. The West German armed forces in 1989, for instance, boasted almost 500,000 active troops, with a further 850,000 reservists. Their main equipment featured 5,000 main battle tanks, 2,136 armoured infantry fighting vehicles, 3,500 armoured personnel carriers, 2,500 artillery pieces, 2,700 anti-tank guided weapons, almost 5,000 air-defence guns, and 800 surface-to-air missiles. Very little of this materiel was of much use for the new tasks of distant crisis management facing the EU in the 1990s.

Although NATO, in its new Strategic Concept of November 1991, drew attention to the need to shift focus away from massed tank and artillery battles in Central Europe to the new and more diverse crisis management challenges of the post-Cold War world, the emphasis initially was doctrinal rather than programmatic (NATO, 1991). New procurement projects have lead-times of around 15 years, but few European governments were able to imagine, let alone to anticipate, the new force-projection challenges that would be facing them in the twenty-first century. All were keen to cash in on the post-1989 'peace dividend'. On average, European defence budgets fell by more than 20 per cent during the period between 1989 and 1998. The budgets of France, Germany and the UK fell by, respectively 12 per cent, 24 per cent and 28 per cent during this period (SIPRI, 1999). The UK immediately embarked on a series of defence reviews culminating in the 1998 'Strategic Defence Review' (UK MOD, 1994, 1995). France moved rapidly from a defence policy of rigorous national autonomy towards one geared towards integrated European operations (Ministère de la Défense, 1994; Howorth, 1998). The majority of European militaries, however (with the notable exceptions of Belgium and the Netherlands), remained unreformed and unchanged for the greater part of the decade. Europe, in short, revealed a dual 'capabilities gap'. There was a growing gap between the advanced weapons systems available to the United States military and the increasingly antiquated systems of the EU member-states, and there was also an emerging gap between those existing EU systems and the real military requirements of the European Union in the post-Cold War world (Hill, 1993).

The quest for a European security and defence identity (ESDI)

In the early 1990s, defence planners began to address the problem of developing a serious EU military capacity that would allow the Union to assume responsibility for the new crisis management tasks of the post–Cold War world. At a meeting at Petersberg (near Bonn) in June 1992, the Western European Union (WEU) had defined three such tasks, corresponding to three levels of combat intensity: 'humanitarian and rescue tasks; peacekeeping tasks; [and] tasks of combat forces in crisis management, including peacemaking' (Ortega, 2005). These 'Petersberg Tasks' implied radical transformation of the EU's existing capacity to provide deployable, professional intervention forces geared to 'out of area' crisis management. But where were these forces to be found? The first task was to end conscription and to move towards all-volunteer forces (AVFs). Conscripts, it was generally recognized, tended to have limited training and skills and, largely for political and juridical reasons, were un-deployable outside of their home countries. Belgium and the Netherlands moved swiftly. Belgium announced the abolition of conscription in 1992 and ended it in 1994; the Netherlands followed suit in 1993 and 1996. France and Spain decided to abolish conscription in 1996 after agonizing debates about the connection between military service and democracy. In both countries, the last conscripts left the armed forces in 2001. The motivations for abolishing conscription varied from country to country. Most, such as Belgium, Spain, and many Central and Eastern European states, sought to focus on downsizing and reduction of the military budget; others, including the Netherlands, France, and Italy, were intent on transforming their militaries into deployable forces for overseas crisis management (Williams, 2005). However, by 2005, 16 years after the end of the Cold War, only 13 of the 25 EU states had moved fully to AVFs, although several others had plans to phase out conscription (Table 4.2).

The next step was to arrange for these new professional forces to be equipped to tackle crisis-management missions. Such a transformational process would clearly take time, but crises – in the Balkans and elsewhere – would not wait. As a stop-gap measure, the procedures known as 'Berlin Plus' were devised to allow the EU to bridge the capabilities gap by *borrowing* necessary assets such as strategic lift, C4I (command, control, communications, computers, and intelligence), and logistics from the United States (Box 4.1). EU-only units could be put together from inside NATO by generating European Combined Joint Task Forces (CJTFs) (Terriff, 2003). A European Security and Defence Identity (ESDI) was thus to be forged, 'separable but not separate' from NATO and overseen politically by the WEU.

In the event, these rather awkward procedures proved unsatisfactory. First, the US military proved far less enthusiastic than the politicians to 'lend' their hard-won high-tech assets to ill-prepared and ill-trained Europeans with little experience in the field. Second, the proposals that EU forces be 'double-hatted' – available either to a NATO/US commander or to a hypothetical EU commander – caused disquiet within the officer corps. Third, the Berlin Plus proposals were, to some extent, predicated on a parallel reform of NATO's overall command structure, with a view to giving more command posts to European officers. The US government's reluctance to confer on a European officer the command of NATO's southern HQ (AFSouth) in Naples effectively sank that agreement (Brenner and Parmentier, 2002). It also became clear to most policy-makers that the WEU was too inconsequential a body to assume responsibility for political oversight of EU military missions. Thus, the challenge of improving military capacity in Europe remained essentially unaddressed throughout the 1990s. The project of generating a European security and defence identity *from inside NATO* had proved to be a false start.

Table 4.2 *European armed forces, 2004*

	Professional or conscript[a]	*Number of Personnel*					
		Army	*Navy*	*Air Force*	*Total in 2004*[b]	*Total 1988*	*% Red'n 88-04*
Austria	Conscript	33,200	–[c]	6,700	39,900	54,700	–27%
Belgium	Professional since 1994	24,800	2,450	10,250	39,200	88,300	–56%
Cyprus	Conscript	10,000	–	–	10,000	13,000	–23%
Czech Rep.	Professional since 2005	16,663	–	5,609	22,272	197,000	–89%
Denmark	Conscript	12,500	3,800	4,200	21,180	29,300	–28%
Estonia	Conscript	3,429	331	193	4,934	n/a	n/a
Finland	Conscript	20,500	5,000	2,800	28,300	35,200	–20%
France	Professional since 2001	133,500	43,995	63,600	254,895	457,000	–44%
Germany	Conscript	191,350	25,650	67,500	284,500	489,000	–42%
Greece	Conscript	110,000	19,250	23,000	163,850	214,000	–23%
Hungary	Ended 2004	23,950		7,500	32,300	99,000	–67%
Ireland	Professional	8,500	1,100	860	10,460	13,200	–21%
Italy	Professional since 2005	112,000	34,000	45,875	191,875	386,000	–50%
Latvia	Plans to end 2006	1,817	685	255	5,238	n/a	n/a
Lithuania	Conscript	11,600	710	1,200	13,510	n/a	n/a

Luxembourg	Professional since 1967	900	–	–	900	800	+12%
Malta	Professional	2,237[d]	(joint)	(joint)	2,237	1,200	+86%
Netherlands	Professional since 1996	23,150	12,130	11,050	53,130	102,200	–48%
Poland	Conscript	89,000	14,300	30,000	141,500	406,000	–65%
Portugal	Conscription ended 2003	26,700	10,950	7,250	44,900	73,900	–39%
Slovakia	Conscript ended 2006	12,860		5,160	20,195	n/a	n/a
Slovenia	Professional since 2004	6,550		(530)	6,550	n/a	n/a
Spain	Professional since 2001	95,600	19,455	22,750	147,255	309,500	–52%
Sweden	Conscript	13,800	7,900	5,900	27,600	67,000	–59%
UK	Professional since 1963	116,760	40,630	48,500	205,890	316,700	–35%
Norway[e]	*Conscript*	*14,700*	*6,180*	*5,000*	*25,800*	*35,800*	*–28%*
Turkey[e]	*Conscript*	*402,000*	*52,750*	*60,100*	*514,850*	*635,300*	*–19%*

Notes: Countries set in bold are the original 15 EU member states prior to 2004. [a]Six of the EU-15 (members prior to 2004 enlargement) still field conscript armies. Half of the EU Accession states (those who became members in 2004) retain conscript armed forces, but one of these (Latvia) plans to end conscription in 2006. [b]In some cases, overall numbers are in excess of the sums for the three armed forces because paramilitaries and other forces are included in the official tallies. [c]Austria and Luxembourg have no navy and Luxembourg has no air force. Of the newest ten members, joining in 2004, the Czech Republic, Cyprus, Hungary, Slovakia, and Slovenia have no navy, and Cyprus also has no air force. [d]Maltese armed forces include all three services. [e]Norway and Turkey are included here although they are not EU members because Norway participates in the ESDP through NATO and the Berlin Plus arrangements, participates in EU joint actions, and has pledged personnel and equipment to the ESDP Rapid Reaction Force. http://europa.eu.int/comm/external_relations/norway/intro/ . Turkey is included because it has a complex agreement with the EU through the EU-NATO Partnership and, if it joined the EU, would become by far the largest armed force in the Union.

Source: *The Military Balance 2005–2006*, pp. 45–150.

Box 4.1 Berlin Plus

The 'Berlin Plus' arrangements refer to the agreed framework for NATO-EU cooperation in crisis-management operations. Under these arrangements, the EU enjoys 'assured access to NATO planning', 'presumed access to NATO assets and capabilities', and a pre-designated Europeans-only chain of command under the Deputy Supreme Commander Europe (DSACEUR), a European general. The initial arrangements were discussed between NATO and the WEU at a ministerial meeting in Berlin in June 1996. The devil proved to be in the detail and it took six years of hard bargaining (the 'Berlin Plus negotiations') to nail down the specifics. At NATO's Washington Summit in April 1999, negotiations on the Berlin Plus mechanisms were stepped up, but the existence of ESDP called for a shift in negotiating partner away from the WEU and in favour of the EU.

In January 2001, the talks entered a new phase involving the EU and NATO directly. After two years of hard bargaining this led, in December 2002, to the NATO-EU Declaration on ESDP (16 December 2002) and the Berlin Plus Arrangements (17 March 2003). The details of these arrangements are to be found in Box 5.1, Chapter 5.

From identity to policy: ESDI to ESDP

The decision taken in 1998 by incoming UK Prime-Minister Tony Blair, to move resolutely towards improved European capacity, broke the log-jam that ESDI had been unable to shift. The Saint Malo Declaration of 4 December 1998 represented a triple crossing of the Rubicon which had major consequences for European military capacity. First, as we saw in Chapter 3, it directly conferred on the EU the political decision-making capacity for crisis-management missions that the WEU had manifestly been ill-equipped to assume. Second, it insisted that 'the Union must have the capacity for autonomous action, backed up by credible military forces, the means to decide to use them, and a readiness to do so, in order to respond to international crises.' The quest for autonomous EU military capacity has proceeded ever since. Third, the Declaration posited a new relationship between the EU and NATO, contributing to the 'vitality of a modernized Atlantic Alliance', the precise definition of which has preoccupied planners to this day. We shall assess the EU-NATO relationship in detail in Chapter 5. There is little doubt that Blair's gamble was primarily motivated by a sense that, unless the European members of NATO made a concerted effort to improve their military capacity, the Alliance itself would begin to unravel. The shift from a relatively fruitless quest for a European military *identity* (ESDI) towards the delivery of a European security and defence *policy* (ESDP) was a major leap forward. The acronym ESDP was coined by the European Council in June 1999 to distinguish this relatively ambitious – and autonomous – EU project from the NATO-dependent mechanisms of ESDI. It was not insignificant that the initiative came from the only two EU countries with power-projection capacity. The other European countries were summoned to follow the Franco-British lead.

The British Ministry of Defence took a major role in driving forward the debate on European military transformation. The decisions taken at the EU Council in Helsinki in December 1999, leading to the establishment of a Helsinki Headline Goal (HHG), were inspired by a series of papers drafted in Whitehall, as were most subsequent ESDP military initiatives (Rutten, 2001: 82–91. The HHG was conceived as a rough 'Force Catalogue' from which would be drawn appropriate resources for a range of hypothetical European missions, including the three main 'Petersberg Tasks' (humanitarian assistance, peacekeeping and peace-making). The main elements of the Force Catalogue were to be 60,000 troops, 100 ships and 400 aircraft, deployable within 60 days and sustainable for one year. Much subsequent comment assumed that the Helsinki Headline Goal was an attempt to create a new European Rapid Reaction Force (ERRF). It was not. In the words of one of its principal architects, it was 'a statement of a level of military ambition intended to galvanise political interest in the subject of force and capability development' (Lee, 2005). Via a series of 'Capabilities Pledging Conferences' in November 2000, November 2001, May 2003 and November 2004, this pool of resources was constantly refined and gradually brought into shape. Following the second Capabilities Commitment Conference of November 2001, EU defence officials and military planners in the Headline Goal Task Force (HGTF) sought to ensure at least minimal compliance with the stated objective of operationality by December 2003.

However, there were several major problems with the Helsinki Headline Goal. The first problem was the way forces were to be built up. Voluntary, bottom-up contributions might secure the raw numbers, but they could not guarantee the delivery, still less the mobilization, of a coherent fighting force. Instead, the key concept had to be usability. In 2005, there were still almost 1.7 million troops in uniform in Europe. Of that number, only about 10 per cent were adequately trained even for serious peace-keeping operations, let alone for peace-making, still less for war-fighting. Of those 170,000, probably at most 50,000 could carry out the type of military operation needed in circumstances such as those in Iraq since 2003. Rotation requirements drop the number still more, leaving just 15,000 to 20,000 troops genuinely usable at any given time in serious military missions (Venusberg, 2004: 27). Yet simply increasing quantities was soon perceived as not only insufficient but inappropriate; what was required was far greater quality. The second problem with the HHG had to do with the procurement of a new generation of strategic systems. If the EU were to engage seriously in potentially distant crisis management operations, it needed the tools of modern force projection. The Union had identified the main areas of strategic deficiency as being: air-to-air refueling; combat search and rescue; headquarters; nuclear, biological and chemical defenses; special operations forces; theater ballistic missile defense; unmanned aerial vehicles; strategic air lift; space; and interoperability (Missiroli, 2003: 94). But in order to generate an effective EU capacity in such areas, it was not enough to rely on voluntary efforts, or even to appoint a lead nation to chair a working group. There had to be collective political agreement to drive the process forward towards agreed targets. That implied top-down leadership, pooling, and specialization. Such processes touched on sensitive issues of national sovereignty.

The third – and potentially biggest – problem with the HHG process was the absence of clear debate about the nature of the military operations the EU might aim to mount. The original thinking behind the HHG derived from experiences in Kosovo. What the EU had in mind – especially in the context of the reference in the Saint-Malo Declaration to the notion of autonomous forces – was the ability to carry out a Kosovo-type operation with minimal reliance on US inputs. This could be done in two ways. A Kosovo operation could have been mounted in 1999 with the EU's existing military assets, but unlike the US-led operation, which depended largely on air power, it would have involved substantial numbers of ground troops and resulted in many casualties. Alternately, the EU could aim to develop a US-style capacity to fight high-level network-centric warfare (Arquilla and Ronfeldt, 2001). This would require even greater defence spending and a more significant human resources challenge. Would the price be politically acceptable? If not, would something less than a fully integrated system – what has been called a 'network-enabled' capacity – be affordable? A European Network Enabling Capability (ENEC) would enable linkages between European forces rather than provide a single advanced network. It would allow EU forces to 'plug in' to certain limited aspects of the USA's advanced system (Venusberg, 2004: 12). Would such a system work? Answers were and remain elusive. In the 2003 war in Iraq, the United States and the UK fought in different geographic zones partly because their battlefield communications technologies could not be properly networked. However, in April 2006 the newly established Defence Agency (see below) held a seminar at which it was agreed that 'the European Union needs to look seriously into the potential of this new technology'. The meeting helped prepare the ground for defining 'the EU's ambitions and future strategy in the NEC area' (EDA, 2006b). We shall assess these developments further in Chapter 7.

To confuse capabilities planning even further, the EU decided in 2004 that it would engage in a more extensive range of missions. Article III-309 of the EU's proposed Constitutional Treaty extended the Petersberg tasks to include '*joint disarmament operations*, humanitarian and rescue tasks, *military advice and assistance tasks*, *conflict prevention* and peacekeeping tasks, [and] tasks of combat forces undertaken for crisis management, including peacemaking and *post-conflict stabilization*' (italics denote new items added to the original Petersberg tasks). The new emphasis was firmly on those missions with both a military and a political-civilian component. The 2004 Constitutional Treaty added the need to 'contribute to the fight against terrorism'. Yet that fight would require very different instruments from those needed to drive the Serbian army out of Kosovo (de Wijk,

2002). How could Europe afford both when at the time it seemed unable to afford either? These internal contradictions at the heart of the HHG process required urgent attention. The third EU Capabilities Conference, held in Brussels in May 2003, registered both progress and caution. On the one hand, it noted that the first phase of the European Capability Action Plan (ECAP), launched in 2001 to identify shortcomings in the HHG, had been successfully concluded, with 19 panels activated to address the majority of the shortfalls, and all member-states participating. On the other hand, it recognized that, 'at the upper end of the spectrum of scale and intensity', significant deficiencies still existed.

The conference adopted the ten priority areas noted above in which improvements needed to be ensured, either through additional contributions, or through member-states' existing procurement programmes. The ECAP process began to shift, in summer 2003, away from sheer quantities towards more qualitative approaches and criteria. Project groups were established to focus on solutions such as leasing, multi-nationalization and role specialization. The EU moved towards the recognition of 'coordination responsibility' for key procurement projects: Germany took the lead on strategic air lift; Spain on air-to-air refuelling; the UK on headquarters; and the Netherlands on PGMs (precision guided munitions) for delivery by EU F-16s. Military capacity was becoming organized.

From HHG to Headline Goal 2010: a qualitative breakthrough?

The most urgent need was soon recognized to be that of assembling a highly-trained, deployable, and sustainable force to meet the challenging missions of the revised Petersberg tasks. This process was facilitated by a series of informal meetings of an EU Council of Defence Ministers, which were instrumental in helping move the debate on capacity away from the raw numbers of the HHG and towards a clear set of qualitative criteria. In addition, after the start of the Iraq War in 2003, the EU devised its first ever 'Security Strategy' document, which spelled out the broad outlines of its military objectives. A detailed analysis of the *European Security Strategy* is provided in Chapter 6.

In 2004, the EU entered a new and qualitatively different stage in the process of strengthening military capabilities, with the announcement of the new Headline Goal 2010 (HG 2010) which was formally adopted at the European Council meeting on 17 June (European Union, 2004), the presentation of the 'battle-groups' concept (EU-ISS 2005: 10–17), the establishment of the European Defence Agency (EDA) and the launch of the Civil-Military Planning Cell (CMPC). Defence Ministers also drove forward the drafting of a 'European Capabilities Action Plan (ECAP) Road Map' aimed at monitoring progress in all areas of capabilities (EU-ISS, 2005: 74–80). Building on the Helsinki Headline Goal, HG 2010 commits the Union 'to be able by 2010 to respond to a crisis with rapid and decisive action applying a fully coherent approach to the whole spectrum of crisis-management operations covered by the Treaty on the European Union'. Interoperability, deployability and sustainability were at the heart of the project. The member-states identified a list of specific milestones within the 2010 horizon, including the establishment of both the EDA and the CMPC by the end of 2004; the implementation of an EU strategic lift command by 2005; the ability by 2007 to deploy force packages at high readiness broadly based on EU battle-groups; the availability of an EU aircraft carrier and associated air wing and escort by 2008; and 'appropriate compatibility and network linkage of all communications equipment and assets' by 2010.

HG 2010, by focusing on small, rapidly deployable units capable of high-intensity warfare, successfully shifted the objective from quantity to quality. It also resolved, at least partially, the contradiction between a Kosovo-style capability and the requirements of the 'war on terrorism'. The newly created battle-groups (Table 4.3), of which up to 15 are projected for 2007, can, if necessary, be used for both types of operation. Battle-groups (BG) are units of 1,500 troops prepared for combat in jungle, desert or mountain conditions, deployable within 15 days and sustainable in the field for up to 30 days with potential extension to 120 days. They are defined as 'the minimum militarily effective, credible, rapidly deployable, coherent force package capable of stand-alone operations or for the initial phase of larger operations'. The battle-group is based on a combined-arms battalion-size force and reinforced with combat support (CS) and combat service support (CSS) elements. It is associated

Table 4.3 *EU nation-state participation in 15 new battle-groups*

Participating countries	*Target date for deployability*
France	2005
UK	2005
Italy	2005
Spain	2006
Germany, France, Belgium, Spain	2006
France, Belgium, Luxembourg	2006
Italy, Spain, Greece, Portugal	2006
Germany, Netherlands, Finland	2007
Germany, Czech Republic, Austria	2007
Italy, Hungary, Slovenia	2007
Poland, Germany, Slovakia, Latvia, Lithuania	2007
Sweden, Finland, Norway, Estonia, Ireland?	2007
UK, Netherlands	2007
Greece, Bulgaria, Romania, Cyprus	2007
Czech Republic, Slovakia	2007

Source: European Union web-site, 2006.

with a force headquarters and with designated operational and strategic enablers such as strategic lift and logistics (EU-ISS, 2005: 296–8). At a meeting of the Council of Defence Ministers on 21 November 2004 it was announced that 13 battle-groups would be established, all to be operational by 2007 or sooner. Two more groups were announced in November 2005. Member-states can also offer niche capabilities, of which the following have been agreed: Cyprus, a medical group; Lithuania, a water purification unit; Greece, the Athens Sealift Coordination Centre; France, the structure of a headquarters for a multinational and deployable force (ESDP Fact-Sheet, 2005). Cyprus also agreed to provide infrastructure, and Ireland to participate in a battle-group (Power, 2006; Collins, 2006). By 2007, the EU should have the capacity to undertake two concurrent operations, even almost simultaneously if necessary.

The European Defence Agency

A European Defence Agency (EDA) subject to the authority of the European Council was called for in the draft Constitutional Treaty of August 2004; armaments cooperation had hitherto taken place outside the EU framework. Two main reasons lay behind the change. The first was the relative failure of previous attempts to coordinate procurement and armaments cooperation. The second was the accelerating reality of ESDP and the associated need to link capabilities to armaments production. The urgency of these drivers was reflected in the fact that in June 2003 the EU agreed not to await ratification of the Treaty in order to launch the EDA but to create it immediately. The stated objectives of the EDA were to:

- contribute to identifying the Member States' military capability objectives and evaluating observance of the capability commitments given by the Member States;
- promote harmonization of operational needs and adoption of effective, compatible procurement methods;
- propose multilateral projects to fulfil the objectives in terms of military capabilities, ensure coordination of the programmes implemented by the Member States and management of specific cooperation programmes;
- support defence technology research, and coordinate and plan joint research activities and the study of technical solutions meeting future operational needs;
- contribute to identifying and, if necessary, implementing any useful measure for strengthening the industrial and technological base of the defence sector and for improving the effectiveness of military expenditure (Schmitt, 2004).

The EDA (www.eda.eu.int), which was created in summer 2004, is guided by a Steering Board formally meeting at the level of Defence Ministers, but occasionally in the format of National Armaments Directors or Research and Technology Directors. The Steering Board met no fewer than 14 times in the Agency's first two years, nine times at the level of defence ministers. The

Steering Board is headed by the High Representative for the Common Foreign and Security Policy (or Union Minister for Foreign Affairs if that post is eventually created) and managed by a Chief Executive. After a fierce turf battle between France and the UK, Nick Witney, the former head of the UK MOD's International Security Policy Division, was named as the first Chief Executive. The Board has four Directorates: Capabilities; R&T; Armaments; Industry and market. The EDA offers the first real opportunity for the EU to bring its defence planning, military capability objectives, and armaments coordination in line with the urgent tasks it faces on the ground. The EU governments are thus poised to move towards more rational armaments and defence planning and an integrated European defence market. All these agendas are interconnected: 'Like it or not, governments and defence industries are roped together in a common endeavour' (Witney, 2005). The dynamics of ESDP suggest that national plans will progressively evolve within a European framework (Figure 4.1).

Figure 4.1 The EDA's capability development process

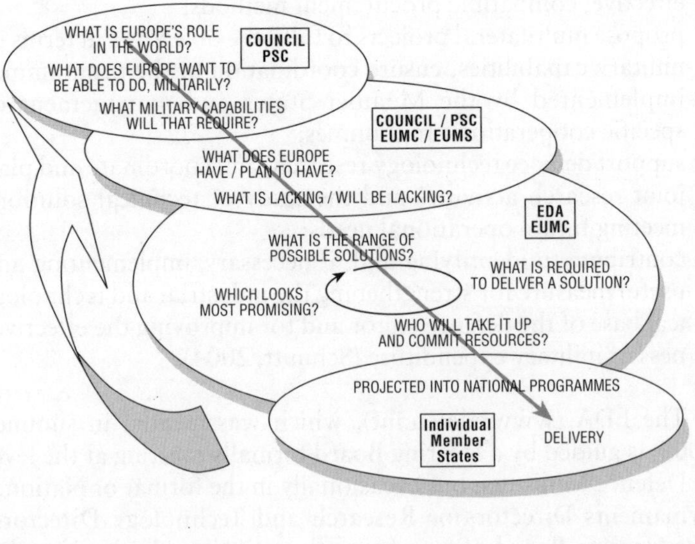

Source: www.eda.europa.eu/cpdv/cpdv/htm (EDA Capabilities Development, 2006)

Reviewing progress in July 2006, the EDA's Chief Executive, Nick Witney was able to record two major developments (EDA, 2006). The first was the launch, on 1 July 2006, of the first genuinely European Defence Equipment Market, with a unanimously agreed Code of Conduct designed to increase cross-border transparency and competition, obtain better value for money, broaden business opportunities for defence contractors and strengthen the global competitiveness of Europe's defence industry. For the first time, European governments committed themselves to purchase defence equipment from each other if the tender was the best available, rather than automatically to award the contract to a national supplier. This move could well revolutionize the European procurement market. The second breakthrough was the publication, in May 2006, of the first serious audit of EU member state spending on Research and Technology, impelled by the October 2005 European Council meeting at Hampton Court. With the EU being outspent by the USA to the tune of 6:1 in R&T, there was strong consensus within the EDA that the Europeans need to spend much more on R&T, spend it more wisely and more collectively. This will be the first real challenge for the EDA in the years ahead.

The civil–military planning cell (CMPC)

Another ESDP breakthrough came in 2003 in the field of operational planning. This was a contentious issue which had, for several years, pitted the UK against France. Paris had always been keen to develop autonomous EU operational planning capabilities, but London had resisted, arguing that this was an expensive duplication of an existing NATO capability. The UK insisted that, in the event of an 'EU-only' operation (that is, without reference to NATO and without the support of NATO planning via Berlin Plus), such missions should have recourse to the national operational planning facilities of the UK (Northwood), of France (Creil) and, to a lesser extent, those of Germany (Potsdam), Italy and Greece. However, at a contentious defence summit among France, Germany, Belgium and Luxembourg on 29 April 2003, at the height of the Iraq crisis, the summiteers decided to forge ahead and create an 'EU' operational planning cell at a Belgian army base in Tervuren, a suburb of Brussels. This provoked outrage in Washington and London and, for a moment, seemed destined to derail the entire ESDP project (IISS, 2003). However, later that summer Tony Blair sought to mend fences with his European partners, and a compromise was reached involving three distinct operational planning facilities. For EU operations under Berlin Plus, a dedicated EU unit has been attached to NATO at SHAPE Headquarters in Mons, Belgium. For most 'EU-only' operations, including most battle-group missions, an appropriate national headquarters will be adapted to planning for multi-national operations. For certain EU-only operations, particularly those involving combined civil and military dimensions, a dedicated and autonomous EU civil–military planning cell (CMPC) is being developed at ESDP headquarters in Brussels. This facility grew in 2006 to around 120 EU military personnel, and began its substantive work on the generation of a strategic planning branch and an operations centre (ESDP, 2006: 7–9).

The challenges ahead

By the end of 2004, the EU was beginning to look like an increasingly credible potential military actor. In May 2006, the EU published its sixth semestrial *Capability Improvement Chart*, listing no fewer than 64 'capabilities' and their progress towards meeting qualitative readiness targets (or, in some cases, their shortcomings (European Council, 2006). Significantly, some major improvements were found in areas with heavy 'legacy' inputs, including composite army aviation battalions and mechanized infantry battalions. Some challenges had been fully solved (nuclear, biological and chemical battalions, combined air operations centre). Some qualitatively significant areas, such as Operational Headquarters, Deployable Laboratories and Medical Units, were recording better progress than expected. But other areas requiring substantial investment, such as strategic transport, air-to-air refuelling, intelligence, surveillance and target acquisition (ISTAR), space assets, suppression of enemy air defences (SEAD), and precision-guided munitions (PGMs), were still facing serious shortfalls or needing longer time-lines for delivery. Success at reaching the European Capability Action Plan (ECAP) targets remained dependent on meaningful political commitments by member states to invest in shortfall areas and to continue the quest for multinational solutions. The EDA was intended to act both as a catalyst and as a benchmark. Following the Council's approval in May 2005 of the migration in whole or in part of 11 ECAP Projects Groups to a more integrated process coordinated by the EDA, 8 ECAP Project Groups had already completed this migration. The remaining ECAP Project Groups were pursuing their work under guidance from the EU Military Committee.

The process of defining priority areas for quality and capacity was greatly assisted by the lessons drawn from the first experiences of the EU in armed combat. Beginning in January 2003, the EU had launched (by June 2006) no fewer than 16 international missions under the aegis of ESDP. These missions are evaluated in detail in Chapter 7. The majority of them were not military missions at all and we shall evaluate the civilian objectives of ESDP later in this chapter. It cannot be argued, as a result of the six military missions conducted to date, that the EU has emerged as a major new strategic actor in world politics. For the most part the missions were small in scale and limited in scope. However, they do represent significant progress in a number of important respects. First, they are the first overseas missions undertaken by the EU and belie the sceptics who have long insisted that the EU, being incapable of coordinating grand strategy, should stick to what it does best in the area of foreign security policy: trade and aid. Second, the military missions, covering two continents, and addressing some of the most sensitive challenges of regional stability, suggest that the EU both can and does conceptualize its 'intervention role' in a broad geo-strategic context. Third, the military missions have covered a wide variety of functions, ranging from policing, to border controls and from tackling international crime rings to robust peace-keeping operations. That spread reflects the range and complexity of the civil-military culture which underlies the ESDP in general and the ESS in particular. But there remain major challenges ahead for the military sector.

One major remaining challenge is that of recruitment and training. Standardization and the quest for interoperability across the continent is a growing feature of military training. Most future EU missions are likely to be multinational, as part of a UN, NATO or EU force. Significant standardization of equipment will have to await the recommendations of the European Defence Agency and the rationalization of procurement. It is, somewhat ironically, through NATO's Partnership for Peace programmes that the majority of the EU member-states are currently improving their capacity for interoperability. These programmes affect formerly neutral countries such as Austria and Sweden as well as new-accession countries such as Hungary and Romania. Language skills are highly prized, but English is increasingly becoming the *de facto* language for multinational force communication. Even Operation *Artemis*, which was overwhelmingly French in composition and command, was officially conducted in English. In 2002, the first of a series of international conferences for cadets from the military academies of all EU member states (as well as for a number of observers from the US military academy at West Point) was organized at Saint-Cyr in France; a second such conference was held in 2003 at the Belgian Royal Military Academy. France and a number of other countries urged the EU to inaugurate a joint EU military training academy, but the resistance of other countries (notably the UK) reduced this ambition to that of a revolving European Security and Defence College (ESDC) established by the Council in July 2005. The ESDC consists of a network of national institutes, colleges, academies and institutions within the EU that deal with security and defence policy issues. The mission of the college is to provide training in the field of ESDP at all strategic levels. Among its principal objectives are to 'further enhance the European security culture within ESDP' and to 'provide Member States' administrations and staff with knowledgeable personnel familiar with EU policies, institutions and procedures'. The ESDC organizes its training activities into high-level courses (HLC) and orientation courses (OC). Participants in the ESDC training activities are usually military or civilian personnel working on ESDP issues for EU member states, acceding states or the EU institutions. Specific orientation courses may also be open to participants from third states and international organizations. During the first (2005/06) high-level course, five residential modules were organized for 60 students in Brussels, Berlin, Shrivenham (UK), Vienna/Budapest and Stockholm. Topics included: history and context of ESDP; ESDP civilian and military capabilities; ESDP crisis-management operations; ESDP in a regional context and future perspectives of ESDP. The orientation courses attracted 330 students (EU-ISS 2006: 234; ESDP 2006: 10–12).

Notwithstanding these developments, the fact remains that Europe's 25 separate militaries are trained to very different levels of combat intensity (as shown in Table 4.4). Whereas most US troops are trained to be able to cope with the requirements of full-scale warfare involving elements of C4ISTAR, satellite intelligence, sensor-to-shooter networks, and nuclear deterrence (levels 9 and 10, on the 1–10 scale), only the UK and France have forces trained to this level. A few EU militaries – Germany, Italy, the Netherlands, Spain and Sweden – can approach the challenge of advanced expeditionary warfare (levels 7 to 8), involving special forces, sea control, air support, air-to-air refuelling, strategic lift, precision guided munitions (PGMs), and theatre ballistic missile defence (TBMDs). As for the rest, force training does not go beyond levels 4 to 5, giving them a capability for medium-level 'Petersberg' peace-support tasks. A sizeable number of countries – Finland, Ireland, Cyprus, Estonia, Latvia, Lithuania, Malta, Slovakia and Slovenia – are unable to deal with more than the lowest-level Petersberg missions (intensity levels 1 to 3).

Nevertheless, European military capacity, after almost a decade of stagnation from 1989 to 1999, has come a long way in a few short years. Progress in procurement, planning, rationalization, force transformation and general 'usability' has been impressive since the turn of the millennium. But the EU still has a long way to go before it can overcome all its shortcomings and emerge as a fully credible coordinated military actor able to carry out the full range of Petersberg tasks. The EU does not aspire to become a military actor on a par with the United States, nor does it think in classical terms of territorial defence. The crisis management tasks it aims to carry out represent a new, professional 'security fire-fighting' service adapted to the modern world. But the unprecedented nature of its objectives also poses one of its most difficult dilemmas. In order to embark on the type of low-casualty operations implicit in network-centric warfare, the EU would need to invest far more than is currently available in new R&D projects and in personnel management. That may be justifiable in the United States because the US military, in addition to policing the world, is also configured to guarantee the defence of the United States. However, the more limited ambitions of ESDP rule out such spending levels in Europe.

Table 4.4 *Armed forces along the conflict intensity scale*

Level of intensity	*Type of operation*	*Countries*	*Required capabilities*
1	Petersberg tasks with low intensity	Luxembourg, Malta	General purpose ground forces
2		Cyprus, Estonia, Finland, Hungary, Ireland, Latvia, Lithuania, Slovakia, Slovenia	
3			
4	Petersberg tasks with medium intensity	Czech Republic, Poland	NBC protection, specialized forces; Civil-Military Cooperation;
5		Austria, Belgium, Denmark, Greece, Portugal	Medical Evacuation
6		Germany, Italy, Netherlands, Spain, Sweden	
7	High Intensity Petersberg, Advanced		Special forces; sea control; air support; air-to-air refueling;
8	expeditionary warfare	France, United Kingdom	strategic lift; PGM; TBMD
9	Full scale warfare		C4ISTAR, Network-centric warfare; satellite intelligence;
10		United States	sensor-to-shooter network; nuclear deterrence

Source: Adapted from Venusberg Group, *A European Defence Strategy*, Gütersloh: Bertelsmann, 2004, p. 68.

Defence spending: more or better?

Above all, the EU needs to address its wasteful spending patterns. The calls for the EU to spend more on defence are too numerous to count. Yet it is not necessarily *greater* spending that is required. Better and *wiser* spending would certainly help. The EU-25, in 2004, spent almost US$230 billion on defence – approximately half the $456 billion US defence budget for that year (Table 4.5). That is almost four times the defence budget of the second biggest military spender on earth (China, at $62.5 billion) and more than that of the six next biggest military powers put together (China, Russia, Japan, Saudi Arabia, India and South Korea: total $226.5 billion). The European Union collectively gets very little bang for this enormous amount of money. Out of that $230 billion, the EU still attempts to fund 25 armies, 21 air forces and 18 navies, for no reason that is any longer obvious or clear. Just three countries in the EU – France, the UK and Germany – together spend 61 per cent of the combined EU-25 expenditure. If Italy, as the fourth largest spender, is added to the trio, these countries account for almost 75 per cent of the EU-25 defence expenditure. By contrast, the average expenditure of the other 21 EU states comes to just $2,869 million, less than the defence budget of, for example, Vietnam ($3,177 million). For as long as this duplication exists, return on investment will be sub-optimal. A major rationalization of the EU's defence spending is overdue. The duplication of infrastructure and support services for these separate armed forces amounts to a huge waste of resources. Alone, most EU member states would be in no position even to defend their own territory from a serious existential threat. But only once the EU has clearly established what it hopes to achieve, with what force levels and with what state of equipment, can it have any clear idea about how much money is needed. Until then, its military force transformation programmes will remain incomplete.

Towards collective defence?

What are the prospects that the EU might one day move towards some form of collective defence? Proposals to institute some kind of mutual assistance clause among EU member states have a long and distinguished pedigree – even pre-dating the EU itself since

Table 4.5 *EU member states' defence expenditure (2004), with comparison to the United States*

	US$ 2004	*US$ per capita 2004*	*Per cent of GDP 2004*	*Active-duty (000s) 2004*
France	51,698 m	855 (1)	2.5 (2)	254.0
UK	49,618 m	823 (2)	2.3 (3)	205.0
Germany	37,790 m	458 (10)	1.4 (14=)	284.0
Italy	30,537 m	525 (7=)	1.8 (5=)	191.0
Spain	12,588 m	312 (12)	1.2 (20=)	147.0
Netherlands	9,607 m	588 (5)	1.6 (8=)	53.0
Greece	5,866 m	550 (6)	2.8 (1)	163.0
Sweden	5,307 m	590 (4)	1.5 (11=)	27.0
Poland	4,605 m	119 (22)	1.9 (4)	141.0
Belgium	4,361 m	421 (11)	1.2 (20=)	36.0
Demark	3,558 m	657 (3)	1.4 (14=)	21.0
Portugal	2,830 m	268 (15)	1.6 (8=)	44.0
Finland	2,483 m	476 (9)	1.3 (18=)	28.0
Austria	2,222 m	271 (14)	0.8 (23=)	39.0
Czech Rep.	1,976 m	192 (18)	1.8 (5=)	22.0
Hungary	1,530 m	152 (19)	1.5 (11=)	32.0
Iceland	0,907 m	228 (17)	0.5 (25)	10.0
Slovakia	0,729 m	134 (20)	1.7 (7)	20.0

Slovenia	0,511 m	254 (16)	1.6 (8=)	6.0
Lithuania	0,311 m	86 (24)	1.4 (14=)	13.0
Cyprus	0,227 m	293 (13)	1.4 (14=)	10.0
Luxembourg	0,243 m	525 (7=)	0.8 (23=)	0.9
Latvia	0,179 m	77 (25)	1.3 (18=)	5.0
Estonia	0,172 m	128 (22)	1.5 (11=)	4.0
Malta	0,052 m	131 (21)	1.0 (22)	2.0
EU-15 Totals	219,615 m			1,502.6
CEE-10 Totals	10,292 m			225.0
EU-25 Totals	229,907 m			1,757.6
EU-15 Average	14,641 m	503	1.51	
CEE-10 Average	1,029 m	157	1.51	
EU-25 Average	9,196 m	364	1.51	
Norway	*4,431*	*968*	*1.8*	*25*
Turkey	*10,115*	*146*	*3.3*	*514*
United States for comparison)	455,908	1,555	3.8	1,473

Notes: Countries set bold are members of NATO. Those in italics acceded to the EU in 2004. Turkey and Norway have again been added for comparison. Norway would rank as the biggest defence spender per capita in Europe. Turkey would rank as the *largest army* with the *highest percentage of GDP*.

Source: IISS, *The Military Balance 2005–2006*.

such a clause was one of the main aims and achievements of the Brussels Treaty of 1948. According to Article V of the WEU ('Modified Brussels') Treaty of 1954:

> If any of the High Contracting Parties should be the object of an armed attack in Europe, the other High Contracting Parties will, in accordance with the provisions of Article 51 of the Charter of the United Nations, afford the Party so attacked all the military and other aid and assistance in their power.

However, not only was the WEU commitment officially subsumed under NATO's Article 5 commitment in 1949, but the status of the WEU text, given the organization's *de facto* demise in 1999, remained uncertain. A group of EU member states, led by France and Germany, had proposed merging the EU and WEU in March 1997, effectively bringing the mutual assistance commitment under the aegis of the EU. But this proposal was vehemently opposed by John Major's government and vetoed at Amsterdam in June 1997 by the incoming Prime Minister, Tony Blair. The events of 11 September 2001 served to remind EU member states that mutual assistance was not included in the Petersberg Tasks. Again, two separate drivers emerged to take matters forward on this issue.

Within the context of the Convention's Working Group on defence, the issue of a mutual assistance clause aroused fierce passions. To cut a very long story short, the following note from the Group's Secretariat relating to a meeting on this issue on 29 October 2002 gives a sense of the range of opinion:

> On the issue of a solidarity commitment, there was a clear difference of views within the group. Several suggested that it would be useful to have some sort of commitment, which in any case reflected the existing general commitments to solidarity in the Treaty. Some recognized that not all Member States would be able to sign up to such a commitment and that it would therefore have to include either an 'opt-in' or 'opt-out' provision. Some suggested that any such provision would depend in part on the future of the collective defence guarantee within WEU (Article V). Others said that they would not wish to see any form of collective commitment. Some argued that it would be politically unacceptable; others preferred not

> to include anything which might undermine existing commitments such as that within NATO. (Convention 2003)

Notwithstanding this degree of complexity, the Working Group recommended *both* the introduction into the Treaty of a solidarity clause outlining procedures in the event of a *terrorist* attack *and* an 'opt-in' facility whereby those member states who wished to take over the mutual assistance commitments of the WEU Treaty should be authorized to do so within the framework of the Union. In parallel, the Franco-German 'motor' continued to pursue the notion of the 'European Union of Security and Defence' (UESD) including 'a general clause on solidarity and common security, binding all member states in the European Union, and allowing for a response to risks of any sort that threaten the Union'.

These various proposals drew fierce opposition from both neutral and Atlanticist member states. No fewer than 24 Convention members sponsored amendments, in the final Convention plenary process, to delete the mutual assistance clause altogether. On the other side of the argument, one leading European security expert, Francois Heisbourg, had argued, in a seminar organized by the Convention's Working Party on Defence, that it was precisely because, in the wake of 9/11, NATO's collective defence guarantee under article 5 had been jettisoned by the USA, that the EU needed to introduce its own collective defence clause nevertheless. The thinking was sharpened somewhat by the new formulation, in Article I-40(2), of the paragraph on *common defence*:

> The common security and defence policy shall include the progressive framing of a common Union defence policy. This will lead to a common defence, when the European Council, acting unanimously, so decides.

This was considerably stronger than the wishy-washy wording in Article 17 of the Treaty of Amsterdam:

> The common foreign and security policy shall include all questions relating to the security of the Union, including the progressive framing of a common defence policy, which might lead to a common defence, should the European Council so decide.

It served as the basis for the proposal, in Article I-40(7) of the Constitutional Treaty, that those member states which did not wish to await the European Council's decision, should be allowed to anticipate it:

> Until such time as the European Council has acted in accordance with paragraph 2 of this Article, closer cooperation shall be established, in the Union framework, as regards mutual defence. Under this cooperation, if one of the Member States participating in such cooperation is the victim of armed aggression on its territory, the other participating States shall give it aid and assistance by all the means in their power, military or other, in accordance with Article 51 of the United Nations Charter. In the execution of closer cooperation on mutual defence, the participating Member States shall work in close cooperation with the North Atlantic Treaty Organization. The detailed arrangements for participation in this cooperation and its operation, and the relevant decision-making procedures, are set out in Article III-214.

Those 'detailed arrangements' in III-214 read as follows:

> 1 The closer cooperation on mutual defence provided for in Article I-40(7) shall be open to all Member States of the Union. A list of Member States participating in closer cooperation shall be set out in the declaration [*title*]. . .
> 2 A Member State participating in such cooperation which is the victim of armed aggression on its territory shall inform the other participating States of the situation and may request aid and assistance from them. Participating Member States shall meet at ministerial level, assisted by their representatives on the Political and Security Committee and the Military Committee.

This remained quite unacceptable both to neutrals, who feared involvement despite the apparent 'opt-in' mechanism, and to Atlanticists still suspicious about the implications for NATO. Three major elements of the proposals remained contentious: the voluntary nature of participation, the vagueness of the reference to 'close cooperation' with NATO, and the very principle of anticipating the EU's decision on common defence. Moreover, the political symbolism of such arrangements was far more obvious than its practical value.

In the event, the controversial proposals on a mutual assistance clause were also factored in to the tripartite compromises of late 2003. Under the Italian presidency, a new text was proposed which effectively drew some of the potential teeth in the original Convention draft. Not only did the crucial first sentence on anticipating the decision of the EU disappear altogether, along with any reference to 'mutual defence', but the requirement to 'give' aid and assistance to a member state under attack was watered down to one in which member states 'shall have an obligation' of aid and assistance. The requirement to work in 'close cooperation' with NATO was replaced by the considerably more robust statement that:

> Commitments and cooperation in this area shall be consistent with commitments under NATO, which, for those States which are members of it, remains the foundation of their collective defence and the forum for its implementation. (6 August 2004 Text I-41(7))

Finally, the 'detailed arrangements' under III-214 were completely scrapped, along with the article itself. On the other hand, a new 'solidarity clause' in the event of a terrorist attack or a natural or man-made disaster, which had been introduced into the Convention's draft (I-42) remained unaffected by this redrafting, as did the detailed arrangements for its implementation (III-231). These items were retained in the August 2004 text as I-43 and III-329.

The debate on a mutual assistance (or mutual defence) clause was confused and confusing. Many of the proposals were wrapped up with parallel proposals on what eventually became structured cooperation. Symbolism often took precedence over pragmatism. Agendas were multiple and cross-cutting. Some might argue that the fact that the opponents of any such clause succeeded, in the final draft constitutional text, of stripping it of much of its bite, suggests that little progress has been made since Amsterdam when Blair took it off the agenda altogether. However, in the context of a Constitution which has already enshrined structured cooperation, the very fact that a specific clause on mutual assistance was included in the text at all represents a significant step forward. What eventually emerged was a largely common-sense recognition that, in the event of attack against a member state, the others will do what they feel they can (or wish to) do to help out. It is a small step towards the recognition of common interests, rights and responsibilities. In conjunction with other such steps, it acquires real political significance. The EU is explicitly pulling ever more closely together, even in these areas which were once the last (and indeed the first) bastion of sovereignty.

Civilian crisis management: the continuation of politics by other means?

While much has been written about the military aspects of ESDP's crisis-management capabilities, the area of Civilian Crisis Management (CCM) has been seriously neglected by researchers. Almost all the books published on ESDP to date – with the notable exception of Duke (2002) – ignore this dimension altogether. With the 2006 publication of a Chaillot Paper by the EU's Institute for Security Studies, an initial – and impressive – rectification of this neglect was achieved (Nowak, 2006). The concept of Civilian Crisis Management did not make its mark in ESDP literature until the Helsinki Council meeting in December 1999 when the term was first used in the Presidency Report. In particular, in the Annexes to that Report, there were specific recommendations on the 'non-military crisis-management' of the EU. This rather 'negative' framing of the concept set the tone for discussions on civilian capabilities over the next two years. These were clearly seen as a *complement* to the military capacities to which Helsinki gave its name. Work had been started following the Cologne Council in June 1999 on inventories listing the civilian tools available to the Union which, at Helsinki, it was noted, 'clearly show that the Member States, the Union, or both have accumulated considerable experience or have considerable resources in a number of areas such as civilian police, humanitarian assistance, administrative and legal rehabilitation, search and rescue, electoral and human rights monitoring etc.' (Rutten, 2001: 89). Such a list immediately highlights one of the trickiest aspects of CCM: coordination between the Council and the Commission. Although the Council, through ESDP, was beginning to establish CCM capabilities, most of these already existed in some aspect or other of the various activities of the Commission. At Helsinki, an *Action Plan* was established which aimed at:

> strengthening the synergy and responsiveness of national, collective and NGO resources in order to avoid duplication and improve performance, while maintaining the flexibility of each contributor to decide on the deployment of assets and capabilities in a particular crisis, or via a particular channel; enhancing and facilitating the EU's contributions to, and activities within, other organizations, such as the UN and the OSCE . . . and ensuring inter-pillar coherence. (Rutten, 2001: 90)

It was agreed to establish a 'coordinating mechanism' to this effect. At the Lisbon Council in March 2000, it was decided to create a Committee for Civilian Crisis Management (Rutten, 2001: 108) and, in Brussels, Javier Solana also established a mechanism within the Council Secretariat to enable coordination with the Commission. From the outset, those responsible for CCM were conscious that coherence was going to prove this policy area's most serious challenge and potentially its Achilles heel (Marquina, 2005).

It was the Portuguese Presidency which gave the first real impulsion to CCM. The Feira Council meeting in June 2000 established a distinctive sub-section of ESDP devoted to CCM. Basing its decisions on the findings of a seminar which had taken place in Lisbon on 3–4 April, the Feira Council adopted the four priority areas identified in that study as the basis of the EU's CCM: police; strengthening the rule of law; strengthening civilian administration and civil protection (Rutten, 2001: 134). The main emphasis, however, was on the development of a police reaction capacity and a target figure of 5,000 deployable officers by 2003 was agreed, with the further proviso that 1,000 should be rapidly deployable (within 30 days). On the rule of law, member states were invited to 'establish national arrangements for selection of judges, prosecutors, penal experts and other relevant categories within the judicial and penal system, to deploy at short notice to peace support operations' and thought was also to be given to training of international judges as well as to modalities for the local recruitment of court personnel and prison officers. As for civil administration, the aim was to refine 'the selection, training and deployment of civil administration experts for duties in the re-establishment of collapsed administrative systems'. A final priority was to be 'civil protection, including search and rescue in disaster relief operations' (*ibid.*: 133–5).

As had been the case with the Helsinki Headline Goal, the initial methodology was to establish targets and then, via a series of pledging conferences, to strive to meet them (Nowak, 2006a: 19). The French Presidency (July to December 2000) was so focused on re-writing the Treaty that little was accomplished under the heading of CCM other than the convening of a number of meetings of the Committee for Civilian Aspects of Crisis Management (CIVCOM), which had been established in May 2000. This key committee, comprising national representatives and officials from the Commission and the Council Secretariat, is intended to facilitate inter-pillar cooperation as well as coordination between member states and the EU. It also advises the COPS about issues of coherence and comprehensiveness in CCM (*ibid.*: 23). In summer 2000, further guidelines for police resources were laid down and a seminar held with delegates from the UN, the OSCE and the Council of Europe on developing capacity in the field of the rule of law. Again, as with the military targets, the dominant thinking derived from Kosovo, although experiences in Guatemala, Croatia, Albania, El Salvador, Bosnia-Herzegovina and East Timor were also examined. Although the emphasis was clearly on learning *how to react* to crises, those involved in CCM were also beginning to consider ways of using the knowledge being accumulated to conceptualize conflict *prevention*, an objective for which the EU was theoretically ideally suited but in practical terms magnificently unprepared (Hill, 2001). Over the next few years, one of the distinctive features of CCM was its gradual shift from reaction to pro-action.

It was the Swedish Presidency (January to June 2001) which made the first real conceptual and programmatic breakthrough in CCM with a lengthy report on ESDP which, without ignoring the military dimension, was overwhelmingly concerned with civilian aspects (Rutten, 2002: 30–61). The Göteborg Council also generated the first major ESDP report on 'The Prevention of

Violent Conflicts' (*ibid.*: 64–8). Göteborg introduced a Police Action Plan intended to allow the EU to deploy police officers rapidly in international operations led by the UN or OSCE as well as in autonomous operations. Emphasis was placed on planning at political-strategic level; command and control of police operations; the legal framework for such operations; cross-EU police interoperability; and training and financing mechanisms. Methodologically, the police capabilities were to be demand-driven and a Police Unit was established within the Council Secretariat. Guiding principles were also established for the participation in EU Police Missions of non-EU member states (Rutten, 2002: 41–2). The first Police Capabilities Commitment Conference took place on 19 November 2001 at which further progress was made on all the Göteborg objectives – especially numbers. The Swedish Presidency was also successful in defining concrete objectives for rule-of-law capabilities which were explicitly conceptualized as being indispensable to the successful conduct of police operations.

Considerable thought was devoted to ways in which legal, judicial and penal expertise from inside the EU could help *strengthen* local resources or even *substitute* for them pending return of the process to local ownership. Again, the Kosovo precedent, where initial substitution had been essential, was invoked. The need for continuity between the short term (crisis management) and the long term (state-building) was stressed. A 2003 target of 200 officials 'adequately prepared for crisis management missions in the field of the rule of law' was established. Complementarity between these resources and the other EU instruments was seen as 'of paramount importance', as was the general raising of standards (the first overt plea for a shift from quantities to quality – which predated a similar evolution in the military realm) and the need to establish a clear strategy for implementation. The first Rule of Law Commitment Conference was held in Brussels on 16 May 2002 and both quantitative and qualitative steps forward were identified. Member states committed 282 officials for crisis-management operations, of whom up to 60 could be deployed within 30 days, and 43 officials were ear-marked for fact-finding missions (a development which was to have genuine significance later). On the qualitative side, the raw numbers were broken down proportionately to tasks and needs (72 judges, 48 prosecutors, 38 administrative service personnel, 72 penitentiary officials and 34 others), training modules for participants were devised, guidelines for criminal procedures in CCM operations were discussed, and progress was made towards a comprehensive concept for the rule of law which differentiated between strengthening and substitution (Haine, 2003: 82–4). In the two other priority areas of civil administration and civil protection, progress was less visible, although by May 2002 the Council Secretariat had generated some Basic Guidelines for crisis management in the area of civil administration, including procedures for generating a pool of experts in such areas as registration of property, elections, taxation, social and medical services and infrastructure, all geared to helping establish a transitional functional administrative framework.

As Agnieszka Nowak has recorded, in the field of civil protection, there was initial resistance from the Commission to the very notion of Council involvement but by 2002 targets had been established and met: 'two to three assessment and/or coordination teams of ten experts capable of dispatching within 3–7 hours, as well as intervention teams of 2,000 personnel and some specialised services to be dispatched within a week'. In addition, synergies with the Commission's resources were maximized through the establishment in January 2002, under Council initiative, of a Community Civilian Protection Mechanism allowing the EU to intervene either via member states' own resources or via Community mechanisms (Nowak, 2006a: 22–3). During the Spanish Presidency (January to June 2002), a further report was issued outlining the necessary stages for progress in this area (Haine, 2003: 89–90). The stage was set for another qualitative move forward towards implementation and deployability. The Laeken Council, in December 2001, had declared that the EU's crisis-management resources – both military and civilian – would be operational by 2003.

On 19 November 2002, EU ministers convened in a first Civilian Crisis Management Capability Conference to take stock of progress to date. They welcomed the fact that the quantitative targets set at Göteborg for 2003 had already been met and noted that the first ever EU civilian crisis-management mission – the EUPM in BiH – was fully prepared to deploy in January 2003. The remainder of their report was devoted to stressing the need for ever closer coordination and coherence between all the agencies and instruments operating in this field (Haine, 2003: 145–6). Much of the year 2003 was tied up with two major issues – the war in Iraq and the launch of the EU's first missions (see Chapter 7). In addition, the European Security Strategy, which attached significant importance to CCM, was adopted. Under the Greek Presidency (January to June), work was started on the wider use of EU monitoring missions as a generic crisis management instrument (Missiroli, 2003: 157) and under the Italian Presidency (July to December) progress was made on establishing modalities for EU cooperation with the OSCE in the field of conflict prevention and CCM (*ibid.*: 269), a Police exercise ('Lucerna 03') was held to test the interoperability of Integrated Police Units, and serious progress was made on a strategic approach to training programmes for CCM activities (*ibid.*: 301–2). 2004, however, was to witness major new steps forward.

Under the Irish Presidency (January to June 2004), a draft Action Plan for CCM was elaborated and endorsed at the European Council meeting on 17 June. Building on the call in the European Security Strategy for 'greater capacity to bring all necessary civilian resources to bear in crisis and post-crisis situations', and for a new focus on 'operations involving both military and civilian capabilities', the Action Plan featured a horizontal and integrated approach to CCM. The aim was to be able to draw on the full range of potential EU resources (Community, CFSP/ESDP and member states) and to deploy 'multifunctional civilian crisis management resources in an integrated format'. This implied the tailoring of CCM 'packages' to the specific circumstances of each crisis, with a heightened emphasis on the quality of the personnel trained and selected for CCM missions. The range of expertise was to be broadened to cover human rights, political affairs, security sector reform, mediation, border control, disarmament, demobilization and reintegration (DDR) and media policy. In the context of the imminent enlargement of the EU to 25 (May 2004), it was agreed to convene a Civilian Capabilities Conference for November at which work on a Civilian Headline Goal would be developed. Applying the initial lessons learned from the missions launched in 2003, considerable attention was devoted to maximizing of synergies between the many EU agencies involved in CCM (including civil–military coordination), to the refinement of planning and mission support, to short-notice deployment, procurement, financing and interoperability issues – all of which had been identified as wanting. In addition, the need for synergies between different training programmes was prioritized and the proposal to create a European Security and Defence College noted. The entire emphasis of the Action Plan was on the shift from quantity to quality, a development which mirrored a similar shift in the military realm with the adoption, at the same time, of the Headline Goal 2010 (EU-ISS 2005: 121–8).

The Civilian Capabilities Commitment Conference of 22 November 2004 was the occasion for a ministerial stocktaking of general progress in CCM. With the advent of ten new member states, new commitments of personnel generated figures well in excess of the targets for experts in: police (5,761), rule of law (631), civilian administration (562) and civil protection (4,968). However, the stress was placed once again on qualitative criteria for recruitment and training. The ministers expressed general satisfaction that the different objectives of the June 2004 Action Plan were being vigorously pursued and once again drew attention to the shortcomings indicated by experience in the field (EU-ISS 2005: 288–90). Great hopes were placed in the elaboration of a Civilian Headline Goal 2008 (CHG 2008) which was finalized by the Council in December 2004. A CHG Project Team was established in the Council Secretariat, with the full involvement of the Commission. The CHG 2008 process, tightly linked to the military HG 2010, is overseen by COPS and supported by CIVCOM. As with the HG 2010, a number of key steps were identified:

- Elaboration of key planning assumptions and illustrative scenarios for stabilization and reconstruction (including substitution missions), conflict prevention, the targeted strengthening of institutions and civilian support for humanitarian operations. This was successfully concluded by April 2005
- Elaboration of Capabilities Requirements List (July 2005)
- Assessment of national contributions to the Capabilities Requirements List and identification of shortfalls (end 2005)
- CHG follow-up process (ongoing with semestrial reports to the Council)

Cooperation between the EU and the UN was highlighted, in line with the European Security Strategy's insistence that the UN has the 'primary responsibility for the maintenance of peace and international security'. EU–UN synergies had already proved their worth in two missions (the EUPM in BiH and Operation *Artemis* in DRC) and a lengthy document was generated in the context of CHG 2008 modalities for practical cooperation with the UN (EU-ISS 2005: 363–70). The first concrete decision under the CHG 2008 process was to establish rapidly deployable Civilian Response Teams (CRTs) and work on developing such teams continued throughout the year (Nowak, 2006a: 32).

On 21 November 2005, a Civilian Capabilities Improvement Conference was convened at foreign ministerial level in the context of the multiplication of CCM missions launched in the course of that year (see Chapter 7). Further capability areas were identified, including specialists in border policing, sexual and violent crime, human trafficking and human rights; and a number of shortfalls were recorded (forensic specialists, judges and administrative staff with financial expertise). A Civilian Capability Improvement Plan stressed several key objectives, most of which derived from sorry experience in the field of making do with inappropriate personnel and ill-adapted mission support instruments such as equipment procurement and disposal and logistics. Work on the CRTs was given high priority, especially the establishment of terms of reference and a pool of 100 appropriate experts, a concept for induction training and special emphasis on rapid deployment of police forces (EU-ISS 2006: 346–9). A further Conference was planned for the end of 2006. Considerable effort was also devoted, both by the Commission and by the Council Secretariat, to the development of conceptual frameworks for the EU's engagement in security sector reform (Nowak, 2006a: 32–3).

How can all this effort be appraised and evaluated? The targets set for 2008 are ambitious and intended to provide the EU with a highly refined and qualitatively appropriate set of instruments for engagement in a very wide variety of CCM missions. The lessons of the EU's experiences with missions undertaken to date are being constantly applied and ministers have clearly identified CCM as one of the key distinctive features of ESDP where value added can be considerable, both in its own right, but also when combined with military instruments. On the positive side, the attempts to perfect the conceptual underpinnings of CCM are exemplary, as is the explicit new emphasis on quality and appropriate training. Raw numbers are no longer regarded as useful. The stress on coherence, coordination and synergies is a welcome sign that inter-agency battles will be strongly resisted by policy-framers. The shift from reactive to proactive mode is important, as is the explicit attempt to be in a position to tailor crisis-management instruments to the specifics of the mission. On the negative side, it has taken seven years from one Helsinki Council meeting to another (December 1999 to December 2006) in order to pin down some rather elementary precepts about the need for appropriate personnel. There is a repetitive element to the many official documents on CCM which never fail to stress that 'greater efforts' and 'greater coherence' will be required. However strongly ministers word their exhortations on synergies and coherence, the existing institutional mechanisms of the Commission and the Council constitute so many fundamental structural obstacles to the implementation of those precepts.

The missions embarked on to date have all revealed serious problems of inter-agency rivalry. In particular, the lack of any significant agreement on a natural division of labour between the Commission's many responsibilities for CCM (Gourlay, 2006) and those recently embraced by the Council remains an obvious failure which demands urgent attention (Gourlay, 2006a). Despite constant repetition of the need to establish a viable funding method for CCM missions (and indeed for military missions), this crucial enabler 'has largely been improvised; does not provide a sustainable and coherent framework for future actions; and could indeed threaten the overall credibility of EU foreign policy' (Missiroli, 2006: 45). Moreover, despite signs of a shift towards proactivism, the EU still lacks anything resembling a strategic approach to intervention. To date, the EU has only engaged in missions which offered themselves up to it. There is a growing need to take proactivism to its next stage and to identify the types of situations and circumstances where the EU might act preventively in a strategic fashion (Serrano 2006). As we shall see in Chapter 7, the EU by the end of 2006 had embarked on ten CCM missions, all of which had provided valuable lessons for those responsible for planning further ones. The objectives laid out in CHG 2008 are important and attempt to draw as many lessons as possible from experience. But it will be the results of future missions which will allow the analyst properly to judge whether CHG 2008 transcends the declaratory and actually helps the EU to improve on its record.

Conclusion

The European Security Strategy document clearly stated the EU's intention to be a 'global player' and to 'share in the responsibility for global security and in building a better world' (ESS, 2003: 4). After reviewing the main threats to the EU and the wider world (terrorism, proliferation of WMD, regional conflicts, state failure and organized crime), the document states that 'none of the new threats is purely military; nor can any be tackled by purely military means. Each requires a mix of instruments' (p. 12). Since the end of the Cold War, the international community has acquired considerable experience – most of it through the United Nations – in humanitarian intervention, post-conflict reconstruction and nation-building or state-building (Chesterman, 2004). At the same time, the limits of naked military power, unaccompanied by significant post-conflict reconstruction plans, have been clearly demonstrated in Afghanistan and Iraq (Diamond, 2005; Phillips, 2005). The 'mix of instruments' referred to in the ESS, is, almost literally, limitless, covering the entire range of policy instruments at the disposal of states and the international community. The European Union is in a particularly strong position to apply such a range of instruments and the ESDP project is precisely about the optimum means of procuring, marshalling, coordinating and deploying them. The ESS defines two strategic objectives: building security in the EU's own neighbourhood; and creating an international order based on effective multilateralism. Yet, despite the historic links between, on the one hand, the European member states and, on the other hand most countries and regions of the world, the EU itself was until comparatively recently totally maladapted to pursue those strategic objectives. It had no vestige of military power and only the first glimmerings of civilian crisis-management capabilities. In a very short time since the dawn of the new century, the EU has begun to address both of those deficiencies. It has focused relentlessly on the development of the necessary instruments with which to pursue a security and defence policy. This chapter has charted its progress in both the military and the civilian areas. While progress has been tangible and impressive in both, there remain many major challenges yet to be tackled, not the least of which remains that of generating maximum synergy between the military and the civilian (Kohl, 2006). The issue of rationalizing defence spending cannot be delayed much longer. Whether the glass is perceived as being half full or half empty, is largely a matter of perception. What is not a matter of perception is the EU's record as a global actor. To date, that record is hardly impressive. One of the biggest problems in pinning down an appropriate strategy for the EU itself is that of its relations with the only global superpower. It is to this issue that we now turn.

Chapter 5

Selling it to Uncle Sam . . . ESDP and Transatlantic Relations

The presence, in the 1998 Saint Malo Declaration, of the ominous-sounding word 'autonomous' immediately sparked a series of reactions to the ESDP project among US policy-makers and analysts. In 2007, the ripples from the '"a"-word' continue to fan out across the pond. This chapter will analyse three sets of issues which were opened up by Saint Malo and ESDP. These issues need to be considered within the broader framework of the evolution of transatlantic relations generally since the end of the Cold War. The first set concerns the different types of reactions which were forthcoming from within the American political class. From the official 'Yes, but . . .' reaction which characterized both the Clinton and the George W. Bush administrations, via the enthusiastic 'Yes please!' and the sceptical 'Oh Yeah?' viewpoints to the outright opposition voiced by the 'No Way!' brigade, it is clear that ESDP had the capacity to divide the Americans just as US security policy succeeded in dividing the Europeans. It is this latter division which forms the basis of the second set of issues raised in this chapter. How has ESDP reinforced or mitigated the basic division among the EU member states between 'Atlanticists' and 'Europeanists'? (Stahl *et al.*, 2004). Donald Rumsfeld's mischievous categorization of Europeans into 'old' and 'new' in 2003 reflected a real division within the EU over the Iraq War. Was that division structural and lasting or contingent and fleeting? The third set of issues has to do with the complex, tortuous – and still ongoing – relations between this new security kid-on-the-block and its staid and rather elderly cousin NATO. In December 2002, the EU and NATO signed a formal Declaration on ESDP (see Box 5.1 later in the chapter) setting out their joint and seemingly consensual views on the nature of their ongoing partnership. Nevertheless, relations have continued to be tense, in large part because of the asymmetries and imbalances between the nature and objectives of the two organizations, themselves a reflection of the shifting world order since 1989. As we saw in Chapter 2, many analysts believe that ESDP is inevitably prejudicial to NATO's future. Although this book argues that there is no *inevitable* tension between the two projects, it cannot be discounted that the pursuit of incompatible policy preferences in both the USA and the EU might one day bring them into collision. This stark reality is further complicated by the parallel processes of enlargement which have characterized the EU and NATO. For the countries of the former Soviet bloc, NATO membership has proved much easier to secure than membership of the EU. Most of these countries have tended to see in the relationship with the USA (via NATO) their surest passage to a secure future (Michta, 1999; Krupnick, 2003; Quinlan, 2002). However, it is more likely that, in the long run, structured stability and security will actually derive from their membership of the European Union (Jacoby, 2004; Vachudova, 2005).

US reactions to ESDP

Transatlantic relations within the NATO Alliance have never been plain-sailing (Schmidt, G., 2001; Freedman, 1983), and disputes over burden-sharing remained a quasi-permanent feature of the relationship throughout the Cold War and beyond (Gnesotto, Sloan and Kamp, 1999). Every decade a major crisis rattled the Alliance (1950s: Suez; 1960s: flexible response; 1970s: Yom Kippour War; 1980s: INF crisis; 1990s: Balkans), yet NATO nevertheless always managed to emerge from the crisis intact. However, in the early twenty-first century the advent of ESDP and the concurrent quarrels between a number of EU governments and the administration of George W. Bush shook the Alliance to its core (Gordon and Shapiro, 2004). This new dispute arose from two interconnecting trends. The first was the gradual and inevitable re-prioritization of 'European affairs' in US grand strategy after the Cold War. As the tectonic plates shifted, US interests and focus moved away from Europe towards the Pacific and the Gulf. The place of Europe in US foreign and security policy remained in a state of considerable uncertainty – a situation that was unsettling for both partners.

Secondly, and concurrently, as the EU emerged as an international actor – one which was actively seeking greater 'autonomy' – the future of the transatlantic relationship seemed clouded in obscurity. Both sides revealed elements of schizophrenia as a result of this dual transition. The United States formally welcomed the EU's shift towards greater self-reliance – but remained fearful of potential EU challenges to US leadership. The European Union exulted in its new-found freedom of manoeuvre – but remained fearful of US abandonment. Two US analysts, one hostile to NATO, the other supportive, gave the flavour of the stakes as perceived in Washington at the start of the twenty-first century:

> The US–EU controversy about ESDP . . . is the proverbial tip of the iceberg. Underlying the current discord are fundamental questions about the nature of the US–European relationship, about American grand strategy and about NATO itself. Inevitably, the new administration will have to come to grips with the question of whether the Alliance – in its current form – has a future. (Layne, 2001)

> Notwithstanding the noticeable change of tone in US–European relations since the re-election of President George W. Bush, the transatlantic partnership remains at risk. . . this is a critical juncture that parallels the start of President Truman's second term in office in 1949, when decisions and the events that prompted them were to shape the history of the following four decades. (Serfaty, 2005)

Any attempt to categorize the various US reactions to ESDP in terms of 'schools of thought' would be tantamount to conferring on the 'debate' more coherence and more visibility than it has actually demonstrated. It would also artificially reduce the overlap between the different positions (Hamilton, 2002: 148; Sloan, 2000: 4–5). Furthermore, it would have to control for the evolution of the various positions over time. There is no doubt that US attitudes towards Europe in general and ESDP in particular shifted from being dominated by sceptics and critics in 1999–2000 to being increasingly characterized by proposals for partnership in 2005–6. At the most basic level, US reactions can be divided into two: those who believe (however much or however little) that ESDP will benefit the USA and the transatlantic relationship; and those who believe it will harm them. However, each of these two groups divides further into two opposing perspectives on the perceived outcome.

The formal position of both the Clinton administration and the George W. Bush administration (the only two, to date, which have had to deal with ESDP) has been characterized by Stanley Sloan as 'Yes, but . . .'. It should be recalled that, in the early months after the end of the Cold War, the administration of President George H.W. Bush remained deeply suspicious of European intentions. At the critical NATO summit in Rome, in October 1991, when the Allies met to adopt a 'New Strategic Concept', Bush opened the meeting by facing up squarely to his European partners with the ominous words: 'If your ultimate aim is to provide for your own defence, then the time to tell us is today!' Nobody blinked (Kelleher, 1995: 58). President Clinton proved, in general, to be far more open-minded about a new European contribution (Sloan, 2000: 10–14). Throughout the 1990s, and in particular during the protracted saga of ESDI, the objective in both the USA and the EU was to find a formula which would retain the US commitment to Europe, respect US leadership and also allow the Europeans greater autonomy (Howorth, 2003a). After the Saint Malo Declaration, official Washington reacted cautiously. On 7 December 1998, Secretary of State Madeleine Albright penned the first formulation of the 'Yes, but . . .' reaction in the *Financial Times* (Albright, 1998). She began on a positive note:

> We welcome the call from Tony Blair, the UK prime minister, for Europeans to consider ways they can take more responsibility for their own security and defence. Our interest is clear: we want a Europe that can act. We want a Europe with modern, flexible military forces that are capable of putting out fires in Europe's backyard and working with us through the alliance to defend our common interests. European efforts to do more for Europe's own defence make it easier, not harder, for us to remain engaged.

But, as we saw in Chapter 2, she immediately coupled this enthusiasm with three caveats, subsequently know as the '3 Ds': there should be no *decoupling*, no *duplication* and no *discrimination*.

On decoupling, Albright insisted that European decision-making should not be 'unhooked from broader Alliance decision-making'. The unfortunate symbolism of this stricture was more significant than its practical reality. To state, on behalf of a politico-military alliance, that it should not be allowed to fall apart bears comparison with a husband authorizing his wife to take a weekend trip on her own on condition that it not lead to divorce. Alliances, like marriages, are based on trust. The warning about decoupling, which suggests a fundamental lack of trust, had two equally unfortunate connotations. The first was the implication that the EU allies were *actively seeking* to 'unhook' the Alliance, an accusation which had little basis in fact. The second connotation was that the USA *would not allow* decoupling, which was even more offensive to the extent to which it appeared to involve some measure of *threat* (Schake, 2003).

Albright's second concern was that ESDP should not *duplicate* resources and assets which already existed in the Alliance. US fears, immediately after Saint-Malo, focused on the EU's potential to *rival* the USA in military hardware. This fear was not unconnected with the other ambition expressed in the Saint-Malo Declaration: 'a strong and competitive European defence industry and technology'. If read as a stricture aimed at eschewing wasteful policies on procurement, the *no duplication* caveat made sense. As a warning to the Europeans not to try to enter into competition with US defence firms, it was disingenuous. As a suggestion that the USA had military assets to spare, it was – as 9/11 was rapidly to demonstrate – just plain wrong. 9/11 also underlined the obvious truth that, if there was Alliance scarcity, particularly in strategic systems – long-range transport, logistics, command and control etc. – it made good sense to fill those gaps. Hence the subsequent theses on 'constructive duplication' (Schake, 2003).

Albright's third caveat concerned fears of ESDP *discrimination* against European members of NATO outside the EU. In particular, this concern focused on the contribution of Turkey and Norway to European security. Under the post-1992 arrangements for European defence cooperation inaugurated by the WEU, these countries were designated 'associate members' of WEU and were, to all intents and purposes, treated as full members of the club (Van Eekelen, 1998: 135–9). However, under the impending institutional arrangements for ESDP, these two vital NATO allies suddenly found themselves excluded from discussions on European security – just as four non-NATO 'neutrals' (Ireland, Austria, Sweden and Finland) were ushered into the security policy chamber with a full seat at the table. The USA exerted enormous pressure on the EU to devise some means of including non-EU NATO allies in the ESDP procedures. This problem, which we shall analyse in some detail below (pp. 163–8) was to pose a major conundrum for NATO ESDP relations over the following four years.

What is noteworthy in this initial US reaction to Saint Malo, however, is the failure to fully grasp the implications of a shift from an ESDI-type capacity forged from within NATO ('separable but not separate') to the autonomous aspirations of ESDP itself. US and NATO officials were to continue for years inaccurately (or disingenuously?) to use the acronym ESDI when referring to ESDP. Albright's '3 Ds' articulated the first official expression of conditionality on the part of the Clinton administration. But as officials in Washington pored over the implications of the ESDP project, they gradually added further conditions to the list, conditions which continued to confuse ESDI with ESDP. The signals were very mixed. US Deputy Secretary of State Strobe Talbott, in an important speech in London in October 1999, after insisting that the administration supported 'ESDI', proceeded to add that 'our support will be guided by the answers to two questions: first, will it work? . . . Second, will it help keep the Alliance together?' This hardly came across as a ringing endorsement. A few weeks later, he attempted to dispel the impression created by his earlier speech with the unambiguous statement that: 'We are not against; we are not ambivalent; we are not anxious; we are for it' (Kupchan, 2000: 17). But doubts persisted.

In summer 2000, an article by Philip Gordon, formerly Director for European Affairs at the National Security Council and currently Director of the Center on the United States and Europe at the Brookings Institution, laid out 'six guiding principles' under which ESDP might succeed in giving the EU more capacity without dividing NATO and/or driving the Americans out of Europe. In addition to Madeleine Albright's '3 D's', all of which were repeated, several new conditions were laid out. The first was that Europeans should attach 'far greater priority' to modernizing their military capabilities than to creating new institutions. The suspicion that ESDP was geared more to European integration than to military capacity lingered long in Washington DC. The second additional condition was that Europeans recognize and state clearly that 'NATO remains their first choice when it comes to military force' and that ESDP would not challenge NATO's primacy. The battle over what became known as NATO's 'right of first refusal' for military operations was thus engaged. The third condition was that formal links should be created immediately between the EU and NATO in order to avoid crossed wires and potential areas of transatlantic conflict. A rider to this third stricture was that the *defence industries* of the two sides should also engage in intensified dialogue. (Gordon, 2000) These 'conditions' were not uncontroversial in Europe. Some member states saw them as tantamount to an edict that ESDP should not be allowed to take any steps without first clearing them with NATO. Others accepted them as an understandable US attempt to ensure that the advent of ESDP did not drive a wedge between the two sides (Howorth, 2000b).

Throughout 1999 and well into 2000, in an attempt to dispel misunderstandings, officials from both Brussels and a number of European capitals (primarily London) criss-crossed the Atlantic in an increasingly successful effort to reassure the Clinton administration that ESDP would enhance and strengthen the Alliance rather than weaken and undermine it (Champion, 2000). In 1999, George Robertson, former British Defence Secretary and at that time NATO Secretary General, countered the negativity of the '3 Ds' with the more positive '3 Is': *improvement* in Europe's military capacity; *inclusiveness* for all NATO allies; and *indivisibility* of transatlantic security (Robertson, 1999). Two full years of reassurance were necessary to calm the nerves of the Clinton administration. However, among those officials engaged in the task of reassurance, there was deep despondency in late 2000 when it became clear that the incoming Bush team had even less sympathy for ESDP than the Clinton team and that the European charm offensive would have to be started again from scratch (Interviews in London and Paris, 2000). Under these circumstances, it was not surprising that Tony Blair paid a hasty visit to the USA in February 2001, only weeks after President Bush's inauguration, primarily in order to reinforce that work of reassurance (Riddell, 2003: 133). The result was that by June

2001, when Bush paid his first visit to Europe, matters had reverted to roughly where they were at the time of Madeleine Albright's original '3 Ds'. After his first meeting with NATO's heads of state and government in Brussels on 13 June 2002, Bush declared:

> The United States would welcome a capable European force properly integrated with NATO that provides new options for handling crises when NATO chooses not to lead. Such a force will require EU members to provide the resources necessary to create real capabilities, without waste or duplication. And such a force must be inclusive, so that all allies who wish to contribute are as fully involved as possible. Our security is indivisible. (Bush, 2001)

Yet again we see that the distinction between a type of ESDI – from within NATO – and an autonomous ESDP – outside it – is blurred.

Such confusion was also to be the cardinal feature of Congressional inquiries into 'ESDP' in late 1999. Resolutions were passed in the House of Representatives (2 November) and in the Senate (8 November) confirming US support for NATO and issuing a long series of concerns about the new European security developments. The gist of the Congressional concerns in fact amounted to suggestions that even an ESDI capability *within* NATO would need to be tightly micromanaged, but everything which smacked of an *autonomous* European capacity should be resisted or hedged with very severe conditionality (Sloan, 2000: 27–33). The question of whether or not ESDP would or could actually meet all the conditions laid down by the US administration has never satisfactorily been resolved. But the starting point in official Washington at the turn of the millennium was crystal clear. ESDP was acceptable *only so long* as it did not constitute a challenge to the United States or a threat to NATO and so long as it actually brought to the table military capacity and resources which could be useful to the Alliance. That approach was (and to some extent still is) broadly shared in London and several other EU capitals. But as we shall see below, it was never universally shared across the EU. Those in the USA who support this line tend to believe that the EU can emerge as a strong and competent partner of the United States and that this is infinitely preferable to coexistence with a weak and incompetent ally (Hunter, 2002). US public opinion, it is feared by many people, will not be prepared to indefinitely support a European ally which does not pull its full weight. However, since the US debacle in Iraq and since the re-election of President Bush, there has been, as we shall see shortly, a more widespread acceptance in DC that the Europeans can and will prove to be useful allies.

Beyond the conditional 'Yes, but . . .' approach, there are two rather distinct groups in the USA who have supported ESDP with some measure of enthusiasm. These have been called variously the 'domestic interests' faction (Sloan, 2000: 5) or the 'decouplers' (Hamilton, 2002: 150). In reality, these are rather different approaches. The former tends to believe that the USA should downplay its world role and concentrate on rectifying its many domestic economic and social problems. This view can be found in one variant in a man like the 2000 Democratic presidential candidate Bill Bradley, and in other variants in the ultra-right paleo-conservative commentator Patrick Buchanan, or among the ideologues of the neo-liberal Cato Institute, which has generally tended to see 'entangling alliances' in general and NATO in particular as an expensive and unnecessary negative in US politics (Carpenter, 1994). Some might tend to castigate these views as 'isolationist'. In reality, they represent one coolly realist appraisal of the appropriate balance between US domestic and overseas interests.

An even more positive approach was forthcoming from a leading European specialist, Charles Kupchan, who sees American power as overstretched and entering a period of decline in which robust and positive assistance from the European allies could only be welcomed (Kupchan, 2002). This attitude I have dubbed the 'Yes please!' approach. One US commentator, however, chose to dub Kupchan a 'decoupler' (Hamilton, 2002: 151). In a key article, Kupchan (2000) sought to answer four types of US concern about ESDP. First, as far as decision-making and Alliance cohesion were concerned, US fears that ESDP would decouple the successful NATO pattern of US leadership and European support were, he argued misplaced. In the post-Cold War world, the Alliance was likely to work better with two more equal pillars than with 19 disparate nations. Moreover, Kupchan insisted, Europe's military ambitions were modest and in no way threatening to US interests. A more capable Europe had been on the US wish-list for decades. Second, as far as implementation was concerned, administration fears about duplication and discrimination were also misguided. Duplication, Kupchan insisted, could be a positive-sum game in areas where European assets were significantly wanting. Moreover, Norway and Turkey were such key allies that Kupchan expressed confidence about the eventual association of these states with the ESDP project. A third US concern had been the political implications of a project which suggested that US commitment to Europe was no longer as essential as in the past. This, the worriers felt, would lead to Congressional demands for major US troop reductions in Europe. Kupchan expressed confidence that both sides of the Atlantic remained sufficiently committed to the relationship to ensure that a new balance acceptable to both sides would be struck. Finally, on feasibility, US scepticism about the seriousness of purpose of the Europeans was clearly unjustifiable given Germany's shift towards a new strategic culture, Britain's lead in pushing European capacity forward and the tectonic forces driving the Europeans to look to their own security affairs. All in all, Kupchan expressed confidence that ESDP represented a positive breakthrough in transatlantic relations, one the USA needed (and had itself been urging on the Europeans for decades) and one which would be of real benefit to both sides. There were – and still are – in the USA many leading analysts who view Europe and ESDP positively and see a more balanced Alliance as both necessary and desirable for both sides (Daalder, 2001; Schake, 2003; Merry, 2003–04; Lebl, 2004; Larrabee, 2004; Gordon, 2004; Schweiss, 2005; Serfaty, 2005). But only Kupchan presents this particular combination of US declinism, European resurgence and transatlantic requirements, together with great confidence in a generally applicable positive-sum game. However, it is worth noting that Kupchan's optimism of spring 2000 had, by the autumn of 2006, given way to deep pessimism about the prospects for transatlantic harmony (Kupchan, 2006).

A third attitude to ESDP was epitomized by the extreme scepticism expressed by a man such as former national security adviser Zbigniew Brzezinski (Brzezinski, 2000). Europe, he argued, would not succeed in becoming a military or even a political power, despite its best efforts, because it simply does not have the drive or the political will to achieve this. Its influence and reach will remain essentially economic and commercial: in short, pragmatic and informed by 'convenience'. It will forever lack the emotional and ideological-crusading passion of the US dream. This attitude, I call the 'Oh Yeah?' approach. The USA should not be concerned about 'ESDI', argued Brzezinski, because he considered it to be an insignificant project: 'the so-called European pillar will be made less out of steel and concrete and more out of *papier-maché*' (Brzezinski, 2000: 24). By the same token, the USA, argued Brzezinski, will remain a hegemon across the Euro-Atlantic space, with the EU as an ongoing junior partner, tied to Washington by self-interest based on proximate values and principles. Deepening and widening he saw as incompatible goals. Deepening was not only impractical from a European perspective, but also undesirable from an American perspective, since it would inevitably generate 'severe two-way transatlantic tensions' (*ibid.*: 2000: 17). This means that *enlargement* should be the primary goal of both NATO and the EU, that the two processes should be conducted as far as possible in parallel – with the same strategic vision: namely to extend the scope of influence of the Atlantic partnership as far East as possible, including, one day, Russia, Ukraine, the trans-Caucasus states and Israel. *NATO enlargement* should therefore become the main strategic priority of the USA, as a way of exercizing leadership and of preserving the hegemonic role. This attitude towards the EU and ESDP is fairly widely shared across the US political class and is to be found in both main political parties. It corresponds closely to those we encountered in an earlier chapter who believe ESDP to be largely irrelevant. It is essentially based on the culture of the transatlantic relationship during the Cold War and expresses confidence that, whatever else might have changed as a result of 1989, the basic transatlantic relationship (despite the griping and moaning from Europeans) remains predictable.

The final category of reaction to ESDP is that which I categorize as 'No way!' Advocates of this approach include the former US ambassador to the United Nations, John Bolton (Bolton, 1999), the former Assistant Secretary of Defense for International Security Affairs Peter Rodman (Rodman, 2000), Council on Foreign Relations member Jeffrey Cimbalo (Cimbalo, 2004), John Hulsman, latterly of the Heritage Foundation (Hulsman and Gardiner, 2004), and many others. Their basic arguments are quite simple: further 'deepening' of the

European integration project in general is not in the US national interest, and ESDP in particular is a threat to NATO and to the Atlantic Alliance. It should be resisted and, if possible, prevented. Although formulated in a populist, non-academic language, this type of reaction replicates the IR theorists' belief that the EU is deliberately balancing against the USA. I have dealt with these arguments elsewhere and will not repeat them here. Suffice it to say that the evidence on which much of this negative commentary is based is either shaky or plain false (Howorth, 2005a).

Since the USA became bogged down in Iraq, the predominantly negative US views of ESDP have tended to give way to many more expressions of support. In the meantime, of course, ESDP has gone from the drawing board to the deployment platform and demonstrated its worth. Concurrently, transatlantic relations, despite a more positive official tone on both sides of the Atlantic, have continued to worsen (Anderson, Ikenberry and Risse, 2007; Pew Global Attitudes Survey, 2006). The result has been that US comment on the future of transatlantic relations has tended to divide into two main camps, which have been categorized as 'disaggregators' – those keen to encourage the administration to adopt a policy of divide and rule in Europe – and 'reassurers' – those allegedly willing to cut a deal with Europe based on European support for US policy on terms favourable to the EU (Van Oudenaren, 2005). There is no doubt that overt disaggregators multiplied at the time of the European Constitutional Treaty (Cimbalo 2004, Hulsman and Gardiner, 2004, Steltzenmuhler, 2004). But their likely influence over US policy is extremely limited. As for the 'reassurers', their numbers have grown as problems in Iraq have risen (Gordon, 2004; Asmus, Blinken and Gordon, 2005; Compact, 2005; Sloan, 2006). They will certainly have an important input into the future high-level political discussions between a new generation of US leaders and a new crop of Europeans.

European approaches to the NATO–ESDP relationship

The second set of issues to be addressed in this chapter is connected with the evolution of various *European* attitudes towards NATO and/or the USA in the context of the emerging

ESDP. The key challenge here is to understand the range of views across the EU as to the precise nature of national institutional preference with respect to NATO and ESDP. At one extreme might come a country such as Denmark, the only one with an opt-out from ESDP, which clearly considers that NATO is the only security actor with which it wishes to be associated; or Poland, which, although obliged by the terms of accession to accept the ESDP chapters of the *acquis communautaire*, has tended in practice to prioritize NATO almost to the exclusion of any real involvement with ESDP, although there are already clear signs that the balance is shifting in the other direction. At the other end of the spectrum might be positioned countries such as Finland and Ireland which have traditionally refused to be associated with NATO and have contributed in significant ways to the definition of a European security policy. Between these two positions, different EU member states can be situated at various points across the space. The key question is whether different nation-states have shifted in their relative attitudes towards these two security bodies. Most have.

The United Kingdom is generally considered to be the most 'Atlanticist' of the main EU member states (Croft *et al.*, 2001). NATO preference is not a beauty competition and other EU member states – Germany, the Netherlands, Portugal – have also pursued a clear Atlanticist line. But the UK is generally regarded as the most engaged in and committed to NATO. Traditionally, in the UK view, both defence and security in Europe have been underwritten by the United States through NATO. The UK has therefore shunned or actively opposed various European initiatives (usually orchestrated by France) aimed at implementing a *European* security or defence entity – the EDC in the 1950s; the Fouchet Plan in the 1960s; the re-launch of WEU in the 1970s; the proposed merger of WEU and the EU in the mid-1990s. In addition to considering the American commitment to European security as indispensable, and while jealously safeguarding its own leading role in the Atlantic security network, Britain has also traditionally feared that any *serious* attempt by the Europeans to organize their own security and defence would encourage isolationism or withdrawal in the USA. In this approach, it has been backed by a number of other European states – with either a history of naval interests in the Atlantic (Netherlands, Denmark), or a less central involvement in continental Europe (Norway), or with both (Portugal). The fundamental reason why the UK, under Tony Blair, embraced the Saint Malo project was the stark realization, on the part of the 1997 New Labour government, that – contrary to London's long-standing assumption – the United States considered greater European security self-reliance to be a *sine qua non* of continued US commitment to the Alliance (Howorth, 2000a). In this sense, ESDP, for Tony Blair, was above all a strategy aimed at preserving NATO. At first, the UK had to work hard to persuade some of its traditional Atlanticist partners in Europe of the salience of this approach. Denmark remained unconvinced (Olsen and Pilegaard, 2005). Portugal – more the military than the politicians – showed deep reluctance (Vasconcelos, 2000). Norway battled constantly with the recognition that adaptation to ESDP, while unwelcome, seemed unavoidable (Tofte, 2005; Graeger, 2005). The Netherlands, by contrast, had already 'come to recognize that the long-range commitment of America to NATO may be put at risk if the European allies refuse to pool their forces' (Van Staden, 1997). The Dutch were also pulled in the ESDP direction by their commitment to European integration (Kreemers, 2001).

Gradually, as ESDP acquired substance, and as transatlantic relations continued to suffer from the fall-out of the 2003 Iraq War, all of these countries learned to balance their traditional institutional preference for NATO with an increasing commitment to and belief in ESDP, not as an alternative but as a complement to the Alliance. The United Kingdom and the Netherlands, both of whom prioritize pragmatism over ideology and results over intentions, have taken ESDP increasingly seriously as the need for its services has grown, alongside recognition that it can offer relief to the US military. It was the UK in particular which, in 2004–5, was instrumental in persuading the more Atlanticist-leaning new accession members from Central and Eastern Europe to embrace the battle-groups concept and to participate in a practical way in the EU's security instruments. It could be said, indeed, that countries like the UK and the Netherlands embarked on ESDP with a view to saving NATO, but have progressively come to believe in the project in its own right. NATO remains a fundamental reference for these countries, all of which will continue to do battle to keep the Alliance as alive and relevant as possible. But, as we shall see in the third part of this chapter, NATO has become a distinct actor with its own problems and its future is increasingly disconnected – at least in any direct way – from developments in ESDP.

While it would be too soon to conclude that some of the more Atlanticist states from Central and Eastern Europe have followed the same evolving trajectory as their West European peers, there are some signs that this is happening. Poland has shifted in the balance of its allegiances. Initially, Poland considered that NATO was the only international institution in which it was worth investing serious time and energy and Warsaw displayed an attitude towards ESDP of scepticism and even hostility. This subsequently shifted to a position more in favour of ESDP (Mink, 2003; Zaborowski, 2004: 17) as a consequence of two major developments: growing disillusionment with the US record in Iraq; and the consequences of Polish membership in the EU. Three secondary factors have complemented these two stimuli and accelerated Poland's evolution towards greater acceptance of ESDP. The first has been a growing sense that Warsaw can play a genuinely leading role among major European decision-makers, a status which is not on offer via NATO where the most Poland could hope for would be a special 'niche' function. The second is Poland's embrace of the EU battle-groups concept. Poland is to take the lead role in a group including Germany, Slovakia, Latvia and Lithuania. The third is a growing awareness that Warsaw's desired policy of extending the security hand of friendship to its Eastern neighbours will be more easily – and probably more successfully – implemented via ESDP than via NATO. Like the UK, Portugal and the Netherlands, Poland has shifted from an exclusively pro-NATO stance to one in which positive benefits are seen to derive from both NATO and ESDP. Similar trends have been detected in other Central and Eastern European countries (Howorth, 2003b; Valasek, 2005; O'Brennan, 2006).

The four former 'neutrals' – Sweden, Finland, Austria, Ireland – are all neutral for different reasons, and their approach to neutrality has shifted constantly. Several studies noted that by the end of the 1990s they no longer attached the same significance to the fact of being 'neutral' and all four are in many ways more comfortable with the concept of 'non-aligned' (Ojanen, 2000; Aggestam, 2001; Gustenau, 1999; Knutsen, 2000; Keohane, 2001). In a world of complex interdependence, what is there to be neutral *about*? Yet the culture of neutrality – tightly tied to issues of identity – dies hard. A nation such as Sweden, which has of its own volition remained outside major conflict since the early nineteenth century, is conditioned at least as much by the *belief* that its neutrality underpins its security as by any evidence of realism (Aggestam, 2001, 183). And the negative outcome of the 2001 Irish referendum on the Treaty of Nice confirmed the assumptions of Irish politicians across the political spectrum that the time was not yet ripe to suggest that Ireland officially change its stance of 'military neutrality', so closely associated with Irish identity (Keohane, 2000, ch. 2). Austria is committed to neutrality by Treaty and by Constitution, and Finland by geographical caution, but both countries have internalized neutrality as a key factor in national identity. The new buzz-words for these countries are: 'alliance-free states', 'ex-neutrals', 'non-allied states' or 'post-neutrals'. I shall refer to them as 'post-neutrals'. Any of these terms still implies 'a negative attitude towards something, maintaining a distance from something, or a reservation' (Ojanen, 2000: 2). As 'neutrals', the body they have traditionally been most distant from has been NATO.

At first, these countries were equally sceptical about European defence integration (Ferreira-Pereira, 2005), but since they joined the EU and began to participate fully in its activities, they have gradually integrated the security sector and have made a significant mark on ESDP. The *autonomy* of EU decision-making (particularly *vis-à-vis* NATO), an aspiration usually associated by commentators with France, is also seen as crucial by the post-neutrals. In debates within the COPS, France's position on the autonomy of ESDP has often been strongly supported by the ambassadors from the neutral countries (Interviews in Brussels 2001–6). This is particularly so in the case of planning, where the incipient EU–NATO planning structure is viewed with concern in more than one post-neutral capital. On the other hand, all four states are also unhappy about any moves towards a common EU defence, whether under article V of WEU or under article I-41(7) of the stalled Constitutional Treaty. This was one of the reasons for the inclusion in the Amsterdam Treaty of the 'constructive abstention' clause which effectively gave them an opt-out – although precisely what 'opting out' would mean in the case of common defence is not clear. When Sweden and Finland abandoned their former objections to plans to merge WEU and EU in

October 1999, they did so 'on the condition that they would not have to assist fellow members who were under military attack' (Ojanen, 2000: 2). However, such an attitude, in reality, seems improbable. Keohane (2001: 18) is similarly sceptical about an Irish government remaining 'neutral' in the event of an attack on an EU member state. Post-neutrality is shifting constantly.

Although in the early years of the twenty-first century there were signs in several of the post-neutral countries of a public debate about evolving relations with both NATO and ESDP, this has subsided with the transatlantic crisis over Iraq. Sweden, for instance, once indicated that it might be forced to reconsider its approach to NATO if the Alliance succeeded in embracing the Baltics (Aggestam, 2001). Austria in 2001 was widely tipped as being tempted to apply for membership of NATO (Liebhart, 2003). On the other hand, there were signs that Ireland and Finland might be more amenable to the idea of collective defence if the EU were the key security institution. Most of these straws in the wind have disappeared with the stand-off over Iraq. The participation of the post-neutrals in any crisis management or peace-support mission, would almost certainly require a UN or OSCE mandate. Austria participated in both SFOR (Bosnia) and KFOR (Kosovo) – which were under UN mandates – but refused to grant NATO over-flight rights during the Kosovo air campaign (which had no such mandate). Ireland, Sweden and Finland succeeded in signalling support for the Kosovo campaign without actually participating. This has been an article of faith with all post-neutrals, who would have great difficulty in endorsing the Alliance's more liberal interpretation of the case for intervention. This is not to say that such countries are hesitant about committing troops. In many ways, their contribution – proportionately – is second to none. It was, of course, a Finnish–Swedish joint initiative which resulted in the Petersberg tasks being written into the Treaty of Amsterdam, largely to ensure the political control of the EU over the WEU and to ensure the right of the post-neutrals to participate in EU peacekeeping operations on an equal footing with other member states. All four post-neutrals have long been major contributors to UN peacekeeping, and have taken their full share of EU duties in the Balkans and in Congo. Moreover, all four are committed to participating in ESDP's new battle-groups configurations (see Box 4.2). In short, while the post-neutrals retain a clear distance from NATO – at least to some extent as a result of the policies of the Bush administration – they have begun to play a real part in ESDP, in large part because the overall profile of the EU's security and defence policy corresponds to the security culture with which they are imbued.

Germany – and, in a slightly different way – Belgium and Luxembourg have revealed the most interesting and possibly the most clear-cut shift in the balance of institutional preference as between ESDP and NATO. The remarks that follow pertain predominantly to Germany and draw heavily on the work of Felix Berenskoetter and Bastien Giegerich (2007). For Germany, in 1955, NATO membership constituted a new lease on life. Not only did it provide a 'ladder out of the morass' (Garton Ash, 1993: 21) but it represented a new form of security identity, a type of ontological security (Mitzen, 2006) – defined as the most appropriate fit between a nation's collective identity, its security culture, the security environment and the available security instruments. NATO allowed Germany to assert itself as a purely defensive, essentially civilian power in which the armed forces could only be used for collective defence and only in multilateral – Alliance – mode, via a decision which would in fact be taken elsewhere. Germany, in short, *identified* with NATO and, by the end of the Cold War, had emerged – in terms of human commitment, territorial centrality and doctrinal salience – as the Alliance's most important European member. Thereafter, everything began to change. As the United States slipped effortlessly into its role as the world's only superpower and began increasingly to project power around the globe, carrying NATO in its wake and imposing on the Alliance a new, more interventionist culture, Germany became less and less comfortable and experienced a growing contradiction in its ontological culture which caused it progressively to distance itself from some of the central pillars of the new NATO at the same time as it began to look elsewhere for a security institution more consonant with its ongoing values. Although in the immediate aftermath of the Cold War, the US designated Germany as its principal 'partner in leadership', the Federal Republic was to fail immediately to live up to this role through its collective recoil from physical involvement in the 1991 Gulf War, which represented everything Germany felt it had definitively rejected. For Germans, and particularly for the student generation, the scale and nature of the war in the

Gulf came as a shock to the system tantamount to a 'security psychosis' (Loedel, 1998: 66). Matters only got worse with NATO's shifting security strategy, emphasising intervention, through the Bosnian imbroglio and especially with the Kosovo war in 1999. Germans were faced with an impossible dilemma, being essentially forced to choose between two equally unacceptable normative absolutes: the rejection of war and the rejection of genocide.

Although German political leaders did their best to persuade the public that adaptation to a new world reality required a relaxation of the pacifist-civilian culture which had dominated the Cold War period, the public were not so easily swayed (Dyson, 2005). Berenskoetter and Giegerich (2007) have charted the course which Germany adopted throughout the 1990s in its quest for an alternative security institution. Successively, Bonn looked to the UN, to the CSCE/OSCE, to WEU and eventually to the EU itself for a new security framework more consonant with deeply rooted and unchanging Germany values. Progressively, Germany came to switch its security identity and to construct its ontological security through ESDP which offered choices that were increasingly absent in NATO: crisis management rather than the pursuit of US global strategy, multilateral decision-making rather than pressure from Washington, a range of policy instruments rather than exclusivity to the military and perhaps above all genuine political influence as opposed to marginalization. In particular, the choice between the underlying deployment norms of the European reaction force (mandated, responsive, rare) and that of NATO's post-Prague Response Force (non-mandated, pre-emptive, frequent) offered Germans little alternative but to draw ever closer to ESDP: 'unable to significantly influence American efforts to redefine the terms of Western order . . . domestic adjustments were increasingly linked to the EU as the collective forum within which German identity could be embedded' (Berenskoetter and Giegerich, 2007: 22).

Although Belgium and Luxembourg have not had to contend with the same ontological security dilemmas as Germany, they too have had to contend with the rival attractions of the traditional NATO alliance and the embryonic ESDP in terms of the institutional fit with national security preferences. Both countries have sought to avoid having to make a choice (Dumoulin, Manigart and Struys, 2003; Linster, 2001). Realism alone dictates that small countries like these cannot afford to burn their bridges with the American hegemon. However, for reasons not dissimilar to those which have affected Poland and Germany (growing concerns about the direction of US/NATO policy, particularly in light of Iraq; favourable evolution of EU policy and particularly of ESDP), both Belgium and Luxembourg have, in effect, nudged closer to the latter without ostensibly distancing themselves from the former. Spain, on the other hand, was never a 'NATO unconditional', having only joined the Alliance in 1982 and then only with a status similar to that of France: non-participation in the integrated military command structure or in the military committee. This was in large part because of the fierce opposition to NATO membership on the part of the Socialist Party (PSOE). Spanish leaders had to tread very lightly in nudging an instinctively anti-American public in the direction of Alliance membership, but PSOE Prime Minister Felipe Gonzalez was able, between 1982 and 1986, to achieve precisely that, winning a decisive referendum on Spanish membership with the message that membership of NATO was a necessary springboard to what was perceived as the real prize: EU membership (Gillespie *et al.*, 1995). In this way, Spain achieved some leverage within the Alliance while ever manoeuvring for greater involvement with the EU. In 1996, the choice, on the part of the new Prime Minister, José Maria Aznar, to take Spain fully into NATO remained unpopular (Rodrigo, 1997) despite the fact that NATO's new Secretary General was Javier Solana. Aznar's subsequent decision to align his country fully with George W. Bush during the 2003 Iraq War was even more unpopular and the 2004 parliamentary elections, coming only days after the Madrid terror attacks, translated into victory for the Socialist José Luiz Rodrigo Zapatero who had campaigned on promises to withdraw Spanish troops from Iraq (Woodworth, 2005). Spain has also seen the EU and ESDP as being more likely than NATO to promote its own security policy priority – a Mediterranean security pact. Since 2001, all these countries, in their distinct ways, have edged closer to ESDP and begun to reevaluate the precise nature of their relationship with NATO.

France presents the greatest puzzle. France is America's 'oldest ally' (Cogan, 1994), yet, according to received wisdom, she is a 'reluctant ally' (Harrison, 1981), engaging in 'the politics of ambivalence' (Menon, 2000) and incestuously inspired, in matters of security and defence, by 'a certain idea of France' (Gordon, 1993). With her complex attitude towards NATO and European security, France has long been a source of exasperation inside Washington DC. During the Iraq crisis of 2002–3 Jacques Chirac's policies were judged so unacceptable in the USA that the administration deemed that the country should be 'punished' (Cogan, 2004) – a term which speaks volumes about the true relationship between these oldest allies. Yet, throughout the Iraq crisis, France continued to act as a firm ally of the United States, participating strongly in the US-led military campaign in Afghanistan, deploying more troops on NATO missions than any other alliance member including the USA, sharing invaluable and highly sensitive intelligence with Washington, and continuing high-level cooperation on nuclear weapons programmes (Tertrais, 2003). At the same time, throughout the postwar period, France has constantly promoted a more robust and autonomous type of European security entity (Bozo, 2000). France's balancing act between NATO and the nascent European security project is one of the hardest narratives to read and one which has given rise to numerous misunderstandings.

France 'opted-out' of NATO's integrated military command structures in 1966 largely because General de Gaulle was unconvinced of the credibility of the US nuclear 'umbrella' in the event of war with the USSR (Bozo, 1991). Since NATO's entire strategy hinged on that nuclear 'guarantee', de Gaulle judged that the overall Alliance package was flawed. He was not afraid to say so. For de Gaulle, once an allied country lapsed into what he called 'vassalization', that country became, *ipso facto*, a weaker ally. It ceased to think strategically and thereby to contribute to the vitality and dynamism of alliance options. No less a witness than Henry Kissinger concurred with this judgment: 'the most consistent, the most creative, the most systematic thinking on strategy in Europe today takes place in France' (Kissinger, 1994: 337). However, in the very different conditions of the post-Cold War world, the 'opt-out' from NATO made little sense. In NATO's 1991 'New Strategic Concept', nuclear deterrence was marginalized, while integrated conventional military missions took centre-stage. France, as a leading military power, intended to play a full part in those missions. During the Gulf War of 1991, owing to her lack of operational familiarity with NATO procedures, France was able to play no more than a bit part (Howorth,

1994). Rapprochement with NATO came during the Bosnian crisis in the early 1990s. By late 1992 it was obvious to defence planners in Paris that NATO alone had the operational command capacity to allow for effective military intervention in the Balkans, and France began to call for NATO to play a lead role. Thereafter, return to the NATO Military Committee was only a matter of time. Intervention in Bosnia meant that membership of the key alliance oversight structures, far from being a constraint on French action (as had been the case during the inactivity of the Cold War) had now become a strategic and political imperative (Grant, 1996; Brenner and Parmentier, 2002: 42). France's absence from NATO decision-shaping structures was becoming a serious liability. Initial re-integration was announced by the new 'cohabitationist' government of Edouard Balladur in Spring 1993 (Gautier, 1999: 80–1).

Ironically, it took the socialist President François Mitterrand's replacement by the neo-Gaullist Jacques Chirac for France's new relationship with NATO to move to a new level. After his presidential election in May 1995, Chirac took the lead in pressing for the use of NATO (including US) ground troops to end the Bosnian conflict. Within weeks of his election, on 14 June 1995, Chirac spent more than an hour in tête-à-tête with Bill Clinton, leading, in Richard Holbrooke's words, to a 'marked re-evaluation of American policy'. It is widely acknowledged that it was Chirac who forced the USA 'to deal with the reality – that one way or another, the United States could no longer stay uninvolved' (Holbrooke, 1998: 65; Delafon and Sancton, 1999: 85). Thus, paradoxically, it was France which ensured that NATO finally shifted from its Cold War stance of deterrence and engaged in military combat for the first time ever.

France's overall objective, in the balancing act between NATO and the nascent EU security entity throughout the 1990s, was to retain the former for serious operations involving collective defence while building up the latter for increasingly autonomous European crisis-management missions, the two working in complementary fashion. But the emphasis was constantly on a new *balance*. The ESDI deal struck in Berlin in June 1996 (Box 4.1) was intended to develop a genuine European military capacity which could offer relief for US forces tied down uselessly in Europe and badly needed elsewhere, at the same time as it restructured the Alliance to give greater command authority to the Europeans. We have examined earlier the reasons for the failure of ESDI. The war in Kosovo only heightened a French sense of imbalance. On both sides of the Atlantic, the postwar verdict was 'never again!' From the US perspective, never again would the Pentagon participate in 'war by committee'. From the European perspective, never again would the major military nations of the old continent commit themselves to an engagement not only in which the United States was in a different military league, but also in which the military command was often subverted by SACEUR's double-hatting as USCOMEUR. Prior to the Kosovo war, it was not widely known in Europe that NATO's Supreme Commander (SACEUR) was at one and the same time the Commander of all US forces in Europe (whether NATO-assigned or not – COMEUR).

Nowhere was this lesson drawn more clearly than in Paris. The French Ministry of Defence, in a substantial study, drew in stark terms the 'Lessons from Kosovo' (Ministère de la Défense, 1999). In many areas of military procurement where the US reigned supreme, France recognized herself (and her European partners) to be utterly deficient. The main 'lesson', therefore, was that future procurement efforts needed to be focused on filling these gaps. Although France drew these lessons with respect to her existing *national* assets, her expectation in terms of the future was that gaps would be filled through *European* cooperation. Ostensibly, the aim was not autonomy for its own sake, but autonomy with a view to 'turning the European Union into a key partner with regard to defence, while strengthening the Atlantic Alliance' (Ministère, 1999: 9). But France also found herself engaged in major *political* battles with the USA during the Kosovo crisis. The strategic decisions on high-level bombing were taken by the Pentagon and driven by considerations of US domestic politics rather than of Alliance strategy (Parmentier, 2000: 16). However, political control over the *implementation* of many (but not all) of those plans remained multilateral (Haine, 2004: 42). Jacques Chirac made great play, in his regular televised interviews during the conflict, of the fact that he personally refused to allow many military operations planned in Washington to be carried out: bombing of certain bridges over the Danube, attacks on the maritime infrastructure of Montenegro, attacks on 'non-essential' targets across Serbia. Such opposition was, the President claimed, expressed 'practically every day' throughout the war. It was this procedure of 'war by committee' that caused the USA to say 'never again' (Clark, 2001: 428–30).

The 2001 war in Afghanistan nevertheless produced a repeat of Kosovo. French reconnaissance aircraft and refuelling tankers began operations as early as 21 October (two weeks after the launch of Operation Enduring Freedom) and were gradually reinforced by naval aviation forces, transport planes and fighters. France was the only country, along with the USA, to fly bombing missions over Afghanistan in direct support of US ground troops. From October 2001 to September 2002, French airmen flew 12,000 hours in support of US operations in Afghanistan (approximately 10% of all coalition missions). French ground troops began deploying in early December to help the US army secure Mazur-e-Sharif and by January 2002 5,500 French troops were in the region. On 1 December 2001, the aircraft carrier *Charles de Gaulle* was ordered to the Indian Ocean along with a massive support flotilla. President Bush went out of his way to praise the operation, noting that 'our good ally France deployed a quarter of her navy in *Operation Enduring Freedom*'. Military cooperation with the USA worked seamlessly and around 200 French special forces, under a strict shroud of secrecy, have been operating alongside their US comrades – under US command – since November 2001. French forces, in short, have played a major role, alongside US forces, in Afghanistan (Gascon, 2002: 20–2). However (just as in Kosovo), *political* disagreements with the Americans arose early on in the campaign, largely over the most appropriate strategies to defeat terrorism and over the most effective use of coalition assets. French officers were reported to have refused some of the targets that US planners proposed to them because of concerns about excessive collateral damage (Shapiro, 2002: 3). Complaints were legion in Paris about lack of proper consultation and the Bush administration was heavily criticized for attaching far too much importance to the military campaign against terrorism.

It is against this background that the French decision to confront the USA over the 2003 Iraq War should be viewed. France did not just stand aside and allow her principal ally to pursue its perceived security interests unilaterally or in combination with hand-picked allies. Chirac *actively opposed* the US position – mainly from within the United Nations. As Charles Kupchan has noted, by denying the USA the blessing of the UN,

France 'arguably imposed considerable costs on the United States in terms of resources and lives' (Kupchan, 2006: 81). So much has now been written on this subject that it is sometimes difficult to focus on the really salient issues. And in many ways, the ongoing drama of the war is such that, in both Washington and Paris, statesmen have decided to let bygones be bygones and concentrate on the future. But the key conclusions are nevertheless clear.

France has made it quite clear, through the five regional conflicts of the post-Cold War world (Gulf War 1991, Bosnia, Kosovo, Afghanistan and Iraq), that a military role alongside her US ally is her default position. This does not stem from disinterested Americanophilia. France's attitude is often affected if not driven by her quest for *status*. In addition, the French military makes no secret of its desire to fight alongside the US military – the better to improve its own performance. NATO has proved, in that sense, a powerful force multiplier. France has, as a matter of principle, no problem with the US doctrines of prevention and pre-emption. However, despite having signed up to the Prague Declaration in November 2002, France does not believe that NATO as an organization is optimally configured to assume a global role. The EU collectively is unlikely to give a blank political cheque to US global strategic ambitions. Unanimity within the Alliance to give political authorization to missions anywhere in the world is highly improbable. New EU–US structures at political level are required to forge a more balanced transatlantic partnership. France has been a prime mover in nudging the EU itself towards the construction of ESDP as the 'European Pillar' of that partnership – a partnership in which France believes strongly. Successive French governments really do appear to believe in progress towards a more norms-driven, rules-based, institutionally structured, multi-lateral, international forum of solidarity to manage the crises of the post-Cold War world. France has been instrumental in creating this first serious breach in the Westphalian order despite clinging furiously to some of the basics of that Westphalian order. France also genuinely believes that regional stability in the broader Middle East is: (a) a global public good in its own right; (b) an outcome that can only be worked towards multi-laterally and multi-nationally; (c) politically and culturally linked to the resolution of the Israel-Palestine question. She also believes firmly that the neo-conservative approach to 'exporting democracy' is short-sighted and misguided. France is not 'balancing' (either in hard or soft terms) against the US. She is pursuing her own agenda and that, as she sees it, of the European Union. To the extent to which this might, at one level – and at one level only – make life more complex for US policy preferences, then that is simply a fact of life. The predictability and certainty of life under the Cold War could not last for ever. But France also believes that the eventual outcome will be a healthier and more stable transatlantic partnership.

On the whole, as the above pages suggest, almost all EU member states, whatever their initial point of departure in relation to the complex issue of relations between NATO and ESDP, tend recently to have shifted somewhat in their institutional preferences. The shifts mainly involve slight moves reflecting waning (but by no means expiring) enthusiasm for NATO and growing (but by no means overwhelming) enthusiasm for ESDP.

Institutional relations between the EU and NATO

Whatever the hype around ESDP, and however strong (or, even more pertinently, weak) its political will might be, the fact remains that, even at the time of writing (late 2006), the EU remains dependent, militarily, on NATO for key aspects of some of its most significant military missions. Until the EU's A-400M heavy transport aircraft comes into service (probably in 2009), the EU has severely limited capacity for getting troops and equipment into theatre. Until such time as the EU collectively decides to develop military applications for its Galileo satellite system, it will also remain heavily dependent on the USA for space-based intelligence. It remains dependent on NATO for many aspects of planning, command and control and logistics. In order to begin to build up its military capacity and plan for overseas missions, it cannot avoid entering into a structured dialogue with NATO. And yet, that process has proven to be fraught with three major sets of problems. The first and most immediate set of problems derives from the very nature of the relationship itself. The EU, by the fact of entering into this relationship, was, in effect, expecting that NATO would help it to achieve its autonomy. The USA, by contrast, was hoping that the relationship would perpetuate a partnership which it would continue to dominate. This contradiction was to some extent based on wishful-thinking. The EU insisted that the acquisition of autonomy through ESDP would 'contribute to the vitality of a modernised Atlantic Alliance' (Saint Malo). The USA hoped that by continuing to refer to 'ESDI' and to the 'WEU', it could avoid confronting the advent of ESDP and of EU 'autonomy'. This raised many sensitive issues. There were problems with the very timing and the format of the negotiations, given the vast disparities in current and future power and influence between the two parties. There were problems of conditionality: what was the reality of the relationship if the US was in a position to impose conditions such as the '3 Ds'? There were also problems of hierarchy: should NATO have the 'right of first refusal' in any potential mission? The second set of problems had to do with the asymmetric memberships of the two bodies. Who was included and who was excluded and what were the consequences – in terms of status and legitimacy – of such a situation? In particular, if one of the parties in one of the two bodies had what it considered an existential interest in some aspect of the negotiations and was prepared to block the entire negotiation process, how could such an impasse be resolved? This arose with Turkey's objections to various fundamental aspects of the NATO–ESDP dialogue. Finally, the third set of problems is more broadly political and strategic. Beyond the narrow institutional or military issues of NATO–ESDP relations, there lies the overall problem of the respective political preferences and normative stances of the USA and of the EU. As these have evolved over time, what have been the elements of convergence and of divergence and how could these be reconciled? At the heart of the ESDP–NATO relationship, there lies the complex web of the entire transatlantic relationship.

At the time of Saint Malo, membership of existing 'European' security and defence organizations was clear-cut but messy (see Figure 5.1). NATO embraced 16 allies and was preparing, at its 'Fiftieth Anniversary' summit in Washington DC in April 1999, to admit three new ones – Poland, Hungary, Czech Republic. WEU involved 28 nations: ten full members (all of them also – by definition – members of NATO); three (and, after April 1999, six) non-EU NATO members, known as 'associate members'; four non-NATO EU members, plus NATO member but 'ESDP-opt-out' Denmark, all with 'observer' status; and seven

Figure 5.1 Institutional membership and association, 2007

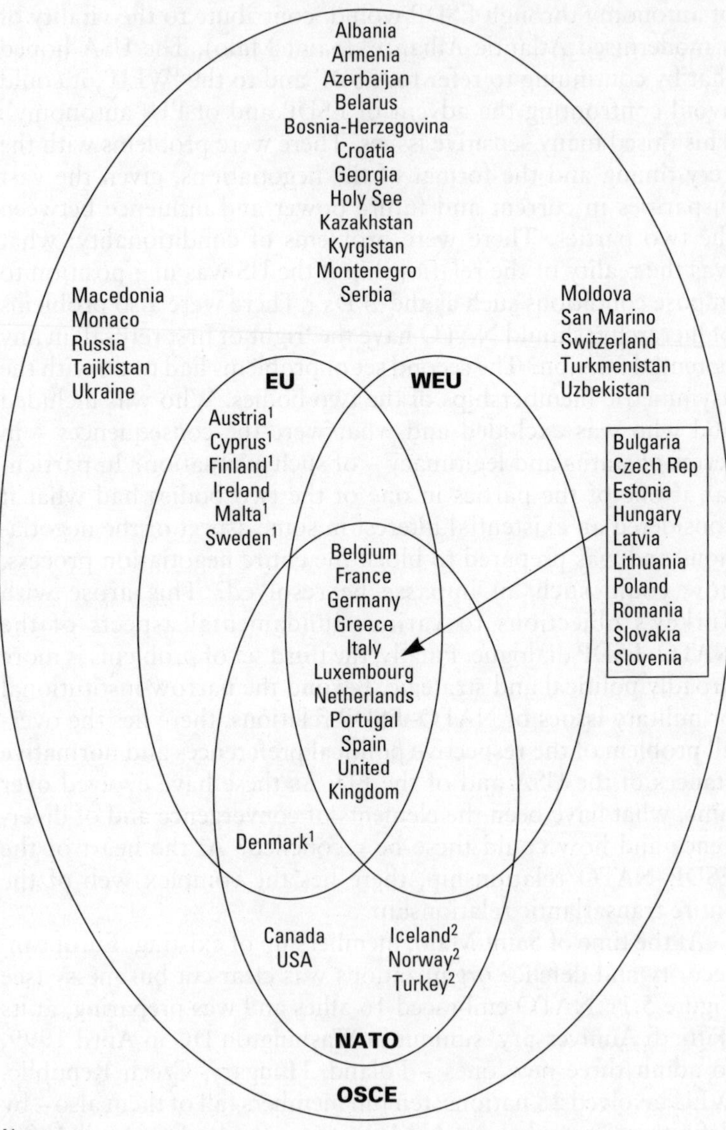

Notes

[1] Observer in the WEU
[2] Associate Member of the WEU

EU/NATO accession candidates from Central and Eastern Europe known as 'associate partners'. For key nations, the assumption by the EU of a defence and security remit involved significant changes as against WEU membership: out went core NATO members Turkey, Norway and Iceland; in came neutral Austria, Finland, Ireland and Sweden. Waiting in the wings were the EU accession candidates. Denmark remained in a category of its own as an isolated 'opt-out' (Wivel, 2005).

Problems of hierarchy

From the very outset, ESDP came under pressure from the USA and from Atlanticist circles in the EU to enter into formal discussions with NATO with a view to reaching agreement on the future security relations between the two organizations and their respective member states. This was recognized in the Saint Malo Declaration itself: 'The reinforcement of European solidarity must take into account the various positions of European states. The different situations of countries in relation to NATO must be respected.' Beginning with Madeleine Albright's December 1998 '3-Ds' article (Albright, 1998) and continuing throughout 1999, repeated proposals were made for the immediate opening of bilateral EU–NATO talks (van Ham, 2000; Donfried and Gallis, 2000; Hunter, 2002). However, there were quite different reactions from within the EU member states to the very principle of negotiations. Those with 'Europeanist' preferences tended to view the pressure with suspicion, detecting in it an attempt on the part of the USA and NATO to micro-manage the development of the infant ESDP even while it was still in gestation. Those with an 'Atlanticist' bias tended to consider such discussions as not only normal but already overdue (Howorth, 2000b). In the first six months of 1999, Germany held the Presidency of both the EU and the WEU. Differences of interpretation between the US approach and the EU approach (as represented by Bonn) rapidly made themselves felt.

In April 1999, NATO met at its grand '50th anniversary' summit in Washington – just as the Kosovo war was becoming critical. The Alliance ostensibly gave its blessing to ESDP (still nevertheless referred to as ESDI). But the Summit Communiqué insisted repeatedly that the new European project should develop in close cooperation with NATO and stated unambiguously that the EU should only envisage autonomous military action 'where the Alliance as a whole is not engaged' – a phrase repeated from the Saint Malo Declaration. The Communiqué insisted that 'non-EU European allies' be permitted 'the fullest possible involvement . . . in EU-led crisis response operations'. It went on to note that 'NATO and the EU should ensure the development of effective mutual consultation, co-operation and transparency, *building on the mechanisms existing between NATO and the WEU*' (emphasis added; Rutten, 2001: 20–39). Throughout much of the 1990s, and particularly after the initiation of ESDI in 1994, NATO had engaged in intense consultations with the WEU over the modalities of cooperation (and particularly the transfer from the former to the latter of key assets) in the event of an operation in which 'NATO as a whole was not engaged'. In effect, that phrase meant 'in which the US chooses not to engage'. The fruits of this dialogue had become known as the NATO–WEU *acquis* (van Eekelen, 1998: 257–67). Naturally, given the relative weakness of WEU, the *acquis* reflected predominantly US preferences. However, the Washington Communiqué's reference to NATO–WEU dialogue was, in a sense, either obsolete or disingenuous for the birth of ESDP implied that the WEU was about to wither away, to be replaced by the EU as a security and military actor in its own right. Indeed, as we have seen, the US propensity to refer to ESDI when clearly what was at issue was ESDP represented at best an ongoing blind-spot on the part of US and NATO circles, at worst an attempt to reverse the autonomous thrust of Saint Malo.

The wording of the Presidency Conclusions of the European Council in Cologne (3–4 June 1999) (Rutten, 2001: 42–5) differed markedly from that of NATO's Washington Communiqué in several major respects. First, the European Union asserted its intention to 'ensure the development of effective mutual consultation, cooperation and transparency *between the European Union and NATO*' (my emphasis). WEU – and its previous *acquis* – had quietly dropped out of the picture. Consultation would have to start again from scratch. Second, instead of the by now ritualistic incantation of the phrase 'where the Alliance as a whole is not engaged', the Cologne text saw ESDP operating 'without prejudice to actions by NATO', which hardly amounted to recognizing an Alliance 'right of first refusal'. Third, whereas the Washington Communiqué had insisted that NATO should remain the instrument of choice for crisis management, the Cologne Presidency Conclusions implied a clear division of labour between NATO, which was seen as 'the foundation of the collective defence of its members' and the EU which would henceforth concentrate on Petersberg-type crisis-management tasks – the traditional French division of labour. Fourth, the hierarchy implicit in the Washington Communiqué between, on the one hand, EU operations conducted through NATO under the Berlin Plus arrangements, and, on the other hand, autonomous missions not having recourse to NATO, seems to be lost in the Presidency Conclusions which suggests that the decision as to which of these would be appropriate is one to be taken by the EU itself. According to Hunter (2002: 57), 'the US administration concluded that the European Union had broken trust over this issue'.

The following 18 months witnessed a messy struggle between various EU bodies and various Atlanticist bodies for control of the future direction of what was only just becoming generally known as ESDP. During the Finnish Presidency of the EU (July to December 1999), considerable pressure from Washington and London ensured that the 'lapses' in the German Presidency report were not repeated. The Helsinki Presidency Report stated boldly in paragraph 27: 'The European Council underlines its determination to develop an autonomous capacity to take decisions and, *where NATO as a whole is not engaged*, to launch and conduct EU-led military operations in response to international crises. *This process will avoid unnecessary duplication and does not imply the creation of a European army* (emphasis added; Rutten, 2001: 82–92). The Clinton administration appeared to be mollified. In reality, the struggle was only just beginning. For several months, there was a serious stand-off about the timing of talks. Atlanticists insisted that these were urgent while Europeanists objecting to being bulldozed. At the time, the author was treated, in an interview with a senior French military officer, to a telling image. It was, said his interlocutor, rather as though the EU, having barely laid down the foundations for its own new construction, was being overwhelmed by consultants from the shiny glass and concrete NATO structure across the road, all proffering free advice on internal partitioning, electric wiring circuits, the positioning of water-pipes and the optimum number of floors (Interview in Paris MOD June 2000).

Problems of inclusion and exclusion

Fashioning direct EU-NATO links also raised complex issues of status and legitimacy. Who should be the priority interlocutors of ESDP? Those EU member states which saw ESDP as an essentially EU project considered that priority should be given to political discussions with EU accession candidates – whether or not they were members of NATO. Atlanticists insisted on prioritizing links with NATO members, whether or not they were candidates for accession to the EU. Thus, in the spring of 2000, a second tug-of-war arose within the EU between these two camps. The argument was over the relative appropriateness of organizing meetings between the EU's still interim COPS, embracing the 15 EU member states' ambassadors, and: *either* the 13 EU accession candidates ('fifteen-plus-thirteen' format), to which might logically be added Norway and Iceland ('fifteen-plus-fifteen'), *or* between COPS and the six non-EU European NATO members ('fifteen-plus-six'). France in particular attempted to outlaw separate meetings in the fifteen-plus-six format on the grounds that the six non-EU NATO members were in any case included in the fifteen-plus-fifteen format. Who was allowed to speak to whom – and when – became an issue of the highest politics. In interviews in Brussels in October 2000, I was informed by one high-ranking Commission official that she had received formal instructions that she was on no account to discuss NATO–EU relations with her husband, a high-ranking official in NATO. Pillow-talk costs lives!

The deadlock was only broken in April 2000 through an eminently commonsense compromise whereby *both* formats were adopted. At the EU Council meeting at Santa Maria da Feira (19–20 June 2000), it was agreed that there would 'be a single inclusive structure in which all the fifteen countries concerned . . . can enjoy the necessary dialogue, consultation and cooperation with the EU' and that, within that structure, there would be special meetings at fifteen-plus-six 'on questions concerning the nature and functioning of EU-led operations using NATO assets and capabilities' (Rutten, 2001: 124–5). These two categories of third country (the 'fifteen' and the 'six') were by no means exhaustive. The Presidency Conclusions of successive European Councils, most notably Nice (December 2000), called for dialogue, cooperation and consultation with 'Russia, Ukraine, other European states with which the Union maintains political dialogue and other interested states such as Canada' (Rutten, 2001: 174). The one country missing from this list was of course the USA. It was through the EU's discussions with these various third countries that the US sought to influence the outcome of the various country to country discussions.

The specific problem of Turkey

Beyond the issue of who was 'in' and who was 'out', however, lay more significant strategic problems. 'Security' by 2000 was understood as an indivisible, positive-sum game – 'I can only be secure if my neighbour is secure'. By this token, the 'excluded', particularly those with strategic significance in the European theatre – Norway with its vast Atlantic seaboard and direct border with Russia, and particularly Turkey with its epicenter between the turbulent Balkans, Middle East and Caucasus – felt a serious sense of grievance about ESDP. As major security actors within NATO, Turkey and Norway had played important roles in WEU. That role abruptly ended with the inauguration of ESDP in 2000. Both countries worried that the primary responsibility for European security, in which they felt themselves to be major stakeholders, was being transferred from the USA (in which they had great confidence) to the EU (in which they had very little). The two countries attempted to negotiate a seat at the EU's defence and security table – in effect membership of the embryonic Political and Security Committee (COPS). This was juridically non-negotiable. Although the EU, in spring 2000, instituted regular security and defence discussions between the COPS and the six non-EU NATO members, as well as with all 15 non-EU European states, Turkey – strongly backed by the USA – found this inadequate in three ways. First, it was widely recognized that most of the scenarios for regional destabilization had their locus in South-Eastern Europe – in Turkey's 'near abroad'. Second, this was particularly significant, viewed from Ankara, in the context of the unresolved disputes between Turkey and Greece over Aegean airspace and territorial waters, and over the divided island of Cyprus. Third, the matter was exacerbated by the EU's longstanding reluctance to engage in discussions over Turkish membership of the Union. Turkey therefore used its

Box 5.1 European Union-NATO Declaration on ESDP (16 December 2002)

The European Union and the North Atlantic Treaty Organization

- Welcome the strategic partnership established between the EU and NATO in crisis management, founded on our shared values, the indivisibility of our security and our determination to tackle the challenges of the new Century;
- Welcome the continued important role of NATO in crisis management and conflict prevention, and reaffirm that NATO remains the foundation of the collective defence of its members;
- Welcome the European Security and Defence Policy (ESDP), whose purpose is to add to the range of instruments already at the European Union's disposal for crisis management and conflict-prevention in support of the Common Foreign and Security Policy, the capacity to conduct EU-led crisis management operations, including military operations where NATO as a whole is not engaged'
- Reaffirm that a stronger European role will help contribute to the vitality of the Alliance, specifically in the field of crisis management;
- Reaffirm their determination to strengthen their capabilities;

Declare that the relationship between the European Union and NATO will be founded on the following principles:

- Partnership: ensuring that the crisis management activities of the two organizations are mutually reinforcing, while recognizing that the European Union and NATO are organizations of a different nature;
- Effective mutual consultation, dialogue, cooperation and transparency;

→

membership of the North Atlantic Council (NAC) to veto the 'Berlin Plus' process whereby the EU might have access to NATO assets. This was, however, a double-edged sword since, at the same time as it denied the EU the ability to mount military missions before it was autonomously equipped to do so, it also

→

- Equality and due regard for the decision-making autonomy and interests of the EU and NATO;
- Respect for the interests of the Member States of the European Union and NATO;
- Respect for the principles of the Charter of the United Nations, which underlie the Treaty on European Union and the Washington Treaty, in order to provide one of the indispensable foundations for a stable Euro-Atlantic security environment, based on the commitment to the peaceful resolution of disputes, in which no country would be able intimidate or coerce any other through the threat or use of force, and also based on respect for treaty rights and obligations as well as refraining from unilateral actions;
- Coherent, transparent and mutually reinforcing development of the military capability requirements common to the two organizations.

To this end:

- The European Union is ensuring the fullest possible involvement of non-EU European members of NATO within ESDP, implementing the relevant Nice arrangements, as set out in the letter from the EU High Representative on 13 December 2002.
- NATO is supporting ESDP in accordance with the relevant Washington Summit decisions, and is giving the European Union, inter alia and in particular, assured access to NATO's planning capabilities, as set out in the NAC decisions on 13 December 2002.
- Both organizations have recognized the need for arrangements to ensure the coherent, transparent and mutually reinforcing development of the capability requirements common to the two organizations, with a spirit of openness.

Source: Jean-Yves Haine (ed.), *From Laeken to Copenhagen. European Defence: Core Documents III*, Paris: EU-ISS, 2003, pp. 178–9. http://www.iss-eu.org/chaillot/chai57e.pdf.

provided an incentive to the EU to precipitate its move towards total autonomy from NATO (Aykan, 2005; Missiroli, 2002).

A series of high-level discussions between UK, US and Turkish diplomats led to an initial solution in December 2001 (involving EU guarantees to Turkey on both non-aggression and consultation). Greece then proceeded to veto these agreements. It was not until December 2002 that a solution to this long-standing dispute was finally negotiated. Ankara settled for 'the fullest possible involvement' in the EU's security and defence decision-shaping process and automatic involvement in the event of an EU mission using NATO assets. Turkey was also given a formal guarantee that ESDP missions would not be deployed in the Aegean and that an EU force would not attack a NATO member state. Greece successfully negotiated a somewhat bizarre reciprocity of this clause (that a NATO force would not attack an EU member state!). Another key 'concession' made to Turkey was that Cyprus would not be allowed to participate in ESDP operations. Technically, this also excluded Malta since the agreed policy was that states lacking partnership agreements with NATO under Partnership for Peace (PFP) would be excluded from ESDP operations. The resolution of this dispute put an end to the two-year stand-off over the Berlin Plus arrangements. However, the politics of Greco-Turkish tensions in the Aegean have by no means been resolved and the EU can not assume that access to NATO assets would be a foregone conclusion in the context of an EU military operation in South-Eastern Europe.

The resolution of the Berlin Plus dispute nevertheless allowed the EU and NATO, on 16 December 2002, to make a landmark Declaration on ESDP (Haine, 2003: 178–80 – Box 5.1) providing a formal basis for a strategic partnership between the two organizations in the areas of crisis management and conflict prevention. The EU and NATO – at least in theory – could henceforth technically develop their relationship in ways which are mutually reinforcing, while recognizing that they are organizations of a different nature. In particular, the EU could theoretically rely on access to NATO's formidable planning capabilities, which had always been the essential prerequisite for any credible EU military operation. In principle, the Europeans could also look forward to more extensive access to other (essentially US) assets. However, in the context of America's ongoing military involvement with Al-Qaeda, Iraq and North Korea, the availability of such assets cannot be taken for granted. Increasingly, the EU will be likely to move further and further down the road to autonomy.

Transatlantic convergence and divergence

More generally, the future of EU–NATO relations remains unpredictable. At its summit meeting in Prague (21–2 November 2002), the Alliance confounded the many pundits who had already pronounced its funeral oration (Layne, 2001; Lieven, 2001; Gedmin, 2002; Kupchan, 2002a) and seemingly sprang back, Phoenix-like, to full-blooded existence. NATO agreed to admit seven new member states (Bulgaria, Estonia, Latvia, Lithuania, Romania, Slovakia, Slovenia) in May 2004, bringing the total membership to 26. It also introduced a new initiative – the Prague Capabilities Commitment – aimed at filling the shortfall in military capacity which threatened to undermine interoperability between EU and US forces. And, most significantly, it agreed to launch the NATO Response Force (NRF), a technologically advanced, flexible, interoperable and sustainable force of some 20,000 troops capable of rapid deployment for high-intensity operations anywhere in the world. Not only did this initiative aim to reconnect EU and US intervention forces, it also aimed to demonstrate to an increasingly sceptical world that the USA remained firmly committed to the Alliance. NATO, it seemed, had finally crossed the Rubicon which many US officials had been advocating throughout the 1990s: the Alliance had 'gone global'. Moreover, it had given itself a new challenge: the war on terrorism. Since February 2001, regular bi-monthly meetings have been taking place between the North Atlantic Council and COPS and, from June 2001, between the EU and NATO Military Committees. At a purely formal, institutional level, relations between ESDP and NATO have been ongoing for several years.

Notwithstanding these developments, many questions remain – both about the politics of EU–US global strategy coordination, and about the prospects for harmonious military cooperation between the NRF and the embryonic European Rapid Reaction Force (ERRF). Although notionally NATO has become an Alliance with a global remit and is no longer bound by the arcane distinction between 'in area' and 'out of area', and although NATO troops have now been deployed in Afghanistan, this does not imply that EU member states will automatically step in line whenever the US administration wishes to deploy NATO forces to some distant trouble spot. The EU is unlikely to endorse any use of the NRF which is not UN-mandated and/or which attempts a *preemptive* strike – at least against a state actor. At the military level, problems of force reservoir, of US troop commitments, of command and control, of right of first refusal, of 'cream-skimming' (the concern that NATO will cream off the best forces for its own use, leaving ESDP with a second-rate force capacity) of training and interoperablity remain to be answered before any judgment can be made about the long-term compatibility of the NRF and the ERRF (Riggio, 2003; Howorth, 2003c).

Moreover, the impact of the 2003 Iraq crisis on intra-Alliance relations was extremely severe. The United Kingdom, from as early as summer 2001, had begun to review its strategic priorities, de-emphasizing the European context and focusing on the global picture. This shift in perspective was accelerated by the terrorist attacks of 11 September 2001 and hardened by the crisis over Iraq. For the UK, loyalty to the United States, in the global 'war on terror', became an absolute priority. While France and other EU member states also broadened their horizons after 9/11 and began to pay closer attention to global challenges, this did not manifest itself in unconditional support for George W. Bush. Indeed, France promoted a discourse on multipolarity which posited that the world was best structured by a small number of regional poles cooperating transparently to construct global order. This view, in addition to fuelling US theses on 'balancing', was seen as heretical in London, which counterposed the notion of unipolarity as an expression of the international community's solidarity in the war on terrorism. The UK roundly denounced multipolarity as divisive of that effort. Franco-British relations (and with them intra-EU and intra-Alliance relations) plumbed new depths in the spring of 2003 as most EU countries (including the accession candidates) lined up in opposing battalions either behind the UK, Spain and Italy or behind France, Germany and Belgium. ESDP, many commentators believed, was severely compromised (Lindstrom, 2003; Howorth, 2003).

As we saw in Chapter 4, a potentially major crisis arose on 29 April 2003 when, against the backdrop of meltdown over policy in Iraq, a mini-summit was held between France, Germany, Belgium and Luxembourg, ostensibly aimed at giving fresh impetus to the European security and defence process. The UK refused to attend. The meeting itself was innocuous enough and the summit's concluding statement insisted that 'the transatlantic partnership remains a fundamental strategic priority for Europe' and that the strengthening of NATO was a major objective (*Déclaration Commune* 2003). But the one proposal which was highlighted by the world's press was for an EU-only operational planning cell, to be established by summer 2004 at a Belgian military facility in Tervuren, a suburb of Brussels. This proposal was widely denounced as an anti-NATO provocation (Sands, 2003; Black, 2003; Dempsey, 2003). From the very outset of the ESDP project, it was clear that, in the event of an 'EU-only' military mission, an autonomous EU planning capacity would be indispensable (Rutten, 2001: 202). Yet, whenever moves to implement such a capacity became real, the US interpreted them as undermining NATO. Despite this, in late 2003, Tony Blair recognized that ESDP cannot proceed without such a capacity. This was not a case of trying to 'play the European card' after a year in which Blair had appeared to back US policy preferences unconditionally. It was a pragmatic acceptance of a strategic reality. The bottom line was spelled out by Dominique de Villepin in his BBC Dimbleby Lecture on 19 October 2003: 'There will be no Europe without a European defence. There will be no European defence without the United Kingdom' (de Villepin, 2003b). From that basic premise, much of the rest follows.

Conclusion: current problems in the NATO–ESDP relationship

At regular intervals, from the spring of 2005 onwards, major US think-tanks and strategic studies organizations produced a flood of substantial studies devoted to the problems of NATO–ESDP relations (Serfaty, 2005; Flournoy and Smith, 2005; Burwell *et al.*, 2006; Serfaty, 2006). All of these pondered long and hard over the unsatisfactory nature of the NATO–ESDP relationship and generated policy recommendations for its improvement. It is perhaps not insignificant that the main EU equivalent of these policy studies (Zaborowski, 2006) made no such effort, but instead focused on specific deep-rooted problem areas where the transatlantic relationship is perceived to be weakest. The American studies all take as their starting point that EU–US relations have been derailed into a siding, that the future direction remains uncertain, but that everything possible must be done to shunt the relationship back onto the mainline. This normative approach is underpinned by quasi-tautological assertions that the EU–US relationship remains the most important relationship for each side. 'Europe matters to America, and America to Europe, because converging concerns, compatible values and overlapping interests make of each the other's partner of choice' states Serfaty (2005: 2–3). 'Politically, the United States and key European states must overcome the political differences that have plagued efforts to build NATO–EU cooperation and begin again with a new commitment to transatlantic cooperation' state Burwell *et al.*, (2006: viii). These expressions of hope and good-will do not tend to find a comparable echo across the Atlantic. Zaborowski, in concluding the 240 page European study entitled, questioningly, *Friends Again?*, noted that 'the ideological gap between the allies is widening' and that 'we may be moving towards a new and a much looser formula for transatlantic cooperation'. He concluded bluntly that, whilst NATO 'has remained a central instrument in US thinking about transatlantic relations, a growing number of issues are being addressed through a direct EU–US framework. This is likely to become a continuing trend, which, in turn, means that NATO's purpose and role may have to be redefined' (Zaborowski, 2006: 213–30). Chancellor Schroeder, in a landmark speech to the Munich Security Conference in February 2005, was even blunter: 'NATO continues to be attractive . . . However, it is no longer the primary venue where transatlantic partners discuss and coordinate strategies' (Schroeder, 2005).

It is widely recognized that the main forum for NATO–ESDP dialogue – the bi-monthly meetings of the North Atlantic Council and the COPS – have failed to deliver any significant agreement. Quite apart from the rather stilted format of the meetings where 'twenty-four' EU ambassadors 'meet' 'twenty-six' NATO ambassadors (almost all from the same member states), the meetings have been deadlocked by Turkey's ongoing worries over Cyprus. Reacting to the EU's decision to admit Cyprus as a divided island, Turkey has insisted that the agenda for NAC–COPS meetings should be restricted to 'Berlin Plus business' – in effect the EU's current operation *Althea* in Bosnia.

Turkey refuses to allow discussion of more substantial Alliance business in the presence of countries – Cyprus and Malta – which are members neither of NATO nor of Partnership for Peace. This has been extended to discussions of intelligence matters, Ankara having vetoed the transmission of almost all NATO intelligence to the EU on the grounds that this might be shared with Cyprus. Classified information may only be transmitted if an EU guarantee is given that the material will not be shared with Cyprus or Malta (Interviews in EUMS, July 2006). There are proposals to re-start the NATO–ESDP dialogue in a new format with one representative of the 32 countries represented by the two bodies, but there is no guarantee that such a move would solve the problem.

Many other proposals have been formulated recently to give new life to the relationship. These range from suggestions as to how military interactions could be improved – functions such as planning, force generation, command structure and political oversight – to proposals for a more formal consultative relationship between the European Defence Agency and NATO's Allied Command Transformation; from strictures on the need for greater intelligence sharing to requests for a 'reverse Berlin Plus', allowing NATO (and, by implication, the USA) to benefit from the EU's growing civilo-military capacity for post-conflict reconstruction and nation-building; from the merging of coordination cells to the coordination of the NATO Response Force and the EU Battlegroups (Burwell *et al.*, 2006: 15–20; Flournoy and Smithy, 2005: 67–71). These are all important and worthwhile proposals, but in and of themselves they point to a broader and growing problem which underpins the entire relationship. Since the election of President George W. Bush, which coincided with the birth of ESDP, the USA has tended to prioritize military instruments over diplomatic, unilateral approaches over multilateral, war-fighting over nation-building and *ad hoc* coalition-forming over Alliance nurturing. The EU, for its part, has done pretty much the opposite. The result is that the EU and the USA, whatever the long-term interests and proximate values that bind them together, currently find themselves in very different places. Dialogue is not impossible, but agreement on the agenda is difficult. It is a similar situation with respect to NATO and ESDP. NATO, by following a US-driven agenda, has transformed itself incessantly. It has enlarged massively, taken on a global remit, declared war on terrorism and established the NATO Response Force. But it remains unclear *what sort of a body NATO currently is*. It is no longer the collective defence organization so valued under the Cold War (even though many of its recent adherents value it primarily for the assumed protection of its article 5). But nor has it really developed into an effective crisis management organization, largely because the USA has not prioritized the instruments – particularly civilian – of crisis management, but also because the EU, through ESDP, *has* made this a priority. In part for that very reason, ESDP has developed rapidly into an effective – albeit still very limited – actor in global crisis management. Whereas, in the four years after Prague, NATO only launched one major mission – Afghanistan – the EU, through ESDP, mounted no fewer than 16 missions. The regularity with which one encounters US calls for a Berlin Plus in reverse is testimony to the fact that it is arguably the EU which has instruments in short supply in the USA rather than the USA which has an excess of instruments badly needed in the EU. Some in Europe see in the current US pressure for Berlin Plus in reverse a not-so-subtle way of trying to limit ESDP to civilian crisis management. Whatever the real agenda, the overall result of these new asymmetries is a growing sense of unease about the compatibility of the two organizations. It may be that the USA and the EU will have to await the election of a new administration in Washington before it becomes clear whether the 'Bush revolution' constitutes a post-9/11 sea-change in EU–US relations or whether it is possible to shift back to the 'normal' great-power jostling of the post-Cold War Clinton era.

Relations between ESDP and NATO remain, at one level, important to the future direction of both bodies. ESDP needs NATO to provide access both to military instruments and to planning facilities and to help the EU acquire an autonomous military capacity. NATO needs ESDP because a coordinated and muscular European capacity is of greater use to the Alliance than a disparate and uncoordinated one and because the EU has developed instruments of nation building and post-conflict reconstruction which NATO lacks and needs. Nevertheless, they remain very different organizations with different objectives and different memberships. As long as suspicions abound as to one another's ultimate strategic purpose, tensions will persist. The USA is bound to remain wary of a 'new kid on the block' aiming at 'security autonomy'. US fears about ESDP developments stem from three main sources. The Bush administration continued to suspect France of posing a major challenge to US leadership. Despite repeated assurances of strong alliance loyalty from all French officials including Jacques Chirac (2003), US leaders – across the political spectrum – continued to assume that French initiatives spelled major problems for transatlantic relations (Burwell, 2006: 26; Friedman, 2003). Washington was also concerned that autonomous EU planning facilities, along with an increasingly muscular EU military capacity, might tempt the Europeans into military adventures which they are ill-prepared to undertake. If things got out of hand, the United States – under Alliance procedures – would be obliged to enter the fray against its wishes and better judgment, and in a worsening strategic environment. Washington is accustomed to an EU that talks above its weight while punching below it. It has had difficulty coming to terms with a different balance between rhetoric and reality. The third US – long-term – fear is that ESDP might one day come to compete with and even rival both NATO and US security policy. This will depend at least as much on US policy as on that of the EU.

The EU, for its part, will remain cautious about an organization which is transforming itself from one whose original explicit purpose was to deliver US engagement in the cause of European security into one whose new unspoken purpose is to deliver European engagement in the cause of US global strategy. The EU will continue to insist on multilateral procedures, on appropriate dialogue and on respect for the primacy and overarching legitimacy of the United Nations. Cooperation with the UN, as well as with the OSCE and the Council of Europe has been ongoing through high-level and working-level contacts. In particular, the EU has prioritised cooperation with these international bodies on crisis management, conflict prevention, the protection of civilians and the international struggle against terrorism. The EU–US relationship remains, for both parties, a first order priority. But the military relationship, so central during the Cold War, has become a second-order priority. Therein lies the major problem for ESDP–NATO relations.

Chapter 6

Towards a European Strategic Culture?

Theorizing strategic culture

Throughout the nineteenth and early twentieth centuries, the government ministry in most leading European nation-states which dealt with defence, military planning and armaments procurement was named, somewhat bluntly, Ministry of War. After the First World War, most countries changed that title to Ministry of National Defence. Today, most of them are called Ministry of Defence. Perhaps one day they will shift register once again and become known as the Ministry of External Security? Whatever their precise title (and the semantics are significant), each of these EU ministries – now 27 of them – still tends, to some extent, to perceive matters of war, peace and security through a *national* lens. Long and often bloody histories, the accidents of geography, national mythologies, as well as overseas experiences have woven deeply rooted cultural narratives of national situation, security and rank. Many elements contribute to these narratives: internal cultural cohesion; interactions with neighbours; defeat and occupation; threat perception; past martial or imperial ambitions and traditions; impermeability and durability of national borders. The result is a cocktail that theoreticians and political scientists have called 'strategic culture' (Booth, 1979; Gray, 1984; Johnston, 1995a). Most of the literature on this issue uses this term, which seems to imply a proactive, 'heroic' and somewhat martial approach to the problem. Less frequently, the term 'security culture' is adopted. I prefer this latter term because it is more neutral politically and because I believe it is more appropriate as a label for whatever collective mindset is in fact taking shape in the EU. However, in deference to convention, for the purposes of this chapter I shall adopt the term 'strategic culture'. In December 2003, the EU published a seminal document, the *European Security Strategy* (ESS – European Council, 2003), which we shall assess at the end of this chapter. That document seems to combine the essential ingredients both of security culture and of strategic culture.

Although it would be an exaggeration to suggest that there are, within the EU, 27 distinct strategic cultures, the exaggeration would only be slight. The ways in which national entities think about defence and security, the role of armies, the function of war and the likelihood of peace are subtly different from one country to another. In an early article on what I called European security culture (Howorth, 2002), I defined a number of dichotomies which I argued would need to be transcended if Europe as a whole was ever to move towards a common approach: differences between allies and neutrals, between Atlanticists and Europeanists, between those favouring professional power projection and those prioritizing conscript-based territorial defence, between emphases on military as opposed to civilian instruments, between large states and small states, between weapons-systems providers and weapons-systems consumers, between nuclear and non-nuclear states. Since that article was written, some of those dichotomies have begun to be resolved, but most have not.

In recent years, a substantial and sophisticated literature has appeared addressing the question of whether developments in ESDP are or are not leading to a new, trans-European, strategic culture – Cornish and Edwards (2005); Toje (2005); Sjursen (2006); and above all Giegerich (2005) and Meyer (2006). Not surprisingly, opinion is deeply divided between those who see elements of convergence and those who detect persistent and structured divergence. There are four main problems surrounding much of this literature. The first is that it is clearly far too soon to say with any certainty whether something that could be identified as a single – or at least a distinctive – European security strategy or strategic culture is actually taking shape. Something is happening, but we are uncertain as to what. As François Heisbourg remarked, quoting Samuel Johnson's comment on the dog which walked on its hind legs: 'It is not done well, but you are surprised it is done at all' (Heisbourg, 2004: 28). Definitive answers to strategic cultural questions cannot yet be supplied. However, it is possible, with the appropriate methodology, to gauge the existence – and the degree – of convergence between the different EU member states around key issues of security and defence. The second problem is that much of the strategic culture literature has been written in the looming shadow of the Iraq crisis and war (2002 to the present). Views as to whether the EU will or will not prove capable of developing a coherent strategic culture are heavily coloured by the context of profound internal divisions over Iraq. Third, distinctions need be made between the literature dealing with the common *foreign* policy and that dealing with *security* policy. The former asks questions about *the nature* of the European project: what kind of actor – or power – does the EU wish to become (Sjursen, 2006a)? The latter is mainly concerned with *implementation*: the development of the will and the capacity to render ESDP credible and useful (Cornish and Edwards, 2005: 801). The requirements of these two policy areas, in terms of an emerging *culture,* cannot be kept entirely separate and there is an important element of overlap, but security and defence policy, while ideally remaining foreign-policy driven, should be analysed in its own terms. It is for this reason primarily that this chapter will focus predominantly on the literature analysing security and defence policy.

The fourth – and most significant – problem is that the vast majority of this literature, and the reasoning informing it, are based on considerations appropriate either to *national* security and defence policy and/or to the role of nation-states. Indeed, the key reference work in the field (Johnston, 1995) relates to strategic culture in *Chinese* history. Although the distinctiveness of *trans-European* security considerations is usually acknowledged in the literature on both CFSP and ESDP, the intellectual discussion is invariably based on considerations which are derived from and appropriate to *national* policy. The problem is that it cannot automatically be assumed that the two phenomena (*national* and *European* strategic culture) are comparable. The EU, to repeat, is not a nation-state and does not behave like one. It behaves differently – both politically and culturally. My analysis will focus more on the pragmatic dimension of commonality in objectives, methods and achievements. One of the first questions in this respect concerns the extent to which the emerging ESDP will reflect the normative 'footprint' adopted by the common foreign policy (the EU as a great power with military teeth versus the EU as a regional power with primarily civilian instruments). Some analysts would like to see much greater progress towards a robust intervention policy with capacities at the highest possible end of military technology (Everts *et al.*, 2004; Venusberg, 2004; Naumann, 2005). Others would wish to limit the emergent security culture to forms of peacekeeping which require international authorization, limited and exceptional military involvement and the dominance of civilian means. The reality is that ESDP, to the extent to which it appears to be developing a unified strategic culture, will almost inevitably emerge as a mix of these two approaches. There are problems with both the neo-realist and the constructivist approaches to the question of strategic culture. I shall begin with a critique of a number of realist analyses which seem to suggest that the EU must learn to act as a nation-state.

The limitations of realism

Those coming at the issue from a neo-realist perspective, however genuinely they may try to probe the prospects of strategic cultural convergence in ESDP, are forced by the logic of their theoretical perspective to conclude that the EU will not prove capable of evolving into a serious security actor. In part, this is because their only possible definition of such an actor is one which resembles the major nation-state powers either of the past or of the present. Sten Rynning, for example, argues that strategic thinking has two inexorable implications. First, it implies zero-sum relations with a clearly designed enemy, and secondly it implies a tight connection between the application of political and military power (Rynning, 2003a: 482). When applied to the EU and ESDP, these traditional neo-realist categories, not surprisingly, fail to fit the bill. Since the EU explicitly claims to be a liberal power promoting values of democracy, the rule of law and individual freedom, it must, this line of argument runs, give itself the (hard power) instruments of that ambition. The problem for the EU, according to Rynning's neo-realist perspective, is that its ambition to 'promote democracy' abroad 'translates into a policy of resolving other people's conflicts by military means if necessary, but without violating international law' (p. 486). This, the argument runs, will encounter two major problems. The first is that, in order to apply coercive power in the traditional manner, the EU will need to transform itself into something approximating a traditional nation-state – presumably by becoming a fully fledged federal state. The second – related – problem is that the nature of contemporary terrorism (asymmetric and messianic) is such that the loose political structures and weak military capabilities of the EU will prove incapable of combating it. Therefore, Rynning concludes, the EU 'does not have the capacity to become a "liberal power"' and should abandon the effort, contenting itself with its traditional instruments of aid and diplomacy and leaving military engagements to 'flexible coalitions outside the EU framework' (by implication NATO, or NATO-enabled coalitions of the willing). This approach to the EU's generation of a strategic culture, coming as it does from a theoretical perspective which sees the EU as if it were a nation-state is difficult to accept. The EU does not wish or intend to become a coercive power of a traditional type, nor does it need – on the contrary – to develop centralized institutions which would enable it to exercise such power. It does not intend to combat terrorism in the manner in which its traditional colonial powers dealt with overseas insurgencies, but via quite different instruments. Not surprisingly, an analysis steeped in neo-realist theory fails to get to grips with the genuinely progressive emergence, within the EU, of convergence on key aspects of security which we shall examine below.

Another deep pessimist in this regard is Julian Lindley-French (2002a, 2004). Again, approaching the issue of coordination or convergence in ESDP from a traditional realist perspective, and with a keen eye for historical parallel, Lindley-French considers the development of a European strategic culture to be 'almost impossible' (2002a: 790). Adopting an overtly states-based framework, he deplores the 'strategic schizophrenia' which plagues European security and defence policy and leads either to 'policy paralysis' or to re-nationalization of defence policy (or both). His analysis revolves exclusively around the actions and aspirations of Europe's great powers (UK, France, Germany and Italy – 'a big country that behaves like a small one' (2002a: 794) – as well as Russia). The remaining states, he argues, 'would rather not know' about strategy and, instead, 'opt for a form of conflict myopia' (p. 802). For Lindley-French, the threats posed in the post-9/11 world by rising powers such as China, rogue states such as Iraq and Iran, terrorist organizations such as Al-Qaeda, and international criminal organizations are every bit as 'real' as the threats emanating from hostile state actors at any time in the past. West European leaders, he concludes, 'like it or not, are back on the world stage' and need the 'mechanisms and capabilities that their place in the world's "Premiership" demands of them' (p. 809). The answer, according to Lindley-French, is a renewed Concert of Europe where the three large powers (four 'if Italy decides it wants to be a major actor') must 'begin a serious effort to develop a transnational strategic concept as the basis for a threat-driven rational response to the new security environment' (p. 810). Lindley-French recognizes that the 'smaller powers will not like it' but considers that, since they have been 'on strategic vacation' since the end of the Cold War, they have no choice but to accept it. In a follow-up article (2004), he deplores the division among Europeans over the Iraq war, but considers that this event was 'a strategic tipping point in both Europe and the transatlantic relationship that will not be reversed'. For Lindley-French, the divisions over Iraq reveal a 'fractured Europe' which is now faced with a 'fundamental strategic choice: either get real about the continuing role of justifiable coercion in international relations and build structures accordingly . . . Or accept that Europe's concept of security is a sham and that the United States will decide by right and might when and how to apply power' (p. 10). For Lindley-French, in true neo-realist fashion, the only driver behind a putative European strategic culture is global systemic pressure. The Europeans will either seize the opportunity, or go under.

A variant on this approach is provided by Lawrence Freedman (2004) who argues vigorously for a straight *bilateral* Franco-British European lead. There are only two countries in the EU which take power and the military seriously, therefore, argues Freedman, let's just face it: we need a *bilateral*, Franco-British lead – rather than Lindley-French's somewhat more politically correct '*tri-rectoire*' (adding Germany). To be fair, Freedman and the other contributors to the volume in which his piece appears were given the specific remit of analysing a 'European way of war' – in other words, the strictly military component of any broader ESDP. From that perspective, Freedman argues that any effective military doctrine will have to be based on a lucid view of the world as it really is – and that only France and the UK possess such a view. The prospect of the

EU-27 generating a military doctrine he sees as negligible – and if they did 'it would stem from a determination to demonstrate political unity and not from the need for a doctrine that would provide effective guidance in an actual conflict' (p. 15). Again, systemic pressures dictate that 'any attempt by governments to draw up an EU military doctrine would be fraught and probably futile'. Such a doctrine therefore should be formulated outside the EU framework and simply accepted by those EU member states who were interested. This is all the more necessary, in Freedman's view, because the emerging 'European way of war' spearheaded by the UK and France is arguably more relevant to the crisis-management and nation-building challenges ahead than is the US way of war. 'Europeans do not have to fight as Americans. Even if they wanted to, it would be totally beyond their capabilities. But, more importantly, in many contemporary conflicts, they are better off fighting the European way' (p. 24). Freedman concludes by arguing that 'the key question is not whether the Europeans can adapt to American doctrine, but whether the Americans can adapt to the European way of war' (p. 26). Freedman has little doubt that the 'European way' is the better way, the way of the future and that it can be blueprinted in Paris and London.

The realist analysts we have just encountered (along with many others) take it for granted that the EU as an entity of 27 nation-states with different strategic cultures has no chance whatsoever of gradually forging a coherent and consensual strategic culture of its own. Movement in international relations is dictated by systemic forces, to which nation-states (or groups of powers) must respond. The role of ideas and cultural intersubjectivity is negligible, the environment is as dangerous and hostile as ever and the need for military seriousness of purpose paramount. The only hope for West Europeans is therefore to build a robust, coercive capacity around those nation-states which understand such a notion and are capable of delivering its practical implementation. This approach – which is versed in a sombre reading of history and strategic doctrine – is very far removed both from the aspirations of those who are charged with creating an EU strategic culture, and from the approach adopted by the other leading school of IR theory: constructivism.

The promise of constructivism

The bulk of the discussion of EU strategic culture is informed by constructivist precepts which most often posit the centrality of *identity* at the heart of the concept. In some ways this is as problematic as the systemic drivers at the heart of realism, and hangs a question mark over the viability of ESDP. If it is assumed as a working hypothesis that, in order to function effectively, ESDP must generate a common European identity and construct a single strategic narrative, then the obvious conclusion to be drawn is that EU security policy is likely to remain sub-optimal in terms of potential until such a convergent identity can be forged – which is clearly far from being the case in 2006. One study which gauged the experiences of three countries (Sweden, Germany and the UK) during the Kosovo conflict against their persistent national security narratives, reached a negative conclusion: 'Kosovo could have become a common experience that united the European countries and told a joint story. However, this did not happen. It appears that national strategic cultures are pre-eminent in obstructing the creation of a common narrative about the ESDP' (Heiselberg, 2003: 35). Quite apart from the perils of expecting too much too soon, there is a fundamental flaw in this type of approach. It is true that, from the late eighteenth century onwards, the requirements of *national defence* against invading foreign armies dictated national conscription, mass mobilization, the construction of negative national stereotypes about *the other* and the forging of a heroic national consciousness geared to collective survival – in short a national strategic culture. Yet the strategic situation of the EU in the post-Cold War and early twenty-first century is very different. There are no discernible *existential* threats massing on the borders of the Union and, to the extent to which there are any discernible collective beliefs about *the other*, these tend to emphasise tolerance, human rights and multiculturalism – inclusiveness rather than exclusion. They are reinforced by multilateral diplomacy. Moreover, the new approaches to security stress indivisibility, positive-sum games and collective endeavour. At the same time, developments in international law, the effects of globalization, alongside the persistence of pockets of what Robert Cooper has called 'pre-modern' society (Cooper, 2003: 16–18) have presented the international community in general and the EU in particular with the challenge of humanitarian intervention: the use of military force in support of emerging international norms. In this connection, one might ask whether the generation of an EU-wide strategic culture *based on the same identity-driven criteria as the existing national strategic cultures* is necessary or even appropriate. European nation-states were forged by violence and war. The EU has been constructed through peace and dialogue.

Although much has been said and written about the lack of (and normative desirability for) a *European identity* (Shore, 2000; Habermas and Derrida, 2003; Robyn, 2005), such a development has never been essential to the *functioning* of the EU in other policy areas. The differentiation between *being* and *doing* in Europe is fundamental to this debate (Howorth, 2000c). However much the European Commission and certain European intellectuals might wish the EU's 490 million citizens to converge towards ever greater cultural commonality and a European identity, the absence of any serious such development has not, to date, prevented the EU from functioning rather well. Europeans have not been called upon or expected to *identify with* the EU in order to accept the logic of its adopting a single voice in trade and competition policy. The smooth functioning of the Coal and Steel Community, the springboard for the entire EU project, was assured despite the reality that an overwhelming majority of European citizens knew nothing of its existence. The Common Agricultural Policy, while keeping certain rural communities alive which might otherwise have died out, would itself probably become a dead duck if it depended for its survival on the existence of a common European identity. Although some countries relinquished their national currencies only with reluctance because of the element of national identification with, say, the deutschmark, the franc or the drachma, the efficiency and functionality of the €uro have been largely unaffected by issues of identity. Similarly, there is no obvious reason why the expert skills of professional armed forces, operating in international format to pursue crisis management missions, usually mandated by the United Nations, should require the forging of a trans-European *identity* in order to be possible (Baun, 2005).

However, the centrality of issues of identity to much of the strategic culture literature does not mean that convergence on an underlying mindset informing the objectives of ESDP is unlikely or impossible. Nicole Gnesotto (2000) defined a common security culture extremely broadly as: 'the aim and the means to incite common thinking, compatible reactions, coherent analysis – in short, a strategic culture that is increasingly European, one that transcends the different national security cultures and interests'. The European Security Strategy document indeed calls for the development of such a convergent 'strategic culture'. If the debate is framed less around issues of identity and more around capacity, objectives and implementation, there are obvious grounds for concluding that such a convergence is already taking place. Cornish and Edwards, updating their earlier definition (Cornish and Edwards, 2001: 587), conceptualize strategic culture as 'the political and institutional confidence and processes to manage and deploy military force, coupled with external recognition of the EU as a legitimate actor in the military sphere' (Cornish and Edwards, 2005: 802). They conclude that, whatever its very real shortcomings, ESDP has 'developed markedly' in a range of areas central to trans-European convergence on key aspects of security and defence policy (military capacity, reliability and legitimacy, civil–military integration and a mutually acceptable working relationship with NATO). These are features which we have examined in other chapters of this book and my conclusions tally with those of Cornish and Edwards. At this relatively practical level of EU achievement, the very fact that, six years after Saint Malo, a wide range of different types of overseas missions were being mounted under an EU command and an EU flag offers clear evidence that convergence is taking place. Other analysts, working within the framework of strategic culture and therefore sensitively attuned to the distinctiveness and durability of national cultures, tentatively concur, even to the point of seeing signs of convergence between, on the one hand, the Central and Eastern European states many saw as irrevocably wedded to the USA at the time of the Iraq war, and, on the other hand, those Western European states that opposed the war (Longhurst and Zaborowski, 2004, 2005). However, without going to the lengths of demanding – or waiting for the appearance of – a trans-EU identity, there are more stringent criteria and tests that can be applied, even from the constructivist perspective, to see whether, in reality, the ESDP narrative that is emerging is one of convergence or of divergence.

Two recent major studies which offer a more identity-driven

definition of strategic culture nevertheless conclude that convergence – albeit limited and slow – is taking place despite the absence of any discernible progress towards an EU-wide identity. Bastian Giegerich (2005) and Christoph Meyer (2006) illustrate the best and the most imaginative in recent constructivist analysis of strategic culture. Although each of their approaches, despite some overlap, is methodologically distinct, and although they focus to some extent on different countries, their conclusions are comparable and complementary. Giegerich studied the impact of EU-level security policy on the strategic cultures of eight EU countries (Austria, France, Germany, UK, Denmark, Ireland, Spain and Sweden) and found that adaptation of those national cultures to an emerging European strategic culture was 'gradual and limited but driven by constant interaction and the emergence of collective norms' (Giegerich, 2005: 238). Meyer compared the evolution of both public and elite opinion in four countries (Germany, France, UK and Poland) through an analysis of changing threat perceptions, mediatised crisis learning, and institutional socialization and found 'areas of shared consensus and convergence, particularly regarding a more activist interpretation of goals regarding humanitarian intervention, an increasing support for the role of the EU as a military actor, and a growing concern over domestic and international authorization' (Meyer, 2006: 169). Both scholars stress that the process of convergence is limited and very slow (this being a value which is both highly personal and relative) and that the challenges to the emergence of a genuinely trans-EU strategic culture remain strong. But both nevertheless detect clear signs of convergence.

Giegerich's work concentrates on adaptation pressures and the ways in which they are met in the different countries studied. The changing security environment has produced a range of pressures on national strategic cultures, most of them implying the need for convergence around emerging European norms. Germany has faced the most severe test of adaptation in that the interventionist, Europeanist features of ESDP run counter to most of Germany's post-1945 strategic culture. France has faced the least pressure for adaptation in that ESDP is, arguably, the consecration of a 50-year old French dream: to project French strategic culture to a European level. Austria and the UK fall somewhere in between. In the former case, EU demands for force projection generated high adaptation pressures since

Austrian armed forces are constitutionally limited to territorial defence. Acceptance of EU crisis management deployments was facilitated by their compatibility with neutrality – which was imposed on Austria by international treaty. The civil–military mix of instruments at the heart of ESDP presented medium adaptation pressures, while both the cooperative and the Europeanist dimensions of the policy were easily integrated. What Giegerich calls 'ideational misfit' was potentially serious in Austria, but has in fact proven to be manageable via a perceptible adaptation of national strategic culture to European norms. In Britain, the major adaptation pressure has been in the area of a required shift of priority from a NATO-first culture to an EU-first. The signs are that, while the UK is prepared to Europeanize those elements of its national strategic culture which are compatible with NATO, it is not prepared seriously to adapt when this is not the case. Germany has adapted the most (see above pp. 149–50) since considerations of the purpose of armed forces provoked massive adaptation pressures, while the desirable mix of instruments and the arena for cooperation also proved problematic. What Giegerich has demonstrated is that where adaptation pressure is the highest, the response of the national strategic culture can often be to disconnect from the EU format. This has been the case with the UK's refusal to distance itself from the US/NATO and with Austria's and Germany's persistent inability to move unambiguously towards the normative acceptance of force projection. Where adaptation pressures are low, there is an implicit compatibility if not an identity between the national and the European norms but it would be stretching the truth to claim that the European was taking precedence over the national. It is in the area where medium adaptation pressures exist (say, for several countries, to accept a mix of civil and military instruments, or, for others, to shift towards an EU rather than a NATO priority) that one sees the greatest evidence of Europeanization of strategic culture. In general, Giegerich concludes that France and Britain, who were the main drivers of ESDP, 'successfully uploaded their preferences to the European level' while Germany and Austria 'were mostly agenda-takers' (p. 245). Giegerich's study (2005), subsequently published in book form, offers a very rich analysis of the working of strategic culture as well as suggesting important research projects to further its understanding.

Christoph Meyer, in his recent book on *The Quest for a European Strategic Culture* (Meyer, 2006) proposes a rigorous conceptual framework based on four 'scalable norms' which allow the analyst to situate member states' positions along a series of continuums. He offers the following working definition for strategic culture:

> the socially transmitted, identity-derived norms, ideas and patterns of behaviour that are shared among a broad majority of actors and social groups within a given security community, which help to shape a ranked set of options for a community's pursuit of security and defence goals. (Meyer, 2005: 528)

Meyer sets out to answer, through an astute combination of theoretical and empirical approaches, three main questions: have national strategic cultures converged since 1989; how can the persistence and transformation of national strategic norms be explained; what are the main areas of normative consensus and of incompatibility? He selected four key European states (UK, France, Germany, Poland) with a view to testing maximum levels of diversity across the strategic norms under investigation (*goals* for the use of force; the *way* in which military force is used and particularly the issue of risk tolerance; the preferred mode of *cooperation* – EU or US; and the level of domestic and international *legitimacy* required). The starting point for normative evolution was 1989, when, for instance, force usage and risk tolerance varied from a very broad scope in France and the UK (even embracing external coercion and disproportionality) to a very narrow scope in Germany (strict territorial defence, reactive and proportionate); cooperation with the USA varied from very high in the UK and Poland to very low in France; and authorization requirements varied from very high in Germany to low in the UK and France (Meyer, 2006: 7). In order to assess the origins of normative change, Meyer employs three types of methodological inquiry: a sociological focus on the role of EU institutions and epistemic communities; a realist-derived analysis of the shift in threat perception; and a sociological analysis of the role of the media in shifting public norms. He also seeks to probe sensitive and salient differences between elite attitudes and public opinion.

Meyer's findings are unequivocal, nuanced and significant. As far as goals for the use of force are concerned, there has been an understandable convergence in terms of threat perception. The general absence of any credible existential external threat has led to a greatly reduced salience among the EU member states for the issue of territorial defence. This in turn has led to much wider acceptance of the legitimacy of humanitarian intervention, itself fuelled by mediatized coverage of inter-ethnic violence. Meyer sees this indeed as 'the area with the highest degree of norm compatibility' (Meyer, 2006: 141). There has even been convergence on democracy promotion, although the picture here is less clear-cut. On preemption, elites are generally favourable whereas public support for the war on terror varies markedly from country to country. As for cooperation with the USA, despite differences between elites (more split) and publics (more universally negative), the 'common meeting ground for these opposing trends is the growing support for the European Union as an actor in security and defence matters, which has been brought about through the combined impact of institutional socialization and the negative experience of European influence on US decision-making and action in the cases of Kosovo and Iraq' (Meyer, 2006: 144). These trends have to be nuanced by two major exceptions at elite level: an ongoing French resistance to acceptance of US leadership; and growing UK scepticism about the usefulness of the EU as a security actor (a finding, incidentally, which is not consistent with my own research) (Meyer, 2006: 145–6). As far as legitimate authorization for the use of force is concerned, although Meyer details important nuances both between the four countries and between elites and the public, the overall finding was 'strong attachment to UN-authorization, multilateralism and a rule-based order' (p. 149). On the way in which force should be used, Meyer found a solidifying 'European consensus [on] maximum restraint against civilian targets and a preference to exhaust non-military means first' (p. 152).

In a series of further refinements, Meyer offers a contrast to these elements of normative compatibility and convergence by highlighting elements of ongoing normative incompatibility. But even here, there is evolution. On the fundamental issue of Franco-British differences over attitudes towards the US ally, he finds that 'the gap is closing' as a result of shifts in both British public opinion and the advent of a younger generation of French policy-makers. My own interviews would concur strongly with this. There are unresolved elements of incompatibility regarding collateral damage, particularly in high-risk situations (more acceptable in France and the UK than in Germany); territorial defence (still salient in Poland); preemption (anathema in Germany); and abandonment of 'sovereignty' over defence policy (unthinkable in the UK). These are significant areas where signs of a common strategic culture are difficult to discern. Nevertheless, 'the key result of the overall study is that strategic cultures in Europe have become more similar concerning the use of force . . . the acceptance of the EU as an appropriate framework for security and defence policy and the de-prioritization of the partnership with the United States'. In addition, domestic and international authorization expectations have converged, as has opinion about the use of force overseas to tackle security threats. But Meyer is careful to stress that 'normative convergence in these areas does not mean that national beliefs have become fully compatible . . . only that differences have narrowed' (p. 11). Meyer's book is the first major study of European strategic culture to be published and as such both merits serious reflection by scholars and justifies the lengthy synopsis given above. Together with Giegerich, he has trailblazed a highly productive and indicative theoretical-empirical approach to the understanding of this important concept.

Lingering questions

However, even the existing literature does not exhaust the subject, and several other issues remain to be discussed. To Meyer's proposed norms might be added several others. First, there is the issue of the acceptable degree of commonality – from loose cooperation to full integration – which might characterize the approach of different member states. While many in Germany, for instance, have long believed that security and defence policy should be transferred to pillar one and dealt with under QMV, other member states (beginning with France and the UK) would go to the stake to resist any such move. A second norm might be the type and sophistication of weapons systems which different member states might be prepared to contribute towards as part of a joint arsenal – from 'legacy' conventional systems to network-centric systems and even nuclear weapons.

Between member states who currently spend the minimum on weapons systems and those for whom, politics willing, the sky might be the limit, there would be a huge range of opinion on such an issue. Again, the level of potential national contribution to ESDP operations would be a divisive factor between those member states reluctantly prepared to be strong-armed into making an occasional commitment and those eager and willing to be considered for every mission. It will only be when the gap begins to narrow in these and other issues that we will be able to conclude that an EU strategic culture is in formation.

One major issue which remains a problem, not only for the neutrals but equally for a large majority of EU member states, is the nuclear issue. The EU's challenge in devising a hypothetical coherent nuclear policy is at least threefold: culturally, the post-neutrals and others have vigorously espoused the cause of nuclear disarmament; politically, most of the non-nuclear EU NATO members have preferred to nestle beneath the US 'umbrella' rather than even think about their relationship with the French or British deterrents; strategically, France and the UK have insisted that their respective nuclear arsenals are for national purposes only. Under such circumstances, is a European nuclear policy in security and defence even imaginable? Matters may be about to change. In the immediate post-Cold War years, France attempted to re-invent nuclear doctrine by speaking of 'concerted deterrence', whereby French nuclear weapons might be considered – existentially – to cover broader EU spaces. The quasi-universal hostility aroused by President Chirac's resumption of nuclear testing in 1995 put an abrupt end to such speculation (Howorth, 1995). Nuclear policy, given its capacity to generate discord, has been the one item which has been consciously absent from the ESDP agenda. However, three recent developments are conspiring to bring it back to centre-stage. First, nuclear weapons are becoming an important currency in various crisis zones (South Asia, East Asia and the Middle East) and are once again the stakes in rivalries within the P-5 (Permanent Members of the UN Security Council). Second, the crisis in arms control and non-proliferation discussions has become generalized, affecting both non-signatory and signatory states. The fiasco over the review conference of the Nuclear Non-Proliferation Treaty (NPT) in 2005 highlighted the extent to which the twin issues of nuclear weapons and nuclear power and those of proliferation and disarmament are henceforth doubly inseparable. Third, the US administration's determination to shift from nuclear deterrence to missile defence is forcing the Europeans to reassess their long standing attitudes towards the nuclear dilemma (Schmitt and Grand, 2001). This is a vast subject, which can only be touched on very briefly. Britain and France are united in their determination to retain their nuclear capabilities and have, for ten years, intensified their cooperation via the Franco-British Joint Commission on Nuclear Policy and Doctrine. They are also united in their determination to keep nuclear policy discussions out of the hands of the Council of Ministers, but they disagree over the extent and nature of their respective cooperation with the USA. Both of those features are subject to change. As the missile defence debate heats up, it is going to become harder for all European countries to avoid engaging with the underlying logic behind the American case for 'defence'.

The proliferation of WMD and the existence of 'states of concern' confront the EU with a stark strategic choice: deterrence or defence? Development of a defensive capacity is not incompatible with the maintenance of deterrence, but *without* a defensive capacity, deterrence becomes even more important than during the Cold War. And since 11 September 2001, the very concept of deterrence has acquired new complexity. The chances of EU states electing to commit the huge resources necessary to construct a European missile defence system seem negligible. They will therefore be obliged to formulate a strategy on the mechanics of deterrence: by whom? against whom? with what? under which scenarios? Could one envisage a coherent ESDP which did not address the question of how the EU would respond in the event of an ABC (atomic, biological or chemical) missile attack on, say, Athens or Rome? For the moment, the EU member states prefer not to discuss such distasteful topics (Freedman, 2001a), although the inclusion in the Constitutional Treaty of 2004 of a clause about common support in the event of a major terrorist attack represents a sign of the changing times (Box 6.1). However, a debate on the adoption by the EU of nuclear deterrence would strain to the utmost the foundation stones of an EU strategic culture. To refuse to adopt a deterrent posture in the absence of missile defences would be to disavow the underlying military rationales of the EU's two most important military

Box 6.1 A common approach to terrorist threats?

'1 The Union and its Member States shall act jointly in a spirit of solidarity if a Member State is the object of a terrorist attack or the victim of a natural or man-made disaster. The Union shall mobilise all the instruments at its disposal, including the military resources made available by the Member States, to:

(a) – prevent the terrorist threat in the territory of the Member States;
– protect democratic institutions and the civilian population from any terrorist attack;
– assist a Member State in its territory, at the request of its political authorities, in the event of a terrorist attack;

(b) assist a Member State in its territory, at the request of its political authorities, in the event of a natural or man-made disaster.

2 The detailed arrangements for implementing this Article are set out in Article III-329'

Source: Constitutional Treaty, Article I-43.

powers and to indirectly commit the EU to ever greater *conventional* defence expenditure. But to adopt such a stance would be to fly in the face of the deeply embedded anti-nuclear ethos of a large majority of member states. Nuclear issues, understandably, are the absent guest at the ESDP table.

One assumption which has been implicit throughout the above discussion is that, unlike in policy areas such as, say, transport or food safety, where 'muddling through' has become a European characteristic, crisis management and military intervention cannot be undertaken without clearly agreed and efficient procedures for rapid decision-making, well-oiled chains of command and solid public support for policy initiatives. If this is true, either ESDP will relatively rapidly generate an efficient collective working culture, based on significant convergence among the nation-states over issues which have previously been marked by considerable divergence, together with a political will to prevail; or it will fail. Those are the stakes. A common strategic culture implies, at the very least, the gradual adoption of a *common mindset* across the EU, with the *entire – enlarging – Union* itself defined as the policy framework. National policy preferences, while not disappearing overnight, will have to be offset against a growing awareness of the ways in which security policy is perceived by partner countries. Such awareness is already making some headway in the domain of the Common Foreign and Security Policy. Formerly, national approaches to geo-strategic issues and/or regions (force projection, relations with Russia, disarmament, the Balkans, the Mediterranean, Africa) were shaped overwhelmingly by national history and geography. More recently, the experiences and lessons of the post-Berlin Wall world, together with the gradual adoption by the EU of common strategies, have resulted in a gradual harmonization, if not (yet) of *approach* to problem-solving, at least of *understanding* of the nature of the problem. While the Barcelona Process and the MEDA project are naturally of most immediate concern in Madrid, Paris and Rome, they are neither ignored nor misunderstood in Berlin, Copenhagen or Stockholm. While relations with Poland, the Baltic States and Russia are most proactively driven by Berlin, Stockholm, Warsaw and Helsinki, they are also supported and nuanced by inputs from Athens, Lisbon and London. Compare this with the diametrically opposite policies towards Yugoslavia which were forthcoming from Bonn, Paris, London and Brussels at the outset of the Balkans crisis in 1991. EU policy towards Russia is an excellent example of the potential impact of 'peripheral' countries such as Sweden and Finland on the CFSP approaches of the traditional more powerful and central actors. There is still a long way to go along the path to a common culture, but the first – and in some ways the most important – steps have already been taken.

The advent of a common *strategic culture*, however, will involve much more than the effacement of differences. First, at the institutional level, it will require a *socialization process* – in Brussels – among the growing ranks of officials concerned with policy-shaping: Political and Security Committee, Military Committee, Military Staff, Council Secretariat, High-Representative-CFSP, Policy Unit, Commission (Relex). While national capitals will inevitably tend to reflect, first and foremost, the heritage of history and geography, those charged explicitly with embracing the EU dimension – however much they might formally remain servants of national governments – will need to transcend such narrow foci. As we have seen in Chapter 3, the evidence suggests that this, too, is beginning to happen. Second, there will have to be growing agreement on the *implications of divergence* among member states and how to handle it. When events such as the Iraq crisis of 2002–3 or the Lebanon crisis of 2006 occur, it is likely that, because of the unresolved issue of attitudes towards the USA, member states will line up on different sides of a clear strategic divide. This should not be taken as the brutal uprooting of the fragile but growing plant that is EU strategic culture. Instead, EU member states ought to have in hand a strategy for managing these differences. It should contain two major elements. The first is that national leaders and national capitals should avoid exacerbating the situation by stirring up personal animosities or national stereotypes – as happened during the Iraq crisis. The second is that there should be automatic recourse to extraordinary meetings of the European Council in order to talk through the differences and attempt to find a way of bridging them.

This leads to a third imperative. Any putative EU strategic culture will need to develop a coherent *security discourse*. Political scientists have recently stressed the importance, in the formulation of policy and above all in *policy-adjustment*, of discourse (Schmidt, 2002; Schmidt and Radaelli, 2004). Discourse has thus been allocated both an ideational dimension, with cognitive and normative functions, and an interactive dimension with coordinative and communicative functions (Schmidt, 2000, 2006). At the ideational level, it is important for policy-makers and leaders, especially those who are launching new policy programmes and projects, to construct a discourse which explains, not only *cognitively*, *why* the new approach is necessary, but also, *normatively*, *how* it fits with traditional norms and values. To date, there has been precious little effort to present these cognitive and normative adjustments to security policy in convincing ways. At the interactive level, the discourse has to be *coordinated* between policy elites and decision-makers in such a way as to ensure that everybody is singing from the same hymn-sheet, but above all, it has to be *communicated* to a range of publics coming from different politico-cultural traditions in such a way as to command their electoral support. EU leaders have hardly begun to embark on the huge task of constructing these various discourses. In most countries, the person in the street has only the vaguest idea of the specifics of the European security and defence policy. The task of enlightening the public cannot be delayed much longer. Until this task is complete, it will not be appropriate to speak of the emergence of a European strategic culture.

At this point, some might be tempted to throw in the towel and declare the overall task to be impossible. The problem with reaching agreement on all these substantive issues – tough enough in its own right – is compounded by the fact that each individual problem – and its solution – is indissociable from each of the others. This is a very tall order, yet it is implicit in the challenge of forging an EU *strategic culture*. Those who are opposed on principle to the idea of Europe as a security actor use the complexity of the task as a pretext to denounce the project itself as impossible and/or dangerous. Those who are determined to forge ahead with ESDP tend to minimize both the complexity and the ambition of the task. Interests, institutions and military realities, while evolving perceptibly, will not shift without resistance. But they are already subsumed in an existing culture and will become a significant part of the emerging one. It is only by taking a long and lucid look at the challenges of forging a strategic culture that we can grasp the interconnected ramifications of this massive historical project. The emergence of a common strategic culture will be the result of both active and passive forces. Those forces have resulted in the adoption of a complex mix of policy instruments, some derived from neo-realism (a muscular rapid-reaction force, sanctions, and a hypothetical nuclear deterrent), some from liberal internationalism (development aid, commercial incentives, civilian assistance), some from moral universalism (conflict prevention, crisis management, nation-building) which, in combination, will provide decision-makers with an unparalleled panoply of resources with which to tackle any given problem. The coordination of these different impulses is, by far and away, the biggest challenge facing ESDP. The challenges posed by the forging of a European strategic culture are arguably greater than those posed by the establishment of the Union itself. But without it, the ESDP simply will not work. The first major attempt at policy level to formulate a coherent approach to ESDP at strategic cultural level was the publication, in December 2003, of the *European Security Strategy* paper. We have referred on several occasions already to this seminal paper. It is high time we took a look at it.

The European Security Strategy: new norms for a new world?

The ESS (often also referred to as the 'Solana Document') sets out in geo-political terms the normative strategic thinking behind ESDP (European Council, 2003). The document has now been subjected to intense comment and analysis – at least in Europe. Analytical critiques of the ESS are: Haine (2003a), Biscop and Coolsaet (2003), Bailes (2005), Biscop (2005), Martisen (2004), Toje (2005), Dannreuther and Peterson (2006). Political analyses include Patten (2004) and Heusgen (2005). An analysis of the normative dimension in terms of the extent to which the document corresponds to the notion of a 'civilian power Europe' is in Whitman (2006). My aim in the following pages is first to explain how this document came to exist and second to assess its most salient aspects.

The idea of drafting a text which attempted to encapsulate a hypothetical trans-European 'strategic culture' emerged early on in the life of ESDP. The Netherlands Institute of International Relations at Clingendael was first off the mark in 2000 with a paper outlining a 'European Strategic Concept' (Van Staden, 2000). Two years later, the Belgian Royal Institute for International Relations (IRRI-KIIB) embarked on a study which generated a 'European Security Concept for the 21st Century' (Coolsaet and Biscop, 2004). The Solana Document arose out of a trans-European desire, in early summer 2003, to move beyond the squabbles which had marked the run-up to the Iraq War. This was particularly so in that it had in many ways been the US National Security Strategy document of September 2002 which had helped set Europeans at each other's throats. The COPS was a forum in which the desire for a common European document became palpable and, according to several witnesses, several ambassadors to that body launched the initiative to draft a common strategic document (Meyer, 2006: 132). In particular, the French and German ambassadors succeeded in persuading their respective governments that the drafting of a common EU strategy would be an appropriate ambition. In the climate of early summer 2003, the UK was also amenable to such a project, and in May 2003 the EU foreign affairs ministers charged Javier Solana with the generation of a text. An initial document was rapidly drafted – largely by Robert Cooper – and presented to the European Council meeting at Thessaloniki on 20 June 2003. Heads of state and government requested a final draft for their meeting in December 2003. In autumn 2003 a series of seminars was held at which the draft was discussed by various experts: at the Aspen Institute Italia (Rome), the EU Institute for Security Studies (Paris) and the Swedish Institute for International Affairs (Stockholm). Many minor amendments were introduced (Solana refused doggedly to entertain more than minor amendments) and the final text, *A Secure Europe in a Better World*, was presented to and accepted by the European Council in Brussels on 12 December 2003. The document can be accessed at: (http://ue.eu.int/uedocs/cmsUpload/78367.pdf)

Sven Biscop published the first full-blown analysis of the paper (Biscop, 2005) and Roland Dannreuther and John Peterson have compared it to the American National Security Strategy document of September 2002, suggesting that both texts defined their objectives in *revolutionary* terms, 'pursuing strategies that sought to change the world essentially in their own images' (Dannreuther and Peterson, 2006: 2). The shortcomings and inadequacies of the ESS document have been widely noted (Heisbourg, 2004; Venusberg, 2004) and the following remarks take it as read that the document is no more than a first shot at stating how the EU believes it intends to relate to the rest of the world. The ESS reflects a number of key concepts which have informed the overall normative approach of ESDP. The first is that of 'comprehensive security' which dates back to the Helsinki Final Act and reflects the intense discussions over a new definition of security which characterized the 1990s (Kirchner and Sperling, 2002). *Security*, in this concept, is seen as indivisible (I cannot be secure if my neighbour remains insecure). To this extent, conceptually it is the precise opposite of *defence* (my security derives from my neighbour's weakness and insecurity). As originally defined at Helsinki, the security concept addresses basic human rights and fundamental freedoms, economic and environmental cooperation as well as peace and stability. Furthermore, the notion of *cooperative security* involves 'the perfectly sensible, though not very precise, notion that security is multi-dimensional in character, demanding attention not only to political and diplomatic disputes but also to such factors as economic underdevelopment, trade disputes, and human rights abuses.' It relies on 'consultation rather than confrontation, reassurance rather than deterrence, transparency rather than secrecy, prevention rather than correction and interdependence rather than unilateralism' (Evans, 1994: 4).

All this is closely linked, as noted by Biscop (2005) to the second key concept, that of *global public goods* which emerged out of debates within the UN – physical security and stability; enforceable legal order; open and inclusive economic order; general wellbeing; health, education and a clean environment) (Ferroni and Mody, 2002). These goods are interdependent and, in general cannot either be conceptualized or even exist in isolation. Thirdly, the notion of comprehensive security is increasingly linked to the new theories of *human security* (UBC, 2005), which is defined as 'freedom for individuals from basic insecurities caused by gross human rights violations'. Mary Kaldor, the coordinator of a special EU human security paper written specifically for Solana as a complement to the ESS, sees the notion as comprising three elements:

- Seven principles for operations in situations of severe insecurity: the primacy of human rights, clear political authority, multilateralism, a bottom-up approach, regional focus, the use of legal instruments, and the appropriate use of force. The report puts particular emphasis on communication, consultation, dialogue and partnership with the local population in order to improve early warning, intelligence gathering, mobilization of local support, implementation and sustainability.
- A 'Human Security Response Force', composed of 15,000 men and women, of whom at least one third would be civilian (police, human rights monitors, development and humanitarian specialists). The Force would be drawn from dedicated troops and civilian capabilities already made available by member states as well as a proposed 'Human Security Volunteer Service'.
- A new legal framework to govern both the decision to intervene and operations on the ground. This would build on the

> domestic law of host states, the domestic law of sending states, international criminal law, international human rights law and international humanitarian law. (Kaldor and Glasius, 2006)

As Richard Whitman has suggested, analysts have reacted to the ESS largely in terms of their own intellectual trademark (realist, pragmatist or humanist) (Whitman, 2006: 11–14). However, what is at issue is not the ways in which analysts have reacted, but rather the 'big picture' principles laid down by the ESS itself. The document itself inevitably constitutes something of a compromise between different cultures and approaches among the EU's member states. The first section deals with the global security environment and gives recognition to the mixed perceptions of globalization that exist. It pays greater attention to the root causes of poverty and global suffering than its US equivalent ([US National Security Strategy] 2002). It identifies five key threats: terrorism, weapons of mass destruction (WMD), failed states, organized crime, and regional conflicts. The EU document is more nuanced than its US equivalent, stressing the 'complex' causes behind contemporary international terrorism and recalling the destabilizing effects of regional conflicts such as Kashmir, the Great Lakes and the Korean peninsula, all of which feed into the cycle of terrorism, WMD, state failure and even international criminality. Nonetheless, it is unequivocal in stating that the EU faces essentially the same challenges as the United States.

The second section outlines the EU's 'strategic objectives'. Two features are stressed: that 'the first line of defence will often be abroad' – via conflict prevention; and that none of the new threats is 'purely military' or manageable through purely military means. The strategic objectives rest on two main pillars: *building security in the European region*, and *creating a viable new international order*. The former entails developing, through a comprehensive 'neighbourhood policy', a 'ring of friends from the Caucasus to the Balkans and around the Mediterranean'. It is, unsurprisingly, absent from the US equivalent document. The latter is only fleetingly entertained in the US text. The EU document is strong in its assertion of a commitment to upholding and developing international law and in recognizing the UN as the main source of international legitimacy. However, the most innovative aspect of this section is the new emphasis on using the EU's powerful trade and development policies in a conditional and targeted way.

The final section addresses the policy implications for the EU. The EU needs to be 'more active, more capable and more coherent'. One of the boldest statements of the document (which guaranteed applause in the United States) is the need to develop a strategic culture that fosters 'early, rapid and, where necessary, robust intervention'. The Strategy, it is claimed, will contribute 'to an effective multilateral system leading to a fairer, safer and more united world'. Clearly, it is far too soon to judge the strategy by its actions or its effects. At present, the most that can be done is to try to break down the key features of the ESS in terms of its discursive message to the outside world. It is in that respect that the EU is attempting to put down markers for a new normative approach to international relations.

Biscop argues that the key features of the ESS, most of which distinguish it from US approaches to security, are: integration, prevention, global scope, multilateralism and a new definition of power.

Integration signifies the conscious mobilization of an entire panoply of policy instruments in a coordinated whole. This 'includes, *inter alia*, external trade, development cooperation, humanitarian aid, international environmental policy, international police, justice and intelligence cooperation, immigration policy, foreign policy (multilateral diplomacy and the promotion of the values of the EU) and the politico-military field)' (Biscop, 2005: 24). We have seen that these elements lie at the heart of the EU's approach to civilian crisis management.

Prevention involves dealing with a host of issues at as early a stage as possible, 'meaningful engagement' (Menon, Nicolaidis and Welsh, 2004) for the long-term (no quick fixes!). Mobilizing instruments and resources from the above range, prevention develops a new approach to development policy by attempting 'through cooperative partnership arrangements, to change whole societies and the behaviour and attitudes of people within them' (Duffield, 2002: 42). A prevention strategy takes the delivery of *global public goods* throughout the world to be the only way in which generalized stability and well-being might ever become possible. The EU is increasingly attempting to incorporate a preventive framework into ESDP.

Global scope. The EU's strategic interests have been perceived as being structured by concentric circles fanning outwards from the core to the near abroad to the global context (Van Staden *et al*., 2000). These interests are not in conflict but are seen to be complementary and ultimately indivisible. The ESS makes clear in its first section that the EU considers it has a duty 'to share in the responsibility for global security and in building a better world'. Furthermore, as we have seen, it states boldly that 'the first line of defence will often be abroad'. As we shall see in the next chapter, the EU's overseas missions have begun to act on this understanding.

Multilateralism. The ESS, as a comprehensive security strategy operates explicitly through dialogue, bargaining, cooperation, partnership and institutionalized, rules-based multilateralism. This is what is implied by 'effective multilateralism'. It relies on and aims to foster global governance. Its key feature is its *transformative* aspect to the extent to which it aims to persuade others to embrace reform as a public good in its own right. Coercion is not excluded, but it is seen explicitly as a last resort. Robert Cooper has theorized the problems of adopting such a 'post-modern' approach to security in a world which is still structured by many pre-modern states and societies (Cooper, 2003: 42–4)

New definition of power. The EU accepts that it must develop into an effective power, but not one comparable to the power of the USA. Indeed, the very word 'power' is absent from the ESS. The intense debates within the EU scholarly and policy-making community of the early twenty-first century between those who felt that, by adopting even the vestiges of 'hard' power, the EU was abandoning its ethos as a 'civilian' power have faded. Most now accept that both types of power are required and that they complement one another (Cornish and Edwards, 2005). The objectives of EU power were nevertheless set out in the Laeken Declaration of December 2001 and reflect very well the implications of the ESS: 'a power resolutely doing battle against all violence, all terror and all fanaticism but which also does not turn a blind-eye to the world's hear-rending injustices. In short, a power wanting to change the course of world affairs in such a way as to benefit not just the rich countries but also the poorest. A power seeking to set globalization within a moral framework, in other words to anchor it in solidarity and sustainable development' (Rutten, 2002: 114).

Taken together, these attributes strongly suggest the gestation of a new normative approach to international relations. It comes very close to articulating the bases of a European strategic culture. That, at any rate, is the rhetoric. Time alone will tell how coherently and how tightly this will develop into a deliverable reality.

Conclusion

The emergence of an EU strategic culture is one of the greatest challenges facing ESDP. The 27 members of the Union have all experienced their own history and their own national narrative, and it is extraordinary that so much of the substance of these national narratives assumes a disconnect between its own reality and the broader European canvas. It is as if English, French, Italian, Polish or Slovenian history took place outside a European context – the nation *against* its broader environment. The very notion of writing an inclusive *European* history, devoted to bringing out commonalities, is very fresh. And yet, the entire European integration project is the living epitome of the need for that collective memory. Those who have struggled with the challenge of theorizing an emergent EU strategic culture have above all been faced with the brick wall of European nationalisms – in the plural. How can a proud European nation, which has forged its historical path by differentiating itself from its predatory (or subservient) neighbours, simply abandon centuries of glorious national endeavour and accept that the EU in 2007 (or 2025) will be faced with an external environment which ignores the niceties (however bloody) of European national difference?

This is where theoretical considerations become critical. If one assumes – as so many realists do – that the world will for ever remain structured by nation-states, each seeking its petty place in the grand scheme of things, imagining a European strategic culture is indeed difficult if not impossible. If, however, one believes that things are happening in Europe; that past divisions are being transcended; that societies and nations and cultures are being constructed afresh through intercultural interaction; that the international system is being reconfigured around a small number of poles (six, eight or ten depending on the analyst); and that the challenge of the future is to contribute collectively towards the vast universal challenge of tackling the root causes of poverty, inequality, exclusion and dismissal, then it is indeed possible to analyse the current state of European thinking on security and defence issues and to emerge with a degree of optimism. The decision taken by the German cabinet in late October 2006 to accept that German armed forces can – and indeed must – participate in *crisis-management missions* to right humanitarian wrongs and correct gross imbalances in power relations not between states but between rulers and peoples, suggests that it is indeed possible to imagine that a European strategic culture is in the making. Ideas are being translated into political programmes. The European Security Strategy itself is an instance of discourse in the cause of human advancement. There is, of course, a long way to go. In particular, leaders are going to have to find the courage to explain the ESDP project properly to their citizens – which means explaining it as a *European* project and not as a vital *national* add-on to what would otherwise be a hopelessly inefficient European mess. Much hypocrisy and hubris remains to be weeded out. But the signs are incontrovertible that a strategic culture of a very different sort is being put together in the European Union. We must now turn to an assessment of the ways in which that strategic culture has been put into initial practice.

Chapter 7

Back to the Front? The EU's Overseas Missions

Thinking about intervention

It was in the run-up to the Helsinki Council in December 1999, that the EU first began to think – collectively – about the specific operational requirements of a putative security and defence policy. At the time, as we saw in Chapter 4, the obvious reference was Kosovo. One of the principal reasons behind the Saint Malo initiative had been a joint Franco-British concern about the lack of EU military capacity in the event of a crisis such as Kosovo. It is the 'Kosovo syndrome' which, in large part, explains the specifics of the Helsinki Headline Goal: the ability rapidly to deploy forces capable of tackling the full range of Petersberg tasks in operations potentially demanding up to corps level strength (60,000 troops) as well as 100 ships and 400 aircraft. As for the potential deployment of forces generated under the Helsinki process, these are the Petersberg tasks, covered by Article 17 (2) of the Treaty on European Union (Treaty of Nice): 'Questions referred to in this Article shall include humanitarian and rescue tasks, peacekeeping tasks and tasks of combat forces in crisis management, including peacemaking.' Only two years after Helsinki, at the Laeken European Council meeting in December 2001, it was asserted that 'the EU should be able to carry out the full range of Petersberg tasks by 2003' (Rutten, 2002: 123). Serious strategic commentators (IISS, 2001; CDS, 2001) tended to view this claim as spurious, notwithstanding the Laeken rider which cautioned: 'efforts must be made if the Union is to be able to carry out the most complex operations as efficiently as possible'. Nevertheless, by the end of 2003, the EU had embarked on no fewer than four overseas missions, including two police missions and two military missions and in 2004 it launched its biggest ever mission, Operation EUFOR-*Althea* in

Bosnia-Herzegovina. While *Althea* fell short of the category 'most complex' (which is code for the high-end Petersberg task designated as 'tasks of combat forces in crisis management, including peacemaking' – in other words, war-fighting), it was a robust, UN- and NATO-backed operation involving some 7,000 peacemakers. This chapter will evaluate the 16 missions undertaken to date by the European Union under the aegis of ESDP and will formulate some reflections on the likely future course of such operations. Many of these missions were given a code name, usually taken from Greek mythology – and thereby imbued not only with a European flavour but also with symbolic meaning. Thus the robust military operation in Congo in summer 2003 was codenamed *Artemis* after the Greek goddess of the wilderness, the hunt, wild animals and fertility; the first police operation in Bosnia was named *Concordia* after the Roman goddess of marital harmony; the first rule-of-law mission in Georgia was named *Themis*, meaning law of nature, the goddess of good counsel and the embodiment of divine order, law and custom.

Those who favour theoretical approaches to these issues will not be surprised – or disappointed – to learn that political scientists and international relations specialists disagree fundamentally on *how* to analyse the international actions of the European Union. Some scholars, coming broadly from the realist school, argue that the EU's external action should be analysed and evaluated holistically in the same way as that of a nation-state. In this view, the 'common' aspect is only one part of a much larger whole, in which the national foreign and security policies of member states are also a vitally important part (Hazel Smith, 2002). Others insist that radical distinctions must be made between three different types of EU foreign policy: those activities (mainly overseas trade) carried out by QMV under Pillar One; those activities subsumed under CFSP and ESDP in Pillar Two; and the national foreign policies of the member states (White, 2001). A third school argues that, since the EU lacks the institutional attributes of a state, the appropriate way of understanding its external impact is to assess the institutional processes whereby it arrives at policy decisions (Michael E. Smith, 2003). Those who wish to follow this debate might start with an analytical article which attempts to guide the reader through it (Bono, 2004). My approach is more empirical. In what follows, I shall concentrate primarily on understanding the nature of the activities the EU has engaged in, on evaluating them in terms of their own stated objectives and on offering some reflections on the overall coherence of the 'EU-method' of crisis management. This will be in line with a growing literature on EU crisis management, on which much of what follows inevitably draws (ICG, 2001, 2005; Duke, 2002; Tardy, 2004; Deighton, 2006; Nowak, 2006).

The 16 missions undertaken to date can be broken down in several ways. Major-General Graham Messervy-Whiting who as the first Chief of Staff of the European Union Military Staff in 2001 was the man responsible for kick-starting the planning of such missions, has proposed a breakdown according to the four main objectives of the 'effective multilateralism' dimension of the European Security Strategy: support for the United Nations; support for the transatlantic relationship; regional stabilization; and spreading good governance (Messervy-Whiting, 2006: 40). The European Union itself rather grandly presents the missions according to geographical zone: Western Balkans, South Caucasus, South East Asia, Middle East, Africa.* For the purposes of this chapter, I shall adopt a more functional breakdown. Thus, we find that there have been four military missions, two military support missions, five police missions, two border control missions, two rule-of-law training missions and one peace-monitoring mission. The first point to notice is that, of the 16, only four have been 'genuine' military missions, with a further two carrying significant military aspects. The remaining ten have been, in essence, 'civilian crisis management' (CCM) missions. While three of the four military missions involved several thousand troops, most of the civilian missions involved between a few dozen and several hundred individuals (for a grand total of fewer than 1,500) (see Box 7.1). They have taken place in 15 different countries on three continents. Artificial distinctions between *military* missions and *civilian* missions, however, must be avoided. Javier Solana has insisted repeatedly that all ESDP missions involve both elements and

---

* For the full details of EU overseas operations, see http://www.consilium.europa.eu/cms3_fo/showPage.asp?id=268&lang=EN&mode=g

Box 7.1 EU/ESDP operations

1. Police missions

	EUPM	PROXIMA	EUPAT	EUPOL -KINSHASA	COPPS
Country	Bosnia	FYROM	FYROM	Congo	Palestine
Dates of mission	1/03–12/07	12/03–12/05	12/05–06/06	03/05–ongoing	01/06–12/08
No. of police	526	200	30	30	75
No. of countries	34	25	8	7	18
Budget	€38 m. p.a	€22 m (total)	€1.5 m	€9 m* (4.3 Braud)	€6.1 m
UN mandate	Yes	Yes	Yes	Yes	No
Head	Kevin Carty	Bart D'Hooge/ Jürgen Scholz	Jürgen Scholz	Adilio Custodio	Marc Otte
Aegis	Dayton/SAA	Ohrid	Ohrid	MONUC	Bilateral

2. Border control and military/technical assistance missions

	Rafah	Mold/Ukr Border	EUSEC RD Congo	AMIS
Country	Pal/Isr/Egypt	Moldova Ukraine	DRC	Sudan/Darfur
Dates	11/05–11/06	01/12/05–12/07	06/05–06/06	06/05–06/06
No. of personnel	55–75	70–120	8 advisors	20 advisors
No. of countries	18 countries	16	6 countries	7 countries
Budget	€11,474,200	€20 m	€1.6 m	€1.9 m
UN mandate	No	No	Yes	Yes
Head	Pietro Pistolese (I)	Ferenc Banfi (H)	Pierre Joana (F)	Pekka Haavisto (SF)
Aegis	Trilateral	Bilateral/Trilat	Bilateral	EU-UN-AU

3. Peace Monitoring and Judicial Training Missions

	Aceh Monitoring	EU-Just-Lex	EU-Just Thémis
Country	Indonesia	Iraq	Georgia
Dates	09/05–03/06	02/05	07/04–07/05
No. of personnel	130	20	10 experts
No. of countries	9	10	8
Budget	€15 m	€10m	€4.65 m
UN mandate	No	No	No
Head	Peter Feith	Stephen White	Sylvie Pantz
Aegis	ESDP	ESDP	ESDP
Command chain	PSC-Mis-HR/SG	PSC-Mis-HR/SG	PSC-Mis-HR/SG

4. Military Missions

	Concordia	Artemis	EUFOR-Althea	EUFOR-RD Congo
Country	Macedonia	DR Congo	BiH	DR Congo
Dates	31/03/03–15/12/03	05/06/03–01/09/03	12/04–date	06/06–12/06
No. of personnel	400	1,800	7,000	2,000
No. of countries	26	17	33	18
Budget	€6.2m + clwtf	€7m.	Costs lie where they fall	€149m
UN mandate	No	Yes	Yes	Yes
Head	Adm. Rainer Feist	Gen. Bruno Neveux	Adm. Hans-Jochen Wittauer	Gen Karl-Heinz Viereck
Aegis	ESDP	ESDP	ESDP	ESDP
Command chain	Berlin Plus	EU-only	Berlin Plus	EU-only

* Plus an EU contribution to MONUC of €400 m.

that the distinctiveness of ESDP derives precisely from its 'civ–mil' synergies.

In order to gain perspective on these missions, it is important to bear in mind that the entire CFSP budget of the EU, out of which ESDP operations are mainly funded, was only €62.6 million in 2005 and €102.6 million in 2006. (Missiroli, 2006: 50). This relatively paltry sum represents only 0.05 per cent of EU spending and compares very unfavourably with the €500 million budget (in 2005) of a non-governmental organization such as *Médecins sans Frontières* (Braud, 2006: 72). However, it is supplemented by complementary sums allocated for special purposes, such as the African Peace Facility which will reach €300 million over the next three years and is drawn from the 9th European Development Fund of the Cotonou Agreement ([ICG] 2005: 5–6). The funding of EU missions remains an unresolved conundrum of considerable seriousness.

Monitoring and assistance missions

It is perhaps appropriate to begin with the Aceh Monitoring Mission (AMM), which was the most distant mission, and the main one to give some credence to the EU's claim to be a 'global player' (Braud and Grevi, 2005). AMM's remit was to oversee the peace agreement between the government of Indonesia (GOI) and the Free Aceh Movement (GAM) which in 2005 put an end to thirty years of civil war. This purely civilian mission, comprising some 130 EU monitors backed by another 96 from the ASEAN member states, supervised the decommissioning and destruction of weapons, the demobilization of the GAM and the reintegration of its soldiers into civil society, and the return of a civil rights regime in the troubled province – although in summer 2006, reports of the re-emergence of Sharia law in Banda Aceh, accompanied by public canings, were disturbing in this regard (ICG, 2006; Perlez, 2006). AMM was launched on 15 September 2005 and initially mandated for a six month stay. In May 2006 the EU agreed to the GOI's request for AMM to continue its mandate until the date of the local elections (*Pilkada*) in Aceh. Initially scheduled for September, these elections were postponed for technical reasons until 11 December 2006 and the EU mission accordingly prolonged until the end of December 2006 as well as being reinforced with an elections observation mission. The AMM was successfully concluded on 15 December 2006. The EU remains committed to the development of Indonesia, contributing 85 per cent of all international funds for long-term reconstruction, and signing a Partnership and Cooperation Agreement in spring 2007.

Why did the EU get involved in Aceh? The first reason was that the peace negotiations between the contending parties were themselves initiated in Helsinki under the auspices of the Crisis Management Initiative (CMI), a non-governmental organization chaired by former Finnish President Martti Ahtisaari. Initially, a majority of the COPS ambassadors were strongly opposed to what was widely perceived as a distant distraction. Only Finland, Sweden, the Netherlands (the former colonial power) and France were in favour. However, the Finns were very persuasive, particularly with respect to the British, who had initially been sceptical but were looking, as holders of the six-month EU presidency in late 2005, for a practical way of demonstrating that the French and Dutch vetoes of the Constitutional Treaty did not spell the end of ESDP. Secondly, the mission offered several benefits, including the first serious testing of the EU's CCM procedures and the first operationalization of the EU's Brussels-based Civil–Military Planning Cell (CMPC). Thirdly, and crucially, the Indonesian government and the GAM were insistent that the EU was the only international organization appropriate to take on this mission. The UN was unacceptable to Jakarta because of the way it had handled (in their view *mishandled*) the peace process in East Timor. ASEAN as the hypothetical lead organization was, for various reasons, unacceptable both to the GOI and to the GAM. The EU therefore came under heavy pressure to accept, particularly when it was pointed out that without the monitoring mission there was a serious risk that the ceasefire would not hold – as had been the case on five previous occasions. This was, in short, a perfect opportunity to demonstrate the growing international clout of the EU as well as to take on a crucial and significant mission testing many of the civilian instruments developed precisely for this purpose (Chapter 4). Force generation was a clear success, with a 'surprisingly swift, extensive and high-quality response to the Council Secretariat's hurried call for tender' (Braud and Grevi, 2005: 24). Indeed, so dedicated were many of the volunteer monitors that they found themselves obliged, as a result of the EU's initial inability to agree on a funding mechanism, to front-load their own expenses to the tune of €7,000 and even, in some cases, to pay for their own travel to Indonesia! The details of the deplorable in-fighting over organizational and funding matters between the Council and the Commission have been extensively recounted by Braud and Grevi (2006: 23–8) and there is no point in repeating them here.

How can one evaluate this mission? Although all the details of a final settlement – above all political – in Aceh remain elusive, the EU has demonstrated its potential to push forward a peace process already in train. It has exemplified its own commitment, in the European Security Strategy, to support regional organizations – in this case ASEAN – as crucial partners in the quest for peace and stability around the world. The specific objectives of the AMM (amnesty and reintegration of GAM fighters, security arrangements, the dispute settlement mechanism and above all political reform) were largely accomplished with the adoption by the Indonesian Parliament, in summer 2005, of the Law on the Governing of Aceh which paved the way for crucial local elections. This was rendered easier as a result of both parties' commitment to making the peace agreement work. But the mission also highlighted deficiencies requiring urgent attention. Problems with financing, procurement, logistical support and rapid deployment mechanisms, as called for in the Civilian Headline Goal 2008, remained on the ESDP agenda after the mission was concluded. In many ways, the AMM was an instance of determined 'muddling through'. Such an approach will be quite unacceptable, not to say unworkable, in the event of a much more challenging peace-monitoring mission in the future – for instance in Kosovo.

Less impressive was the EU's record in responding to the humanitarian crisis that convulsed the Sudanese region of Darfur from 2003. Sudan is Africa's largest country and Darfur is roughly the size of France. Fighting between two local rebel groups, the Sudan Liberation Movement/Army (SLM/A) and the Justice and Equality Movement (JEM) on the one hand, and the Arabic militia *Janjaweed* backed by the Government of Sudan (GOS) on the other hand, rapidly affected close to three million people, with almost 2 million becoming internally displaced persons (IDPs), and hundreds of thousands fleeing across the border into neighbouring Chad. The crisis became the first major challenge for the recently (2002) created African Union (AU). UK Secretary of State for International Development, Hilary Benn, deemed it 'the most serious humanitarian emergency in the world today'. An initial ceasefire agreement was reached in the Chad capital N'Djamena in April 2004 and in May an AU monitoring mission – African Mission in Sudan (AMIS) – was established with 60 military observers protected by 300 AU troops. This force rapidly proved irrelevant since both sides ignored the ceasefire and in October 2004 the AU created AMIS II, a 3,320 strong force of troops and police to engage in monitoring and verification of the N'Djamena agreement. Troop levels grew progressively to around 8,000. There were persistent rumours that the EU was preparing a military intervention force. The Chairman of the EU Military Committee, General Gustav Hägglund, in an interview with the *Financial Times* on 12 April 2004, stated that he saw 'no reason why the EU could not go to Sudan', arguing that this would be a perfect implementation of the battle-group concept. In late July 2004, General Mike Jackson, UK Chief of the General Staff, told the BBC that 'if need be, we will be able to go to Sudan. I suspect we could put a brigade together very quickly indeed' (Williams and Bellamy, 2005: 34). In reality, the challenge of Darfur proved too severe a politico-military test for the fledgling ESDP – as indeed it was also to prove with respect to NATO, despite President Bush's February 2006 proposal to send in 20,000 NATO troops (Dempsey, 2006).

Instead, the EU has, since January 2004, provided a large range of services and support facilities to both the African Union in general and to AMIS II in particular. On the civilo-diplomatic side, it raised almost €1 billion via the Commission, the Council and the member states; it was the prime mover behind UN Security Council Resolution 1593 referring the situation to the International Criminal Court; it gave steadfast support to the UN Special Representative, Jan Pronk; and proved to be a major force in the peace talks which led, on 5 May 2006, to the somewhat more promising Darfur Peace Agreement signed in Abuja, Nigeria. At the same time, on the military side, it deployed 100 troops and 50 policemen to support AMIS II, coordinated strategic airlift for over 2,000 AU troops, contributed massively to the funding of the AU mission and appointed a special representative, Pekka Haavisto, to coordinate EU aid and assistance. The

EU presents this package of measures as further evidence of its 'effective multilateralism' under the guise of 'working with partners'. At the same time, Brussels claims that this rather modest level of involvement respects the 'African ownership' principle whereby former colonial powers seek to take a back seat in crises, deferring to the AU as the principal stakeholder. That principle, of course, can also be viewed as a proxy for avoiding direct involvement (Braud, 2006). Two academic specialists have argued that 'the most likely explanation for [the EU's] failure to contemplate intervention in Darfur was that its leaders lacked the political will to muster the necessary resources' (Williams and Bellamy, 2005: 34). Analysts acknowledge the leading role which the EU has taken in the Darfur crisis, but note that there are serious limitations to its ability to develop its partnership with the AU. The relationship is very new, since neither the African Union nor ESDP existed at the turn of the century. Moreover, the EU is not a single actor and the biggest problem has been that of coordination between its different levels asnd agencies. While the COPS is charged with giving political direction to the mission, it is too distant from the reality on the ground to be able to do this effectively. Moreover, the major funding from the African Peace Facility is provided by the European Commission which tries hard to micro-manage its disbursement even though the entire AMIS II support operation is directed by the Council. (ICG, 2005a: 5–12). There was far too little coordination between the different donors and sporadic turf-wars between ESDP and NATO, despite the fact that the two organizations were carrying out almost identical functions (HRW, 2005). Moreover, despite attempting on two occasions to leverage its funding to impose much needed reorganization of AMIS II's structures and procedures, the EU's recommendations were systematically ignored. Some have commented that the EU, by prioritizing the AU as its preferred partner for African missions has missed several opportunities to play a stronger role in partnership with other organizations such as NATO and the UN (Braud, 2006: 78). One main difference between the Aceh mission and the Darfur mission is, of course, the fact that, in the former case there was a genuine peace to be monitored, one supported by both parties, while in the latter case there is merely a peace 'agreement', one which is systematically violated by both parties.

It is relatively easy from the comfort of a university chair to accuse the EU and the international community of abandoning 'the responsibility to protect' (Williams and Bellamy, 2005) or to conclude that 'the sun of humanitarian intervention has set for now' (Weiss, 2004: 149). A more balanced judgment might conclude that the EU has proved to be a leading agent for assistance during a major regional crisis, pending take-over by the United Nations – scheduled for December 2006. The EU mission was extended for a third time in September 2006 to last until the arrival of the UN replacement mission. Short of sending in a massive armed force (which it probably does not possess and which would ride roughshod over the important principle of African ownership) it is difficult to see quite what more the EU could have done in this particular case. Sudan's vast geographical expanses have been subject for centuries to fissiparous political and tribal tendencies. The country forms the crossroads in the age-old struggle between Arabs and Africans, has a fragile truce to a separate long-standing civil war in the South, has a government in Khartoum which seems impervious to international pressure and is adept at obstructionism, and possesses regional borders which make very little sense. As both the EU and NATO concluded, further military involvement ran the very real risk of those bodies becoming bogged down in a Sudanese quagmire potentially for many years, subject to Arab and Muslim accusations of acting as a 'Trojan Horse' in the global battle for Western hegemony. Only a regional political solution – sustainable over the long term – can effectively put an end to this major crisis. The EU has thrown both energy and money into the quest for a solution, but the results are unsatisfactory and very limited. The EU's capacity to do other than provide band-aid to the deeply torn African continent appears circumscribed. While the stakes for the whole of Africa in the outcome to this regional crisis remain exceptionally high, the EU has ultimately proven unable to contribute in a manner consistent with its future ambitions and historical responsibilities for Africa. Re-reading the ESS with Darfur in mind, one is struck by the shortfall between the rhetoric and the reality. There are clear lessons here for ESDP's future involvements both in Africa and elsewhere.

Less dramatic than the Darfur crisis have been a number of other, more limited regional crises in which the EU has offered assistance through its ESDP instruments. The following section will briefly assess four such missions. Two missions for the training of judges, jurists and penitentiary officers – in Georgia and in Iraq – have successfully delivered, respectively, 300 and 800 trained officials capable of contributing to the establishment of the rule of law in societies emerging from totalitarianism. Two border control missions have also been mounted in areas where the shift to stability and good governance is critical for regional security: at Rafah, the main crossing point between Gaza and Egypt; and on the Moldova/Ukrainian border. The objective of these missions is to tackle international smuggling, criminality and even terrorism, to inculcate best practice and to stabilize critical choke-points for the passage of human cargoes.

The Georgian rule of law mission, EUJUST-*Thémis*, was explicitly situated in the context of the European Neighbourhood Policy, which aims to foster a ring of well governed countries around the EU. After the 'rose revolution' in December 2003 which brought the 37 year old Mikheil Saakashvili to power, Georgia made energetic overtures to the European Union. The country is not only a highly fragile state surrounded by pockets of instability, but also, as of 2007, shares a (Black Sea) border with the EU's new member states, Romania and Bulgaria. The EU, which has a vital stake in the success of reform in the country, responded with a number of initiatives, including the appointment of the Finnish diplomat Heikki Talvitie as Special Representative (EUSR) to the South Caucasus, increases in technical assistance, humanitarian aid, food support and rehabilitation programmes in South Ossetia and Abkhazia (Lynch, 2006: 12), as well as the ESDP initiative EUJUST-*Thémis* to help solve the country's principal internal problem: a corrupt and antiquated rule of law and criminal justice system which essentially harked back unchanged to Soviet days (Helly, 2006: 89). *Thémis* built on a number of rule-of-law projects which the Commission had already been funding but, by being mounted through the Council under ESDP, presented the added-value of sending a strong political signal to the Georgian government about the EU's support for the reform programme. The mission – which was to last one year – comprised ten legal experts under a French Head of Mission, Sylvie Pantz, working in close cooperation with all relevant Georgian ministries and other legal and penitentiary institutions and with a team of eight Georgian legal experts.

According to the terms of the Joint Action (2004/523/04) establishing the mission, its objective was 'the development of a horizontal governmental strategy guiding the reform process for all relevant stakeholders in the criminal justice sector, including the establishment of a mechanism for coordination and priority setting for criminal justice reform'. The EU Council notes, laconically, that, respecting its May 2005 deadline, 'the high-level group finished its work and submitted the strategy to the Government of Georgia' which duly approved it under Saakashvili's signature on 9 July 2005. That, however, was not the whole story. The EU had consciously set up this mission with a view to learning lessons which could be applied in future missions. Apart from teething problems such as a lack of reliable phone and fax lines and the absence of internet services, there were serious problems of communication resulting in major Georgian interlocutors remaining in complete ignorance about the very existence of the mission (Cronin, 2004) as well as major problems of coherence between the different agencies of the EU. According to one leading expert on *Thémis*, the mandate was 'too ambitious and too difficult to implement' (Helly, 2006: 99). Moreover, the EU was not the only player in town. Georgian policy-makers were also being advised by experts from the American Bar Association and the US Department of Justice who offered a rather different legal philosophy. The implementation of a definitive system in Georgia is still in abeyance and everything henceforth depends on EU follow-up. However, according to two policy analysts, the EU has proved reluctant to become too closely engaged with Georgia both because of fear of Russia's reaction and because of reluctance to envisage eventual Georgian membership of the Union (Leonard and Grant, 2005). The main lessons emerging from this first ESDP experiment in civilian crisis management were twofold. First, that such an operation could be applied 'as a preventive measure in situations of relative stability or when a risk of destabilisation is detected'. But, secondly, that success will ultimately depend on 'assertive political follow-up from the EUSR backing up an efficient and energetic implementation managed by the Commission in the framework of the ENP' (Helly, 2006: 102). A follow-up mission was initiated but it was terminated without further success on 28 February 2006 (European Council, 2006a: 5).

In July 2005, immediately following the conclusion of

EUJUST-*Thémis,* and in response to an invitation from the Iraqi Transitional Government, the EU launched a second integrated rule-of-law mission, this one in Iraq – EUJUST-*Lex*. The mission consisted of integrated training in the fields of management and criminal investigation for senior officials from the judiciary, the police and the penitentiary in order to help promote an integrated criminal-justice system in Iraq. During the first year of the programme, almost 700 judges, investigating magistrates, senior police and penitentiary officers had participated in integrated training courses in 10 member states. All training activities, which were conducted in Arabic and Kurdish, took place inside the EU. The mission had a liaison office in Baghdad. On 12 June 2006, mindful of the time-frame lessons of *Thémis,* the Council agreed to extend EUJUST *Lex* for a further period of 18 months. Head of the mission was Stephen White, a former UK Head of the Senior Police Leadership Development Programme, who had extensive experience of policing in Northern Ireland as well as of consultancy work in Iraq itself. Information about the mission remains classified and, under the terms of the Council Joint Action which established it, all staff involved, both during and after the mission 'shall exercise the greatest discretion with regard to all facts and information' relating to it (Joint Action 2005/190/CFSP Article 6/2). This ESDP initiative is seen as complementary to other rule-of-law training programmes for Iraq, including those organized by NATO, the UN, the USA and the EU member states. Follow-up programmes are envisaged in coordination with the Commission as part of the EU's overall commitment to the sustainability of the justice system in Iraq. It is impossible, in the current state of public knowledge about this mission, to formulate an objective evaluation of it.

Two border assistance missions (BAMs) were also launched under the aegis of ESDP. The first, inaugurated on 30 November 2005, was at the Rafah crossing point (RCP) between Gaza and Egypt. This is the only Gaza entry and exit point not directly controlled by Israel and is therefore of crucial importance to the Palestinian economy and to the viability of any future Palestinian state. When Israel withdrew from Gaza in September 2005, the RCP was stormed by local Palestinians, hundreds of whose homes had been bulldozed by retreating Israeli settlers. The rioters arc-welded holes through the steel barriers enabling thousands to pass unchecked into Egypt. Uncontrolled traffic in the opposite direction – potentially permitting a chaotic influx of weapons, exiled extremists and even terrorists into Gaza – was an Israeli nightmare and, under pressure from Tel Aviv and Washington, Egypt promptly closed the crossing point. However, on 15 November 2005 Israel and the Palestinian National Authority (PNA) concluded an 'Agreement on Movement and Access' at Rafah which called for a Third Party monitoring presence. The EU accepted the invitation from both parties to fulfil this function and rapidly set in motion the EU BAM-Rafah mission. The operation monitors, verifies and evaluates the performance of the PNA border control, security and customs officials working at the Terminal and ensures that the PNA complies with all applicable regulations. It also contributes to Palestinian training and capacity building in all aspects of border control and customs operations and contributes to the liaison between the Palestinian, Israeli and Egyptian authorities. It was initially given a 12 month mandate but this was subject to extension. EU Liaison Officers work with the Israeli authorities in Kerem Shalom to resolve any disputes arising out of the border mission.

Operations began on 26 November 2005 when the RCP opened for five hours a day, extending within a month to nine hours. When the mission enters its full deployment phase the border will open 24 hours a day. Only Palestinian ID cardholders are permitted to cross the border. Officials made special efforts to facilitate the exit and re-entry of the pilgrims for the Hajj, opening for 20 hours a day in December 2005 and January 2006. At full strength, the EU contingent will involve 75 police and customs officers from eighteen member states. By February 2006, 100,000 people had used the crossing point.

However, problems immediately arose with the election of Hamas in January 2006, since the Israeli authorities announced their refusal to allow Hamas ministers to cross the border (Pirozzi, 2006: 5). In April 2006, Palestinian President Mahmoud Abbas sent members of his personal Presidential Guard to man the crossing in a move denounced by Hamas as a power-grab. An explosive incident was narrowly avoided in May 2006 when Abbas's officers stopped Sami Abu Zuhri, chief spokesman for the Hamas government, and removed from him a body-belt containing over €600,000 in cash. Zuhri's bodyguards were simultaneously stripped of their weapons. As one Canadian reporter remarked, 'even as all else in the Palestinian realm appears to be coming undone, the Rafah Border Terminal has come together with the same routine efficiency one encounters at, say, the airports of Heathrow, Pearson or La Guardia' (Potter, 2006). With the onset of military exchanges in Gaza, the RBC was closed on 25 June 2006, leading to the stranding of thousands on either side of the frontier. After two holes were detonated in the border wall near Rafah on 15 July, the crossing was temporarily re-opened on 18 July 2006 in the direction of Gaza only, allowing almost 5,000 people to cross through. While the EU mission is clearly of cardinal importance to the smooth running of border controls in Gaza during peace-time, the mission became effectively irrelevant in the presence of renewed armed conflict between Israel and the Palestinians.

The second EU BAM was established on the Ukraine–Moldova border on 30 November 2005 at the joint request of the Presidents of Moldova and Ukraine. This border is an especially sensitive one in that it skirts the Eastern extremity of the disputed Russian-backed enclave of Transnistria and has long been a hot-bed of criminality, trafficking in people, drugs and weapons, money-laundering, smuggling and other illicit activities. Ukrainian and Moldovan business circles 'have become adept at using the parallel Transnistrian economy to their own ends, regularly participating in re-export and other illegal practices' ([ICG] 2004: i). The EU has a vital interest in stabilising the area since in 2007 Moldova became an EU border state and since the Transnistria issue complicates EU relations with Russia. The border mission, whose overall budget will rise to €20 million, is an advisory, technical body and has no executive powers. It is a joint ESDP-Commission initiative operating in close cooperation with the EU Special Representative to Moldova, the Dutch diplomat Adriaan Jacobovits de Szeged, whose mandate is largely devoted to helping solve the Transnistrian conundrum (Popescu, 2005). Its aims are to assist Moldova and Ukraine to harmonize their border management standards and procedures with those prevalent in EU member states; to assist in enhancing the professional and operational capacities of the Moldovan and Ukrainian customs officials and border guards; to improve risk-analysis capacities; and to improve cooperation and complementarity between the border guards, customs services and other law enforcement agencies. Strategically, if this border mission can be made to work effectively, it will put enormous pressure on the Transnistrian authorities to reach a settlement with Moldova. The mission was scheduled to last two years, but is likely to be extended. It has its headquarters in Odessa, and mans six field offices. In summer 2006, it included 70 EU experts seconded from 16 EU member states and assisted by 50 local officials. The mission provides on-the-job training and advice to Moldovan and Ukrainian officials, reinforcing their capacity to carry out effective border and customs controls and border surveillance. It contributes to building confidence and strengthening cross border cooperation. This mission, like that in Georgia, operates in conjunction with the EU's Neighbourhood Policy.

At the second meeting of the mission's advisory board in May 2006, it was decided to step up the intensity of border controls, particularly in order to clamp down on the smuggling of illicit foodstuffs. During a ten-day cross-border operation in late May and early June 2006, more smuggled goods were seized than in the previous three months. It was also decided to increase the EU personnel from 70 to 108 and to open two additional field offices. Although it is intended that greater border transparency will create a more favourable environment for settling the Transnistria problem, the EU recognizes that any overall solution can only be the outcome of a political process to which Brussels is, since late 2005, contributing through the so-called 5+2 negotiations (Ukraine, Moldova, Russia, Transnistria, OSCE plus the USA and the EU). In the view of one leading expert, this conflict is both the closest to the EU physically and the 'most solvable' (Popescu, 2005: 43). Although the EU has occasionally called for Russian withdrawal from Transnistria, Brussels has never really confronted Moscow over this issue. Javier Solana, in an uncharacteristic departure from EU policy in March 2006, appeared to argue, in an interview with Moldova's leading daily, that the Transnistria conflict was an internal affair between the two Moldovan parties, implying that it did not directly stem from Russian involvement (Socor, 2006). Sensitive and progressive handling of what is a many-sided dispute is the only solution. The EU border mission in Ukraine/Moldova is a significant practical move to improve regional relations in an area where eventual EU membership for both countries is possible. It is certainly a vibrant symbol of the EU's ability and desire to deploy civilian crisis management tools wherever they can serve a useful purpose. Ultimately, it is likely that an ESDP police mission to Moldova will become necessary.

Police missions

ESDP's greatest innovation has gradually emerged as that of the police mission. This reflects the considerable energy which has been committed to Civilian Capabilities in the context of the Civilian Headline Goal 2008 (Chapter 4). In post-conflict or crisis-management situations, the most urgent need is often for local security forces and above all for a highly professional police force. The EU has made a serious initial commitment in this regard both through deployment of police officers and through local police training schemes in Macedonia, Bosnia, Congo (Kinshasa) and Palestine. Furthermore, a Council Secretariat proposal was floated in 2004 to send a police mission to Darfur but the idea was abandoned after objections from both Khartoum and the African Union. This is a relatively new departure for the EU – previously trail-blazed by the UN and by OSCE – and one which is proving as necessary and pragmatic on the ground as it is politically symbolic of a new approach to security and stability. Police missions are 'at the forefront of the operationalisation of the civilian component of the ESDP' in terms of numbers of missions and personnel deployed (Merlingen and Ostrauskaitė, 2006). However, the EU's record to date is mixed at best.

The most high-profile of the five police missions mounted to date – as well as the most difficult and challenging – was ESDP's first-ever overseas mission, the EU Police Mission in Bosnia and Herzegovina (EUPM) first launched on 1 January 2003 and renewed with a modified mandate in November 2005 to run until December 2007. The mission took over from the United Nations International Police Task Force (IPTF) which had been assisting with policing in BiH since the Dayton Agreement in 1995. EUPM's terms of reference were to establish in BiH a sustainable, professional and multiethnic police service operating in accordance with best European and international standards. Under the guidance of the EU Special Representative (EUSR), Paddy Ashdown, EUPM is intended to support, advise and guide the preparation and implementation of police restructuring. In addition, it aims to improve, through proactive mentoring, monitoring and inspecting, police managerial and operational capacities, especially at the State level, in order to enhance BiH's capacity to fight organized crime. Most of Europe's drugs and sex-trade traffic as well as illegal immigration circuits operate via criminal networks out of the Balkans. The EUPM was also tasked with monitoring the exercise of political control over the police. At its height, the mission involved over 500 EU police officers and BiH officials from 34 countries including all EU member states except Denmark. The mission was the EU's first serious foray into the operationalization of *security sector reform*, a recent post-conflict state-building concept at the heart of the European Security Strategy (Osland, 2004: 546; Helly, 2006a). Officially, the EU claims a number of successes, including the transformation of the State Investigation and Protection Agency (SIPA) into an operational police agency with enhanced and executive powers to fight major and organized crime; solid development of other state-level institutions, in cooperation with the European Commission, not least the Ministry of Security (MoS) and the State Border Service (SBS); development of local ownership of the reform process through the establishment of the Police Steering Board, co-chaired by EUPM and local authorities; progress towards police reform with the EUPM playing a key advisory role.

Unfortunately, this self-congratulatory balance sheet is not shared by independent analysts of the EUPM record. The widely respected International Crisis Group, in a negative November 2005 report, considered that 'no matter what criteria are used to assess EUPM performance, the indicators are depressing'. It concluded that 'a weak mandate has been interpreted in the narrowest possible fashion, permitting it to avoid many responsibilities' (ICG, 2005b: 12). This verdict was reiterated in the EU's main weekly newspaper (Lyon, 2005). Kari Osland also drew negative conclusions from EUPM's record of addressing the challenges set by its own mission statement and drew attention to the lack of political will in Brussels to address the problem of Serb obfuscation (Osland, 2004: 557). The fundamental problem facing the EUPM – that of persuading the political authorities in BiH – and particularly the governing Serbian Democratic Party (SDS) in Republika Srpska (RS) – to cooperate with the EU was identified in the first independent study of EUPM, published even before it began its work (Nowak, 2003: 30). Part of the problem, however, also derives from shortcomings in the EU's conceptual understanding of the role of policing in post-conflict situations. Two specialists have offered a trenchant critique of the overall EU approach (Merlingen and Ostrauskaitè, 2006). They argued that a purely functional definition of policing (social peacekeeping or crime fighting) is inadequate and stress that policing is a 'form of social ordering work'. As such, it cannot be neutral but is geared to the protection or projection of a certain ideal of social order. In particular police aid operations involve the 'import' into a given social and political context of international norms which may not be appropriate and will always be difficult to impose. The EUPM mission statement stressed the need to ensure local ownership of the process which is essential for sustainability. However, it is also crucial to ensure that local ownership is not dominated by forces opposed to the overall process of security sector reform (Osland, 2004: 547). This ultimately proved to be the most difficult challenge for the EUPM. Overseas police missions by definition aim to bring about the transformation of the local by the international. They can involve two methods: *strengthening* (of local police forces) or *substitution* (direct policing by the international authorities). The former can be minimalist (responding to urgent needs through 'quick fixes') or maximalist (involving political institution-building). The main problem with the EUPM was that, from the outset – as was also the case with the other EU police missions we shall assess below – it was limited to strengthening rather than to substitution and that it focused on the high to medium police management levels rather than on that of community policing. The main procedure, *co-location*, involves the appointment of international advisors alongside their equivalents at the various levels. While analysts accept that the EUPM was more successful than its predecessor, the UN's IPTF, at commanding the respect of its Bosnian hosts, the absence of co-location at street level has ignored one basic precept of police reform: 'no reform can hope to succeed that does not enlist the support of the ordinary constables who construct the reality of the policing experience' (Merlingen and Ostrauskaitè, 2005: 231 citing Fielding 1988). Co-location also raised serious questions about the coherence of European 'best practice' in policing (given the considerable diversity of practice across the Union).

These are structural challenges which face any international policing mission – and from which previous missions by the UN and the OSCE also suffered.

However, in addition to these structural challenges, the EUPM also suffered from slowness in delivery, inadequate equipment, heterogeneity of police personnel, and turf wars between the mission itself and the efforts of the EUSR. Another analyst drew attention to the counter-productive effects of using the police as a transmission mechanism for the values the EU wants BiH to embrace, arguing that this undermined the basic functions of the police 'to the point that the institution is now in a parlous state'. She concluded, referring to both the UN and the EU missions, that while the BiH police forces were, in fall 2005, 'no longer part of the problem, they still cannot be regarded as part of the solution' (Celador, 2005: 372–3). But the biggest problem of all, according to the ICG, has been the lack of political will to take on the ruling party in RS. The EU considered, in 2005, that only two obstacles remained before BiH could begin negotiations on a Stabilization and Association Agreement (SAA): police reform and reform of the public broadcasting system. The criteria for police reform were stringent and unambiguous: exclusive competence for police matters at state level; no political interference in policing. Despite the fact that, according to the ICG report, no movement whatever was noticeable towards either of these elements in Republika Srpska (ICG, 2005: 7–12), the EU nevertheless went ahead, in October 2005, with negotiations on a SAA, arguing that the entire country should not suffer for the recalcitrance of one political party (the SDS). The ICG recommended that the EUPM should not have its mission extended but should be closed down completely and replaced by a far more robust mission, more along the lines of the initial UN-IPTF, whose mandate included working at local level, replacing corrupt or politically inspired police officers and generally being far more proactive in matters of police reform ([ICG 2005b: 14). For the EU, this ran counter to the key principle of local ownership. To some extent, the December 2004 arrival in BiH of the military mission EUFOR-*Althéa* (see below) revitalized the fight against organized crime and successfully engaged in areas where EUPM had been reluctant to tread. But the mixed balance-sheet which hangs over EUPM does not augur well for the EU's other police missions.

These have, to date, been present in three very different countries – FYROM, Congo and Palestine. The original mission in FYROM (Operation *Proxima*) succeeded the EU's first military mission, *Concordia* in the same country. It ran from December 2003 to December 2005 and was replaced by a follow-up mission, the EU Police Advisory Team (EUPAT) with a six-month mandate from 15 December 2005 to 14 June 2006. The remit of these two missions was similar in one sense to that of the EUPM (mentoring, monitoring and advising the Macedonian police, fighting organized crime and promoting European police standards). But it was also different in that it was tasked with supporting the government's police reform measures. Although *Proxima* involved 200 EU police officers from 25 countries, EUPAT was scaled down to 30 officers in 2006. Both operations epitomised the 'dual track' approach of the EU whereby the European Commission supports long-term structural change in the Ministry of the Interior and Police Forces, while the Council, through ESDP, tackles 'urgent needs' in support of the political Framework Agreement. *Proxima* involved 28 separate programmes covering all functions in the uniformed police, criminal police, the Department for State Security and Counter-Intelligence, and internal control (police misconduct complaints). The mission was supplemented by a team of border control police officers at major border crossings and international airports. It encountered many problems of implementation and operationality, largely deriving from the fact that it was the latest arrival after a host of international bodies with competing mandates, some of which were politically driven. The FYROM government effectively asked for the mission to be terminated fearing that its very presence would compromise the country's chances of accelerated progress towards EU membership. Other problems stemmed from encrusted interagency turf battles and institutional incoherence (Ioannides, 2006: 76–82). In short, *Proxima* and EUPAT basically offered the EU ample opportunity to learn from their mistakes in the policing business.

In the Democratic Republic of Congo (DRC), the EU has a multi-faceted record of attempts to consolidate the peace process. The military mission *Artemis* (see below) in 2003 prevented a major humanitarian disaster in Ituri province and paved the way for the UN force MONUC. The EU was also instrumental in establishing a special Congolese police force in

Kinshasa (the Integrated Police Unit – IPU) with the specific remit of protecting the personnel, institutions and infrastructure of the transitional government. The COPS decided in December 2003 on a three-strand approach involving the establishment of a training centre in Kinshasa, the training programme itself, and follow-up monitoring and mentoring. The subsequent establishment of EUPOL-Kinshasa, launched in December 2004, has involved the monitoring, mentoring and advising of the IPU in the period during the run-up to the Congolese elections in July 2006. The mission was extended in November 2005, given the likelihood of continuing electoral uncertainty until late 2006, and was due to run until December 2006. The members of the mission – 28 officers from France, Portugal, Italy, Netherlands, Belgium, Canada and Turkey – have also been active participants in the Reflection Group for the Reform and Reorganization of the Congolese National Police. They operate on the basis of co-location at senior management level, thus offering to some extent the same structural problems that were noted above with respect to EUPM. However, in the case of Congo, it is more appropriate to limit the EU presence to the higher echelons in view of the likely difficulties of culture clash if European police constables were to attempt to co-locate with Congolese officers on the beat in major African cities. This was the first ESDP civil mission for crisis management in Africa, working in tight cooperation with the UN's MONUC force and marks an important step in relations between the EU and the UN (Grevi, Lynch and Missiroli, 2005). There is no doubt that the mission played a role in the smooth running of the Congolese elections on 30 July 2006. The cost to the EU (less than €5 million) is insignificant. EUPOL-Kinshasa is a mission with equal components of practical value-added and political symbolism.

Finally, on 14 November 2005, the Council established an EU Police Mission (EUPOL COPPS-Palestine) in the Palestinian Territories under the aegis of ESDP. This forms part of the EU's major effort to bolster the Palestinian National Authority (PNA) which has seen the Union emerge as the majority bank-roller of the embryonic Palestinian state. The EU is also present in the region with a Commission Delegation to Israel in Tel Aviv and a Commission Technical Assistance Office for the West Bank and Gaza based in Jersusalem. The EU Special Representative for the Middle East Peace Process, Marc Otte, was formerly Head of the

ESDP Task Force in Javier Solana's Policy Unit. The operational phase started on 1 January 2006 with an initial duration of three years. The EUPOL COPPS has a long-term reform focus and aims to provide enhanced support to the Palestinian Authority in establishing sustainable and effective policing arrangements. It consists of two parallel tracks, an operational plan (material needs and infrastructure) and a transformational plan (reform of system and structure). Although the mission embarked on its remit with confidence and commitment, the Palestinian elections in late January 2006 created a hiatus through which it is difficult from a distance to discern any clear developments. The majority of the Palestinian security forces originate from the military wing of the PLO and are considered loyal to President Mahmoud Abbas. A power struggle immediately ensued between Abbas and Hamas in spring 2006 since these forces were technically under the control of the Prime Minister and the Interior Minister, both of which shifted to Hamas (Pirozzi, 2006: 6). The last official EU declaration on the mission came in the 12 June *Presidency Report on ESDP* to the European Council: 'The EU is keeping its activities in the Occupied Territories under review to ensure consistency with Quartet policy on assistance to the new Palestinian Authority' (p. 6). It is therefore impossible to make any pronouncements on its value or success.

The EU Gendarmerie (http://www.eurogendfor.org/home.htm)

The European Gendarmerie Force (EGF) is an initiative of 5 EU member states – France, Italy, Netherlands, Portugal and Spain – aimed at improving the EU's crisis management capability in sensitive areas requiring interface between military and police forces. It was officially inaugurated in January 2006 under the command of French Gendarmerie Brigadier-General Gérard Deanaz and was declared fully operational on 20 July 2006. Notionally, it can deploy up to 800 gendarmes in less than 30 days and embraces a force of 2,300. The EGF responds to the need rapidly to conduct the entire spectrum of civil security actions, either on its own or in parallel with a military intervention. It aims to facilitate the handling of critical situations that require management by police forces. Three distinct functions are envisaged. During the initial phase of an operation, the EGF could enter the theatre along with a military force to carry out police duties. In the transitional phase of a mission, it could act alone or in conjunction with a military force to facilitate cooperation with local and international police units. During the military disengagement phase, it would facilitate the handing over of responsibilities to civilian authorities. Its tasks cover the entire range of police operations, from traffic control to border patrols, from criminal investigations to training, from public surveillance to property protection. Based in Vicenza, Italy, the EGF HQ is now developing a comprehensive and coherent operational system. Although it has yet to be deployed, from mid-March until the end of April 2006, the EGF conducted its second Command Post exercise, in the framework of a comprehensive International Crisis Management involvement under the aegis of the European Union. The scenario simulated the collapse of police structures in a neighbouring state leading to the intervention of the EGF to carry out the full range of policing activities including both substitution and strengthening of the local force. EGF aims to provide the International Community with a valid and operational instrument for crisis management, first and foremost at the disposal of the EU, but also of other International Organizations, such as NATO, the UN and the OSCE and *ad hoc* coalitions

EU military operations

On 31 March 2003, the EU launched its first-ever military operation, a peace-keeping mission in the Former Yugoslav Republic of Macedonia (FYROM), taking over from a NATO force. It deployed 357 troops, from all EU states except Ireland and Denmark and from 14 additional nations, an average of 13 troops per participating state. Several member states provided one symbolic individual! In a small mountainous country, it succeeded in helping keep the peace between bands of lightly-armed irregulars and the Macedonian 'army', which boasts a defence budget less than half that of Luxembourg. This was an operation high in political symbolism and modest in terms of military footprint. The mission was challenged in early September 2003 by growing unrest in northern villages but the EU forces successfully assisted the Macedonian security forces in reestablishing order. By the end of the mission, it was clear that the biggest problem in Macedonia was no longer armed conflict but criminality – hence *Concordia* was succeeded on 15 December 2003 by the police operation *Proxima* (see above). Concordia's primary value was that it allowed the EU to test its recently agreed procedures covering every aspect of the mounting of a military operation, albeit a modest one, such as command and control, use-of-force policy, logistics, financing, and legal arrangements and memoranda of understanding with host nations (Messervy-Whiting 2003). It was also significant in that it was the first practical implementation of the Berlin Plus procedures (Mace, 2004; Abele, 2003). NATO and the EU had previously cooperated closely in FYROM, with Javier Solana and NATO Secretary General Lord Robertson jointly defusing in 2001 a potentially explosive stand-off between Albanian 'rebels' and the Macedonian authorities, the former using the leverage of the Stabilization and Association Agreement, the latter NATO forces. Thereafter, a succession of NATO missions (*Essential Harvest*, *Amber Fox* and finally *Allied Harmony*) managed the security situation and oversaw disarmament of irregulars. Each mission was overwhelmingly composed of EU forces and each involved fewer troops than its predecessor, *Allied Harmony* consisting of only 400 troops. From an operational standpoint, ESDP's *Concordia* could have deployed without the back-up of Berlin Plus. However, from a political perspective, the main EU Atlanticist nations insisted that the resolution of the Berlin Plus procedures should precede the mission. It was only when Berlin Plus was formally signed on 17 March that *Concordia* could deploy (two weeks later). In fact, NATO remained a major background presence. Although the COPS exercised political control over the mission, *Concordia* made use of NATO operational planning at SHAPE, while force HQ was at NATO HQ Skopje. In addition, an EU Command Element was located at NATO's AFSouth HQ in Naples, an extra level of command which was considered superfluous by some French officials (Gourlay, 2003: 5). This political disagreement within the EU was symptomatic of the internal differences over interpretation of Berlin Plus. In addition, the EU and NATO disagreed over border control in FYROM, the latter seeing it as a military issue and the former as a civilian responsibility (Mace, 2004: 483). Nevertheless, *Concordia* was deemed a successful operation by most commentators, although the ICG insisted there was 'no room for complacency' (ICG, 2003).

From June to September 2003, the EU launched its first-ever *autonomous* mission, *Artemis*, in the Democratic Republic of Congo. Operation *Artemis*, which was also the EU's first operation outside Europe and the first EU operation under Chapter VII of the UN Charter, offers even richer lessons about EU capabilities than *Concordia* (Cornish, 2004). The objective was to secure the area around Bunia in Ituri province which had been the scene of violent confrontations between Ugandan and Congolese armed forces, variously backed by a range of local tribal militias in the war which had convulsed the DRC since 1998. Over 50,000 people had been massacred in the area since 1999. The UN force in DRC, MONUC, proved unable to cope and Kofi Annan called for international assistance. France, backed by the UK, proposed an EU force, partly impelled by the dynamism of Franco-British cooperation in Africa since the mid-1990s, and partly as a way of helping heal the wounds of European disagreements over Iraq earlier in the year (Ulriksen, Gourlay and Mace, 2004: 511). The terms of reference of the mission, which deployed fully on 12 June 2003, included the stabilization of security, the improvement of the humanitarian situation in Bunia, protection of the airport and of the refugee camps and protection of UN personnel and other civilians in the area. This was explicitly regarded as an interim mission to allow the UN to assemble a more permanent force by September. An impartial assessment suggests that the mission, which involved rapid force projection to a distance of 6,500 kilometres into unknown and non-permissive terrain, was a success. France was the 'framework nation', supplying 1,785 of the 2,200 troops deployed. Sixteen other 'troop contributing nations' were involved, offering strategic air-lift (Germany, Greece, United Kingdom, Brazil and Canada) engineers (UK), helicopters (South Africa) and special-forces (Sweden). Operational planning was conducted from the French *Centre de Planification et de Conduite des Opérations* (CPCO) at Creil, to which were seconded officers from 13 other countries, thus demonstrating the potential for multi-nationalization of a national Permanent Joint Head Quarters. The operation, whose military details have been closely analysed (Cornish, 2004; Ulriksen *et al.*, 2004) demonstrated EU capacity for: rapid deployment (7 days after

UNSC Resolution 1484 on 30 May), logistics, a single command structure, well and appropriately trained forces, clear rules of engagement allowing for tactical evolution in the theatre, good incorporation of multinational elements, excellent inter-service cooperation, and adequate communications. NATO procedures were adopted throughout, even though the mission was conducted with no recourse to NATO assets or planning. The twin challenges of command chain and logistics were successfully met, even though deficiencies were noted in certain aspects of secure communications as well as transmissions, lift and manning at the force HQ (Ministère de la Défense 2004). *Artemis* demonstrated conclusively that the EU can undertake a peacekeeping operation, and on a significant scale, even at some distance from Europe.

The mission, despite its apparent success, nevertheless drew fire from a number of critics. Several NGOs, with observers on the ground, considered *Artemis* too limited in time and space. The International Crisis Group (which appears regularly to criticize EU missions) issued a report only days after *Artemis* deployed and judged the mission 'totally insufficient', arguing that only a mission which was 'more forceful', more 'geographically extensive' and 'maintained for much longer' could respond adequately to the crisis in Ituri ([ICG] 2003a). Similarly, a *Médecins sans Frontières* report castigated *Artemis* for having been 'unable to ensure genuine protection for civilians' (MSF, 2003: 14). These criticisms, which were also aimed at the UN itself, are based, to some extent on a misunderstanding of the terms of reference of the mission, whose mandate was strictly limited to the area around Bunia. As Ulriksen, Gourlay and Mace have chronicled, the EU forces engaged in high-intensity combat with the rebel militias, the Swedish commander stating that Bunia was the toughest challenge for Sweden's armed forces since the UN campaigns in Katanga in the 1960s (p. 519). However, critics charged that *Artemis* succeeded in demilitarizing Bunia only by driving the militia elsewhere, where they continued to massacre civilians. It is this accusation which lies at the heart of the NGO reports. Yet *Artemis* was not mandated to demilitarize the entire province of Ituri and can hardly be criticized for failing to do more than it was tasked to do. Another (minor) controversy surrounds the issue of whether or not *Artemis* can be seen as a precedent for future EU missions.

Cornish concluded that 'it is appropriate to regard [it] as a practical experiment in politico-military collaboration in the EU, from which to draw lessons for the broader ESDP' (Cornish, 2004: 19). Ulriksen, Gourlay and Mace concluded that the mission – the 'shape of things to come' – was indeed a precedent for EU intervention in Africa, especially in view of US reluctance to engage in that continent (pp. 521–3). Catherine Gégout, however, analyzing the mission from a strictly realist perspective, concluded that *Artemis* did not 'stem from a reaction to a crisis situation in Africa' but merely from a 'will to promote the EU's own image' (Gégout, 2005: 443). Since, in realist terms, it was clearly an aberration, it can only be explained as a 'one off'. For realists, ESDP continues to defy the rules of the international game . . .

The third EU military operation is more difficult both to evaluate and to fault. The transfer from NATO to the EU of responsibility for the Stabilization Force (SFOR) in Bosnia-Herzegovina, in December 2004 (Operation EUFOR-*Althea*), represented an even greater test of the EU's military muscle (http://www.euforbih.org/). The initial NATO force deployed in Bosnia-Herzegovina (IFOR, December 1995) had involved some 60,000 troops under the Dayton Agreement. This was scaled down repeatedly, reaching a total of 12,000 in the follow-up SFOR by January 2003. Projections for 2004 foresaw a further reduction to about 7,000 troops organized in ten battle-groups of around 750 soldiers each. Operation *Althéa* has been the EU's most ambitious military mission to date. In addition to stabilizing Bosnia-Herzegovina, *Althéa* allowed the EU to experiment with large-scale helicopter manoeuvres, to combat drug-running, to organize the voluntary surrender of small arms, and to undertake liaison and observation team (LOT) activities, peace support training schemes, and psychological operations (see Box 7.2). EU forces were drawn from 22 member states as well as from 11 non-EU states, including Morocco. The EU operates under the 'Berlin Plus' procedures agreed with NATO. *Althéa* had clear and explicit objectives. In the short term, the challenge was to ensure a seamless transition from SFOR and to maintain a secure environment for the implementation of the Dayton Peace Agreement (Annexes 1-A and 2 of Dayton). In the medium term, the mission aimed to help BiH move towards EU membership, through the signature of a Stabilization and

Box 7.2 Operation Althéa: types of military mission

- Door to door collection of small arms and munitions, harvesting several thousand guns and hand-grenades, hundreds of thousands of rounds of ammunition and assorted mines, anti-tank rockets and explosives. All weapons destroyed.
- Deterring and controlling illicit trafficking in fuel and logging – the most extensive and best organized criminal activity in the Balkans.
- Provision of engineering teams to train and monitor the de-mining activities of the BiH armed forces.
- The use of Liaison Observation Teams (LOTs) in the villages to establish trust with the local population through established residence, visibility and constructive involvement with communities and the local police.
- Border controls to reduce smuggling, people trafficking and international criminal activities.
- Collaboration with the Integrated Police Unit to help arrest individuals wanted by the International Criminal Court. To date, however, this has not netted the two most wanted suspects, former Bosnian Serb leader Radovan Karadzic and Serb General Radko Mladic.

Association Agreement; and in the long term to create a stable, viable and multi-ethnic BiH working harmoniously with its neighbours. Operation *Althéa* is explicitly framed as part of a broader EU policy towards the Balkans which deploys a wide range of political, economic, commercial, cultural and police instruments to smooth transition towards eventual EU membership. The essential difference between NATO's SFOR and *Althéa* was that the former represented 'emergency surgery' as the last stage of the road from Dayton, while the latter represented 'rehabilitation' as the first step on the road to Brussels. As such, *Althéa* was far more of a civil–military mix than a purely military operation. The operation exemplified the increasing demands on European soldiers for a broad range of skills and training.

The first Force Commander of *Althéa*, UK Major General David Leakey, admitted to being somewhat bemused to find that his main orders from Javier Solana appeared to be essentially non-military. One of his 'key military tasks' was to support the HR's Mission Implementation Plan, and one of his 'key supporting task' was to help the fight against organized crime. Above all, *Althéa* was to be 'new and distinct' and to 'make a difference' (Leakey, 2006: 61–2). The Mission Implementation Plan comprised four elements (economy, rule of law, police and defence reform) which, at first sight, seemed ill-suited for military leverage. Leakey soon realized that the challenge in BiH was that of adopting a holistic approach to the remaining obstacles to reform, which included smuggling, customs/tax avoidance and general corruption as obstacles to economic governance, political obfuscation and corruption (particularly in Republika Srpska) as well as extensive crime networks which were retarding the rule of law, and the protection of war criminals which was obstructing defence reform. At first, *Althéa's* involvement in the fight against crime was not openly welcomed by the EUPM which sensed a turf battle. However, the military mission's approach involved detecting and surrounding criminal activities before handing the situation over to the BiH authorities supported by the EUPM. Leakey claims that all of these operations were relatively successful and that *Althéa* worked harmoniously with all the EU agencies in Bosnia (the EU Presidency, EUPM, EU Monitoring Mission, the EC's Customs and Fiscal Assistance Office and the European Commission Delegation as well as the EUSR – Paddy Ashdown) as well as with the relevant BiH authorities (Leakey, 2006: 63–8). In this way, what began as a purely military mission was transformed into a complex civil–military project in which the entire range of EU instruments was brought to bear in a holistic approach. To date, there have been no independent analyses of the *Althéa* mission and it is too early to offer a critical appraisal. There has been critical comment on the overall approach of the EU in Bosnia – and in particular of the 'high-handed' proactivism of the EUSR Paddy Ashdown – who has been accused of ignoring the task of consensus-building among the three main constituencies in BiH and of imposing his own personal perspective on 'what I think is right' (Chandler, 2005). Whether such judgments are fair in the context of a highly complex and still largely encrusted stand-off between previously warring parties, history will eventually indicate. But at time of writing, *Althéa* appears to have carried out its mission with efficiency, adaptability and success. The force command was transferred in December 2005 to Major General Gian Marco Chiarini and in December 2006 to Admiral Hans-Jochen Witthauer. The mission is ongoing.

A fourth military operation under ESDP was finally launched in June 2006 in support of the United Nations mission in Congo (MONUC) during the crucial presidential election period (July to October). The mission, codenamed EUFOR RD Congo followed the model of *Artemis* in being an autonomous EU mission under Chapter VII of the United Nations. It comprised 2,000 EU troops under the operational command of German Lieutenant-General Karlheinz Viereck based at the Germany Permanent Joint HQ in Potsdam (the first time this PJHQ was used). Germany and France supplied two-thirds of the troops, the others coming from 16 European countries including Turkey. The force HQ was in Kinshasa under the command of French Major-General Christian Damay. An advance contingent of several hundred troops was deployed to Kinshasa and a reserve 'over the horizon' force of 1,200 was based in neighbouring Gabon, only to be called up in the event of troubles requiring their presence. The mission had a very limited remit: to support MONUC in stabilizing the country, to protect civilians in the area of deployment, to protect Kinshasa airport and to carry out whatever protection and rescue missions might prove necessary. The mission was to last four months from the date of the Congolese elections (30 July 2006).

From the outset, this ESDP mission courted controversy. The UN request for assistance in overseeing the elections was formulated in December 2005, but it was only in March 2006 that an initial EU answer was forthcoming. This is as compared with the seven days it took for the EU to agree to *Artemis*. Two main problems arose. The first was the reluctance of the UK to be involved, given its major deployments in Iraq and (increasingly) in Afghanistan. The second was the fact that France wanted to pressure Germany into leading this mission as a demonstration that the Franco-German partnership was still alive and well. Germany was very reluctant and initial reports suggested that Berlin had ruled out participation. Eventually, a deal was struck whereby, of the 780 German troops deployed, only 100 or so went to Kinshasa, the remainder forming part of the reserve in Gabon. Many criticisms of the mission were voiced. The first argued that the size of the force (1,000 maximum deployed in DRC itself) was inadequate given that the elections were nationwide in a country three times the size of France with 50,000 polling stations. This was surely 'tokenism' at its height? (Haine and Giegerich, 2006). Second, critics noted that the EU troops were overwhelmingly based in Kinshasa, which had essentially been pacified for some time. None was deployed to the eastern part of the country where troubles were likely to occur in towns such as Goma, Bukavu or Kisangani. Third, this tokenism was heightened by the stationing of the reserve force in Gabon. 'I've never understood what this force is doing', quipped presidential candidate Christophe Mboso, 'are the elections taking place in Gabon?' Fourth, critics noted that the mission would end at precisely the time when the troops might most be needed – after the announcement of the result. Military misadventures compounded these weaknesses. Soon after the force deployed, French military jets flying low over the compound of one of the candidates – ex-rebel leader Jean-Pierre Bemba – sparked a riot which left six Congolese civilians dead. The following day, a Belgian air-force drone, on its maiden flight, crashed into a house in Kinshasa, injuring five (Rettman, 2006). However, the elections did take place throughout the country practically without incident, although the extent to which this could be attributed to the EU force is subject to debate.

Unlike *Artemis*, EUFOR RD-Congo is unlikely to go down in the annals as an ESDP success story. Accusations that it was primarily intended to get some good coverage for the EU are hard to avoid. However, it was consciously framed as part of the EU's comprehensive approach to the DRC, which involved, in addition to *Artemis* and the Kinshasa police mission, a separate advisory and assistance mission for security sector reform, EUSEC RD Congo, launched in June 2005 for 12 months. EUSEC RD Congo had a staff of nine advisors from six EU countries, helping the Congolese army establish an efficient administrative structure, with solid finances and a reliable system for the payment of soldiers' wages (a major problem in the past with vast sums for 'ghost soldiers' being siphoned off into military leaders' bank accounts in Switzerland). In addition, the EU financed the Congolese elections to the tune of 80 per cent and was instrumental in shaping the Congolese constitution and legal framework. When taken together, the four EU missions in Congo do amount to a sizeable measure of assistance, even though many might have wished for the EU to assume a far more ambitious role in several crisis-ridden African countries.

These military operations were complemented in November/December 2005 and April 2006 by two significant EU-only military exercises (Milex 05 and EVAC 06) which focused, respectively, on the activation of a fully fledged EU Operation Headquarters and on that of an ambitious evacuation mission. A further exercise, scheduled for September/October 2006, focused on the development of procedures for a Comprehensive EU Crisis Management capability.

Conclusion

The 16 EU missions analysed above are too recent to allow for any comprehensive or (still less) definitive judgment on the operational aspects of ESDP. The fact that such missions have taken place 'on three continents', while significant in itself, does not amount to consecrating a global role for EU intervention. The bulk of the operations have been in the Western Balkans, which is surely the EU's most urgent priority neighbour, and a second area of focus has been crisis-ridden Africa (especially Congo), the source of increasingly heavy migratory pressure. One should not underestimate the scale and range of these missions, most of which have been put together with remarkable speed and, on the whole, efficiency. Together, they certainly amount to an important new development, from which the EU is learning all the time and going from strength to strength – while, in parallel, the Constitutional crisis is taken by many to spell paralysis. The EU has shown that it is taken seriously as an international partner by the United Nations and that its neighbours welcome and benefit from its involvement. It has also demonstrated its capacity to emerge – and grow – as a military actor. In general, there are a number of open questions (Grevi *et al.*, 2005). The first is the extent to which the operations will depend indefinitely on certain lead countries – with others playing bit parts. This is unlikely to prove sustainable over time. The second is the question of when and whether the EU will prove able to engage in a serious military mission at the level of high intensity combat. With the exception of *Artemis*, the EU's military muscle has not yet been seriously tested. Thirdly, there is the ongoing problem of financing of such missions, a technical issue which has been examined in detail by Antonio Missiroli (Missiroli, 2003a, 2006). Until sustainable budgetary instruments have been agreed, ESDP missions will remain highly experimental. Fourthly, there is an urgent need for far greater coherence in the implementation of ESDP. The various operations in Bosnia-Herzegovina, for instance, fall under the auspices of many different DGs in Brussels. Turf battles are legion and extremely prejudicial to the smooth running of the operation – a prime example is the clash of cultures between the administrative frameworks for EUPM and for EUFOR-*Althéa* in BiH (Orsini, 2006). Above all, the civil–military crisis management procedures in Brussels need drastic streamlining (Nowak, 2006: 139–40). Overseas missions will not work if they are micro-managed by committees. This structural reform of the ESDP process is without doubt the most crucial challenge ahead for an EU which wishes to intervene helpfully and effectively on the world stage.

Chapter 8

The Major Challenges Ahead

The EU's world in 2025

Officials whose job it is to carry out forward planning in the area of security and defence policy generally adopt a 15–20-year time-frame. This is a realistic perspective in which to detect fundamental shifts in the security environment and it is a necessary framework within which to conceive and implement the procurement of whatever weapons systems, armaments and other policy instruments might be thought to be appropriate to deal with those shifts. What is the world going to look like in 2025? What will be the long-term trends in key areas such as demography, economics, energy sources, the environment, and science and technology which will impact on the EU's security? What developments are likely in the main regions of the world – particularly among rising 'poles' such as China, India and Latin America – which will affect global balances? What type of operations is the EU likely to have to prepare for in the longer term and with what range of instruments? As this book was nearing completion, several substantial reports were published which attempted to answer precisely these questions (Gnesotto and Grevi, 2006; EDA, 2006c; SDA, 2006; Keohane, 2006). This chapter draws heavily on these reports, particularly that of the EU–ISS.

The first main point to stress is that, in relation to the rest of the world in 2025, each member state of the European Union will have interests which are practically indistinguishable from those of any other. The EU will increasingly be seen by the rest of the world, and will need to respond to it, as an ever more homogeneous entity. No major challenge to the EU's security is likely to derive from internal phenomena. This will be true even in the context of further enlargement since the criteria for membership demand the prior resolution of any potential conflicts of interest between member states. All major challenges to EU security will therefore come from outside the Union (Gnesotto and Grevi, 2006). Moreover, the world outside the EU will present a dual and paradoxical structure. It will be more interconnected, but also more disaggregated than today. It will be more interconnected in the sense that the impact of globalization will reach further and deeper into all parts of the world. But it will also be more disaggregated in two ways. First, globalization will affect different countries and different regions in different and unequal ways. Second, the rise of new regional poles will replace the somewhat artificial forms of the post-Cold War world's much discussed 'unipolarity'. Multipolarity will be the dominant feature of the world in 2025. The relative fortunes and security of the EU will therefore be affected in two different ways. Through greater global interconnectedness, developments everywhere will have an impact on the EU. But as a result of multipolarity, the EU may find itself making choices akin to those involved in traditional balance of power calculations.

For these reasons, it is also reasonable to formulate a second general point. Just as the major challenges will derive from outside the EU, none of those challenges can be satisfactorily met without some *collective* input from the EU. In a world structured by seven or eight significant poles, the capacity of individual nation-states in Europe (even large ones) to exercise direct influence on global or regional outcomes will be increasingly limited. To quote one key study '[l]ooking at the major economic, energy, environmental and demographic trends shaping the world to come, it is apparent that not making collective choices at the European level effectively amounts, over the long-term, to abdicating sovereignty' (Gnesotto and Grevi, 2006: 207). One of the main reasons behind European integration in the first place was the recognition that, *vis-à-vis* the United States, the member states of the EU would be likely to achieve far more in the key areas of trade, tariffs and competition policy if they operated as a single actor than if they behaved as a congeries of competing nations. This will be even more true – and in a broader range of policy areas – when the EU finds itself as one part of a complex multi-polar system in which a small number of 'big beasts' are vying for resources and influence.

It is the nature and evolution of this multipolar system which constitutes the third general point with respect to the security environment in 2025. Multipolarity can come in several different forms. Neo-realism, were it to escape its theoretical focus on the nation-state, would expect multipolarity to reflect the same basic conditions of anarchy which presided over the Westphalian system. In other words, given the absence of any overarching authority, a multipolar world made up of seven or eight poles would be unstable, conflict-prone and violent. The same balance of power logic which presided over the fate of Europe in the early modern period would thus be extended to the entire planet. Given Europe's shrinking resources and competitive edge (see below), this might not be a world in which the EU would be likely to win many battles. Another possibility for such a multipolar world would be the gradual emergence of a new form of bipolarity in which the so-called liberal democratic poles might find themselves pitted against the rest on either ideological or religious grounds. One such scenario sketched out by Samuel Huntington foresaw a global confrontation between, on the one hand, Europe, the USA, Russia and India and, on the other hand, China, Japan and most of the Islamic world (Huntington, 1996: 315). Other groupings might equally be imagined. Timothy Garton Ash foresees growing solidarity between states of the 'free world' in a complex and generous campaign to bring the benefits of democracy and open markets to all other states in the world (Garton Ash, 2004). Neo-realism argues that bipolar systems are the most stable. However, in a world bristling with nuclear and other weapons of mass destruction, this would not be a scenario which would offer much comfort to Europeans. It is therefore towards a third type of multipolarity that the EU should direct all its energies – a structure in which multi-polarity embraces multilateralism, in which all poles accept the basic constraints of international law and regulation and in which all are engaged in a serious effort to reverse the growing gap between rich and poor, included and excluded. If, in 2006, approximately one billion people on earth belong to 'rich' countries, two billion belong to countries trying to join the ranks of the rich, and three billion live in abject poverty, the respective figures for the nine billion inhabitants of the earth in 2025 are predicted to be two, three and four billion (Cohen, 2006). In other words, one billion more people will have joined the ranks of those for whom despair is a way of life.

Weaknesses and vulnerabilities

In short, the world will be smaller, more volatile and almost certainly more dangerous in 2025. The EU will have no alternative but to act collectively within it. The 'effective multilateralism' which underlies the EU's Security Strategy document speaks directly to the challenges of international order, in which the Union will interact with other regional bodies such as the African Union in Africa, ASEAN in Southeast Asia, Mercosur or the putative Association of Latin American States in South America, the UN and the IAEA in seeking to stem the proliferation of nuclear weapons. The EU will have every incentive to fashion a type of multipolarity which is consistent both with multilateralism and with collective security. One valuable asset of the EU in this regard is legitimacy, which some have foreseen as 'the hard currency of future international relations' (EU-ISS, 2006a: 198). Legitimacy is not a value which any nation or group of nations enjoys as of right – it is an attribute which is conferred on one actor through the recognition of others. The EU's habitual preference for multilateralism, international law, cultural diversity, negotiation and compromise will give it an edge in the process whereby multiple poles increasingly compete over both interests and values. The perceived legitimacy of the EU's positions among the other poles will be an important attribute in reaching agreements.

The world of 2025 will nevertheless be one in which the current strengths of the EU will have been significantly diminished. The economic strengths of the EU will be relatively weaker. China will have overtaken the EU as an overall economic giant and may even have overtaken the United States. India will have emerged as the world's third largest economy, overtaking Japan (Das, 2006). GDP will grow more slowly in the EU than in any of its major competitors. Job losses will continue to mount as companies step up 'offshoring' of both production and service activities. While key industries such as telecommunications, automobiles, engineering and aeronauticals are expected to remain competitive, the EU's recent edge in high-technology industries has already been eroded by competition from China and India. The EU's relatively low level of investment in research and development (1.93% of EU GDP, against 2.59% for the USA, 3.15% in Japan and 1.31% in China) makes the challenge of turning the EU, by 2010, into the 'most competitive knowledge-based economy in the world' – the so-called Lisbon target – impossible to meet (Murray and Wanlin, 2005). Globalization will therefore continue to pose challenges to the EU which will have an immediate effect on employment, income levels and general security. Social security and health budgets are predicted to rise considerably, leaving comparatively fewer resources for security and defence *per se*. At the same time, globalization will emerge as the most powerful factor shaping international politics (Friedman, 2005) and it will assume less Westernized, more plural and more local forms. As countries such as China, India, Russia and Brazil seek to join the world system instead of shunning it, they will, in their turn, have a growing influence over it, which can only redound to the comparative disadvantage of both the EU and the USA (Goldman Sachs, 2003).

Demographic trends will prove to be an additional – and worsening – problem for Europe. First, with the lowest fertility rates in the world (currently 1.5), the EU will simply not be producing enough descendants – either to fuel growth or to man the ranks of the armed and police forces required by ESDP (the recruitment pool of 16 to 30-year-olds will fall by over 15%). Secondly, with an ever-ageing population, the EU will be increasingly dependent on immigration to solve the pensions problems of an over-65 cohort numbering almost 50 per cent of that of the working population (15 to 64-year-olds) (European Commission, 2006). Projections for immigration suggest annual intakes over the entire period of between 600,000 and 1 million. A strategy will be required to identify the optimum sources of that manpower given the problems of forging a multicultural society. Such a policy will be all the more critical given the high fertility rates among the EU's southern neighbours. The population of Africa is set to expand over the next 20 years by almost 50 per cent (despite AIDS), rising to 1.3 billion. In the Middle East and North Africa (MENA), population growth will be almost as high and the prospects for employment among these burgeoning masses are poor at best. The situation will be rendered even more volatile as desertification and a deteriorating rural environment generate uncontrolled urbanization – estimated to be higher for the MENA region (70%) than for other parts of the world. These migratory pressures on the EU will be aggravated by the fact that other potential sources of employment for MENA labour – the states of the Gulf Cooperation Council – are being closed off. Foreign workers make up almost 90 per cent of the workforce in the United Arab Emirates and Qatar, and 60 per cent in Saudi Arabia and Bahrain (Gnesotto and Grevi, 2006: 23). A long-term EU security policy must include a strategic plan for the economic development and overall stabilization of Europe's southern neighbours.

Another major challenge for the EU will be energy security. Anticipated EU demand (+15%) will continue to grow faster than supply, with overall world demand in 2030 being 50 per cent higher than in 2006. Competition will intensify. Oil and natural gas will be the two largest sources for the EU. Twenty per cent of the EU's oil passes through the Straits of Hormuz and 12 per cent through the Malacca Straits, two of the most unstable waterways in the world. Fifty per cent of the EU's natural gas comes from one Russian company – Gazprom – which refuses to play by the rules of international trade. Dependency on energy imports will grow from 50 per cent in 2006 to 70 per cent in 2030, with imports of oil rising to 90 per cent and gas to 80 per cent (Willenborg, 2004: 15). This vulnerability will be exacerbated by the volatility of oil prices, given endemic instability in the major area of supply – the Middle East. Power generation is predicted to require an increase of around 50 per cent over the next 20 years, with the majority of that increase coming from gas supplies, largely from Russia. It is estimated that the EU will need to invest around €625 billion to meet this increased demand (Gnesotto and Grevi, 2006: 64). The political implications of this rising energy dependency are more significant than the technical challenges. The EU will be bidding in a global market where other players will have both more urgent demands and, increasingly, more global clout. China's consumption of oil is predicted to rise from 5.3 million barrels per day (2006) to 13.3 m.b.d (2030), and its consumption of gas from 36 billion to 157 billion cubic meters. Similar projections are made for India. The European Commission, in association with the International Energy Agency, has developed guidelines to avoid over-dependency on too few suppliers and to put in train measures to increase capacity, efficiency, transparency, diversity and emergency stocks (European Commission, 2006a; Mandil, 2006; Bahgat, 2006). But the security of the EU's energy supplies, in an increasingly competitive global market, will be a geo-strategic challenge of major proportions, particularly given serious uncertainties about the political future of the main oil suppliers – Saudi Arabia, Iran, Iraq and Algeria.

Closely associated with the problems of energy security will be the growing problems of international environmental sustainability. Over the period 2006 to 2025, no major disasters are predicted, although on current trends the Arctic ice-cap could disappear by 2060 (EEA, 2005). Global warming will affect European water resources with increasing droughts and decreasing river discharges, both factors having a deleterious effect on agricultural yield. During the 2003 heatwaves, both France and Austria suffered a 30 per cent decrease in crop yield. The EU is committed under the Kyoto protocol to reduce its greenhouse emissions to 8 per cent below the 1990 figure by 2010. Current projections suggest that there will actually be an increase by 2010 of 3 per cent and by 2030 of 5 per cent. Greenhouse emissions from developing countries will represent a much greater attack on the environment than that presented by the EU. None of these trends points towards a more stable world. To quote Gnesotto and Grevi:

> In short, looking ahead to 2025, the world will be more populated, more exploited, more arid and more polluted than it is today. In other words, it will become a far less hospitable place. The wellbeing of billions of people will be put under more or less severe strain . . . more efforts will need to be made to deliver 'global public goods' to those in need, whose absolute numbers will expand. These include, among others, access to health and education and benefiting from a clean environment. In other words, a viable long-term security strategy must focus on prevention across the different dimensions of external relations and reflect the notion of comprehensive security traditionally upheld by the European Union and outlined by the European Security Strategy. (Gnesotto and Grevi, 2006: 192)

Troublesome neighbours?

Europe's immediate neighbourhood in 2025 will be even more volatile and less stable than in 2006. Russia remains an unpredictable partner, one whose leaders, according to one expert, 'have given up on becoming part of the West and have started creating their own Moscow-centered system' (Trenin, 2006). Lack of industrial diversification, an ill-defined private sector, the dominance of the energy sector, rampant social problems, declining demography, limited and reversible elements of democracy, and vast social inequalities and imbalances combine to make Russia a weak neighbour which arguably offers Europe less long-term security than when it was a strong one. The EU's dependency on Russian energy sources is likely to be exacerbated by competing demands for those resources from other global players, thus heightening the EU's vulnerability. Strategic cooperation between China and Russia – most notably via the recently created Shanghai Cooperation Organization, grouping China, Russia, Kazakhstan, Kyrgyzstan, Tajikistan and Uzbekistan – could develop either into a trading bloc or, in a worst case scenario, into a military alliance challenging NATO for supremacy (Antonenko, 2006). Russia was initially very keen to be involved with ESDP, which it tended to see as a way of driving a wedge between the EU and the USA. In recent years, that interest has subsided and the notion of security cooperation between the EU and Russia has tended to concentrate exclusively on energy policy.

The Middle East, which, assuming Turkish membership of the Union, will become an immediate neighbour before 2020, is arguably the least stable region on earth. The Israel–Palestine conflict will continue to overshadow and affect other theatres of instability in the area. Over the next 20 years, the political viability of the areas currently covered by Iraq, Saudi Arabia, Lebanon, Syria and Jordan will continue to be called into question by the long-term effects of the chaotic great power carve-up of the former Ottoman Empire after the First World War (Haass, 2006). Ironically, Iran – which figures as part of George W. Bush's 'axis of evil' – is probably the most stable state in the region. The EU is already faced with the massive dilemma of coping with a hypothetical nuclear-armed Iran. The challenge such a prospect poses is not necessarily so dramatic in and of itself. Some American analysts are confident that a nuclear Iran can be contained and that the key strategic questions for the future are how to nudge Iran towards a policy of defining nuclear weapons exclusively as defensive systems, and how to persuade Iran not to spread its capabilities further a-field (Schake and

Yaphe, 2001: ix). But from a European perspective, an Iranian bomb would be almost certain to spark a proliferation race in the region, with Egypt, Turkey and possibly even Syria trying hard to get in on the action. This is a challenge which Javier Solana has been tackling on an almost daily basis since 2005. European solutions to the problem may ultimately differ from US solutions.

Turkish membership of the EU would radically transform the strategic challenges facing ESDP. If the EU's immediate borders ceased to lie along the relatively benign line between an 'East' and a 'West' which runs through the areas traditionally demarcating the transition between Europe and Russia and instead move half way into Asia Minor, the prospect of 'instability on the borders' – which prompted Tony Blair to argue in favour of further enlargement – will become critical. With Turkey inside the Union, the EU's immediate neighbours become some of the most turbulent areas in the world: Georgia, Armenia, Iran, Iraq, Syria. Lebanon will lie one hundred miles to the South and the Israeli-occupied Golan heights a further hundred miles beyond. To cope with this new geo-strategic environment, the EU would require far more numerous and more robust peace-keeping forces than it is currently anticipating. Some have suggested that Israeli membership of the European Union would be the best possible way of defusing the never-ending stand-off between Israel and Palestine (Asmus and Jackson, 2005). A December, 2003 poll revealed that a majority of Israelis desire membership for their state: 60 per cent support the idea of Israeli membership in the European Union, and a further 25 per cent 'tend to support' the idea (European Commission, 2004). Analysts have looked into the long-term prospects of EU–Israeli security and defence cooperation and formulated proposals for institutionalized security dialogue, interoperability, cooperation in defence research and development, and growing partnership in intelligence (Shapiro and Becker, 2004). Such developments, were they to become realities, would radically transform the entire Middle Eastern strategic landscape.

In North Africa, popular unrest as a result of inadequate social and economic progress, feeding into Islamic fundamentalism, will continue to undermine most regimes from Egypt to Morocco. The EU's 'Barcelona Process' of developing partnerships with the various countries of the entire Mediterranean area has been slowing down for a number of years and requires a major new re-launch. Sub-Saharan Africa, already the theatre of 80 per cent of the world's civil wars, and rife with state failures, is unlikely to become more stable in this period. Given its burgeoning demographic growth, migratory pressures on the EU, already very strong in 2006, will only grow stronger.

Finally, the EU will have to live, for the next 20 years, with a growing threat from terrorism. That threat is likely to come far less from the 'global' level exemplified by Al Qaeda. Philippe Errera identified 'three circles of threat' from Islamist terrorism (Errera, 2005) which are currently being confused and conflated in operationally unhelpful ways. The three circles identified by Errera are, first, the Al Quaeda leadership, which is progressively being 'degraded' and as such is less and less of a threat; second, locally based groups sharing some of Al-Quaeda's ideology but which remain 'territorialized' in important ways and therefore restricted to their areas of operation (Chechnya, Kosovo); third, *Jihadist* individuals or groups of individuals who should be considered 'home-grown bottom-up franchisees' of the greater Islamist cause. The July 2005 London bombers are the classic example of this latter circle. They are arguably the biggest problem of all, but they are also the one which does not directly call on the instruments of an external security or defence policy. Nevertheless, in seeking to define a coherent counter-terrorism policy for the next decades, the EU will have to work ever more closely with its major partners among the world's poles, all of which have an equal stake in eliminating the threat. Foremost among those poles, in this instance, will be the United States (Rees 2006).

Defence policy planning

Given this highly – and increasingly – unstable global and regional environment, what are the priorities and imperatives for security and defence policy planners? Two immediate issues have been identified by the European Defence Agency in its 2006 report: adapting to the changing role of force; and adapting to the technological revolution. It is a truism to say that the EU has turned its back on the use of military force in the Clausewitzian sense of 'the continuation of politics by other means'. There seems little doubt that the emerging European strategic culture will continue to rule out traditional notions of expeditionary warfare or military conquest as they were developed in Europe from the seventeenth century onwards. Quite apart from the fact that such approaches have been totally absent from the EU since its inception fifty years ago, modern communications and media technology also militate against them. The problems of legitimacy encountered by the world's only superpower in Vietnam and in Iraq have highlighted the very real limits to the use of naked military power. Politically, 'victory' is assured less by the application of military force than by the manner in which that force is applied. The use of military force is thus 'increasingly constrained by legal and policy considerations based on general international law and the law of armed conflict' (EDA, 2006c: 10). The EU as such is therefore highly unlikely to become involved in traditional state-to-state conflict.

This is not to say that the EU will not find itself, over the years, forced to make contingency plans for the development of high intensity war-fighting capacity in the context of a hypothetical peace-making intervention between two large contending armed forces. As we have seen in Chapter 4, while troops trained for high intensity warfare can easily 'step down' the intensity scale to deal with peace-keeping and humanitarian missions, forces trained only for the latter are incapable of assuming the former challenges. One future scenario foresees the EU's 'first war' as taking place in 2010, involving a major (30,000 troop) expedition in putting an end to a rapidly escalating war between Serbia and a recently independent Kosovo (Keohane, 2006). It is difficult to imagine that, when faced with the option of developing such a war-fighting force, EU military and political leaders will decide to mortgage their future intervention capacity by denying themselves access to such capabilities.

This is all the more true in that military technology and the development of 'smart' weaponry have conferred on advanced military powers (of which the USA and – to a much lesser extent – the EU are currently the only examples) such an advantage in the field that potential adversaries will have no prospect of prevailing. The predominant role of information technology in the application of military force has consequences for manpower (troops can be replaced by machines), for strike accuracy and precision (collateral damage can no longer be excused as the inevitable consequences of warfare) and for protection (deaths among combat forces will be constantly reduced). Yet, to stay abreast of this burgeoning technology will require vast networks of highly trained researchers working transnationally to combine expertise in an ever wider range of technological developments. It will also require considerable resource inputs which currently appear to be beyond the political tolerance of an EU likely to be subjected to massive demand for resources in other sectors. These major decisions on the *nature* of the EU's future armed forces will generate intense political debate across the member states.

These issues pose what in some ways is the most significant challenge of all, at the interface between the political and the military: rationalization both of procurement and of defence budgets across the EU. It is difficult to see how the EU, if it seeks to deliver on its ambitions to become a serious player in security and defence policy can put off indefinitely the challenge of rationalizing and even synthesizing the defence budgets of its member states. This poses the issue of military pooling and of specialization. How can a given nation-state be persuaded to concentrate its limited efforts on a narrow sector of the overall security project – say, the development of air-to-air refuelling – while leaving the air defences of its territorial space to the specialized air-force of another member state? There is an urgent need over the next 20 years to spend *more wisely* the $230 billion the EU-25 spent on 'defence' in 2004. A sum of money more than three times the defence budget of the second biggest military spender on earth (Russia at $65,200 bn) and equivalent to that of the *six* next biggest spenders put together (Russia, China, Japan, Saudi Arabia, India, South Korea) ought to be more than enough to meet the limited military ambitions the EU has so far set itself. How much longer can the EU afford to field 25 armies, 21 air forces and 18 navies? Such ongoing military questions cannot be disconnected from the overall problem of strategic coordination between ESDP and NATO. As the latter seeks to become a global alliance, incorporating distant partners and eventual members such as Japan, Australia, New Zealand and, who knows, maybe also South Africa and India, such developments will have major consequences for the EU's own evolution as a strategic player.

How will all this affect the future of ESDP operations? The

working assumption in Brussels is that future ESDP missions will be 'expeditionary, multi-national and multi-instrument' (EDA, 2006c: 13). Their purpose will be to demonstrate EU political will to contribute to the resolution of crises. As often as not, forces will be deployed not in order to participate in battles already raging, but in order to prevent conflict from breaking out. The missions will typically involve the full range of instruments at the disposal of the Union, usually in association with other inter-governmental and non-governmental organizations. The strictly military dimension to ESDP missions is unlikely to be the most important. The lessons learned in the Balkans, Afghanistan and the Middle East over the past 15 years are incontrovertible. 'Success' cannot be measured in terms of initial military inputs, but in terms of eventual political outcomes. These will require close attention to the finer points of nation-building – promotion of human rights, rule of law, security sector reform and good governance. The instruments required for these approaches will be an integral part of ESDP missions. While access to information will be an increasing *sine qua non* for overseas missions, so too will it empower adversaries. Some argue that cyberspace has become 'a new common environment . . . analogous to the sea in previous centuries' (EDA, 2006c: 14). Missions will need to factor in the requirement of responding to asymmetrical counter-measures which will demand creative adaptability across the range of policy instruments.

Current planning assumptions for the next 20 years, formulated by the European Defence Agency, involve concentration on four strategic 'enablers': Synergy, Agility, Selectivity and Sustainability. All of these features will take EU forces further down the same road as that already taken by the US military. **Synergy** involves the growing integration of land, air, space and maritime forces (often referred to in the jargon as 'jointery') using a combination of smart weaponry, real-time intelligence and focussed logistics to produce maximum effects with minimum collateral damage. This will require the EU to commit resources to high technology features such as stealth, signature reduction and thermal masking. **Agility** refers to the growing need for rapidity of reaction, the swift creation of an appropriate 'force package' (troops from different services and equipped with the necessary instruments) and deployability – involving forces probably drawn from a wide range of countries. Such forces will probably have to work alongside other international organizations such as the UN and NATO, with the capacity to operate at will across the entire theatre of operations, switching seamlessly from open country combat to urban combat. **Selectivity** implies the capacity to choose between a range of different instruments for carrying the offensive to the adversary. In particular, it will involve the development of 'non-kinetic' capabilities such as computer network attack, electromagnetic or directed-energy capacity, military deception and psychological operations, all designed to limit lethality while disabling the opposition. **Sustainability** implies short-circuiting an adversary's ability to impede or to deny both access and, particularly, continued supply to the forces on the ground. The buzz-word here is 'sustainment pipelines', involving secure logistics linkages between support elements and combat elements. Political sustainability also implies maximum attention to force protection (EDA, 2006c: 16–19). Public opinion in EU member states will have limited tolerance for significant numbers of casualties. These features will all require significant developments in the fields of knowledge exploitation and knowledge management (turning data into actionable information), interoperability (the use of common equipment across a range of international force units), manpower balance calculations (reducing dependency on manpower and increasing the role of technology) and rapid procurement of new state of the art equipment. It is also clear that the EU's remaining defence industries will have to compete with US industry on the terms set by the latter – particularly in investment, research and development and synergizing between civilian and military technology. The 'new thinking' which has emerged from the activities of the newly established (2005) European Defence Agency is unequivocal. In order to carry out the military tasks which will be required of it in the year 2025, the EU is – like it or not – going to have to become more and more comparable to the US military. This is a message which will be welcomed in some countries and vigorously rejected in others. A debate is being launched about the type of military force that the European Union and its member states will be able to deploy in 20 years; that debate will be ongoing throughout the entire period.

Continuing political-cultural challenges

Finally, a number of major challenges face the EU on the political and normative/cultural fronts. First, on the political front, the main challenge is clear: how to move towards ever-greater collective European efficiency in the security and defence sector while retaining as much essential national sovereignty as possible. Can the EU-27 accept a *de facto* leadership role in ESDP on the part of a small number of member states – three in some scenarios (UK, France and Germany), up to six in other scenarios (UK, France, Germany, Italy, Spain, Poland)? How will the big-states/small-states dichotomy work out? Will political ownership and control of the ESDP project necessarily move – progressively – from the national capitals towards more centralizing agencies in Brussels? How compatible would this be with further EU enlargement? Secondly, these questions feed into the cultural frame we examined in Chapter 6. Will the EU continue to refine its distinctive civil-military footprint and consolidate its position as a *sui generis*, unprecedented international actor? Will the different cultural imperatives of countries like Ireland, Sweden, France, Estonia and Britain manage to synthesize in a collective and universally accepted norm? Or will ESDP be forced, by the very scale and growing ambition of its project, to morph into a small-scale version of the United States. Will EU leaders make a real effort to educate their publics about the project, and will the publics gradually internalize what is essentially an external instrument? Given the underlying significance attached in this book to 'events', I shall not attempt to argue for a particular pathway. But it is hard to see how the EU can avoid making choices in favour of ever-greater security and defence coordination and even integration: what I called earlier coordigration. By the time a second edition of this book is called for, some of the answers to these questions may be becoming clearer.

Appendix

A Secure Europe in a Better World: European Security Strategy*

Introduction

Europe has never been so prosperous, so secure nor so free. The violence of the first half of the 20th Century has given way to a period of peace and stability unprecedented in European history.

The creation of the European Union has been central to this development. It has transformed the relations between our states, and the lives of our citizens. European countries are committed to dealing peacefully with disputes and to co-operating through common institutions. Over this period, the progressive spread of the rule of law and democracy has seen authoritarian regimes change into secure, stable and dynamic democracies. Successive enlargements are making a reality of the vision of a united and peaceful continent.

The United States has played a critical role in European integration and European security, in particular through NATO. The end of the Cold War has left the United States in a dominant position as a military actor. However, no single country is able to tackle today's complex problems on its own.

Europe still faces security threats and challenges. The outbreak of conflict in the Balkans was a reminder that war has not disappeared from our continent. Over the last decade, no region of the world has been untouched by armed conflict. Most of these conflicts have been within rather than between states, and most of the victims have been civilians.

As a union of 25 states with over 450 million people producing a quarter of the world's Gross National Product (GNP), and with a wide range of instruments at its disposal, the European Union is inevitably a

---

* Document proposed by Javier Solana and adopted by the Heads of State and Government at the European Council in Brussels on 12 December 2003.

global player. In the last decade European forces have been deployed abroad to places as distant as Afghanistan, East Timor and the DRC. The increasing convergence of European interests and the strengthening of mutual solidarity of the EU makes us a more credible and effective actor. Europe should be ready to share in the responsibility for global security and in building a better world.

I The security environment: global challenges and key threats

Global challenges

The post Cold War environment is one of increasingly open borders in which the internal and external aspects of security are indissolubly linked. Flows of trade and investment, the development of technology and the spread of democracy have brought freedom and prosperity to many people. Others have perceived globalisation as a cause of frustration and injustice. These developments have also increased the scope for non-state groups to play a part in international affairs. And they have increased European dependence – and so vulnerability – on an interconnected infrastructure in transport, energy, information and other fields.

Since 1990, almost 4 million people have died in wars, 90% of them civilians. Over 18 million people world-wide have left their homes as a result of conflict. In much of the developing world, poverty and disease cause untold suffering and give rise to pressing security concerns. Almost 3 billion people, half the world's population, live on less than 2 Euros a day. 45 million die every year of hunger and malnutrition. AIDS is now one of the most devastating pandemics in human history and contributes to the breakdown of societies. New diseases can spread rapidly and become global threats. Sub-Saharan Africa is poorer now than it was 10 years ago. In many cases, economic failure is linked to political problems and violent conflict.

Security is a precondition of development. Conflict not only destroys infrastructure, including social infrastructure; it also encourages criminality, deters investment and makes normal economic activity impossible. A number of countries and regions are caught in a cycle of conflict, insecurity and poverty.

Competition for natural resources – notably water – which will be aggravated by global warming over the next decades, is likely to create further turbulence and migratory movements in various regions.

Energy dependence is a special concern for Europe. Europe is the world's largest importer of oil and gas. Imports account for about 50% of energy consumption today. This will rise to 70% in 2030. Most energy imports come from the Gulf, Russia and North Africa.

Key threats

Large-scale aggression against any Member State is now improbable. Instead, Europe faces new threats which are more diverse, less visible and less predictable.

Terrorism: Terrorism puts lives at risk; it imposes large costs; it seeks to undermine the openness and tolerance of our societies, and it poses a growing strategic threat to the whole of Europe. Increasingly, terrorist movements are well-resourced, connected by electronic networks, and are willing to use unlimited violence to cause massive casualties.

The most recent wave of terrorism is global in its scope and is linked to violent religious extremism. It arises out of complex causes. These include the pressures of modernisation, cultural, social and political crises, and the alienation of young people living in foreign societies. This phenomenon is also a part of our own society.

Europe is both a target and a base for such terrorism: European countries are targets and have been attacked. Logistical bases for Al Qaeda cells have been uncovered in the UK, Italy, Germany, Spain and Belgium. Concerted European action is indispensable.

Proliferation of weapons of mass destruction is potentially the greatest threat to our security. The international treaty regimes and export control arrangements have slowed the spread of WMD and delivery systems. We are now, however, entering a new and dangerous period that raises the possibility of a WMD arms race, especially in the Middle East. Advances in the biological sciences may increase the potency of biological weapons in the coming years; attacks with chemical and radiological materials are also a serious possibility. The spread of missile technology adds a further element of instability and could put Europe at increasing risk.

The most frightening scenario is one in which terrorist groups acquire weapons of mass destruction. In this event, a small group would be able to inflict damage on a scale previously possible only for States and armies.

Regional conflicts: Problems such as those in Kashmir, the Great Lakes Region and the Korean Peninsula impact on European interests directly and indirectly, as do conflicts nearer to home, above all in the Middle East. Violent or frozen conflicts, which also persist on our borders, threaten regional stability. They destroy human lives and social and physical infrastructures; they threaten minorities, fundamental freedoms and human rights. Conflict can lead to extremism, terrorism and state failure; it provides opportunities for organised crime. Regional insecurity can fuel the demand for WMD. The most practical way to tackle the often elusive new threats will sometimes be to deal with the older problems of regional conflict.

State failure: Bad governance – corruption, abuse of power, weak institutions and lack of accountability – and civil conflict corrode States from within. In some cases, this has brought about the collapse of State institutions. Somalia, Liberia and Afghanistan under the Taliban are the best known recent examples. Collapse of the State can be associated with obvious threats, such as organised crime or terrorism. State failure is an alarming phenomenon, that undermines global governance, and adds to regional instability.

Organised crime: Europe is a prime target for organised crime. This internal threat to our security has an important external dimension: cross-border trafficking in drugs, women, illegal migrants and weapons accounts for a large part of the activities of criminal gangs. It can have links with terrorism.

Such criminal activities are often associated with weak or failing states. Revenues from drugs have fuelled the weakening of state structures in several drug-producing countries. Revenues from trade in gemstones, timber and small arms, fuel conflict in other parts of the world. All these activities undermine both the rule of law and social order itself. In extreme cases, organised crime can come to dominate the state. 90% of the heroin in Europe comes from poppies grown in Afghanistan – where the drugs trade pays for private armies. Most of it is distributed through Balkan criminal networks which are also responsible for some 200,000 of the 700,000 women victims of the sex trade world wide. A new dimension to organised crime which will merit further attention is the growth in maritime piracy.

Taking these different elements together – terrorism committed to maximum violence, the availability of weapons of mass destruction, organised crime, the weakening of the state system and the privatisation of force – we could be confronted with a very radical threat indeed.

II Strategic objectives

We live in a world that holds brighter prospects but also greater threats than we have known. The future will depend partly on our actions. We need both to think globally and to act locally. To defend its security and to promote its values, the EU has three strategic objectives:

Addressing the threats

The European Union has been active in tackling the key threats.

- It has responded after 11 September with measures that included the adoption of a European Arrest Warrant, steps to attack terrorist financing and an agreement on mutual legal assistance with the U.S.A. The EU continues to develop cooperation in this area and to improve its defences.
- It has pursued policies against proliferation over many years. The Union has just agreed a further programme of action which foresees steps to strengthen the International Atomic Energy Agency, measures to tighten export controls and to deal with illegal shipments and illicit procurement. The EU is committed to achieving universal adherence to multilateral treaty regimes, as well as to strengthening the treaties and their verification provisions.
- The European Union and Member States have intervened to help deal with regional conflicts and to put failed states back on their feet, including in the Balkans, Afghanistan, and in the DRC. Restoring good government to the Balkans, fostering democracy and enabling the authorities there to tackle organised crime is one of the most effective ways of dealing with organised crime within the EU.

In an era of globalisation, distant threats may be as much a concern as those that are near at hand. Nuclear activities in North Korea, nuclear risks in South Asia, and proliferation in the Middle East are all of concern to Europe. Terrorists and criminals are now able to operate world-wide: their activities in central or southeast Asia may be a threat to European countries or their citizens. Meanwhile, global communication increases awareness in Europe of regional conflicts or humanitarian tragedies anywhere in the world.

Our traditional concept of self-defence – up to and including the Cold War – was based on the threat of invasion. With the new threats, the first line of defence will often be abroad. The new threats are dynamic. The risks of proliferation grow over time; left alone, terrorist networks will become ever more dangerous. State failure and organised crime spread if they are neglected – as we have seen in West Africa. This implies that we should be ready to act before a crisis occurs. Conflict prevention and threat prevention cannot start too early.

In contrast to the massive visible threat in the Cold War, none of the new threats is purely military; nor can any be tackled by purely military means. Each requires a mixture of instruments. Proliferation may be contained through export controls and attacked through political, economic and other pressures while the underlying political causes are also tackled. Dealing with terrorism may require a mixture of intelligence, police, judicial, military and other means. In failed states, military instruments may be needed to restore order, humanitarian means to tackle the immediate crisis. Regional conflicts need political solutions but military assets and effective policing may be needed in the post conflict phase. Economic instruments serve reconstruction, and civilian crisis management helps restore civil government. The European Union is particularly well equipped to respond to such multifaceted situations.

Building security in our neighbourhood

Even in an era of globalisation, geography is still important. It is in the European interest that countries on our borders are well-governed. Neighbours who are engaged in violent conflict, weak states where organised crime flourishes, dysfunctional societies or exploding population growth on its borders all pose problems for Europe.

The integration of acceding states increases our security but also brings the EU closer to troubled areas. Our task is to promote a ring of well governed countries to the East of the European Union and on the borders of the Mediterranean with whom we can enjoy close and cooperative relations.

The importance of this is best illustrated in the Balkans. Through our concerted efforts with the US, Russia, NATO and other international partners, the stability of the region is no longer threatened by the outbreak of major conflict. The credibility of our foreign policy depends on the consolidation of our achievements there. The European perspective offers both a strategic objective and an incentive for reform.

It is not in our interest that enlargement should create new dividing lines in Europe. We need to extend the benefits of economic and political cooperation to our neighbours in the East while tackling political problems there. We should now take a stronger and more active interest in the problems of the Southern Caucasus, which will in due course also be a neighbouring region.

Resolution of the Arab/Israeli conflict is a strategic priority for Europe. Without this, there will be little chance of dealing with other problems in the Middle East. The European Union must remain engaged and ready to commit resources to the problem until it is solved. The two state solution – which Europe has long supported – is now widely accepted. Implementing it will require a united and cooperative effort by the European Union, the United States, the United Nations and Russia, and the countries of the region, but above all by the Israelis and the Palestinians themselves.

The Mediterranean area generally continues to undergo serious problems of economic stagnation, social unrest and unresolved conflicts. The European Union's interests require a continued engagement with Mediterranean partners, through more effective economic, security and cultural cooperation in the framework of the Barcelona Process. A broader engagement with the Arab World should also be considered.

An international order based on effective multilateralism

In a world of global threats, global markets and global media, our security and prosperity increasingly depend on an effective multilateral system. The development of a stronger international society, well functioning international institutions and a rule-based international order is our objective.

We are committed to upholding and developing International Law. The fundamental framework for international relations is the United Nations Charter. The United Nations Security Council has the primary responsibility for the maintenance of international peace and security. Strengthening the United Nations, equipping it to fulfil its responsibilities and to act effectively, is a European priority.

We want international organisations, regimes and treaties to be effective in confronting threats to international peace and security, and must therefore be ready to act when their rules are broken.

Key institutions in the international system, such as the World Trade Organisation (WTO) and the International Financial Institutions, have extended their membership. China has joined the WTO and Russia is negotiating its entry. It should be an objective for us to widen the membership of such bodies while maintaining their high standards.

One of the core elements of the international system is the transatlantic relationship. This is not only in our bilateral interest but strengthens the international community as a whole. NATO is an important expression of this relationship.

Regional organisations also strengthen global governance. For the European Union, the strength and effectiveness of the OSCE and the Council of Europe has a particular significance. Other regional organisations such as ASEAN, MERCOSUR and the African Union make an important contribution to a more orderly world.

It is a condition of a rule-based international order that law evolves in response to developments such as proliferation, terrorism and global warming. We have an interest in further developing existing institutions such as the World Trade Organisation and in supporting new ones such as the International Criminal Court. Our own experience in Europe demonstrates that security can be increased through confidence building and arms control regimes. Such instruments can also make an important contribution to security and stability in our neighbourhood and beyond.

The quality of international society depends on the quality of the governments that are its foundation. The best protection for our security is a world of well-governed democratic states. Spreading good governance, supporting social and political reform, dealing with corruption and abuse of power, establishing the rule of law and protecting human rights are the best means of strengthening the international order.

Trade and development policies can be powerful tools for promoting reform. As the world's largest provider of official assistance and its largest trading entity, the European Union and its Member States are well placed to pursue these goals.

Contributing to better governance through assistance programmes, conditionality and targeted trade measures remains an important feature in our policy that we should further reinforce. A world seen as offering justice and opportunity for everyone will be more secure for the European Union and its citizens.

A number of countries have placed themselves outside the bounds of international society. Some have sought isolation; others persistently violate international norms. It is desirable that such countries should rejoin the international community, and the EU should be ready to provide assistance. Those who are unwilling to do so should understand that there is a price to be paid, including in their relationship with the European Union.

III Policy implications for Europe

The European Union has made progress towards a coherent foreign policy and effective crisis management. We have instruments in place that can be used effectively, as we have demonstrated in the Balkans and beyond. But if we are to make a contribution that matches our potential, we need to be more active, more coherent and more capable. And we need to work with others.

More active in pursuing our strategic objectives. This applies to the full spectrum of instruments for crisis management and conflict prevention at our disposal, including political, diplomatic, military and civilian, trade and development activities. Active policies are needed to counter the new dynamic threats. We need to develop a strategic culture that fosters early, rapid, and when necessary, robust intervention.

As a Union of 25 members, spending more than 160 billion Euros on defence, we should be able to sustain several operations simultaneously.

We could add particular value by developing operations involving both military and civilian capabilities.

The EU should support the United Nations as it responds to threats to international peace and security. The EU is committed to reinforcing its cooperation with the UN to assist countries emerging from conflicts, and to enhancing its support for the UN in short-term crisis management situations.

We need to be able to act before countries around us deteriorate, when signs of proliferation are detected, and before humanitarian emergencies arise. Preventive engagement can avoid more serious problems in the future. A European Union which takes greater responsibility and which is more active will be one which carries greater political weight.

More capable. A more capable Europe is within our grasp, though it will take time to realise our full potential. Actions underway – notably the establishment of a defence agency – take us in the right direction.

To transform our militaries into more flexible, mobile forces, and to enable them to address the new threats, more resources for defence and more effective use of resources are necessary.

Systematic use of pooled and shared assets would reduce duplications, overheads and, in the medium-term, increase capabilities.

In almost every major intervention, military efficiency has been followed by civilian chaos. We need greater capacity to bring all necessary civilian resources to bear in crisis and post crisis situations.

Stronger diplomatic capability: we need a system that combines the resources of Member States with those of EU institutions. Dealing with problems that are more distant and more foreign requires better understanding and communication.

Common threat assessments are the best basis for common actions. This requires improved sharing of intelligence among Member States and with partners.

As we increase capabilities in the different areas, we should think in terms of a wider spectrum of missions. This might include joint disarmament operations, support for third countries in combating terrorism and security sector reform. The last of these would be part of broader institution building.

The EU-NATO permanent arrangements, in particular Berlin Plus, enhance the operational capability of the EU and provide the framework for the strategic partnership between the two organisations in crisis management. This reflects our common determination to tackle the challenges of the new century.

More coherent. The point of the Common Foreign and Security Policy and European Security and Defence Policy is that we are stronger when we act together. Over recent years we have created a number of different instruments, each of which has its own structure and rationale.

The challenge now is to bring together the different instruments and capabilities: European assistance programmes and the European Development Fund, military and civilian capabilities from Member States and other instruments. All of these can have an impact on our security and on that of third countries. Security is the first condition for development.

Diplomatic efforts, development, trade and environmental policies, should follow the same agenda. In a crisis there is no substitute for unity of command.

Better co-ordination between external action and Justice and Home Affairs policies is crucial in the fight both against terrorism and organised crime.

Greater coherence is needed not only among EU instruments but also embracing the external activities of the individual member states.

Coherent policies are also needed regionally, especially in dealing with conflict. Problems are rarely solved on a single country basis, or without regional support, as in different ways experience in both the Balkans and West Africa shows.

Working with partners There are few if any problems we can deal with on our own. The threats described above are common threats, shared with all our closest partners. International cooperation is a necessity. We need to pursue our objectives both through multilateral cooperation in international organisations and through partnerships with key actors.

The transatlantic relationship is irreplaceable. Acting together, the European Union and the United States can be a formidable force for good in the world. Our aim should be an effective and balanced partnership with the USA. This is an additional reason for the EU to build up further its capabilities and increase its coherence.

We should continue to work for closer relations with Russia, a major factor in our security and prosperity. Respect for common values will reinforce progress towards a strategic partnership.

Our history, geography and cultural ties give us links with every part of the world: our neighbours in the Middle East, our partners in Africa, in Latin America, and in Asia. These relationships are an important asset to build on. In particular we should look to develop strategic partnerships, with Japan, China, Canada and India as well as with all those who share our goals and values, and are prepared to act in their support.

Conclusion

This is a world of new dangers but also of new opportunities. The European Union has the potential to make a major contribution, both in dealing with the threats and in helping realise the opportunities. An active and capable European Union would make an impact on a global scale. In doing so, it would contribute to an effective multilateral system leading to a fairer, safer and more united world.

Source: European Council (2003) *A Secure Europe in a Better World*, Brussels, 12 December 2003, accessed at: http://ue.eu.int/uedocs/cmsUpload/78367.pdf.

Bibliography

Abele, Alexander B. (2003) 'The EU Rapid Reaction Force and Operation "Concordia" in Macedonia, *Armed Conflict and Military Intervention*', accessed at: www.juridicum.at/component/option,com_docman/task,doc_download/gid,103/Itemid,91/

Adamski, Janet, M.T. Johnson and Christina M. Schweiss (2006) *Old Europe, New Security*. London: Ashgate.

Aggestam, Lisbeth (1999) 'Role Conceptions and the Politics of Identity in Foreign Policy', *ARENA Working Paper* 99/8. Oslo, Centre for European Studies, University of Oslo, accessed at: http://www.arena.uio.no/publications/working-papers1999/papers/wp99_8.htm - 15.04.2005 kl. 11:05

—— (2000a) 'A Common Foreign and Security Policy: Role Conceptions and the Politics of Identity in the EU', in L. Aggestam and A. Hyde-Price, *Security and Identity in Europe: Exploring the New Agenda*. Basingstoke: Palgrave Macmillan, 86–115.

—— (2000b) 'Germany', in I. Manners and R.G. Whitman (eds), *The Foreign Policies of European Union Member States*. Manchester: Manchester University Press, 64–83.

—— (2001) 'An End to Neutrality? Continuity and Change in Swedish Foreign Policy', in R. Niblett and W. Wallace (eds), *Rethinking European Order. West European Responses, 1989–1997*. New York: Palgrave Macmillan.

Albright, Madeleine (1998) 'The Right Balance will Secure NATO's Future', *Financial Times* 7 December (accessed in Rutten, 2001: 10–12).

Alexander, Martin and Tim Garden (2001) 'The Arithmetic of Defence Policy', *International Affairs*, vol. 77/3: 509–29.

Allen, David J. (2004) 'So Who Will Speak for Europe? The Constitutional Treaty and Coherence in EU External Relations', *CFSP Forum*, vol. 2/5, September.

Alliot Marie, Michele (2005) 'Security Could be Europe's Great Rallying Point', *Financial Times*, 5 December.

Anderson, Jeffrey, G., John Ikenberry and Thomas Risse (eds) (forthcoming) *The End of the West: the Deep Sources of The Transatlantic Crisis*.

Andréani, Gilles, Christoph Bertram and Charles Grant (2001) *Europe's Military Revolution*. London: Centre for European Reform, accessed at: http://www.cer.org.uk/pdf/p22x_military_revolution.pdf

Annersley, Claire (2000) 'New Labour and Foreign Policy', in Steve Ludlam and Martin Smith (eds), *New Labour in Power*. Basingstoke: Palgrave Macmillan.

Antonenko, Oksana (2006) 'Policy Brief on *Shanghai Cooperation Organisation*'. London: Centre for European Reform.

Arquilla, John and David Ronfeldt (2001) *Networks and Netwars: The Future of Terror, Crime, and Militancy*. Santa Monica, CA: RAND.

Art, Robert J. (2004) 'Western Europe Hedges its Bets', in T.V. Paul, J.J. Wirtz and M. Fortmann (eds), *Balance of Power: Theory and Practice in the Twenty-First Century*. Stanford, CA: Stanford University Press.

—— (2005) 'Hard Balancing Times Are Here Again', *International Security*, vol. 30/2 Fall.

—— (2006) 'Correspondence: Striking the Balance', *International Security*, vol. 30/3, Winter 2005–6, 177–85.

Asmus, Ronald D. (2002) *Opening NATO's Door. How the Alliance Remade Itself for a New Era*. New York: Columbia University Press.

——, Anthony J. Blinken and Philip H. Gordon (2005) 'Nothing to Fear', *Foreign Affairs*, vol. 84/1: 174–7.

—— and Bruce Jackson (2005) 'Does Israel Belong in the EU and NATO?', *Policy Review*, vol. 125 February/March: 47–56.

Assinder, Nick (2000) 'Euro Army Widens Political Splits', *BBC News: Talking Politics*, 20 November.

Aybet, Gülnur (2001) *Dynamics of European Security Cooperation*. Basingstoke: Palgrave Macmillan.

Ayka, Mahmut Bali (2005) 'Turkey and European Security and Defence Identity/Policy (ESDI/P): A Turkish View', *Journal of Contemporary European Studies*, vol. 13/3, December: 335–59.

Bahgat, Gawdat (2006) 'Europe's Energy Security: Challenges and Opportunities', *International Affairs*, vol. 82/5: 961–75.

Bailes, Alison J.K. (2005) *The European Security Strategy: An Evolutionary History*, SIPRI Policy Paper no. 10. Stockholm: SIPRI.

Bali Aykan, Mahmut (2005) 'Turkey and European Security Identity/Policy (ESDI/P): A Turkish View', *Journal of Contemporary European Studies*, vol. 13/3, 335–59.

Barry, Charles (1996) 'NATO's Combined Joint Task Forces in Theory and Practice', *Survival*, vol. 38/1, Spring: 81–97.

Baun, Michael (2005) 'How Necessary is a Common Strategic Culture?', *Oxford Journal on Good Governance*, vol. 2/1.

Becher, Klaus (2004) 'German Forces in International Military Operations', *Orbis*, vol. 48/3: 397–408.

Benoit, Bertrand and Ben Hall (2003) 'Blair Backs EU Plans for Joint Defence Project', *Financial Times*, 23 September.

Bensahel, Nora (1999) 'Separable but not Separate Forces: NATO's Development of the Combined Joint Task Force', *European Security*, vol. 8, Summer: 52–73.

Berenskoetter, Felix S. (2005) 'Mapping the Mind Gap: A Comparison of US and European Security Strategies', *Security Dialogue*, vol. 36/1, 71–92.

—— and Bastien Giegerich (2007) 'From NATO to ESDP: Analysing Shifts in German Institutional Preferences after 1990', *International Security* (forthcoming).

Binnendijk, Hans David C. Gompert and Richard L. Kugler (2005) 'A New Military Framework for NATO', *Defense Horizons* no. 48, Washington, DC, May.

Biscop, Sven (2005) *The European Security Strategy: A Global Agenda for Positive Power*. Aldershot: Ashgate.

—— (ed.) (2005a) *E Pluribus Unum? Military Integration in the European Union*. Brussels: IRRI-KIIB (*Egmont Paper* 7).

—— and Rick Coolsaet (2003) *The World is the Stage – a Global Security Strategy for the European Union*, Policy Paper 8, *Notre Europe*, (Paris), accessed in May 2004 at: http://www.notre-europe.asso.fr/IMG/pdf/Policypaper8.pdf

Black, Ian (2003) 'France, Germany Deepen UK Rift', *The Guardian*, 30 April.

Blair, Tony (1999) 'Doctrine of the International Community', Chicago, April, accessed at: http://www.number-10.gov.uk/output/Page1297.asp

—— (2000) 'Committed to Europe, Reforming Europe', Ghent City Hall, 23 February, accessed at: http://www.number-10.gov.uk/output/Page1510.asp

—— (2002) 'A Clear Course for Europe', 28 November, accessed at: http://www.number-10.gov.uk/output/Page1739.asp

—— (2003) 'Prime Minister's Speech on Europe', Warsaw, 30 May, accessed at: http://www.number-10.gov.uk/output/Page3787.asp

Bolton, John (1999) 'Risking NATO's Future?', *Washington Times* 15 December.

Bonnén, Preben (2003) *Towards a Common European Security and Defence Policy*. Münster: Lit Verlag.

Bono, Giovanna, (2004) 'Introduction: the Role of the EU in External Crisis Management', *International Peacekeeping*, vol. 11/3, Autumn, 395–403.

Booth, Ken (1979) *Strategy and Ethnocentrism*. London: Croom Helm.

Bozo, Frédéric (1991) *La France et l'OTAN: De la Guerre Froide au Nouvel Ordre européen*. Paris: Masson.

Bozo, Frédéric (2000) *Two Strategies for Europe: de Gaulle, the United States and the Atlantic Alliance*. Lanham, MD: Rowman and Littlefield.

—— (2003) 'The Effects of Kosovo and the Danger of Decoupling', in Jolyon Howorth and John Keeler (eds), *Defending Europe*. New York: Palgrave Macmillan.

Braud, Pierre-Antoine (2006) 'Implementing ESDP Operations in Africa', in Deighton (2006), 71–81.

—— and Giovanni Grevi (2005) *The EU Mission in Aceh : implementing peace*. Paris: EU-ISS, (*Occasional Paper* no. 61).

Brawley, Mark R. and Pierre Martin (eds) (2000) *Alliance Politics, Kosovo, and NATO's War: Allied Force or Forced Allies?* New York: Palgrave, 2000.

Bremner, Charles (2003) 'Paris and Berlin Prepare Alliance to Rival NATO', *The Times*, 28 April.

Brems, Knudsen, T. (2004) 'Denmark and the War against Iraq: Losing Sight of Internationalism?' in P. Carlsen and H. Mouritzen. *Danish Foreign Policy Yearbook 2004*. Copenhagen: Danish Institute for International Studies. 49–90.

Brenner, Michael J. (2002) *Europe's New Security Vocation*. Washington, DC: NDU (McNair Paper 66).

—— (2003) 'The CFSP Factor: A Comparison of United States and French Strategies', *Cooperation and Conflict*, vol. 38/3, 187–209.

—— and Guillaume Parmentier (2002) *Reconcilable Differences: U.S. French Relations in the New Era*. Washington, DC: Brookings.

Brimmer, Esther (ed.) (2002) *The EU's Search for a Strategic Role: ESDP and its Implications for Transatlantic Relations*. Washington, DC: Center for Transatlantic Relations.

Brooks, Stephen G. and William C. Wohlforth (2005) 'Hard Times for Soft Balancing', *International Security*, vol. 30/1, Summer, 72–108.

Brooks, Stephen G. and William C. Wohlforth (2006) 'Correspondence: Striking the Balance', *International Security*, vol. 30/3, Winter, 2005–6, 186–91.

Brzezinski, Zbigniew (2000) 'Living with the New Europe', *The National Interest*. Summer.

Buffotot, Patrice (ed.) (2001) *La Défense en Europe. Nouvelles Réalités, Nouvelles Ambitions*. Paris: Documentation Française (Notes et Etudes Documentaires 5136–37).

Buras, Piotr and Kerry Longhurst (2004) 'The Berlin Republic, Iraq, and the Use of Force', *European Security*, vol. 13/3, 215–45.

Burgess, James Peter and Ola Tunander (eds) (2000) *European Security Identities. Contested Understandings of EU and NATO*. Oslo: International Peace Research Institute.

Burwell, Frances G. David C. Gompert, Leslie S. Lebl, Jan M. Lodal and Walter B. Slocombe (2006) *Transatlantic Transformation: Building a NATO-EU Security Architecture*. Washington, DC: The Atlantic Council of the United States, Policy Paper.

Bush, George and Brent Scowcroft (1998) *A World Transformed*. New York: Knopf.

Bush, George W. (2001) 'Excerpted Remarks to the North Atlantic Council', NATO, 13 June, http://www.nato.int/docu/speech/2001/s010613g.htm

Buzan, Barry, Ole Waever and Jaap de Wilde, (1998) *Security: a New Framework for Analysis*. Boulder, CO: Lynne Rienner.

Carpenter, Ted Galen (1994) *Beyond NATO: staying out of Europe's wars*. Washington, DC: Cato Institute.

Casey, Gerry (2001) 'The Euro Army', *Archives SligoWeekender*, 01 June, accessed at: http://archives.tcm.ie/sligoweekender/2001/06/01/story7930.asp

CDS (2001) 'Achieving the Helsinki Headline Goal', *Centre for Defence Studies Discussion Paper*. Kings College: University of London, November.

Celador, Gemma Collantes (2005) 'Police Reform: Peacebuilding through "Democratic Policing"?', *International Peacekeeping*, vol. 12/3, Autumn, 364–76.

Champion, Marc (1999) 'British Envoy Visiting US to Allay Fears: Plans for European Force Within NATO Raise Concerns in Congress', *The Wall Street Journal*, 26 January.

Chandler, David, 'Introduction: Peace Without Politics', *International Peacekeeping*, vol. 11/3, Autumn, 307–21.

Chesterman, Simon (2004) *You the People: the United Nations, Transitional Administration and State-Building*. Oxford: Oxford University Press.

Chirac, Jacques (2003) 'Interview with the *New York Times*', 22 September 2003, at: http://www.nytimes.com/2003/09/22/international/22CHIRAC_FULL.html?ex=1109048400&en=d7d4042c8c061a0e&ei=5070

Cimbalo, Jeffrey L. (2004) 'Saving NATO from Europe'. *Foreign Affairs*, vol. 83/6.

Clark, Wesley K. (2001) *Waging Modern War*. New York: Public Affairs.

Clarke, Michael and Paul Cornish (2002) 'The European Defence Project and the Prague Summit'. *International Affairs*, vol. 78/3, 777–88.

Coates, Crispin (2000) 'Spanish Defence Policy: Eurocorps and NATO Reform', *Mediterranean Politics*, vol. 5/2, 170–89.

Coates, David and Joel Krieger (2004) *Blair's war*. Oxford: Polity.

Cogan, Charles G. (1994) *Oldest Allies, Guarded Friends: The United States and France Since 1940*. Westport, CT: Praeger.

—— (2001) *The Third Option: the Emancipation of European Defense 1989–2000*. Westport, CT: Praeger.

—— (2004) 'The Iraq Crisis and France: heaven-sent opportunity or problem from hell?', *French Politics, Culture and Society*, vol. 22, Fall, 120–34.

Cohen, Daniel (2006) *Globalisation and Its Enemies*. Cambridge: MIT Press.

Collester, J. Bryan (2000) 'How Defense 'Spilled Over' into the CFSP' in Maria Green Cowles and Michael Smith (eds), *The State of the European Union: Volume 5 – Widening and Deepening*. Oxford: Oxford University Press.

Collins, Stephen (2006) 'O'Dea Anticipates Irish Role in EU's Nordic Battle-Group', *Irish Times*, 12 May.

Compact (2005) *A Compact Between the United State and Europe*, accessible at: www.brookings.edu/comm/news/20050216compact.htm

Convention (2003) Summary of the meeting held on 29 October 2002,' *CONV 399/02* (12 November).

Coolsaet, Rik and Sven Biscop (2004) *A European Security Concept for the 21st Century*. Brussels: IRRI_KIIB, 'Egmont Paper 1'.

Cooper, Robert (2003) *The Breaking of Nations. Order and Chaos in the Twenty-First Century*. New York: Atlantic Monthly Press.

Cornish, Paul (2004) *Artemis and Coral: British Perspectives on European Union Crisis Management Operations in the Democratic Republic of Congo*. Unpublished report, Kings College: London.

—— and Geoffrey Edwards (2001) 'Beyond the EU/NATO Dichotomy: the beginnings of a European strategic culture', *International Affairs*, vol. 77/3.

—— and —— (2005) 'The strategic culture of the European Union: a progress report', *International Affairs*, vol. 81/4.

Croft, Stuart (2000) 'The EU, NATO and Europeanisation: the Return of the Architectural Debate', *European Security*, vol. 9, 1–20.

Croft, Stuart Andrew Dorman, Wyn Rees and Mathew Utley (2001) *Britain and Defence 1945–2000: a Policy Re-evaluation*. London: Longman.

Cronin, David (2004) 'Uphill struggle for EU 'rule of law' mission in Georgia', *European Voice*, 28 October.

Crowe, Brian (2003) 'A Common Foreign Policy After Iraq?', *International Affairs*, vol. 79/3, 533–46.

Cumming, Chris (2002) 'EuroArmy: For Peace or War?', accessed at: http://www.garnertedarmstrong.ws/Mark_Wordfroms/manews0012.shtml

Cutler, Robert M. and Alexander von Lingen (2003) 'The European Parliament and European Union Security and Defence Policy', *European Security*, vol. 12/2, 1–20.

Daalder, Ivo H. (2001) 'A US View of European Security and Defence Policy', *Brookings*, March.

—— and M. E. O'Hanlon (2000) *Winning Ugly: NATO's War to Save Kosovo*. Washington, DC: Brookings Institution Press.

Dannreuther, Roland and John Peterson (eds) (2006) *Security Strategy and the Transatlantic Alliance*. London: Routledge.

Das, Gurcharan (2006) 'The India Model', *Foreign Affairs* 85/4, July/August.

Déclaration commune des chefs d'Etat et de gouvernement d'Allemagne, de France, du Luxembourg et de Belgique sur la défense européenne, Bruxelles le 29 avril 2003, accessed at: http://www.defense.gouv.fr/sites/defense/archives/declarations_des_hautes_autorites_de_letat_-_1999_a_2004/discours_divers/2003/d060503/060503.htm

Deighton, Anne (ed.) (1997) *Western European Union 1954–1997: Defence, Security, Integration*. Oxford: European Interdependence Research Unit.

—— (2002) 'The European Security and Defence Policy', *Journal of Common Market Studies*, vol. 40/4,

—— (ed.) (2006) *Securing Europe: Implementing the European Security Strategy*. Zurich: Zürcher Beiträge.

De Jonge Oudraat, Chantal (2002) *The New Transatlantic Security Network. AICGS Policy Paper No. 20*. Washington, DC: American Institute for Contemporary German Studies.

Delafon, Gilles and Thomas Sancton (1998) *Dear Jacques Cher Bill: Au Coeur de l'Elysée et de la Maison Blanche 1995–1999*. Paris: Plon.

Dempsey, Judy (2003) 'Defence Plan could rival NATO', *Financial Times*, 29 April.

—— (2006) 'Pressure rises over NATO's Darfur Role', *International Herald Tribune*, 19 February.

Den Boer, Monica and Jörg Monar (2002) '11 September and the Challenge of Global Terrorism to the EU as a Security Actor' in Geoffrey Edwards and Georg Wiessala (eds) *The European Union: Annual Review of the EU 2001/2002*. Oxford: Blackwell.

De Wijk, Rob (2002) 'The Limits of Military Power,' *Washington Quarterly*, Winter 2002.

Diamond, Larry (2005) *Squandered Victory: The American Occupation and the Bungled Effort to Bring Democracy to* Iraq. New York: Henry Holt.

Diedrichs, Udo and Mathias Jopp (2003) 'Flexible Modes of Governance: Making CFSP and ESDP Work,' *The International Spectator*, vol. XXXVIII/3.

Dobbins, James (2005–06) 'New Directions for Transatlantic Security Cooperation', *Survival*, Winter 2005–6.

Donfried, Karen and Paul Gallis (2000) *European Security: the Debate in NATO and the European Union*. Washington, DC: Congressional Research Service (CRS) Report to Congress, April 25.

Donno, Daniela (2006) 'Defending Democratic Norms? The European Union's Selective Enforcement of Democracy Clauses'. Working Paper, Yale University: New Haven, CT.

Duffield, John S. (1995) 'NATO's Functions After the Cold War', *Political Science Quarterly*,

—— (1999) 'Political Culture and State Behavior: Why Germany Confounds Neorealism', *International Organization* 53/4, 765–803.

—— (2002) *Global Governance and New Wars*, London: Zed Books.

Duke, Simon (2000) *The Elusive Quest for European Security: from EDC to CFSP*. Basingstoke: Palgrave Macmillan.

—— (2002) *The EU and Crisis Management: Development and Prospects*. Maastricht: EIPA.

—— (2002a) 'Preparing for European Diplomacy?', *Journal of Common Market Studies*, vol. 40/5, December.

—— (2003) 'The Convention, the Draft Constitution and External Relations: effects and implications for the EU and its international role', Maastricht, European Institute for Public Administration (EIPA), Working Paper 2003/W/2.

—— (2005) 'The Linchpin COPS. Assessing the workings and institutional relations of the Political and Security Committee', Maastricht, EIPA, Working Paper 2005/W/05.

Dumoulin, André, Raphael Mathieu and Gordon Sarlet (2003) *La Politique Européenne de sécurité et de défense (PESD). De l'opératoire à l'identitaire*, Brussels: Bruylant, 2003, 940 pages.

——, Philippe Manigart and Wally Struys (2003) *La Belgique et la Politique Européenne de Sécurité et de Défense*, Brussels: Bruylant.

Dyson, Tom (2005) 'German Military Reform 1998–2004: Leadership and the Triumph of Domestic Constraint over International Opportunity', *European Security*, vol. 14/3, 361–86, September.

Echikson, William (1999) 'Coming Soon: A Euro-Army', *Business Week*, 20 December Available at: http://www.businessweek.com/1999/99_51/b3660214.htm

EDA (2006) *EDA Bulletin*, Issue 2, July, accessed at: http://www.eda.europa.eu/reference/eda/EDA%20-%20Bulletin%2002.pdf

—— (2006a) 'Defence Research and Technology Spend', Brussels, 29 May, accessed at: http://www.eda.europa.eu/facts/Defence%20R&T%20Spend.pdf

—— (2006b) *EDA Seminar on Network-Enabled Capability*, 25 April http://www.eda.europa.eu/news/2006-04-25-0.htm

—— (2006c) *An Initial Long-Term Vision for European Defence Capability and Capacity Needs*, October, accessed at: http://www.eda.europa.eu/ltv/061003%20-%20EDA%20-%20Long%20Term%20Vision%20Report.pdf

Errera, Philippe (2005) 'Three Circles of Threat', *Survival*, vol. 47/1, Spring.

ESDP (2005) *ESDP Newsletter, No.*1, December, accessed at: http://www.consilium.europa.eu/uedocs/cmsUpload/051214_NewsletterFinal.pdf

—— (2006) *ESDP Newsletter*, No.2, June, accessed at: http://www.consilium.europa.eu/uedocs/cmsUpload/ESDP_Newsletter_ISSUE2.pdf

—— Fact-Sheet (2005) *EU Battle Groups*, accessed at: http://www.consilium.europa.eu/uedocs/cmsUpload/BattlegroupsNov05factsheet.pdf

European Commission (2004) The European Commission's Delegation to Israel, *Poll: Vast Majority Of Israelis Want Israel To Join EU*, 2004. Available at http://web.radicalparty.org/pressreview/print_250.php?func=detail&par=8907

—— (2006) *The Impact of Ageing on Public Expenditure. Projections for the EU 25 Member States on Pensions, Health Care, Long-Term Care, Education and Unemployment Transfers (2004–2050)*, The Economic Policy Committee Special Report no. 1, 14 February.

—— (2006a) *A European Strategy for Sustainable, Competitive and Secure Energy*, Green Paper, Brussels 8 March.

European Convention (2002) Final Report of Working Group VIII – Defence, 12 December, accessed at: http://register.consilium.eu.int/pdf/en/02/cv00/00461en2.pdf

European Council (2003) *A Secure Europe in a Better World*, Brussels, December 12, 2003, accessed at: http://ue.eu.int/uedocs/cmsUpload/78367.pdf

—— (2004) *Headline Goal 2010*, accessed at: http://ue.eu.int/uedocs/cmsUpload/2010percent20Headline percent20Goal.pdf.

—— (2006) *Capabilities Improvement Chart 1/2006*, accessed at; http://www.consilium.europa.eu/ueDocs/cms_Data/docs/pressData/en/esdp/89603.pdf

—— (2006a) *Presidency Report on ESDP*, 12 June.

European Environment Agency (EEA) (2005) *The European Environment: State and Outlook*, EEA State of Environment Report no. 1, November.

EU-ISS (2004) *European Defence: A proposal for a White Paper. Report of an independent Task Force*, Paris, EU-ISS, May: http://www.iss-eu.org/chaillot/wp2004.pdf

EU-ISS (2005) *EU Security and Defence. Core Documents 2004. Volume V*, Paris EU-ISS (*Chaillot Paper 75*), February.

—— (2006) *EU Security and Defence. Core Documents 2005. Volume VI*, Paris EU-ISS (*Chaillot Paper 87*), March.

Evans, Gareth (1994) 'Cooperative Security and Interstate Conflict', *Foreign Policy*, Issue 96, 3–20.
Evans-Pritchard, Ambrose and George Jones (2002) 'Britain Caves in on Euro-Army', *Daily Telegraph*, 16 March.
Everts, Steven, (2002) *Shaping a Credible EU Foreign Policy*. London: Centre for European Reform.
Everts, Steven, and Daniel Keohane (2003) 'The European Convention and EU Foreign Policy: Learning from Failure', *Survival*, vol. 45/3, pp. 167–86.
Everts, Steven *et al.*, (2004) *A European Way of War*. London: CER.
Farrell, Theo (2001) 'Transnational Norms and Military Development: Constructing Ireland's Professional Army', *European Journal of International Relations*, vol. 7/1: 63–102.
Ferguson, Niall (2004) *Colossus: The Price of America's Empire*. New York: Penguin.
Ferreira-Pereira, Laura C. (2006) 'Inside the Fence, But Outside the Walls: Austria, Finland and Sweden in the Post-Cold War Security Architecture', *Cooperation and Conflict*, vol. 41/1, 99–122.
Ferroni, Marco and Ashoka Mody (eds), (2002) *International Public Goods: Incentives, Measurement and Financing*. New York: Springer.
Fielding, Nigel (1988) *Joining Forces: Police Training, Socialisation and Occupational Competence*. London: Routledge.
Finnemore, Martha (2003) *The purpose of intervention: changing beliefs about the use of force*. Ithaca, NY: Cornell University Press.
Fleckenstein, Bernhard (2000) 'Germany: Forerunner of a Postnational Military', in Charles, Moskos *et al.*, *The Postmodern Military: Armed Forces After the Cold War*. Oxford: Oxford University Press.
Flournoy, Michèle A. and Julianne Smith (dir.) (2005) *European Defense Integration: Bridging the Gap Between Strategy and Capabilities*. Washington, DC: CSIS Report.
Forster, Anthony and A. Blair (2002) *The making of Britain's European foreign policy*. New York: Longman.
Forster, Anthony and William Wallace (2002) 'What is NATO for?', *Survival*, vol. 43/4.
Freedman, Lawrence (ed.) (1983) *The Troubled Alliance: Atlantic Relations in the 1980s*. London: Heinemann.
Freedman, Lawrence (2001) 'Rethinking European Security' 'in Helen Wallace (ed) *Interlocking Dimensions of European Integration*. Basingstoke: Palgrave Macmillan.
—— (2001a) 'Europe and Deterrence', in Schmitt and Grand (eds), 81–102.
—— (2004) 'Can the EU develop an effective military doctrine?' in Steven Everts *et al.*ii, *A European Way of War*. London: CER, 13–26.

Friedman, Thomas (2003) 'Vote France off the Island', *New York Times* 9 February.
—— (2005) *The World Is Flat: A Brief History of the Twenty-First Century*. New York: Farrar, Strauss and Giroux.
Fukuyama, Francis (1992) *The End of History and the Last Man*. New York: Free Press.
Fuller, Thomas (2003) 'Summit talk of close European military ties upsets US', *International Herald Tribune*, 17 October.
Fursdon, Edward (1980) *The European Defence Community: A History*. London: Macmillan.
Gardner, Hall (ed.) (2004) *NATO and the European Union: New World, New Europe, New Threats*. Aldershot: Ashgate.
Gärtner, Heinz, Adrian Hyde-Price and Erich Reiter (2001) *Europe's New Security Challenges*. Boulder CO: Lynne Rienner.
Garton Ash, Timothy (1993): *In Europe's name. Germany and the divided continent*. New York: Random House.
—— (2004) *Free World: America, Europe and the Surprising Future of the West*. New York: Random House.
Gascon, Garance (2002) « Armée Multiethnique pour l'Afghanistan », *Terre Magazine*, 138, October.
Louis Gautier (1999) *Mitterrand et son Armée 1990–1995*. Paris: Grasset.
Gedmin, Jeffrey (2002) 'The Alliance is Doomed', *Washington Post*, 20 May.
Gégout, Catherine (2002) 'The French and British Change Position in CESDP: A Security Community and Historical Institutionalist Perspective', *Politique Européenne*, vol. 1/8.
—— (2005) 'Causes and Consequences of the EU's Military Intervention in the Democratic Republic of Congo: a Realist Explanation', *European Foreign Affairs Review*, vol. 10, 427–43.
Geyde, Robin and Ambrose Evans-Pritchard (2003) 'More Nations Condemn Euro-Army', *Daily Telegraph* 1 May.
Giegerich, Bastien (2005) 'National Policies Toward ESDP: 1999–2003', PhD Dissertation, London Schoool of Economics, 2005.
Giegerich, Bastien and William Wallace (2004) 'Not Such a Soft Power: The External Deployment of European Forces', *Survival*, vol. 46/2, 163–82.
Gillespie, Richard (2002) 'Spain's Pursuit of Security in the Western Mediterranean.' European Security, vol. 11/2, 48–74.
Gillespie, Richard, F. Rodrigo and J. Story (eds) (1995) *Democratic Spain: Reshaping External Relations in a Changing World*. London: Routledge.
Ginsberg, Roy H. (2001) *The European Union in International Politics: Baptism by Fire*. Lanham, MD: Rowman and Littlefield.

—— (2002) *Ten Years of European Union Foreign Policy: Baptism, Confirmation, Validation*. Washington, DC: Böll Foundation.

—— (2003) 'European Security and Defence Policy: The State of Play.' *EUSA Review*, vol. 16/1.

Glarbo, Kenneth (1999) 'Wide-Awake Diplomacy: Reconstructing the Common Foreign and Security Policy of the European Union', *Journal of European Public Policy*, vol. 6, 634–51.

Gnesotto, Nicole (1998) *La Puissance et l'Europe*. Paris: FNSP.

—— (2000) 'For a common European security culture', *WEU-ISS Newsletter*, no 31, October.

—— (ed.) (2004) *EU Security and Defence Policy: the first five years (1999–2004)*. Paris: EU-ISS.

—— and Giovanni Grevi (eds) (2006) *The New Global Puzzle: What Works for the EU in 2025?*, available on-line at: http://www.iss-eu.org/books/NGP.pdf

——, Stanley Sloan and Karl-Heinz Kamp (1999) *Burden Sharing in NATO*, 3 volumes, Paris: IFRI.

Goldman Sachs Report (2003) *Dreaming with BRIC's – The Path To 2050*, Global Economics Paper no. 99, accessed at: http://www2.goldmansachs.com/insight/research/reports/report6.html

Gompert, David C. and F. Stephen Larrabee (1997) *America and Europe: A Partnership for a New Era*. Cambridge: Cambridge University Press.

Gordon, Philip H. (1993) *A Certain Idea of France: French Security Policy and the Gaullist Legacy*. Princeton, NJ: Princeton University Press.

—— (1994) 'Berlin's Difficulties: The Normalization of German Foreign Policy', *Orbis*, vol. 38(2): 225–43.

—— (1997–98) 'Europe's Uncommon Foreign Policy' in *International Security*, vol. 22/3, 74–100.

—— (2000) 'Their Own Army?', *Foreign Affairs*, vol. 79/4, July/August.

—— (2002) 'NATO after 11 September', in *Survival*, vol. 43(4).

—— (2004) 'Letter to Europe', *Prospect*, July.

Gordon, Philip H. and Jeremy Shapiro (2004) *Allies at War: America, Europe and the Crisis Over Iraq*. Washington, DC: Brookings.

Gourlay, Catriona (2003) 'EU Operations Update: Past, Present and Future', *European Security Review* no. 19, October.

—— (2006) 'Community Instruments for Civilian Crisis Management' in Nowak (2006), 49–67.

—— (2006a) 'Civil-Civil Coordination in EU Crisis Management', in Nowak (2006), 103–22.

Graeger, Nina (2005) Norway between NATO, the EU and the US: A Case Study of Post-Cold War Security and Defence Discourse', *Cambridge Review of International Affairs*, vol. 18/1, April.

Grant, Charles (1998) *Can Britain Lead in Europe?* London: Centre for European Reform.

Grant, Robert P. (1996) 'France's New Relationship with NATO', *Survival*, vol. 38/1.

Gray, Colin S. (1984) 'Comparative Strategic Culture', *Parameters*, Winter, 26–33.

Gray, Colin S. (1999) 'Strategic Culture as Context: The First Generation of Theory Strikes Back', *Review of International Studies*, vol. 25(1): 49–69.

Greenwood, Sean (1989) 'Return to Dunkirk: The Origins of the Anglo-French Treaty of March 1947,' *Journal of Strategic Studies*, vol. 6.

Gregory, Shaun (2000a) *French defence policy into the twenty-first century*. Basingstoke: Palgrave Macmillan.

Grevi, Giovanni, Dov Lynch and Antonio Missiroli (2005) 'ESDP Operations', Paris, EU-ISS: http://www.iss-eu.org/esdp/09-dvl-am.pdf

Guay, Terrence and Robert Callum, 'Future Prospects of Europe's Defence Industry', *International Affairs*, 78(4), October 2002.

Gustenau Gustav (1999) *Towards a common European policy on security and defence: an Austrian view of challenges to the 'post-neutrals'*, WEU-ISS Occasional Paper 9.

Haas, Peter (1992) 'Introduction: Epistemic Communities and International Policy Coordination', *International Organization*, vol. 46, 1–35.

Haass, Richard (2006) 'The New Middle East', *Foreign Affairs*, vol. 85/6, December, 2–12.

Habermas. Jurgen and Jacques Derrida (2003) 'February 15 or What Binds Europeans Together: a Plea for a Common Foreign Policy, Beginning in the Core of Europe', *Constellations*, vol. 10/3, 291–97 (originally published as 'Unsere Erneurung', *FAZ*, 13/05/2003).

Hagman, Hans-Christian (2002) *European Crisis Management and Defence: The Search for Capabilities*. London: Oxford University Press (Adelphi Paper 353).

Haine, Jean-Yves (ed.) (2003) *From Laeken to Copenhagen: European Defence: Core Documents 3*, Chaillot Paper no. 57. Paris: European Union Institute for Security Studies EU-ISS, available at http://www.iss-eu.org/chaillot/chai57e.pdf

Haine, Jean-Yves (2003) 'European Strategy: First Steps', *EU-ISS Newsletter No.7* (July) available on-line at www.iss-eu.org

—— (2004) 'A Historical Perspective', in Nicole Gnesotto (dir), *EU Security and Defence Policy: the first five years 1999–2004*. Paris: EU-ISS.

—— (2004) 'ESDP and NATO', in Nicole Gnesotto (dir), *EU Security and Defence Policy: the first five years 1999–2004*. Paris: EU-ISS.

Haine, Jean-Yves and Bastien Giegerich (2006) 'In Congo, a cosmetic EU operation', *International Herald Tribune* 13 June.

Hamilton, Daniel (2002) *American Views of European Security and Defence Policy*, in Brimmer, Esther (editor, 2002), *The EU's search for a strategic role: ESDP and its strategic implications for Transatlantic Relations*, Washington, DC: Center for Transatlantic Relations.

Harnisch, S. and Hans W. Maull (2001) *The Foreign Policy of the Berlin Republic*, Manchester: Manchester University Press.

Harrison, Michael M. (1981) *The Reluctant Ally: France and Atlantic Security*, Baltimore, MD: Johns Hopkins University Press.

Hatfield, Richard (2000) 'The Consequences of St Malo', Speech at IFRI, Paris, 28 April.

Heisbourg, François (2000) *European Defence: Making it Work*, Paris WEU-ISS (Chaillot Paper no. 42) www.iss-eu.org/chaillot/chai42e.pdf

—— (2000b) 'Europe's Strategic Ambitions: The Limits of Ambiguity.' *Survival*, vol. 42/2, 5–15.

—— (2000c) 'European Defence Takes a Leap Forward', *NATO Review*, Spring/Summer.

—— (2004) 'The 'European Security Strategy' is Not a Security Strategy', in S. Everts, L. Freedman, C. Grant *et al.*, *A European Way of War*. London: Centre for European Reform.

Heiselberg, Stein (2003) *Pacifism or Activism: Towards a Common Strategic Culture Within the European Security and Defense Policy?*, Copenhagen, DUPI, IIS Working Paper 2003/4, 36 pages.

Helly, Damien (2006) 'EUJUST-Themis in Georgia: an ambitious bet on rule of law', in Nowak 2006, 87–102.

Helly, Damien (2006a) 'Developing an EU Strategy for Security Sector Reform', *European Security Review*, 28.

Heusgen, Christoph 'Is there such a thing as a thing as a European Strategic Culture?, *Oxford Journal on Good Governance*, Volume 2 Number 1 March 2005, Oxford: Oxford Council on Good Governance, 29–32.

Hill, Christopher (1993)'The Capability-Expectations Gap, or Conceptualising Europe's International Role,' *Journal of Common Market Studies*, vol. 31/3, 305–28.

—— (2003) *The Changing Politics of Foreign Policy*. Basingstoke: Palgrave Macmillan.

Hoffmann, Stanley (1966) 'Obstinate or Obsolete? The Fate of the Nation State and the Case of Western Europe', *Daedalus*, vol. 95/2, 862–915.

—— (1982) 'Reflections on the Nation State in Western Europe Today', *Journal of Common Market Studies*, vol. 21/1–2, 21–37.

Holbrooke, Richard (1998) *To End a War*. New York: Random House.
Howorth, Jolyon (1994) 'French Policy in the Conflict', in Alex Danchev and Dan Keohane (eds), *International Perspectives on the Gulf Conflict*. London and New York: Macmillan and Saint Martins, 175–200.
—— (1994b) 'The Debate in France over Military Intervention in Europe', in Lawrence Freedman (ed.), *Military Intervention in European Conflicts*. Oxford: Blackwell, 1994.
—— (1995) '"HiroChirac" and the French nuclear conundrum: a testing time for the pursuit of grandeur', *French Politics and Society*, vol. 13/3, 1–17.
—— (1998) 'French defence reforms: national tactics for a European strategy?' *Brassey's Defence Yearbook 1998*. London: Brassey's, 130–51.
—— (2000) *European Integration and Defence: the Ultimate Challenge?* Paris, WEU-ISS (Chaillot Paper no. 43) www.iss-eu.org/chaillot/chai43e.pdf
—— (2000a) 'Britain, NATO and CESDP: fixed strategy, changing tactics', *European Foreign Affairs Review*, vol. 5, no. 3, 1–20.
—— (2000b) 'Britain, France and the European Defence Initiative', *Survival*, vol. 42, no. 2, 33–55.
—— (2000c) '*Being* and *Doing* in Europe since 1945: contrasting dichotomies of identity and efficiency', in J. Andrew (ed.), *Why Europe?*, Basingstoke: Palgrave Macmillan, 85–96.
—— (2001) 'Les relations UE-OTAN: le point de vue du Royaume-Uni', in Jacques Beltran et Frédéric Bozo (sous la direction de), *Etats-Unis-Europe: réinventer l'Alliance*. Paris: IFRI, 2001, 133–56.
—— (2002) 'The CESDP and the Forging of a European Security Culture', *Politique Européenne*, vol. 8, automne, 88–108.
—— (2002a) *The European Security Conundrum: Prospects for ESDP after 11 September*, Paris: Notre-Europe (www.notre-europe.asso.fr).
Howorth, Jolyon (2003) 'France, Britain and the Euro-Atlantic Crisis', *Survival*, vol. 45/4, November, 173–92.
—— (2003a) 'Foreign and Defence Policy Cooperation: European and American Perspectives', in John Peterson and Mark A. Pollack (eds), *Europe, America, Bush: Transatlantic Relations after 2000*. New York: Routledge, 2003, 13–27.
—— (2003b) 'Elargissement de l'U.E.: implications en terme de défense, sécurité et politiques d'achat de materiel militaire', *Reflets et Perspectives de la Vie Economique*, Septembre, 78–97.
—— (2003c) 'ESDP and NATO: wedlock or deadlock?', *Cooperation and Conflict*, vol. 38/3, 235–54.
—— (2004) 'Discourse, Ideas and Epistemic Communities in European Security and Defence Policy', in special edition of *West European*

Politics: 'Europeanisation, Policy Change and Discourse', vol. 27/1, January, 29–52.

—— (2005a) 'Draft Dodger', *Foreign Affairs*, vol. 84/1.

—— (2005b)'The Euro-Atlantic Security Dilemma: France, Britain and the ESDP', *Journal of Transatlantic Studies*, vol. 3/1, 39–54.

—— (2006) 'France and the Iraq War: Defender of International Legitimacy', in Rick Fawn and Raymond Hinnebusch (eds), *The Iraq War*, Boulder, CO: Lynne Rienner, 2006, 49–60.

—— (2006a) 'The European Security and Defence Policy: Neither Hard nor Soft Balancing: Just policy-Making', Paper delivered to the Annual meeting of the American Political Science Association, Philadelphia.

Howorth, Jolyon and Anand Menon (eds) (1997) *National Defence and European Security*. London: Routledge.

Howorth, Jolyon and John T.S. Keeler (eds) (2003) *Defending Europe: NATO and the Quest for European Autonomy*. London and New York: Palgrave Macmillan.

Hübner, Danuta (2002) Representative of the Government of Poland, European Convention *Working Document 25 – WG VIII* (21 November).

Hulsman John C. (2000) 'A Grand Bargain with Europe: Preserving NATO for the Twenty-First Century', *The Heritage Foundation Backgrounder*, no. 1360.

Hulsman, John C. and Nile Gardiner (2004) 'A Conservative Vision for US Policy Towards Europe', *Heritage Backgrounder*, no. 1803, 4 October.

Human Rights Watch (HRW) (2005), 'NATO and EU Must End Squabble Over Darfur Airlift' accessed at http://hrw.org/english/docs/2005/06/09/darfur11105.htm

Human Security (2004) *A Human security Doctrine for Europe: the Barcelona report of the Study Group on Europe's Security Capabilities,* presented to EU High Representative Javier Solana in Barcelona, 15 September 2004. http://www.lse.ac.uk/Depts/global/Human%20Security%20Report%20Full.pdf

Hunter, Robert E. (2000) *The European Security and Defense Policy*: *NATO's Companion – or Competitor?* Monterrey, CA: Rand Publications.

Huntington, Samuel P. (1996) *The Clash of Civilisations and the Re-Making of World Order*. New York: Simon and Schuster.

Hyde-Price, Adrian (2000) *Germany and European Order: Enlarging NATO and the EU*. Manchester: Manchester University Press.

—— (2004) 'European Security, Strategic Culture and the Use of Force', *European Security*, vol. 13/4, 323–43.

International Crisis Group (ICG) (2001), *EU Crisis Response Capability: Institutions and Processes for Conflict Prevention and Management*, 26 June 2001, accessed at: http://www.crisisgroup.org/library/documents/report_archive/A400327_26062001.pdf

—— (2003) International Crisis Group, *Macedonia: No Room for Complacency*, *Europe Report no. 149*, October: http://www.crisisgroup.org/library/documents/europe/49_macedonia_no_room_for_complacency.pdf

—— (2003a) International Crisis Group, *Congo Crisis. Military Intervention in Ituri Africa Report no 64*, 13 June, accessed at: http://www.crisisgroup.org/library/documents/report_archive/A401005_13062003.pdf

—— (2004) International Crisis Group, *Moldova: Regional Tensions over Transnistria*, *Europe Report no. 157*, 17 June, accessed at: http://www.crisisgroup.org/home/index.cfm?id=2811&l=1

—— (2005) International Crisis Group, *EU Crisis Response Capability Revisited*, *Europe Report no. 160*, 17 January 2005, accessed at: http://www.crisisgroup.org/library/documents/europe/160_eu_crisis_response_capability_revisited_edit.pdf

— (2005a) International Crisis Group, *The EU/AU Partnership in Darfur: Not Yet a Winning Combination*, *Africa Report no. 99*, 25 October, accessed at: http://www.crisisgroup.org/home/index.cfm?id=3766&l=1

—— (2005b) International Crisis Group, *Bosnia's Stalled Police Reform: No Progress, No EU*, Europe Report no. 164, 6 September, accessed at: http://www.crisisgroup.org/library/documents/europe/balkans/164_bosnia_stalled_police_reform_no_progress_no_eu.pdf

—— (2006) International Crisis Group, 'Islamic Law and Criminal Justice in Aceh', *Asia Report no. 117*, 31 July: http://www.crisisgroup.org/home/index.cfm?id=4295

IISS International Institute for Strategic Studies (2001), 'The European Rapid Reaction Force', *The Military Balance 2001–2002*, London: Oxford University Press, 283–91.

—— (2003) 'EU Operational Planning: The Politics of Defence', *Strategic Comments*, vol. 9, Issue 10, December.

—— (2004) 'The US Global Posture Review: will redeployment ease the strain?', *Strategic Comments*, vol. 10, Issue 7.

Ioannides, Isabelle (2006) 'EU Police Mission Proxima: testing the 'European approach' to building peace', in Nowak 2006, 69–86.

Irondelle, Bastien (2007) 'Europeanisation without the European Union? French Military Reforms 1991–1996', *Journal of European Public Policy*, forthcoming.

Jacoby, Wade (2004) *The Enlargement of the European Union and NATO: Ordering from the Menu in Central Europe*. Cambridge: Cambridge University Press.

JEPP (2006) *Journal of European Public Policy*, 13/2, March. Special issue on 'What Kind of Power? European Foreign Policy in Perspective'.

Johnston, Alastair Ian (1995) *Strategic Culture and Grand Strategy in Chinese History*. Princeton, NJ: Princeton University Press.

—— (1995a) 'Thinking about strategic culture', *International Security*, vol. 19/4, 32–64.

Jopp, Mathias (1999) 'European Defence Policy: the Debate on Institutional Aspects', Bonn Institüt für Europäische Politik.

Kaldor, Mary and Marlies Glasius (eds) (2006) *A Human Security Doctrine for Europe*. London: Routledge.

Katzenstein, Peter J. (ed.) (1996) *The Culture of National Security: Norms and Identity in World Politics*. New York: Columbia University Press.

Keating, Tamara (2004) *Constructing the Gaullist Consensus: a Cultural Perspective on French Policy Towards The United States in NATO 1958–2000*. Baden-Baden: Nomos.

Kelleher, Catherine (1995) *The Future of European Security*. Washington DC: Brookings.

Keohane, Daniel (2001) *Realigning Neutrality: Irish Defence Policy and the EU*, WEU-ISS, Occasional Paper 24.

—— (2006) *EU Defence 2020*. London: CER.

Keohane, Robert O. and Joseph S. Nye (eds) (1972) *Transnationalism and World Politics*. Cambridge: Cambridge University Press.

—— and —— (1977) *Power and Interdependence: World Politics in Transition*. Boston, MA: Little, Brown.

Kernic, Frank, Jean M. Callaghan and Philippe Manigart (2001) *Public Opinion on European Security and Defense: a Survey of European Trends and Public Attitudes toward CFSP and ESDP*. Garmisch-Partenkirchen: Peter Lang.

Kirchner, Emil and James Sperling (2002) 'The New Security Threats in Europe', *European Foreign Affairs Review*, vol. 7/4, 423–52.

Kissinger, Henry (1994) 'Dealing with de Gaulle', in Robert O. Paxton and Nicholas Wahl (eds), *De Gaulle and the United States: a centennial re-appraisal*. Oxford: Berg, 1994.

Knodt, Michele and S. Princen (eds) (2003) *Understanding the European Union's External Relations*. London: Routledge.

Knutsen, Bjørn Olav (2000) *The Nordic dimension in the evolving European security structure and the role of Norway*. Paris: WEU-ISS Occasional Paper 22.

Kohl, Radek (2006) 'Civil-Military Coordination in EU Crisis Management' in Nowak (2006), 123–38.

Kolodziej, Edward A. (1987) *Making and Marketing Arms: The French Experience and its Implications for the International System*. Princeton, NJ: Princeton University Press.

Korteweg, Rem (2005) *The Discourse on European Defence*. Clingendael: Centre for Strategic Studies.

Kreemers, Bert (2001) 'The role of a 'pocket-sized' medium power in ESDP: the case of the Netherlands' in *Europa: el debate sobre defense y seguridad*. Barcelona: Barcelona University Press.

Krupnick, Charles (2003) *Almost NATO: Partners and Players in Central and Eastern European Security*. Lanham, MD: Rowman and Littlefield.

Kupchan, Charles (2000) 'In Defence of European Defence: an American Perspective', *Survival*, vol. 42/2.

—— (2002) *The End of the American Era: US Foreign Policy and the Geo-Politics of the Twenty-First Century*. New York: Vintage.

—— (2002a) 'The Last Days of the Atlantic Alliance', *Financial Times*, 18 November.

—— (2006) 'The Fourth Age: The Next Era in Transatlantic Relations', *The National Interest*, Fall, 77–83.

Lankowski, Carl and Simon Serfaty (1999) *Europeanizing Security: NATO and an Integrating Europe*, Washington, DC: AICGS.

Larrabee, F. Stephen (2004) 'ESDP and NATO: Assuring Complementarity', *The International Spectator*, XXXIX/1, January–March.

Layne, Christopher (2001) 'Death Knell for NATO? The Bush Administration Confronts the European Security and Defense Policy', *Policy Analysis*, 394, accessed at: http://www.cato.org/pubs/pas/pa394.pdf

Leakey, David (2006) ÉSDP and Civil/Military Cooperation: Bosnia and Herzegovina, 2005' in Deighton 2006, 61–70.

Lebl, Leslie S. (2004) 'European Union Defence Policy: An American Perspective', *Policy Analysis*, vol. 506, June 24.

Lee, Ian (2005) 'The Seven-Year Itch: Reflections on European Security and Defence Policy', Unpublished MS, UK MoD.

Leonard, Mark (2005a) *Why Europe will Run the Twenty-First Century*. London: Fourth Estate.

—— and Charles Grant (2005) 'Georgia and the EU: Can Europe's neighbourhood policy deliver? London: Centre for European Reform *Policy Brief*.

Lieber, Keir A. and Gerard Alexander (2005) 'Waiting for Balancing: Why the World is not Pushing Back', *International Security*, vol. 30/3, Summer, 177–96.

—— and —— (2006) 'Correspondence: Striking the Balance', *International Security*, vol. 30/3, Winter 2005–6, 191–6.

Liebhart, K. (2003) 'Austrian Neutrality: Historical Development and Semantic Change' in A. Kovacs and R. Wodak. *NATO, Neutrality and National Identity: The Case of Austria and Hungary*. Vienna: Böhlau Verlag, 23–49.

Lieven, Anatol (2001) 'The End of NATO', *Prospect*.
Lindborg, Chris (2002) *European Approaches to Civilian Crisis Management*, BASIC Special Report 2002/1.
Lindley-French, Julian (2000) *Leading Alone or Acting Together? The Transatlantic Security Agenda for the Next Presidency*, Paris: WE-ISS, Occasional Paper no. 20, http://www.iss-eu.org/occasion/occ20.pdf
—— (2002) *Terms of Engagement: The Paradox of American Power and the Trasnsatlantic Dilemma post-11v September*, Paris, EU-ISS (Chaillot Paper 52) http://www.iss-eu.org/chaillot/chai52e.pdf
—— (2002a) 'In the Shade of Locarno? Why European Defence is Failing', *International Affairs*, vol. 78/4, 789–811.
—— (2004) 'The Revolution in Security Affairs: Hard and Soft Security Dynamics in the 21st Century', *European Security*, vol. 13, 1–15.
Lindstrom, Gustav (2003) *Shift or Rift : Assessing US-EU Relations after Iraq*, Paris EU-ISS, http://www.iss-eu.org/chaillot/bk2003.pdf
—— (2003a) The *Galileo satellite system and its security implications,* Paris, WEU-ISS (Working Paper 44), http://www.iss-eu.org/occasion/occ44.pdf
Linster, Roger 'Luxembourg, la fidélité aux engagements', in Buffotot (ed.) (2001).
Loedel, Peter H. (1998) 'Searching for security: redefining Germany's security interests' in Mary McKenzie and Peter H. Loedel (eds) (1998), *The Promise and Reality of European Security Cooperation*. Westport, CT: Praeger.
Longhurst, Kerry (2005) *Germany and the Use of Force: The Evolution of German Security Policy 1990–2003*. Manchester: Manchester University Press.
Longhurst, Kerry and Marcin Zaborowski (2004) 'The Future of European Security', *European Security*, vol. 13/4, 381–91.
—— and —— (2005) *Old Europe, new Europe and the transatlantic security agenda*. London: Routledge.
Lynch, Dov (2006) *Why Georgia Matters*, Paris EU-ISS (Chaillot Paper no. 90).
Lyon, James (2006) 'EU's Bosnia Police Mission is "Laughing Stock"', *European Voice*, 15–21 September.
Mace, Catriona (2004) 'Operation *Concordia*: Developing a 'European' Approach to Crisis Management', *International Peacekeeping*, vol. 11/3, Autumn, 474–90.
Mandil, Claude (2006) 'Future Challenges: What World for What Union?', Paper to the Annual Conference of the EU-ISS. Paris: 6 October.
Manners, Ian (2002a) *European [security] Union: from existential threat to ontological security*, Copenhagen Peace Research Institute,

Working Paper 5/2002. http://www.copri.dk/publications/WP/WP 2002/5-2002.doc
—— (2002b) 'Normative Power Europe: A Contradiction in Terms?', *Journal of Common Market Studies*, June, vol. 40, no. 2, 235–58.
—— (2004) 'Normative Power Europe Reconsidered', Paper presented to CIDEL Workshop, Oslo, October.
—— (2004a) 'The Missing Tradition of the ES: including Nietzschean Relativism and World Imagination in Extranational Studies', *Millennium: Journal of International Studies*, March, vol. 32, no. 2, 241–64.
—— (2004b) 'The Value of Peace', in Miriam Aziz and Susan Millns (eds) *Values in the Constitution of Europe* (London: Dartmouth).
—— (2005) *Europe and the World*. Basingstoke: Palgrave Macmillan.
Manners, Ian, and Richard Whitman (2000) *The Foreign Policies of European Union Member States*. Manchester: Manchester University Press.
—— and —— (2003) 'The 'Difference Engine': Constructing and Representing the International Identity of the European Union', *Journal of European Public Policy*, June, vol. 10, no. 3, 380–404.
Margaras, Vasilis (2005) 'Strategic culture: a reliable tool of analysis for EU security developments?' *European Foreign Policy Conference*, London School of Economics, July 1–2, http://www.lse.ac.uk/Depts/intrel/EFPC/Papers/Margaras.doc
Marquina, Antonio and Xira Ruiz (2005) 'A European Competitive Advantage? Civilian Instruments for Conflict Prevention and Crisis Management', *Journal of Transatlantic Studies*, vol. 3/1, 71–87.
Marsden, Chris (2000) 'Political Warfare Erupts in Britain over Plans for European Army', *WSWS News*, 27 November, available at: http://www.wsws.org/articles/2000/nov2000/arm-n27.shtml
Martin, Laurence and John Garnett (eds) (1997) *British Foreign Policy: Challenges and Choices for the 21st Century*. London: Pinter/RIIA.
Martinsen, Martin Per (2004) 'Forging a Strategic Culture: Putting Policy into the ESDP,' *Oxford Journal on Good Governance*, Volume 1/1 Oxford, Oxford Council on Good Governance, 61–6.
McCormick, John (2006) *The European Superpower*. Basingstoke: Palgrave Macmillan.
Mearsheimer, John J. (2001) *The Tragedy of Great Power Politics*. New York: Norton.
Menon, Anand (1996) 'Defence Policy and Integration in Western Europe', *Contemporary Secuerity Policy*, vol. 17, 261–83.
—— (2000) *France, NATO and the Limits of Independence*. Basingstoke: Palgrave Macmillan.

—— (2003) 'Why ESDP is Misguided and Dangerous for the Alliance', in Jolyon Howorth and John T.S. Keeler (eds), *Defending Europe: the EU, NATO and the Quest for European Autonomy*. New York: Palgrave Macmillan.

—— (2004) 'From Crisis to Catharsis: ESDP after Iraq', *International Affairs*, vol. 80/4, July, 631–48.

—— (2006) 'Security Policy: The Logic of Leaderlesseness' in Jack Hayward (ed.) *Leaderless Europe*. Oxford: Oxford University Press, 2006.

Menon, Anand, Kalypso Nicolaidis and J. Welsh (2004) 'In Defence of Europe: A Response to Kagan', *Journal of European Affairs*, vol. 2/3.

Mérand, Frédéric Francois (2003) 'Soldiers and Diplomats: The Institutionalization of the European Security and Defense Policy, 1989–2003', Ph.D. Dissertation. University of California: Berkeley.

Merlingen, Michael and Rasa Ostrauskaite (2005) 'ESDP Police Missions: Meaning, Context and Operational Challenges', *European Foreign Affairs Review*, vol. 10, 215–35.

—— and —— (2006) *European Union Peacebuilding and Policing*. London: Routledge.

Merry, Wayne E. (2003–4) 'Therapy's End: Thinking Beyond NATO', *The National Interest*, Winter.

Messervy-Whiting, Graham (2003) 'The Politico-Military Structure in Brussels: Capabilities and Limits,' discussion paper for the Geneva Centre for Security Policy, Workshop on the EU and Peace Operations, September 22–23.

—— (2006) 'ESDP Deployments and the European Security Strategy', in Anne Deighton (ed.) (2006), 33–43.

Meyer, Christoph O. (2005) 'Convergence towards a European Strategic Culture? A Constructivist Framework for Explaining Changing Norms', *European Journal of International Relations*, vol. 11/4, 523–49.

—— (2006) *The Quest for a European Strategic Culture: Changing Norms on Security and Defence in the European Union*. Basingstoke: Palgrave Macmillan.

Michta, Andrew A. (ed.) (1999) *America's New Allies: Poland, Hungary and the Czech Republic in NATO*, Washington, DC: University of Washington Press.

Millen, Raymond A. (2002) 'European Security and Defense Policy Rapid Reaction Force: A Trojan Horse for NATO', *Strategic Studies Institute Newsletter* September.

Ministère de la Défense, Paris (1994) *Livre Blanc sur la Défense*, Paris, vol. 10/18.

—— (1999) *Les Leçons du Kosovo*, MS.

—— (2004) *Opération Artemis*, MS.

Mink, Georges (2003) 'Pologne: à la recherché d'un rang de puissance internationale', *Ramses 2004 : Rapport Annuel Mondial sur le Système Economique et les Stratégies*, Paris: IFRI.

Missiroli, Antonio (2000) *CFSP, Defence and Flexibility*, Paris: WEU-Institute for Security Studies, (*Chaillot Paper no. 38*).

—— (2002) 'EU-NATO Cooperation in Crisis Management: No Turkish Delight for ESDP?', *Security Dialogue* vol. 33/1.

Missiroli, Antonio (ed.) (2003) *From Copenhagen to Brussels. European Defence: Core Documents IV*, Paris: EU-ISS (Chaillot Paper 67), accessed at: http://www.iss-eu.org/chaillot/chai67e.pdf

—— (2003a) *Euros for ESDP: Financing EU Operations*, Occasional Paper 45, EU Institute for Security Studies. Paris: June.

—— (2006) 'Money Matters: Financing EU Crisis Management', in Deighton 2006, 45–57.

Mitzen, Jennifer (2006): 'Ontological Security in World Politics. State Identity and the Security Dilemma', *European Journal of International Relations*, 12/3, 341–70.

Monde, Le (2003) 'Les 'Quatre' lancent un groupe pionnier dans le domaine de la défense', 30 April.

Moravcsik, Andrew (1998) *The Choice for Europe: Social Purpose and State Power from Messina to Maastricht*. Ithaca, NY: Cornell University Press.

—— (2003) 'The World is Bipolar After All', *Newsweek International*.

MSF (Médecins sans Frontières) (2003), *Ituri: Unkept Promises? A Pretence of Protection and Inadequate Assistance*, Report 25 July, accessed at: http://www.msf.org/source/countries/africa/drc/2003/unkeptpromises/report.doc

Müller-Brandeck-Bocquet, Gisela (2002) 'The New CFSP and ESDP Decision-Making System of the European Union', *European Foreign Affairs Review*, vol. 7, 257–82.

Müller-Willer, Björn (2004) *For our eyes only? Shaping an intelligence community within the EU*. Paris: EU-ISS Occasional Paper 50.

Murray, Alasdair and Aurore Wanlin (2005) *The Lisbon Scorecard V: Can Europe Compete?* London: CER.

NATO (1991) 'The Alliance's Strategic Concept agreed by the Heads of State and Government participating in the meeting of the North Atlantic Council', Rome, November 8. Available on NATO 'Basic Documents' website: www.nato.int/docu/basictxt/b911108a.htm.

Naumann, Klaus (2005) 'Military Needs of a Strategic Culture in Europe', *Oxford Journal on Good Governance*, 2/1.

New Europe (2001) Seminar on *The Future of the European Union*. London: New Europe Research Trust.

Newsweek (2002) 'Europe's Mr Fix It – Javier Solana', 17 June.

Niblett, Robin and William Wallace (eds), (2001) *Rethinking European Order: West European Responses 1989–1997*. London: Palgrave.

Nicolaidis, Kalypso (2005) 'The Power of the Superpowerless' in Tod Lindberg (ed.), *Beyond Paradise and Power: Europe, America and the Future of a Troubled Partnership*. New York: Routledge.

Nowak, Agnieszka (2003) *L'Union en Action: La Mission de Police en Bosnie*, Paris: EU-ISS, Occasional Paper no. 42, http://www.iss-eu.org/occasion/occ42.pdf

Nowak, Agnieszka (ed.) (2006) *Civilian Crisis Management: the European Way*, Paris: EU-ISS (Chaillot Paper no. 90), http://www.iss-eu.org/chaillot/chai90.pdf

Nuttall, Simon J. (1992) *European Political Cooperation*. Oxford: Oxford University Press.

—— (2000) *European Foreign Policy*. Oxford: Oxford University Press.

Nye, Joseph S. (1990) *Bound to Lead: The Changing Nature of American Power*. New York: Basic Books.

—— (2001) *The Paradox of American Power: Why the World's Only Superpower Cannot Go It Alone*. New York: Oxford University Press.

—— (2004) *Soft Power: The Means to Success in World Politics*. New York: Public Affairs Press.

O'Brennan, John (2006) '"Bringing Geo-Politics Back In": Exploring the Security Dimension of the 2004 Eastern Enlargement of the European Union', *Cambridge Review of International Affairs*, vol. 19/1, March.

Ojanen, Hanna (2000) *Participation and Influence: Finland, Sweden and the post-Amsterdam development of the CFSP*, WEU-ISS Occasional Paper 11.

—— (2002) *Theories at a Loss? EU-NATO fusion and the 'low-politicisation of security and defence in European Integration*, Helsinki: Finnish Institute of International Affairs, Working Paper 31.

—— (2006) 'The EU and NATO: Two Competing Models for a Common Defence Policy', *Journal of Common Market Studies*, vol. 44/1, 2006, 57–76.

Olsen, Gorm Rye and Jess Pilegaard (2005) 'The Costs of Non-Europe? Denmark and the Common Security and Defence Policy', *European Security*, vol. 14/3.

Orsini, Dominique (2006) 'Future of ESDP: Lessons from Bosnia', *European Security Review*, no. 29, June.

Ortega, Martin (2001) *Military Intervention and the European Union*, Paris: WEU-ISS (Chaillot Paper no. 45) www.iss-eu.org/chaillot/chai45e.pdf

—— (2004) 'Poland: a new European Atlanticist at a Crossroads?', *European Security*, vol. 13/4, 301–22.

—— (2005) *Petersberg Tasks and Missions for the EU Military Forces*. Paris, EU-ISS, accessed at: http://www.iss-eu.org/esdp/04-mo.pdf

Osland, Kari M. 'The EU Police Mission in Bosnia and Herzegovina', *International Peacekeeping*, vol. 11/3, Autumn, 544–60.

Pape, Robert A. (2005) 'Soft Balancing Against the United States', *International Security*, vol. 30/1, Summer, 7–45.

Parmentier, Guillaume (2000) 'Après le Kosovo: pour un nouveau contrat transatlantique', *Politique Etrangère*, vol. 1/2000, 9–32.

Patten, Chris (2000) 'A European Foreign Policy: ambition and reality', Speech to IFRI and RIIA.

—— (2004) 'A Security Strategy for Europe,' *Oxford Journal on Good Governance*, vol. 1/1 July. Oxford: Oxford Council on Good Governance, 13–17.

—— (2006) *Cousins and Strangers: America, Britain and Europe in a New Century*. New York: Holt.

Perlez, Jane (2006) 'In religious Aceh, Islamic law is taking hold', *International Herald Tribune* 1 August 2006.

Pew Global Attitudes Survey (2006) accessed at: http://pewglobal.org/reports/pdf/DividedWorld2006.pdf

Pfaff, William (1998–9) 'The Coming Clash of Europe with America', *World Policy*, Winter 1998–9, 1–9.

Phillips, David (2005) *Losing Iraq: Inside the Postwar Reconstruction Fiasco*. Boulder, CO: Westview Press.

Pierson, Paul (2004) *Politics in Time: History, Institutions and Social Analysis*. Princeton, NJ: Princeton University Press.

Piks, Rihards (2003) Representative of the Parliament of Latvia, European Convention *Working Document 29 – WG VIII* (4 December).

Pirozzi, Nicoletta (2006) 'Building Security in the Palestinian Territories', *European Security Review*, 28, February.

Pollack Mark A. (1997) 'Delegation, agency, and agenda-setting in the European Community', *International Organization*, vol. 51(1), 99–134.

—— (2003) *The Engines of European Integration: Delegation, Agency and Agenda Setting in the European Union*. Oxford: Oxford University Press.

Popescu, Nicu (2005) *The EU in Moldova – Settling Conflicts in the Neighbourhood*, Paris, EU-ISS (*Occasional Paper no. 60*) October.

Posen, Barry R. (2004) 'ESDP and the Structure of World Power', *The International Spectator*, vol. XXXIX/1.

—— (2004a) 'The Unipolar Moment and ESDP', draft, unpublished paper given to Yale Seminar Series, November 2004.

Potter, Mitch (2006) 'Something that works: the Rafah Crossing', *Toronto Star* 21 May.

Power, Declan (2006) 'Mixed reaction to 'battle-group' decision', *The Post IE*, 12 February.

Quinlan, Joseph P. (2003) *Drifting Apart or Growing Together? The Primacy of the Transatlantic Economy*. Washington, DC: Center for Transatlantic Relations.

Quinlan, Michael (2001) *European Defense Cooperation: Asset or Threat to NATO?* Washington, DC: Woodrow Wilson Centre Press.

—— (2002) 'ESDP and Enlargement', in Esther Brimmer (ed.) *op.cit.*, 23–33.

Rees, Wyn (1998) *The Western European Union at the Crossroads: between transatlantic solidarity and European integration*. Boulder, CO: Westview.

—— (2006) *Transatlantic Counter-Terrorism Cooperation: The New Imperative*. London: Routledge.

Rettman, Andrew (2006) 'Congo drone crash compounds EU soldiers' image problem', *EU Observer* 31 July.

Riddell, Peter (2003) *Hug them close: Blair, Clinton, Bush and the 'Special Relationship'*. London: Politico's.

Rieker, Pernile (2004a) *EU Security Policy: Contrasting Rationalism and Social Constructivism*, Working Paper 659-2004. Oslo: NUPI.

Riggio, Daniele (2003) 'EU-NATO Cooperation and Complementarity between the Rapid Reaction Forces', *The International Spectator*, XXXVIII/3.

Risse, Thomas (2000) 'Let's Argue! Communicative Action in World Politics', *International Organization*, 54.

Risse, Thomas (2002) 'Social Constructivism and European Integration', Working Paper, Freie Universität, Berlin.

Roberts, Adam (2002) 'Counter-terrorism, Armed Force and the Laws of War', *Survival*, vol. 44/1, 7–32.

Robertson, George (1999) 'Sécurité et Interdépendance', *Politique Etrangère*, vol. 4/1999, 863–6.

—— (1999a) Speech to the RUSI conference ('NATO at Fifty') 16 March 1999, accessed at: http://www.basicint.org/europe/NATO/99summit/6-2.htm

Robyn, Richard (2005) *The Changing Face of European Identity*. London: Routledge.

Rodman, Peter (2000) 'The World's Resentment: Anti-Americanism as a Global Phenomenon', *The National Interest*, Summer.

Rodrigo, Fernando (1997) 'Spain and NATO's Enlargement', NATO, 1997, accessed at: http://www.nato.int/acad/conf/enlarg97/rodrigo.htm

Roper, John 'Two Cheers for Mr. Blair? The Political Realities of European Defence Cooperation', in Geoffrey Edwards and Georg Wiessala (eds) *The European Union: Annual Review of the EU 1999/2000*, Oxford: Blackwell, 2000.

Rummel, Reinhardt (2004) 'Soft-Power EU – Interventionspolitik mit zivilen Mitteln', in Hans-Georg Ehrhart and Burkard Schmitt (Hg.), *Die Sicherheitspolitik der EU im Werden: Bedrohungen, Aktivitäten, Fähigkeiten,* Baden-Baden, 259–72.

Rupp, Richard E. (2006) *NATO After 9/11: An Alliance in Continuing Decline*. Basingstoke: Palgrave Macmillan.

Russett, Bruce (1994) *Grasping the Democratic Peace*. Princeton, NJ: Princeton University Press.

Russett, Bruce and John R Oneal (2001) *Triangulating Peace: Democracy, Interdependence, and International Organizations*. New York: Norton.

Rutten, Maartje (2001) *From Saint-Malo to Nice. European Defence: core documents,* Paris: Chaillot Paper 47.

—— (2002) *From Nice to Laeken. European Defence: core documents vol. II*, Paris: Chaillot Paper 51.

Rynning, Sten (2002) 'Shaping Military Doctrine in France:Decision Makers between International Power and Domestic Interests', *Security Studies*, vol. 11, 85–116.

Rynning, Sten (2003) 'A fragmented external role: the EU, defence policy and new Atlanticism', in Michèle Knodt and Sebastiaan Princen (eds), *Understanding the European Union's External Relations*. London: Routledge.

—— (2003a) 'European Union: Towards a Strategic Culture?' *Security Dialogue*, December, vol. 34/4, 479–96.

—— (2005) *NATO Renewed: The Power and Purpose of Transatlantic Cooperation*. Basingstoke: Palgrave Macmillan.

Salmon, Trevor (2005) 'The European Security and Defence Policy: Built on Rocks or Sand?', *European Foreign Affairs Review* 10, 359–79.

Salmon, Trevor and Alistair J.K. Shepherd (2003) *Toward a European Army*. Boulder, CO: Lynne Rienner.

Sandholtz, Wayne and Alex Stone Sweet (eds) (1998) *European Integration and Supranational Governance*. Oxford: Oxford University Press.

Sands, David R. (2003) 'EU Plan draws Rapid Reaction', *Washington Times*, 30 April.

Sangiovanni, Mette Eilstrup (2003) 'Why a Common Security and Defence Policy is Bad for Europe', *Survival*, vol. 45/3, 193–206.

Sbragia, Alberta (2007) 'The United States and the European Union: Comparing Two "Sui Generis" Systems', in A. Menon and M. Schain

(eds) *Comparative Federalism: The United States and the European Union*. Oxford: Oxford University Press.
Schake, Kori and Judith Yaphe (2001) *The Strategic Implications of a Nuclear-Armed Iran*, Washington, DC: National Defense University (McNair Paper 64).
Schake, Kori (2003) 'The United States, ESDP and Constructive Duplication', in Howorth and Keeler (2003): 107–32.
Schmidt, Gustav (ed.) (2001) *A History of NATO: The First Fifty Years*, 3 vols, Basingstoke: Palgrave Macmillan.
Schmidt, Vivien A. (2000) 'Democracy and Discourse in an Integrating Europe and a Globalising World', *European Law Journal*, vol. 6 (3), 277–300.
—— (2002) *The Futures of European Capitalism*. Oxford: Oxford University Press.
—— (2002a) 'Discourse as Framework for Analysis: Policy Construction and Legitimization for Changing Policies and Practices', Chapter 5 of Schmidt 2002.
—— (2005): 'Democracy in Europe: The Impact of European Integration', *Perspectives on Politics*, vol. 3, no. 4: 761–79.
—— (2006) *Democracy in Europe: The EU and National Polities*. Oxford: Oxford University Press.
Schmidt, Vivien A. and Claudio Radaelli (2004) 'Conceptual and Methodological Issues in Policy Change in Europe,' *West European Politics*, vol. 27, no. 4: 1–28.
Schmitt, Burkard (2000) *From Cooperation to Integration: Defense and Aerospace Industries in Europe*. Paris: EU-ISS Cahier de Chaillot.
Schmitt, Burkard (2003) *The European Union and Armaments: Getting a Bigger Bang for the Euro*, Paris: EU-Institute for Security Studies (Chaillot Paper 63).
—— (2003a) *European Armaments Cooperation: Core Documents*. Paris: EU-Institute for Security Studies (Chaillot Paper no. 59).
—— (2004) 'Progress towards the European Defence Agency,' EU-ISS, *Analyses*, Winter.
Schmitt, Burkard and Grand Camille (2001) 'The Case for a Great European Debate' in Schmitt and Grand, 159–69.
Schmitt, Burkard and Grand, Camille (eds) (2001) *Nuclear Weapons: a New Great Debate*, Paris: Chaillot Paper 48.
Schnabel, Rockwell A. and Francis X. Rocca (2005) , *The Next Superpower? The Rise of Europe and Its Challenge to the United States*. Lanham, MD: Rowman and Littlefield.
Schroeder, Gerhard (2005) *Speech at the 41st Munich Conference on Security Policy*, 12 February, accessed at: http://www.securityconference.de/konferenzen/rede.php?menu_2005=&id=143&sprache=en&

Schweiss, Christina M. (2005) 'The NATO-EU Nexus and evolving global security frameworks', Paper to EUSA Conference. Austin, TX: April.

SDA (Security and Defence Agenda) (2006) *Europe's Long-Term Vision of the Defence Agenda in 2025: sharp or fuzzy?* Brussels, 13 June, accessed at: http://www.forum-europe.com/publication/SDALTVSummaryJune2006t.pdf

Serfaty, Simon (ed.) (2005) *The United States, the European Union, and NATO: After the Cold War and Beyond Iraq*. Washington, DC: CSIS Report.

—— (2006) *Moment of Reflection, Commitment to Action*. Washington, DC: CSIS Report, August.

Serrano, Pedro (2006) 'A Strategic Approach to the European Security and Defence Policy' in Nowak 2006, 39–47).

Shapiro, Jeremy (2002) 'The Role of France in the War on Terrorism', *Brookings* working paper: http://www.brookings.edu/fp/cusf/analysis/shapiro.pdf

Shapiro, Shlomo and Klaus Becher (2004) *European-Israeli Security and Defence Cooperation: Expectations and Impediments*. Beer Sheva: The Centre for the Study of European Politics and Society.

Sharp, Jane M. O. (ed.) (1990) *Europe after an American Withdrawal: Economic and Military Issues*. Oxford: Oxford University Press.

Shearer, Andrew (2000) 'Britain, France and the Saint-Malo Declaration: tactical rapprochement or strategic entente?', *Cambridge Review of International Affairs*, XIII/2.

Shore, Cris (2000) *Building Europe: The Cultural Politics of European Integration*. London: Routledge.

SIPRI (1999) Stockholm International Peace Research Institute, *Yearbook 1999*, Stockholm: Oxford University Press, 298.

Sjursen, Helene (ed) (2006) *Journal of European Public Policy* 13/2, March. Special issue on 'What Kind of Power? European Foreign Policy in Perspective'.

Sjursen, Helene (2006a) 'What Kind of Power?', *Journal of European Public Policy*, vol. 13/2, March.

Sloan, Stanley R. (2000) *The United States and European Defence*, Paris, WEU, (Chaillot Paper 39) www.iss-eu.org/chaillot/chai39e.pdf

—— (2003) *NATO, the European Union and the Atlantic Community*. Lanham, MD: Rowman and Littlefield.

—— (2006) 'Building a New Foundation for Transatlantic Relations', *EuroFuture*, Summer.

Smith, Hazel (2002) *European Union Foreign Policy: what it is and what it does*. London: Pluto.

Smith, Martin A. and Graham Timmins (eds) (2002) *Uncertain Europe: Building a New European Security Order?* London: Routledge.

Smith, Michael E. (2003) *Europe's Foreign and Security Policy: the Institutionalization of Cooperation*. Cambridge: Cambridge University Press.

Smith, Steve (2000) 'Wendt's World' *Review of International Studies*, vol. 26/1, 151–63.

Spiegel, Peter and James Blitz, 'US dismay over Blair's stance in EU defence', *Financial Times*, 16 October 2003.

Socor, Vladimir (2006) 'Solana Gaffe Overshadows failure of 5+2 negotiations', *Eurasia Daily Monitor* 6 March: http://www.jamestown.org/edm/article.php?article_id=2370844

Stahl, Berhard, Henning Boekle, Jörg Nadoll and Anna Jóhannesdóttir (2004) 'Understanding the Atlanticist-Europeanist Divide in the CFSP: Comparing Denmark, France, Germany and the Netherlands', *European Foreign Affairs Review* 9, 417–41.

Steltzenmüller, Constanze (2004) 'The Disaggregation Temptation', *Die Zeit Internet Edition*, November 19, accessible at: http://www.zeit.de/2004/48/disaggregation

Stone Sweet, Alec, Wayne Sandholtz and Neil Fligstein (eds) (2001) *The Institutionalization of Europe*. Oxford: Oxford University Press.

Stubb, Alexander C-G. (1996) 'A Categorization of Differentiated Integration,' *Journal of Common Market Studies*, vol. 34/2.

Susman, Gerald I. and Sean O'Keefe (eds) (1998) *The Defense Industry in the Post-Cold War Era: Corporate Strategies and Public Policy Perspectives*. London: Pergamon.

Tams, Carsten (1999) 'The Functions of a European Security and Defence Identity and its Institutional Form' in Helga Haftendoorn *et al.* (eds) *Imperfect Unions: Security Institutions Over Time and Space*. Oxford: Oxford University Press.

Tardy, Thierry (2004) *Peace Operations in World Politics after September 11 2001*. London: Frank Cass.

Terriff, Terry (2003) 'The CJTF Concept and the Limits of European Autonomy,' in Jolyon Howorth and John T.S. Keeler (eds) *Defending Europe: The EU, NATO and the Quest for European Autonomy*. New York: Palgrave Macmillan.

Tertrais, Bruno (2003) 'L'inévitable réconciliation franco-américaine', *Le Figaro*, 26 mai.

Thomas, James P. (2000) *The Military Challenges of Transatlantic Coalitions*. Oxford: Oxford University Press (Adelphi Paper 333).

Tofte, Sunniva (2005) 'Non-EU NATO Members and the post-Cold War European Security Structures: a Case Study of Norway', PhD Dissertation. Bath: University of Bath, UK.

Toje, Asle (ed) (2005) *Oxford Journal on Good Governance*, vol. 2/1 March. Special issue on 'European Strategic Culture'.

Trenin, Dmitri (2006) 'Russia Leaves the West', *Foreign Affairs*, vol. 85/4, July/August.

UBC (2005) *The Human Security Report 2005*, Vancouver, University of British Columbia. http://www.humansecurityreport.info/

UK Ministry of Defence (MOD) (1994) *Front Line First: The Defence Costs Study*. London: HMSO, July.

—— (1995) *Statement on the Defence Estimates: Stable Forces in a Strong Britain*. London: HMSO.

—— (1998) *The Strategic Defence Review*, Chapter 6, 'A Policy for People,' accessed at: http://www.mod.uk/issues/sdr/people_policy.htm.

Ulriksen, Stale, Catriona Gourlay and Catriona Mace (2004) 'Operation *Artemis*: The Shape of Things to Come?', *International Peacekeeping*, vol. 11/3, Autumn, 508–25.

US National Security Strategy (2002) accessed at: *The National Security Strategy of the United States*, available at: http://www.whitehouse.gov/nsc/nss.html

Vachudova, Milada (2005) *Europe Undivided: Democracy, Leverage and Integration after Communism*. Oxford: Oxford University Press.

Vaïsse, Maurice, Pierre Mélandri and Frédéric Bozo (eds) (1996) *La France et l'OTAN*. Brussels: Complexe.

Valásek, Tomás (2005) 'New EU Members in Europe's Security Policy', *Cambridge Review of International Affairs*, vol. 18/2.

Van Eekelen, Willem (1998) *Debating European Security 1948–1998*. Brussels: CEPS.

—— (2006) *The Continuing Debate on European Security*. Brussels: CEPS.

Van Ham, Peter (2000) 'Europe's Common Defense Policy: Implications for the TransAtlantic Relationship', *Security Dialogue*, vol. 31/2, 215–28.

Van Oudenaren, John (2005) 'Containing Europe', *The National Interest*, Summer, 57–64.

Van Staden, Alfred (1997) 'The Netherlands' in Jolyon Howorth and Anand Menon (1997), 87–104.

Van Staden, Alfred *et al.*, (2000) *Towards a European Strategic Concept*. The Hague: Netherlands Institute of International Relations, the Clingendael Institute.

Vasconcelos, Alvaro de (2000) 'Portugal 2000: la voie européenne', *Notre Europe*, *Etudes et Recherches* no. 9, Paris, January.

Védrine, Hubert (2000) *Les cartes de la France à l'heure de la mondialisation. Dialogue avec Dominique Moisi*. Paris: Fayard.

Venusberg Group (2000) *Enhancing the European Union as an International Security Actor: A Strategy for Action*. Gütersloh: Bertelsmann Foundation.
—— (2004) *A European Defence Strategy*, Gütersloh, Bertelsmann Foundation http://www.cap.uni-muenchen.de/download/2004/2004_Venusberg_Report.pdf
Villepin, Dominique de (2003) 'Law, Force and Justice', The Alastair Buchan Lecture, 27 March 2003, accessed at: http://www.iiss.org/conferences/alastair-buchan/the-alastair-buchan-lecture-2003
—— (2003a) *Un Autre Monde*. Paris: L'Herne.
—— (2003b) Dimbleby Lecture, London, 10 October, accessed at : http://www.bbc.co.uk/pressoffice/pressreleases/stories/2003/10_october/17/dimbleby_lecture.pdf
Wagner, Wolfgang (2003) 'Why the EU's Common Foreign and Security Policy Will Remain Intergovernmental, *Journal of European Public Policy*, 10, 576–96.
Wallace, Helen and Wallace, William (2000) *Policy-Making in the European Union*, 4th edition. Oxford: Oxford University Press.
Wallace, William (2001) 'Europe: the necessary partner', *Foreign Affairs*, vol. 80(3), 16–34.
Walt, Stephen (1998–1999) 'The Ties that Fray: why Europe and America are Drifting Apart', *The National Interest*, Winter.
—— (2005) *Taming American Power: The Global Response to US Primacy*. New York: Norton.
Waltz, Kenneth (1979) *Theory of International Politics*. Reading, MA: Addison-Wesley.
Walzer, Michael (2000) *Just and Unjust Wars: A Moral Argument With Historical Illustrations* (New York, Basic Books (3rd edition).
Watanabe, Lisa (2005) 'The ESDP: between estrangement and a new partnership in transatlantic security', *Journal of Contemporary European Studies*, vol. 13/1.
Weiss, Thomas G. (2004) 'The Sunset of Humanitarian Intervention? The Responsibility to Protect in a Unipolar Era', *Security Dialogue*, vol. 35/2.
Wendt, Alexander (1999) *Social Theory of International Politics*, Cambridge: Cambridge University Press.
Wessels, Wolfgang (2001) 'The Amsterdam Treaty in Theoretical Perspectives: which dynamics at work?' in Jorg Monar and Wolfgang Wessels (eds), *The European Union after the Treaty of Amsterdam*, London.
Weston, Sir John (2001) 'Foreign and Defence Policy', in New Europe Seminar on *The Future of the European Union*. London: New Europe Research Trust.

Wheeler, Nicholas J. (2000) *Saving Strangers: Humanitarian Intervention in International Society*. Oxford: Oxford University Press.

Wheeler, Nicholas J. and Tim Dunne (1998) 'Good International Citizenship: a third way for British foreign policy', in *International Affairs*, vol. 74/4.

White, Brian (2001) *Understanding European Foreign Policy*. Basingstoke: Palgrave Macmillan.

Whitman, Richard G. (1998) *From Civilian Power to Superpower: The International Identity of the European Union*. London: Macmillan.

—— (1999) *Amsterdam's Unifinished Business: The Blair Government's Initiative and the Future of the Western European Union*. Paris: WEU-ISS Occasional Paper no. 7.

—— (2006) 'Road Map for a Route March? (De-)civilianizing through the EU's Security Strategy', *European Foreign Affairs Review*, no. 11, 1–15.

Willenborg, Robert *et al.*ii (2004) *Europe's Oil Defences. An Analysis of Europe's Oil Supply Vulnerability and its Emergency Oil Stockholding Systems*. The Hague: Clingendael.

Williams, Cindy (2005) 'From Conscripts to Volunteers: NATO's Transitions to All Volunteer Forces,' *Naval War College Review*, vol. 58/1, Winter.

Williams, Paul D. and Alex J. Bellamy (2005) 'The Responsibility to Protect and the Crisis in Darfur', *Security Dialogue*, vol. 36/1, 27–47.

Winnerstig, Mike (2000) *A World Reformed?: the United States and European security from Reagan to Clinton*. Stockholm: Stockholm University.

Witney, Nick (2005) 'Bridging the Gap between European Strategy and Capabilities', Speech in Brussels, 12 October: http://www.eda.europa.eu/news/2005-10-12-0.htm

Wivel, Anders (2005) 'Between Paradise and Power: Denmark's Transatlantic Dilemma', *Security Dialogue*, vol. 36/3, 417–21.

Woodworth, Paddy (2005) 'Spain's "Second Transition"', *World Policy Journal*, vol. 22/3.

Wyatt-Walter, Holly (1997) *The European Community and the Security Dilemma 1989–1992*. London: Macmillan.

Yost, David S. (1998) *NATO Transformed: The Alliance's New Roles in International Security*. Washington, DC: United States Institute of Peace Press.

Youngs, Richard (ed.) (2004) *Global Europe: New Terms of Engagement*. London: Foreign Policy Centre.

Zaborowski, Marcin (2004) *Germany, Poland and Europe: Conflict, Cooperation and Europeanisation*. Manchester: Manchester University Press.

—— (2004a) *From America's protégé to constructive European: Polish Security Policy in the 21st Century*. Paris: EU-ISS (Occasional Paper no. 56).
—— (ed.) (2006) *Friends Again? EU-US Relations After the Crisis*, Paris EU-ISS, http://www.iss-eu.org/books/transat06.pdf

Index

Note: page numbers in **bold** are major entries.

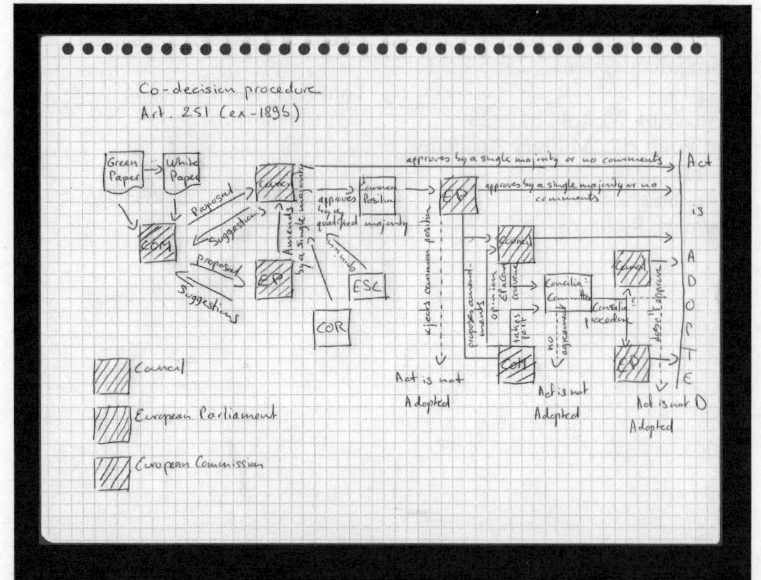
Co-decision procedure
Art. 251 (ex-189b)
Green Paper
White Paper
Proposal
Suggestions
COM
EP
ESC
COR
Common Position
approves by a single majority or no comments
Act is not Adopted
Act is ADOPTED
Council
European Parliament
European Commission